FROMMER'S

COMPREHENSIVE TRAVEL GUIDE

San Antonio & Austin

1st Edition

by Edie Jarolim

D0452090

MACMILLAN • USA

ABOUT THE AUTHOR

Edie Jarolim was a senior editor at Frommer's in New York before she indulged her Southwest fantasies and moved to Tucson, Arizona. She has contribued to numerous travel guides (including *Frommer's Egypt*), and her articles have appeaared in such diverse publications as the London *Guardian,* the *Wall Street Journal,* and *Bride's* magazine. She was tickled to have the chance to write about two of her favorite cities in the state that spawned two of her favorite people, Ann Richards and Molly Ivins.

MACMILLAN TRAVEL

A Simon & Schuster Macmillan Company
15 Columbus Circle
New York, NY 10023

ISBN 0-02-860463-6

ISSN 1080-9104

Special Sales

Bulk purchases (10+ copies) of Frommer's travel guides are available to corporations at special discounts. The Special Sales Department can produce custom editions to be used as premiums and/or for sales promotion to suit individual needs. Existing editions can be produced with custom cover imprints such as corporate logos. For more information write to Special Sales, Simon & Schuster, 1230 Avenue of the Americas, New York, NY 10020.

Manufactured in the United States of America.

Contents

List of Maps

What the Symbols Mean

★ Frommer's Favorites   Hotels, restaurants, attractions, and entertainments you should not miss

$ Super-Special Values   Really exceptional values

In Hotel and Other Listings

The following symbols refer to the standard amenities available in all rooms:

A/C   air conditioning
MINIBAR   refrigerator stocked with beverages and snacks
TEL   telephone
TV   television

The following abbreviations are used for credit cards:

AE   American Express
CB   Carte Blanche
DC   Diners Club
DISC   Discover
ER   enRoute
EU   Eurocard
JCB   Japanese Credit Bureau
MC   MasterCard
V   Visa

Trip Planning with this Guide
USE THE FOLLOWING FEATURES:

What Things Cost   To help you plan your daily budget

Calendar of Events   To plan for or avoid

Suggested Itineraries   For seeing the cities

What's Special About Checklist   A summary of the city's highlights

Easy-to-Read Maps   Walking tours, city sights, hotel and restaurant locations

Fast Facts   All the essentials at a glance: climate, currency, embassies, emergencies, information, safety, taxes, tipping, and more

Frommer's Smart Traveler Tips   Hints on how to secure the best value for your money

Invitation to the Reader

In researching this book, I discovered many wonderful places—hotels, restaurants, shops, and more. I'm sure you'll find others. Please tell us about them, so we can share the information with your fellow travelers in upcoming editions. If you were disappointed with a recommendation, we'd love to know that, too. Please write to:

Edie Jarolim
Frommer's San Antonio & Austin, 1st Edition
Macmillan Travel
15 Columbus Circle
New York, NY 10023

An Additional Note

Please be advised that travel information is subject to change at any time—and this is especially true of prices. We therefore suggest that you write or call ahead for confirmation when making your travel plans. The authors, editors, and publisher cannot be held responsible for the experiences of readers while traveling. Your safety is important to us, however, so we encourage you to stay alert and be aware of your surroundings. Keep a close eye on cameras, purses, and wallets, all favorite targets of thieves and pickpockets.

1

Introducing San Antonio

Cᴀʟʟ ɪᴛ ᴛʜᴇ Fɪᴇꜱᴛᴀ Cɪᴛʏ ᴏʀ ᴛʜᴇ Aʟᴀᴍᴏ Cɪᴛʏ; ᴇᴀᴄʜ ᴏꜰ Sᴀɴ Aɴᴛᴏɴɪᴏ'ꜱ nicknames reveals a different truth. Visitors come here to kick back and party, but they also come to seek out Texas's history—some would say its soul. They come to sit on the banks of a glittering river and sip cactus margaritas, but also to view the Franciscan missions that rose up along the same river more than two and a half centuries ago.

Although now a thriving metropolis with more than a million people—the 10th largest city in the United States—San Antonio for many years straddled the boundary between civilization and the frontier. The only major city founded before Texas won its independence from Mexico, it long drew diverse groups with distinct goals: Spanish missionaries and militia men, southern plantation owners and German merchants, western cattle ranchers and Eastern architects. All left their mark, not only on the city's culture and cuisine, but more tangibly on its winding downtown streets.

Amid San Antonio's typical Southwest sprawl, it is those winding downtown streets most visitors recall, whether they're ardent urban enthusiasts or folks who just get a charge out of briefly abandoning their cars. They recall those downtown streets—and that river. Few who come to San Antonio leave without a memory of a moment, quiet or heart quickening, sunlit or sparkling with tiny tree-draped lights, when that river didn't somehow work its magic on them.

1 Geography, History & Culture

Geography

Three geographical zones meet in San Antonio: The Balcones Fault divides the farms and forests of east Texas from the scrubby brushland and ranches of west Texas, and the Edwards Plateau drops off to the southern coastal plains. Frederick Law Olmsted's description in his 1853 *A Journey Through Texas* is more poetic. San Antonio, he writes, "lies basking on the edge of a vast plain, through which the river winds slowly off beyond where the eye can reach. To the east are gentle slopes toward it; to the north a long gradual sweep upward to the mountain country, which comes down within five or six miles; to the south and west, the open prairies, extending almost level to the coast, a hundred and fifty miles away."

History

Dateline

- **1691** On June 13, saint day of Anthony of Padua, San Antonio River discovered and named by the

➤

THE HISTORY OF SAN ANTONIO IS the stuff of legends, that of the Alamo being but the most famous of an amazing lot. If it were a movie, the city would be an epic with an improbably packed plot, encompassing the end of a great empire, the rise of a republic, and the rescue of the river with which the story began.

What's Special About San Antonio

Walkway

- The River Walk is a wonderland of restaurants, shops, and riverboats lying just below the city's downtown streets.

Historical Highlights

- The Alamo marks the site of the most famous battle for Texas independence.
- The San Antonio Missions take visitors on a trip back to the days of the city's Spanish colonial past.

Architectural Feat

- The 750-foot-high Tower of the Americas has an observation deck with an endless view of the city.

Theaters

- The Majestic Theater used to wow 'em in vaudeville days, and its fantastical overhead sky dome is still a crowd-pleaser.
- The Arneson River Theatre has the audience sitting on one side of the river applauding actors performing on the other.

Museums

- The McNay Art Museum combines a lovely Mediterranean setting with an intimate Impressionist collection.
- The Witte's hands-on exhibits of Texas history and natural science enthrall adults and children alike.

Festival

- Fiesta, the biggest bash in a city that likes to party, features a coronation, river parades, ethnic food fests, rodeos—more than 150 events in all.

For the Kids

- Fiesta Texas boasts the highest and fastest roller coaster in the world, along with rides, shows, and food booths galore.
- Sea World of Texas, the world's largest marine theme park, offers great aquatic displays and lots of places for visitors to get wet.

Regional Food & Drink

- Mexican restaurants serve tasty, inexpensive fare in a festive, informal atmosphere all around town.
- Southwestern cuisine is combined with fresh regional ingredients in innovative ways at some of San Antonio's best restaurants.

ON A MISSION

Having already established an empire—the huge Viceroyalty of New Spain, which covered, at its high point, Mexico, Guatemala, and large parts of the southwestern United States—by the late 17th century Spain was engaged in the far less glamorous task of maintaining it. The remote regions of east Texas had been coming under attack by the native Apache and Comanches; now with rumors of French forays into the Spanish territory flying, search parties were dispatched to investigate.

On one of these search parties in 1691, regional governor Domingo Teran de los Ríos and Father Damian Massenet came upon a wooded plain fed by a fast-flowing river. They named the river—called Yanaguana by the native Coahuiltecan Indians—San Antonio de Padua, after the saint's day on which they arrived. When, some decades later, the Spanish Franciscans proposed to build a new mission halfway between the ones on the Rio Grande River and those more recently established in east Texas, the abundant water and friendliness of the local population brought the plain near the San Antonio River to mind.

And so it was that in 1718, Mission San Antonio de Valero—later known as the Alamo—was founded. To protect the religious complex from Apache attack, the *presidio* (fortress) of San Antonio de Béxar went up a few days later. In 1719, a second mission was built nearby, and in 1731, three ill-fated east Texas missions, nearly destroyed by attacks by both the French and the Indians, were moved hundreds of miles to the safer banks of the San Antonio River. 1731 was also significant for another reason: In March of that year, 15 weary families arrived from the Spanish Canary Islands with a royal dispensation from Philip V to help settle his far-flung New World kingdom. Near the protection of the presidio, they established the village of San Fernando de Béxar.

Thus within little more than a decade, what is now downtown San Antonio became home to three distinct, though related, settlements: a mission complex; the military garrison designed to protect it; and the civilian town known as Béxar (pronounced Bear) until 1837, when it was officially renamed San Antonio. To irrigate their crops, the early settlers were given narrow strips of land stretching back from the river and from the nearby San Pedro Creek; centuries later, the paths connecting these strips, which followed the winding waterways, were paved as the city's streets.

REMEMBER THE ALAMO

As the 18th century wore on, the missions came continuously under siege by hostile Indians, and the mission Indians fell victim to a host of European diseases against which they had no natural resistance; by the end of the 1700s, the Spanish mission system itself was terminal. In 1794, Mission San Antonio de Valero was secularized, its rich farmlands redistributed. In 1810, recognizing the military potential of the thick walls of the complex, the Spanish authorities turned the former mission into a garrison. The men recruited to serve here all hailed from the Mexican town of San José y Santiago del Alamo de Parras; the name of their station was soon shortened to the Alamo.

By 1824, all five missions had been secularized and Spain was once again worried about Texas. Apaches and Comanches roamed the territory freely; with the incentive of converting the native populations eliminated, it was next to impossible to persuade any Spaniards to live there. So, although the Spanish were rightly suspicious of Anglo-American designs on their land, when *empresario* (land agent) Moses Austin arrived in San Antonio in 1820, the government reluctantly agreed to allow him to settle some 300 Anglo-American families in the region. Austin died before he could see his plan carried out, and Spain lost its hold on Mexico in 1821, when the country became independent, but Moses's son, Stephen, convinced the new government to honor the terms of the original agreement.

Dateline

siege by Mexican general Santa Anna; using "Remember the Alamo" as a rallying cry, Sam Houston defeats Santa Anna at San Jacinto.

- **1836–1845** Republic of Texas.
- **1845** Texas annexed to the United States.
- **1861** Texas secedes from the Union.
- **1876** Fort Sam Houston established as new quartermaster depot.
- **1877** The railroad arrives in San Antonio, precipitating new waves of immigration.
- **1880s** King William, first residential suburb, begins to be developed by German immigrants.
- **1939–40** WPA builds River Walk, based on plans drawn up in 1929 by architect Robert H. H. Hugman.
- **1968** HemisFair exposition—River Walk extension, Convention Center, Mansión del Rio and Hilton Palacio del Rio completed for the occasion, along with Tower of the Americas and other fair structures.
- **1988** Rivercenter Mall opens.
- **1993** Alamodome, huge new sports complex, completed.

By 1830, however, the Mexicans were growing nervous about the large numbers of Anglos descending on their country from the north. They had already repealed many of the tax breaks they had initially granted the settlers; now they prohibited all further U.S. immigration to the territory. When, in 1835, General Antonio López de Santa Anna abolished Mexico's democratic 1824 constitution, Tejanos (Hispanic Texans) and Anglos alike balked at his dictatorship and a cry rose up for a separate republic.

The first battle for Texas independence fought on San Antonio soil fell to the rebels; Mexican general Martín Perfecto de Cós surrendered after a short, successful siege on the town in December 1835. But it was the return engagement, that glorious, doomed fight against all odds, that forever captured the American imagination: From February 23 through March 6, 1836, some 180 volunteers—among them Davy Crockett and Jim Bowie—serving under the command of William Travis, died trying to defend the Alamo fortress against a vastly greater number of Santa Anna's men. One month later, the memory of their martyrdom was used to exhort Sam Houston's troops on to victory at the Battle of San Jacinto, thus securing Texas's freedom.

AFTER THE FALL

Ironically, few Anglos came to live in San Antonio during Texas's stint as a republic (1836–45), but settlers came from overseas in droves: By 1850, Mexicans and Anglos were outnumbered by European, mostly German, immigrants. The Civil War put a temporary halt to the city's growth—in part because Texas joined the confederacy and most of the new settlers were Union sympathizers—but expansion picked up again soon afterward; the coming of the railroad in 1877 set off a new wave of immigration. Riding hard on its crest, the King William district, a residential suburb named for Kaiser Wilhelm, was developed by prosperous German merchants.

Some of the immigrants set up Southern-style plantations; others opened factories and shops; and more and more who arrived after the Civil War earned their keep by driving cattle. The Spanish had brought longhorn cattle and *vaqueros* (cowboys) from Mexico into the area; now Texas cowboys drove herds north on the Chisholm Trail from San Antonio to Kansas City, where they were shipped east. Others moved cattle west, for use as seed stock in the fledgling ranching industry.

Over the years San Antonio had never abandoned its role as a military stronghold. In 1849, the Alamo was designated a quartermaster depot for the U.S. Army; in 1876, the much larger Fort Sam Houston was built to take over those duties. Apache chief Geronimo was held at the clock tower in the fort's Quadrangle for 40 days in 1886, en route to exile in Florida; Teddy Roosevelt outfitted his Rough Riders—some of whom he recruited in San Antonio bars—at Fort Sam 12 years later.

A RIVER RUNS THROUGH IT

As the city marched into the 20th century, Fort Sam Houston continued to expand. In 1910, it witnessed the first military flight by an

American; early aviation stars like Charles Lindbergh honed their flying skills here. From 1917 to 1941, four air force bases—Kelly Field, Brooks Field, Randolph Field, and Lackland Army Air Base—shot up, making San Antonio the largest military complex in the United States outside the Washington, D.C., area. The military remains the city's major employer today, with the tourism industry nudging it closely from behind.

Which brings us back again to the river. As the city moved farther and farther from its agrarian roots, the San Antonio River grew less and less central to the economy; by the turn of the century, its constant flooding made it a downright nuisance. When a particularly severe storm in 1921 caused it to overflow its banks, killing 50 people and destroying many downtown businesses, there was serious talk of cementing the river over.

In 1925, the newly formed San Antonio Conservation Society put on a puppet show warning the city council against killing the goose that was laying the golden eggs of downtown economic growth. And in 1927, Robert H. H. Hugman, an architect who had lived in New Orleans and studied that city's Beaux Carré district, came up with a detailed plan for saving the waterway. His proposed River Walk, with shops, restaurants, and entertainment areas buttressed by a series of floodgates, would render the river profitable as well as safe, and also preserve its natural beauty. The depression intervened, but in 1941, with the help of a federal Works Project Administration (WPA) grant, Hugman's vision became a reality.

Still, for some decades more, the River Walk remained just another pretty space; not until the 1968 HemisFair exposition drew record crowds to the rescued waterway did the city begin banking on its banks. In the next 20 years, commercial development of the Big Bend section took off, culminating in the huge Rivercenter shopping and hotel complex in 1988 and still continuing apace today; the South Bank project, anchored by a Hard Rock Cafe, is the latest of the riverside entertainment meccas. Instead of falling victim to the city's suburban spread, the place where San Antonio began was revitalized by its river—just as the Conservation Society had predicted.

Culture

With its German, southern, western, and, above all, Hispanic influences—the city is about 50% Mexican American—San Antonio's cultural life is immensely rich and complex. At the New Orleans–like Fiesta, for example, San Antonians might break confetti eggs called *cascarones,* listen to oompah bands, and cheer rodeo bull riders. Countless country-and-western ballads twang on about San Antone—probably because the name rhymes with "alone"—which is also America's capital for Tejano music, a unique blend of Mexican and German sounds. And no self-respecting San Antonio festival would be complete without Mexican tamales and tacos, Texan chili and barbecue, southern hush puppies and glazed ham, and German beer and Bratwurst.

The city's buildings also reflect its multiethnic history. After the Texas revolution, Spanish *viga* beams began to be replaced by southern Greek Revival columns, German *fachwerk* pitched roofs, and East Coast Victorian gingerbread. San Antonio, like the rest of the Southwest, has now returned to its Hispanic architectural roots—even chain hotels in the area have red-clay roofs, Saltillo tile floors, and central patios—but updated versions of other indigenous building styles are also popular. The rustic elegant Hill Country look, for example, might use native limestone in structures which combine sprawling Texas ranch features with more intricate German details.

2 Recommended Books & Films

Books

Before Frederick Law Olmsted became a landscape architect—New York's Central Park is among his creations—he was a successful journalist; his 1853 *A Journey Through Texas* includes a delightful section on his impressions of early San Antonio. William Sidney Porter, better known as O. Henry, had a newspaper office in San Antonio for a while; two collections of his short stories, *O. Henry's Texas Stories* and *Time to Write,* include a number of pieces set in the city, among them "A Fog in Santone," "The Higher Abdication," "Hygeia at the Solito," "Seats of the Haughty," and "The Missing Chord."

O. Henry wasn't very successful at selling his newspaper, the *Rolling Stone,* in San Antonio in the 1890s, but there's a lively literary scene in town today. Resident writers include Sandra Cisneros, many of whose powerful, critically acclaimed short stories in *Women Hollering Creek* are set in the city; novelist Sarah Bird, whose humorous *The Mommy Club* pokes fun at the yuppies of the King William area; and mystery writer Jay Brandon, whose excellent *Loose Among the Lambs* kept San Antonians busy trying to guess the identities of the local figures fictionalized therein.

Films

For a bit of the myth surrounding the city, you might want to rent *The Alamo,* starring John Wayne, or *San Antonio,* starring Errol Flynn, though neither was shot in town (the 1935 *Fall of the Alamo*—not available on video—was). A number of early aviation movies used Fort Sam Houston as a location, among them the 1927 silent film, *Wings,* the first film to receive an Academy Award for best picture. Some of the better-known films set in San Antonio are *The Getaway* (1972), *Sugarland Express* (1973), *Race with the Devil* (1975), and *Cloak and Dagger* (1983). San Antonian Robert Rodriguez won critical acclaim in 1993 for his low-budget *El Mariachi;* he financed much of it with the money he got from serving as a guinea pig for medical experiments at nearby hospitals. The most recent Hollywood movie made in town was *Father Hood* with Patrick Swayze. Oh, yes—the title star of the children's classic, *The Black Stallion,* was raised on a local ranch.

2

Planning a Trip to San Antonio

Spontaneity is all well and good when you get to where you're going, but advance planning can make or break a trip. San Antonio is becoming more and more popular; it's best to book your vacation here well in advance. If you're thinking of coming for April's huge Fiesta bash, try to reserve at least six months ahead of time to avoid disappointment.

Most people tour San Antonio in summer, though it's not really the ideal season: The weather can be steamy, hotel rooms are at a premium, and restaurants and attractions tend to be crowded. That said, there are plenty of places to cool off around town, and some of the most popular outdoor tourist spots are open only—or have far more extended schedules—this time of year. (If sights such as Sea World and Fiesta Texas top your roster of things to do, call ahead to check when they're closed.) Consider visiting off-season or during the week in high season: San Antonio is the single most popular destination in the state for Texans, many of whom drive in just for the weekend.

What Things Cost in San Antonio	U.S.$
Taxi from the airport to the city center	13.00
Streetcar ride between any two downtown points	.25
Local telephone call	.25
Long-neck beer	2.00
Double at the Fairmount (very expensive)	185.00
Double at the Ramada Emily Morgan (moderate)	90.00
Double at the Best Western Town House Motel (inexpensive)	50.00
Lunch for one at Zuni Grill (moderate)	10.00
Lunch for one at Schilo's (inexpensive)	5.00
Dinner for one, without wine, at Biga (expensive)	25.00
Dinner for one, without wine, at La Calesa (moderate)	14.00
Dinner for one, without wine, at Earl Abel's (inexpensive)	8.00
Coca-Cola	1.00
Cup of espresso	2.00
Roll of ASA 100 Kodacolor film, 36 exposures	5.50
Admission to the Witte Museum	4.00
Movie ticket	1.50–6.25
Ticket to the San Antonio Symphony	12.00–45.00

1 Information

Contact the **San Antonio Convention & Visitors Bureau,** P.O. Box 2277, San Antonio, TX 78298 (☎ toll free **800/447-3372**), for a useful pretrip information packet, including a visitors guide and map, lodging guide, detailed calendar of events, arts brochure, and SAVE San Antonio booklet with discount coupons for a number of hotels and attractions. If you want to find out about hotel-room availability before you leave, call the bureau's lodging line (☎ **800/858-4303**).

Phone the **Texas Department of Transportation** (☎ toll free **800/8888-TEX**) ahead of time to receive the *Texas State Travel Guide,* a glossy book chock-full of information about the state, along with a statewide accommodations booklet. The department also has a toll-free number (☎ **800/452-9292**) to call for information on road conditions, special events, and general attractions in the areas you're interested in visiting; traveler counselors will even advise you on the quickest or most scenic route to your intended destination.

2 When to Go

Climate

Complain to San Antonians about their city's heat on a sultry summer day and you're likely to be assured that it's far more humid in say, Houston, or anywhere in east Texas. This may be true—but it won't make you feel any less sweaty. From late May to early September, expect high temperatures and high humidity with some regularity.

Fall and spring are prime times to visit; the days are pleasantly warm and, if you come in late March/early April, the wildflowers in nearby Hill Country will be in glorious bloom. Temperate weather combined with the lively celebrations surrounding Christmas also make November and December good months to come. January and February can be a bit raw—but if you're from up North you probably won't even notice.

San Antonio's Average Monthly Temperature & Rainfall

	Jan	Feb	Mar	Apr	May	June	July	Aug	Sept	Oct	Nov	Dec
Average	52.0	54.5	60.8	68.2	75.3	81.9	84.0	83.8	79.3	70.5	59.7	53.2
Rainfall	1.66	2.06	1.54	2.54	3.07	2.79	1.69	2.41	3.71	2.84	1.77	1.46

The Fiesta City

San Antonio's nickname refers to its huge April bash, but it also touches on the city's tendency to party hearty. It's only natural that a place with strong southern, western, and Hispanic roots would know how to have a good time: elaborately costumed festival queens, wild-and-wooly rodeos, and, at the drop of a sombrero, Mexican food and mariachis are rolled out year-round. And where else but San Antonio would something as potentially dull as draining a river turn into a cause for celebration?

San Antonio Calendar of Events

February

- **Livestock Show and Rodeo,** Joe and Harry Freeman Coliseum. Starting in early February, San Antonio hosts more than two weeks of rodeo events, livestock judging, country-and-western bands, and carnivals.
☎ **210/225-5851.**

April

- **Starving Artist Show,** River Walk and La Villita. Part of the proceeds of the work sold by nearly 1,000 local artists go to benefit the Little Church of La Villita's program to feed the hungry. ☎ **210/226-3593.**

⭐ **Fiesta San Antonio**

What started as a modest marking of Texas's independence more than 100 years ago is now a huge celebration, with an elaborately costumed royal court presiding over 10 days of revelry: parades, balls, food fests, sporting events, concerts, and art shows.
Where: All over town. **When:** Starting the third week of April. **How:** ☎ **210/227-5191** for details on tickets and events.

May

- **Cinco de Mayo,** Market Square. On the weekend closest to the Fifth of May, Mexico's independence from France is celebrated with music, food booths, and more.
☎ **210/299-8600.**

⭐ **Tejano Conjunto Festival**

This annual festival, sponsored by the Guadalupe Cultural Arts Center, celebrates the lively and unique blend of Mexican and German music born in south Texas. The best *conjunto* musicians in the nation perform here.
Where: Rosedale Park, 340 Dartmouth St. **When:** Four days in mid-May. **How:** Call **210/271-9070** for schedules and ticket information.

- **Return of the Chili Queens,** Market Square. Memorial Day weekend sees the annual celebration of chili, said to have originated in San Antonio, with music, dancing,

craft demonstrations, and, of course, chili aplenty.
☎ **210/299-8600.**

June

• **Fiesta Noche del Rio,** Arneson River Theatre. Every
Thursday, Friday, and Saturday from June through
August, a colorful revue celebrating Latin culture is held
on one side of the river while the audience claps from
across the water. ☎ **210/299-8610.**

August

• **Texas Folklife Festival,** Institute of Texas Cultures. For
four days in early August, ethnic foods, dances, crafts
demonstrations, and games celebrate the diversity of
Texas's heritage. ☎ **210/558-2300.**
• **Carver Jazz Festival,** Majestic Theater. Masters of
American jazz meet the hot new rising stars at this huge
annual jam session in late August. ☎ **210/299-7211.**

September

• **Diez de Seis de Septiembre.** On the weekend nearest
September 16th, Mexican independence from Spain
is celebrated at La Villita, the Arneson River Theatre,
and Guadalupe Plaza. For schedules of events, call the
San Antonio Convention & Visitors Bureau, toll free
☎ **800/447-3372.**
• **JazzSAlive,** Travis Park. Bands from New Orleans and
San Antonio come together for a weekend of hot jazz in
late September. ☎ **210/299-8486.**
• **Great Country River Festival,** River Walk. Late
September is also a time for Texas two-stepping to the
free country-and-western bands that play at the Arneson
River Theater and up and down along the river.
☎ **210/227-4262.**

October

• **Oktoberfest,** Beethoven Home. San Antonio's German
roots show at this early October festival with food,
dance, oompah bands, and beer. ☎ **210/222-1521.**
• **Inter-American Bookfair and Literary Festival,**
Mexican Cultural Institute. Forty international
publishers gather for poetry-and-fiction readings,
workshops, panel discussions, and book exhibits.
☎ **210/271-3151.**

November

★ **Lighting Ceremony and Holiday River Parade.**
Just after Thanksgiving Day, trees and bridges along
the river are illuminated by some 50,000 lights; Santa
Claus arrives on a boat during the floating river parade.
☎ **210/227-4262.**

- **Fiestas Navidenas,** Market Square. On weekends between Thanksgiving Day and Christmas, the Mexican market hosts piñata parties, a blessing of the animals, and surprise visits from Pancho Claus. ☎ **210/299-8600.**

December

- **Rivercenter Christmas Pageant.** River barges in the Rivercenter complex are the untraditional setting for the traditional Christmas story on December weekends leading up to the holiday. ☎ **210/225-0000.**
- **Fiesta de las Luminarias,** River Walk. On the weekends before Christmas, the River Walk is lit up by thousands of candles. ☎ **210/227-4262.**
- **Las Posadas,** River Walk. Singers walk along the river searching for lodging in a moving multifaith rendition of the Christmas story. ☎ **210/224-6163.**

---

3   Tips for Special Travelers

FOR THE DISABLED An excellent resource for travelers with any type of disability is **Travelin' Talk,** Box 3534, Clarksville, TN 37043 (☎ **615/552-6670,** fax 615/552-1182). Whether you want general information about transportation in San Antonio, or have specific questions for an individual in town with a similar impairment, the organization can refer you to a local resource. Members receive a quarterly newsletter and get a discount on the huge Travelin' Talk directory, which lists, among many other things, travel agents and tour operators who specialize in working with the disabled.

FOR SENIORS By joining the **American Association of Retired Persons** (AARP), 601 E St. NW, Washington, DC 20049 (☎ **202/434-2277**), those over age 50 can get good discounts on many hotels, rental cars, and sights; an Amoco Motoring Plan offers trip-routing information and emergency road service. (Always remember to ask about these discounts in advance—for example, when you're booking a room or renting a car, not when you're checking out or returning the vehicle.)

    The nonprofit **Elderhostel,** 75 Federal St., third floor, Boston, MA 02110 (☎ **617/426-7788**), has a variety of inexpensive and interesting study programs, including room and board, for ages 60 and older; they're becoming very popular, so book early. Among the many classes offered in San Antonio in 1994 were "The Truth about Texas Heroes: Or What Really Happened at the Alamo?" and "Folk Art of Latin America."

FOR FAMILIES Those who travel frequently with children will glean some useful hints from the *Family Travel Times* newsletter, Travel with Your Children, 45 W. 18th St., seventh floor, New York, NY 10011 (☎ **212/206-0688**), offering both general and destination-specific information; the March 1994 issue is devoted to San Antonio. A sample issue costs $2, an annual subscription (10 issues) $55. The monthly *Our Kids* magazine, published in San Antonio, includes a calendar that lists daily activities oriented toward children; you can find it in San Antonio at many downtown hotels, HEB supermarkets, Wal-Marts, and Drug Emporiums, or order it in advance from the publisher, 8400 Blanco, Suite 201, San Antonio TX 78216 (☎ 210/349-6667).

FOR STUDENTS   The **Council on International Educational Exchange** (CIEE), 205 E. 42nd St., New York, NY 10017 (☎ 212/661-1414), offers a variety of discounts on airfares, rail fares, and accommodations; send for the organization's *Student Travels* magazine for details. You don't have to be a student—or even a youth—to join **Hostelling International–American Youth Hostels,** Box 37613, Washington, DC 20013 (☎ 202/783-6161), which gives its members discounts at its dorm-style hostels around the world, and also offers rail and bus travel discounts in many places.

4   Getting There

By Plane

San Antonio International Airport (☎ 210/821-3411) is approximately 11 miles north of downtown.

THE MAJOR AIRLINES   The major domestic carriers serving San Antonio are **American** (☎ toll free **800/433-7300**), **Delta** (☎ 210/222-2354 or toll free **800/221-1212**), **Continental** (☎ toll free **800/525-0280**), **Northwest** (☎ toll free **800/225-2525**), **Southwest** (☎ toll free **800/433-5368**), **TWA** (☎ 210/226-0626 or toll free **800/221-2000**), **United** (☎ toll free **800/241-6522**), and **USAir** (☎ toll free **800/428-4322**). **Mexicana** (☎ 210/525-9191 or toll free **800/531-7921**) and **Continental** (☎ toll free **800/231-0856**) offer international service. Smaller commuter airlines that fly into San Antonio include Aerolitoral, Aeromar, and Conquest.

The lowest standard fares to San Antonio require a 14-day advance purchase, a stay over Saturday night, and travel during the week. With these restrictions, almost all the domestic airlines listed above fly from New York to San Antonio for $522. The fares vary more from carrier to carrier when you fly from other cities: Continental, Delta, Northwest, and United offer the best rates from Chicago (around $258) and Los Angeles (around $268). If you're departing from one of the cities that Southwest services, you're likely to get the lowest rates on that airline. Remember that all the airlines run seasonal specials; look out for them as soon as you start thinking about taking a trip.

By Train

The downtown San Antonio **Amtrak** station, 1174 E. Commerce St. (☎ 210/223-3226), provides service three times a week—east to Miami via Houston, Lafayette, and New Orleans and west to

Los Angeles via El Paso, Tucson, and Phoenix. There are also daily round-trips between San Antonio and Chicago via Austin, Fort Worth, Dallas, Little Rock, St. Louis, and Springfield. Round-trip prices range from $188 to $362 to Chicago, $218 to $420 to Miami, and $218 to $422 to Los Angeles, depending on time of year, advance-purchase options, and other variables. Call toll free **800/872-7245** for current fares, schedules, and reservations.

By Bus

San Antonio's **Greyhound** station, 500 N. St. Mary's St. (☎ **210/ 270-5861**), is located downtown about two blocks from the River Walk; buses come and go from all directions to the busy 24-hour terminal. Some sample one-way fares are: $159 from New York, $149 from Miami, $139 from Chicago, $149 from Los Angeles, and $179 from Seattle. However, Greyhound's 14-day advance specials bring the prices down considerably: One 1994 promotion, for example, allowed you to travel between any two points in the mainland United States for $68 one-way, $136 round-trip, as long as you didn't leave on a Friday or a Sunday. For all current price and schedule information, call toll free **800/231-2222.**

By Car

As has been said of Rome, all roads lead to San Antonio. The city is fed by four interstates (I-35, I-10, I-37, and I-410), five U.S. highways (U.S. 281, U.S. 90, U.S. 87, U.S. 181, and U.S. 81), and five state highways (S.H. 16, S.H. 13, S.H. 211, S.H. 151, and S.H. 1604). In San Antonio, I-410 and S.H. 1604, which circle the city, are referred to as Loop 410 and Loop 1604. All freeways lead into the central business district; U.S. 281 and Loop 410 are closest to the airport.

San Antonio is 975 miles from Atlanta; 1,979 miles from Boston; 1,187 miles from Chicago; 1,342 miles from Los Angeles; 1,360 miles from Miami; 527 miles from New Orleans; 1,781 miles from New York; 1,724 miles from San Francisco; and 2,149 miles from Seattle. The distance to Dallas is 282 miles, to Houston 199 miles, and to Austin 80 miles.

3

Getting to Know San Antonio

FOR VISITORS, SAN ANTONIO IS REALLY TWO CITIES. DOWNTOWN, SITE OF the original Spanish settlements, is the compact, eminently strollable tourist hub. Thanks in large part to the River Walk and its waterside development, a once decaying urban center now buzzes with hotels, restaurants, and shops. And thanks in large part to the San Antonio Conservation Society, many of downtown's beautiful old buildings are still intact; some house popular tourist attractions, while others are occupied by the large businesses that are increasingly trickling back to where it all began.

The other city is spread out, mostly low-rise, and connected by freeways—more than its fair share, in fact. San Antonio's most recent growth has been toward the northwest, where you'll find the sprawling South Texas Medical Center complex and, farther out, the ritzy new Dominion Country Club and housing development; the two large theme parks, Fiesta Texas and Sea World of Texas are also in this direction. The old southeast section, home to four of the five historic missions, remains largely Hispanic, while much of the southwest is taken up by Kelly and Lackland air force bases. Whether you fly in or drive in, you're likely to find yourself in the northeast at some point: along with the airport, this section hosts the Brackenridge Park attractions and many of the best restaurants and shops in town.

You'll probably want your own wheels if you're staying in this second San Antonio; downtown, where public transportation is cheap and plentiful, a car tends to be more of a hindrance than a help.

1   Orientation

Arriving

BY PLANE   The two-terminal **San Antonio International Airport** (☎ 210/821-3411), about 11 miles north of downtown, is compact, clean, well marked—even cheerful. Among its various amenities are a postal center, ATM, foreign-currency exchange, game room, and some well-stocked gift shops. Each terminal hosts a branch office of the City of San Antonio Visitor Information Center (see "Tourist Information," below); in Terminal One, there's also an electronic panel on which you can pull up descriptions of selected area hotels and a phone that will connect you directly to any of them that you choose.

Loop 410 and U.S. 281 South intersect just below the airport. If you're renting a car here (see "Car Rentals" in "Getting Around," below), it should take about 15 to 20 minutes to drive downtown via U.S. 281 South.

Most of the hotels within a radius of a mile or two offer **free shuttle service** to and from the airport (be sure to check when you make your reservation). If you're staying downtown, you'll most likely have to pay your own way.

VIA Metropolitan Transit's bus no. 2 is the cheapest (40¢) way to get downtown but also the slowest; it'll take from 40 to 45 minutes. (If you have a long layover at the airport, VIA's Loop 550/551 Limited express bus (75¢) can bring you to the nearby North Star and Central Park malls and let you shop the time away.)

Star Shuttle (☎ **366-3183**), with a booth at each of the terminals, offers van service from the airport to the downtown hotels for $5 per person. It runs around-the-clock, but if you're arriving after midnight you should call 24-hours in advance to prearrange pick up.

There's also a cab queue in front of each terminal. The flag-drop charge on taxis is $1.60; add $1.30 for the first and each additional mile. It should cost you about $12 to $14 to get downtown, including the 50¢ airport departure fee; from 9pm to 5am there's an additional $1 after-hours charge.

BY TRAIN   The **Amtrak** station, 1174 E. Commerce St. (☎ **210/223-3226** or toll free **800/872-7245**), is in St. Paul Square, on the east side of downtown near the Alamodome. You can pick up a public VIA streetcar from here to the major hotel areas; cabs are also available in this area.

BY BUS   The **Greyhound** station, 500 N. St. Mary's St. (☎ **210/270-5861** or toll free **800/231-2222**), is just blocks north of the heart of downtown and within walking distance of a number of hotels. Many public streetcar and bus lines run nearby.

BY CAR   The central part of San Antonio is circled by I-410, always called **Loop 410** in town; **I-10, I-35, I-37, U.S. 90, U.S. 87,** and **U.S. 281** (also known as the McAllister Freeway) all feed into 410, but not in any consistent east-west or north-south directions. **S.L.** (state loop) **1604** forms a larger loop around the outskirts of town.

Tourist Information

The main office of the **City of San Antonio Visitor Information Center** is across the street from the Alamo, at 317 Alamo Plaza (☎ **210/270-8748**). Hours are 8:30am to 6pm daily, except Thanksgiving, Christmas, and New Year's, when the center is closed. Two satellite offices are located in Terminals One (☎ **210/821-3421**) and Two (☎ **210/821-3418**) of the San Antonio International Airport; both are open daily from 10am to 6pm. You'll get recorded information about attractions in town on a prompt system if you call **800/447-3372.**

You can pick up a free copy of *Fiesta* magazine at the San Antonio Visitor Information Center, as well as at most downtown hotels and many shops. This very readable (but advertising-based) tourist publication lists sights, restaurants, shops, cultural events, and some nightlife. Also free—and not ad driven—is San Antonio's alternative paper, the *Current.* It's a bit skimpy compared to many such tabloids, but it's a good source for nightlife listings. If you can track down the *Current*'s *Visitors Guide to the Alamo City* supplement, check out its offbeat takes on the standard tourist attractions and its suggestions for unusual things to do around town.

Arguably the best state-oriented magazine in the country, *Texas Monthly* contains excellent short reviews of restaurants in San Antonio, among other cities; its incisive, witty articles about local politics, people, and events are a great way to get acquainted with Lone Star territory in general. You can buy a copy at almost any bookstore or newsstand around.

City Layout

Although it lies at the southern edge of Texas Hill Country, San Antonio itself is basically flat. As noted above, the city divides into two distinct districts: a compact central downtown surrounded by a western-style, freeway-laced sprawl. Neither section is laid out in a neat grid system; many of downtown's streets trace the meandering course of the San Antonio River, while a number of the thoroughfares in the rest of town follow old conquistador routes or 19th-century cattle-drive trails.

MAIN ARTERIES & STREETS Welcome to loop land. Most of the major roads in Texas meet in San Antonio, where they form a rough wheel-and-spoke pattern: I-410 traces a 10- to 15-mile circumference around downtown, and S.L. 1604 forms an even larger circle around them both. I-35, I-10, I-37, U.S. 281, U.S. 90, and U.S. 87, along with many smaller thoroughfares, run diagonally, but not always separately, across these two loops to form its main spokes. For example, U.S. 90, U.S. 87, and I-10 converge for a while in an east-west direction just south of downtown, while U.S. 281, I-35, and I-37 run together on a north-south route to the east; I-10, I-35, and U.S. 87 bond for a bit going north-south to the west of downtown.

Among the most major of the minor spokes are Broadway, McCullough, San Pedro, and Blanco, all of which lead north from the city center into the most popular shopping and restaurant areas of town. Fredericksburg goes out to the Medical Center from just northwest of downtown. When locals refer to the Strip, they mean the stretch of North St. Mary's between Josephine and Magnolia, known for its nightlife.

Downtown is bounded by I-37 on the east, I-35 on the north and west, and U.S. 90 on the south. Within these parameters, Commerce, Market, and Houston are important east-west throughfares. Alamo and Santa Rosa are major north-south streets, the former on the east side, the latter on the west side.

FINDING AN ADDRESS Few locals are aware that there's any method to the madness of finding downtown addresses, but in fact directions are based on the layout of the first Spanish settlements, when the San Fernando cathedral was at the center of town: Market is the north/south street divider and Flores separates the east from west. Thus, South St. Mary's becomes North St. Mary's when it crosses Market, where the addresses start from 0 in both directions. North of downtown, San Pedro is the east/west dividing line, although not every street sign reflects this fact.

There are few such clear-cut rules in loop land, but on its north-ernmost stretch, Loop 410 divides into east and west at Broadway; at Bandera Road, it splits into Loop 410 north and south. Keep go-ing far enough south and I-35 marks yet another boundary between east and west. Knowing this will help a little in locating an address, and will explain why, when you go in a circle around town—you probably won't do this voluntarily—you'll notice that the directions marked on overhead signs have suddenly shifted.

STREET MAPS The Visitor Information Center (see "Tourist In-formation," above) and most hotels distribute the free street maps published by the San Antonio Convention & Visitors Bureau (SACVB). They mark the main attractions in town and are useful enough as a general reference, especially if you're on foot; they even indicate which downtown streets are one-way—a bonus for drivers. You Are Here, a San Antonio company, publishes a color souvenir map of downtown that's less distorted and more detailed than the SACVB's map; you can pick one up at Booksmiths, 209 Alamo Plaza, or Alamo News, 511 E. Houston St. But if you're going to do much navigating around town, you'll need something better. Both Rand McNally's and Gousha's maps of San Antonio are reliable; you'll find one or the other at most convenience stores, drugstores, bookstores, and newsstands.

Neighborhoods in Brief

Downtown Site of San Antonio's three oldest Spanish settlements, this area includes the Alamo and other historic sites, along with the River Walk, the Alamodome, the convention center, the Rivercenter Mall, and many high-rise hotels, restaurants, and shops. It's also the center of commerce and law; many banks and offices, as well as most government buildings, are located here.

King William The city's first suburb, this historic district directly south of downtown was settled in the mid- to late 1800s by the wealthy German merchants who built some of the most beautiful mansions in town. Only two of the area's many impeccably restored homes are generally open to the public, but a number have been turned into bed-and-breakfasts.

Monte Vista Immediately northwest of downtown, Monte Vista was established soon after King William by a conglomeration of wealthy cattleman, politicos, and generals who moved "on to the hill" at the turn of the century. A number of the area's large houses have been split up into apartments for students of nearby Trinity Univer-sity and San Antonio Community College, but many lovely old homes have been restored in the past 20 years.

Fort Sam Houston Built in 1876 to the northeast of downtown, Fort Sam Houston hosts a number of stunning officers' homes. Much of the working class neighborhood surrounding Fort Sam is now run-down, but renewed interest in restoring San Antonio's older areas is beginning to have some impact here, too.

Alamo Heights Area In the 1890s, when construction in the area began, Alamo Heights was at the far northern reaches of San Antonio. It has slowly evolved into one of the city's most exclusive neighborhoods, and is now home to wealthy families, expensive shops, and trendy restaurants. Terrell Hills to the east, Olmos Park to the west, and Lincoln Heights to the north are all offshoots of this moneyed area; the latter is home to the Quarry, once just that but now a ritzy golf course. The greater portion of these neighborhoods share a single zip code ending in the numbers "09"—thus the local term "09ers," referring to the area's yuppie residents.

Medical Center The neighborhood surrounding the South Texas Medical Center—host to the majority of San Antonio's hospitals and medical facilities, including the University of Texas Health Science Center—is one of the more recently established. Most of the homes are condominiums and apartments, and most of the shopping and dining is in strip malls.

2 Getting Around

By Public Transportation

BY BUS San Antonio's public transportation system is extremely visitor friendly. Among the 90 regular bus routes that **VIA Metropolitan Transit Service** runs around town is no. 7/40, the Via Vistas Cultural Route, which stops at many popular tourist attractions: the McNay Art Museum, the San Antonio Botanical Gardens, the San Antonio Zoo, the Witte Museum, the San Antonio Museum of Art, Alamo Plaza, La Villita, HemisFair Park, the King William Historic District, the Yturri-Edmunds House and Mill, the Buckhorn Museums and Bar, and San Antonio Missions National Historical Park. The cost is 40¢ for regular routes (including the cultural one), 75¢ to $1 for express buses; call **210/227-2020** for transit information or stop in at VIA's downtown center, 112 N. Soledad, for maps.

BY STREETCAR In addition to its bus lines, VIA offers four convenient downtown streetcar routes that cover all the most popular tourist stops. Designed to look like the turn-of-the century trolleys used in San Antonio until 1933, the streetcars cost only a quarter to ride (though fares were recently raised from a dime, still a bargain).

Discount Passes A $2 Day-Tripper pass, good for an entire day of travel on all VIA transportation except express buses, can be purchased at VIA's downtown Information Center. Seniors (62 and over) can get a discount card at this office or at two other VIA offices: 800 W. Myrtle (☎ **210/227-5371**) and the Crossroads Park and Ride in the Crossroads Mall parking lot (☎ **210/735-3317**). It's necessary to go in person with proof of age and a Social Security card; the picture ID that you'll receive on the spot will entitle you to half-off all VIA fares, except the Day-Tripper pass.

By Other Transportation

BY TAXI   Cabs are available outside the airport, near the Greyhound and Amtrak terminals, and at most major downtown hotels, but they're next to impossible to hail on the street; most of the time, you'll need to phone for one in advance. The two major taxi companies in town are **Checker Cab** (☎ 210/222-2151) and **Yellow Cab** (☎ 210/226-4242); see "By Plane" in the "Orientation" section, above, for rates. Most cabbies impose a minimum of $6 for trips from the airport, $3 for rides downtown.

BY CAR   One word of advice about driving downtown: Unless you're familiar with the pattern of one-way streets and with the location of the area's seven parking meters—don't. It's not that the streets in downtown San Antonio are narrower or more crowded than those in most city centers; it's just that there's no need to bother with a car in this public transport–happy part of town.

As for highway driving, because of the many convergences of major freeways here—described in the "Main Arteries & Streets" section, above—if you're not constantly vigilant, you'll find yourself in the express lane to somewhere you really don't want to go. Don't let your mind wander; watch the signs carefully and be prepared to make lots of quick lane changes.

Rush hour lasts from about 7:45am to 9am and 4:30pm to 6pm Monday through Friday. It's best to avoid the I-10/Loop 410 interchange on the northwest side of town during this time, and all parts of I-35 and U.S. 281 north of downtown. (A good alternative route for 281 north is San Pedro.) San Antonio's rush hour may not be bad compared with those of Houston or Dallas, but it's getting worse all the time. Because of San Antonio's rapid growth, you can also expect to find major highway construction or repairs going on somewhere in the city at any given time.

Car Rentals   Advantage (☎ toll free **800/777-5500**), Alamo (☎ **210/828-7967** or toll free **800/327-9633**), Avis (☎ **210/824-0141** or toll free **800/831-2847**), Budget (☎ toll free **800/527-0700**), Dollar (☎ toll free **800/800-4000**), Hertz (☎ **210/841-8800** or toll free **800/654-3131**), and Thrifty (☎ toll free **800/367-2277**) all have desks at both of the airport terminals. Hertz is also represented downtown at the Marriott Rivercenter at Bowie and Commerce (☎ **210/225-3676**).

Almost all of the major car-rental companies have their own discount programs. Your rate will often depend on the organizations to which you belong, the dates of travel, and the length of your stay. Some companies give discounts to AAA members, for example, and some have special deals in conjunction with various airlines. Off-season rates are likely to be lower, and prices are sometimes reduced on weekends (or midweek). Call as far in advance as possible to book a car, and always ask about specials. Typical undiscounted summer rates for a subcompact are $26 a day and $125 a week with unlimited mileage.

In case you were wondering—yes, the Alamo car rental company got its start in San Antonio.

Parking Parking meters are not plentiful in the heart of downtown, though you can find some on the streets near the River Walk and on Broadway. The cost is 25¢ every half hour and the time limit is 2 hours; some meters also accept dimes, so you'll pay 10¢ for every 10 minutes. There are some very inexpensive ($1^1/_2$ hours for a quarter) meters at the outskirts of town; the trick is to find one. Though too few signs inform you of this, parking next to meters is free after 6pm Monday through Saturday and all day Sunday. You can also park legally in no-parking zones during these times. If you don't observe the laws, you'll be ticketed pretty quickly; if you haven't moved your car within 30 minutes after that, it'll be towed.

Except during Fiesta or other major events, you shouldn't have a problem finding a parking lot or garage for your car; rates run from $2.50 to $6 per day—the closer you get to the Alamo and the River Walk, the more expensive they become. Prices tend to go up during special events and summer weekends; a parking lot that ordinarily charges $3.50 a day is likely to charge $5. If you're only staying for a short time, consider leaving your car in the Rivercenter Mall garage and getting your ticket validated at one of the shops; you don't have to buy anything and you'll have two hours of free parking. This is only a good idea, however, if you're allergic to shopping or have an iron will; otherwise, this could end up costing you a lot more in the long run than a pay parking garage.

Driving Rules Right turns on red are permitted after a full stop. Left turns on red are also allowed, but only if you're going from a one-way street onto another one-way street.

BY RIVER TAXI From 9am to 9 or 9:30pm, **Paseo del Rio** (☎ **222-1701**) runs a river taxi that makes a full circle of the river up to the north channel. Just flag down the red-and-white barge that says "River Shuttle," buy a ticket for $3, and tell the driver where you want to be let out. This is not a quick way to get where you're going—the barge has an established route and is constantly stopping for and dropping off people—but it's a fun one.

BY BICYCLE There are no bicycle paths downtown, though the local police get around fine on two wheels; the streets are wide enough for riding in most areas. Many locals bike around other parts of town, but there are no designated lanes or other special accommodations for them. For recreational bicycling, see also the "Sports and Recreation" section of Chapter 6.

ON FOOT Downtown San Antonio is a treat for walkers, who can perambulate from one tourist attraction to another, or stroll along a beautifully landscaped river. Traffic lights even stay green long enough for pedestrians to cross without putting their lives in peril. Jaywalking is a ticketable offense, but one that's rarely enforced.

Fast Facts: San Antonio

Airport   See "Orientation" in this chapter.

American Express   2103 Broadway (☎ 828-4809).

Area Code   The telephone area code in San Antonio is **210**.

Babysitters   Your hotel should be able to recommend a reliable service.

Business Hours   Banks are usually open Monday through Friday, 9am to 6pm; most also have hours on Saturday from 9am to 1pm. Office hours are generally weekdays from 9am to 5pm. Shops tend to be open from 9 or 10am until 5:30 or 6pm Monday through Saturday, with shorter hours on Sunday, but many downtown stores don't close their doors until dark or after in summer. Most malls are open Monday through Saturday from 10am to 9pm, Sunday from noon until 6pm. The majority of bars and clubs boot their last customers out at 2am.

Car Rentals   See "Getting Around" in this chapter.

Climate   See "When to Go" in Chapter 2.

Currency & Exchange   See "Fast Facts: For the Foreign Traveler" in the Appendix.

Dentist   For a referral, contact the Bexar County Medical Society at 202 W. French Place (☎ **210/734-6691**).

Doctor   See "Dentist" above.

Documents Required   See "Preparing for Your Trip" in the Appendix.

Driving Rules   See "Getting Around" in this chapter.

Drugstores   Eckerd and Walgreen are the major chain pharmacies in San Antonio. There's an Eckerd's downtown at 211 Losoya/River Walk (☎ **210/224-9293**). Call **800/925-4733** to find the Walgreen nearest you.

Embassies/Consulates   See "Fast Facts: For the Foreign Traveler" in the Appendix.

Emergencies   For police, fire, or medical emergencies, dial **911**.

Eyeglasses   Downtown, Texas State Optical (TSO), 327 W. Commerce St. (☎ **210/227-4229**), is a trusted name for glasses. Near the airport, Eye Mart, 13417 San Pedro Ave. (☎ **210/496-6549**), offers quick and friendly service.

Hairdressers/Barbers   John Moore's for Hair, 5901 Broadway (☎ **210/826-9669**), has been serving San Antonio's elite in Alamo Heights for over 20 years. On the Strip, Mario's Beauty Salon, at 2603 N. St. Mary's St. (☎ **210/732-2310**), is always open. Owner Mario Iturralde, who's been featured in *Texas Monthly* magazine for his creative hairstyles, will cut hair at almost any hour of the day or night, but late-night appointments must come with a recommendation from another customer. A reliable local chain is Sergio's, with a convenient downtown location at 116 Losoya, across the street from the Hyatt (☎ **210/224-4968**).

Holidays See "Calendar of Events" in Chapter 2 and "Holidays" in "Fast Facts: For the Foreign Traveler" in the Appendix.

Hospitals The main downtown hospital is Baptist Medical Center, 111 Dallas St. (☎ **210/222-8431**). Metropolitan Hospital, at 1310 McCullough (☎ **210/271-2200**), is just north of downtown. There are many hospitals in the northwest's South Texas Medical Center, but Methodist, at 7700 Floyd Curl Dr. (☎ **210/692-4000**), is the largest.

Hot Lines A complete menu for Select Talk (☎ **210/524-4600**), an automated information hot line provided by Southwestern Bell, can be found in the front of the San Antonio Southwestern Bell Yellow Pages. The San Antonio Info-Line (☎ **210/732-4636**) can clue you in on attractions, restaurants, entertainment and events, recreation, shopping, local and professional services, and more.

Information See "Tourist Information" in this chapter.

Laundry/Dry Cleaning A reliable location for cleaning downtown is the multipurpose San Antonio Shoe Hospital, 124 E. Houston St. (☎ **210/223-9159**). Kwik-N-Neat offers one-hour service at 33 San Antonio locations; call **210/735-3331** for the one nearest you.

Libraries For a long time, the main public library was located just blocks from the heart of downtown at 203 S. St. Mary's St. (☎ **210/299-7820**); by the time you read this, the new building at 649 Soledad should be open.

Liquor Laws The legal drinking age in Texas is 21. Underage drinkers can legally imbibe as long as they stay within sight of their legal age spouses or parents; they need to be prepared to show proof of the relationship, however. Open containers are prohibited in public and in vehicles. Liquor laws are strictly enforced.

Lost Property Airport (☎ **210/824-7329**); bus station (☎ **210/270-5826**).

Luggage Storage/Lockers There are lockers at the Greyhound Bus Station and at the Amtrak station.

Maps See "City Layout" in this chapter.

Newspapers/Magazines Shock waves went through town in 1993 when the Hearst Corporation, owner of the *San Antonio-Express,* bought the competing *San Antonio Light*—and promptly shut it down. The *Express* is now the last—and only—word for news in town. See "Tourist Information" above, for magazine recommendations.

Photographic Needs   The Eckerd drugstore at 211 Losoya St. (☎ 210/224-9293) offers many types of film processing, including one-hour service. Barry's Camera and Video at 402 San Pedro Ave. (☎ 210/227-7363) is a reputable camera dealer and repair shop.

Police   Nonemergency (☎ 210/299-7484); general theft (☎ 210/299-7650).

Post Office   The main post office is at the far northeast part of town at 10410 Perrin-Beitel (☎ 210/650-1630), but the most convenient location is downtown at 615 E. Houston St., just across from Alamo Square (☎ 210/227-3399).

Radio/TV   You should be able to find something to suit your radio tastes in San Antonio. KISS at 99.5 FM plays heavy rock; KZEP at 104.5 FM, classic rock; KJ97 at 97.1 FM, country; KSMG at 105.3 FM, oldies. KSYM at 90.1 FM is the only college alternative station in south Texas. For Spanish language music, tune in to KCOR at 93.1 FM. You'll find National Public Radio and some jazz and classical music on KSTX at 89.1 FM; WOAI 7060 on the AM dial is an all-news station.

The local television affiliates are as follows: KMOL on Channel 4, NBC; KENS on Channel 5, CBS; KSAT on Channel 12, ABC; KLRN on Channel 9, PBS. FOX 35 on Channel 35 is the Fox network.

Religious Services   Local religious services are listed in the newspaper; you can find addresses for houses of worship in the Yellow Pages.

Restrooms   You can use the restrooms downtown at the Rivercenter Mall or you can duck into any of the free tourist attractions (yes, you can go to the bathroom at the Alamo, gratis). Most restaurants don't mind quick visits, either—they never know, you might come back for a meal later on.

Safety   There are frequent police patrols downtown at night; as a result, there are not a lot of muggings, pickpocketings, or purse snatchings in the area. But use common sense, as you would anywhere else: walk only in well-lit, well-populated streets. It's not a good idea to stroll south of Durango after dark.

Shoe Repairs   For a quick fix downtown, go to San Antonio Shoe Hospital at 124 E. Houston St. (☎ 210/223-9159).

Taxes   Sales tax recently went down from $8^1/4$% to $7^3/4$% (the extra half cent had gone to pay for the Alamodome). Restaurant tax is also $7^3/4$%. The surcharge on hotels in San Antonio is a whopping 15%.

Taxis   See "Getting Around" in this chapter.

Time   San Antonio is on central daylight time and observes daylight saving time.

Tipping   For restaurants and taxis, a 15% tip is customary. Hotel bellhops, airport porters, and valets in San Antonio are used to getting anywhere from $1 to $2 per bag, depending on the weight or size of the luggage and the service provided. You might tip chambermaids anywhere from $1 to $5 per person per night.

Transit Information   You can get information about VIA Metropolitan Transit's buses and streetcars by calling **227-2020;** see also "Orientation" and "Getting Around" earlier in this chapter.

Weather   ☎ 210/828-3384.

3   Networks & Resources

For Students

San Antonio is not a college town, and there's no general gathering place for college-age folks. The city's major universities, Trinity, 715 Stadium Dr. (☎ **210/736-7011**), and St. Mary's, 1 Camino Santa Maria (☎ **210/436-3011**), are private, as is Incarnate Word College, 4301 Broadway (☎ **210/829-6000**). The best source of local information for student visitors is probably the San Antonio International Hostel, 621 Pierce St. (☎ **210/223-9426**).

For Gay Men & Lesbians

San Antonio's gay and lesbian community is fairly large, but not very visible. For information on community events and for referrals, call the **Gay & Lesbian Switchboard** at **210/733-7300;** you'll get a recording most of the time, but the switchboard is staffed a few nights a week, depending on the availability of volunteers. **Lesbian Information San Antonio** (☎ **210/828-5472**) focuses on gay women's events around town. For a recorded listing of the gay bars in the city, phone **San Antonio Gay and Lesbian Switchboard Bar Information number** (☎ **734-2833**); three of the clubs—the Bonham Exchange, Nexus, and Industria—are reviewed in "San Antonio Nights", Chapter 8. You can pick up a copy of the lesbian newspaper, *Woman Space,* at **Textures Bookstore,** 5309 McCullough (☎ **210/805-8398**), also a good resource for lesbian literature and information on gay happenings around town. The **Esperanza Peace & Justice Center,** 922 San Pedro Ave. (☎ **210/436-9475**), hosts a lesbian social every Friday night.

For Women

Textures Bookstore and the Esperanza Peace & Justice Center, noted above, are good resources for straight as well as lesbian women; Esperanza deals largely with Hispanic culture and concerns. San Antonio's rape hot line number is **800/551-0008.**

4

San Antonio Accommodations

Y OU DON'T HAVE TO LEAVE YOUR LODGINGS TO SIGHTSEE IN SAN ANTONIO: The city has the highest concentration of historic hotels in Texas. Most of these, as well as other, more recently built luxury accommodations, are in the downtown area, which is where you're likely to want to be whether you're here on pleasure or convention business. Prices in this prime location can be high, but not uniformly, and you'll generally get your money's worth. You'll also economize by eliminating the need to rent a car: Most of the tourist attractions are within walking distance or easily accessible by public transportation, and many of the best restaurants are only an inexpensive cab ride from downtown.

In recent years, a number of the old mansions in the King William and Monte Vista Historic Districts have been converted into bed-and-breakfasts; some are reviewed below. For information about additional bed-and-breakfasts in these areas and in other neighborhoods around the city, contact **Bed & Breakfast Hosts of San Antonio,** 177 NE Loop 410, Suite 600, San Antonio, TX 78217 (☎ **210/824-8036** or toll free **800/356-1605** [reservations]); friendly Lavern Campbell will spend the time necessary to match you up with a place that suits your personality and your purse. The **San Antonio Bed and Breakfast Association** (☎ toll free **800/ 950-9903**) and **Alamo City Bed and Breakfast Hotline** (☎ toll free **800/210-8422**) can also help you find a bed-and-breakfast.

Areas around town where moderately priced and inexpensive chain lodgings are concentrated are also included in the listings that follow; the pricier or more distinctive properties in these sections are reviewed fully, while the more familiar standardized hotels or motels are noted in brief.

Wherever you decide to stay, but especially if it's downtown, try to book as far in advance as possible. This is doubly true if you're planning to visit in high season (May through October). Don't even think about coming to town during Fiesta (the third week in April) if you haven't reserved a room six months in advance.

Hotels included in the **Very Expensive** price category generally charge more than $160 per night for a double room; **Expensive** hotels range from $110 to $160 for a double; **Moderate** hotels go from $70 to $110; and **Inexpensive** rooms cost less than $70. Unless otherwise specified, these rates do not include the 15% room tax.

---

1 Downtown

Very Expensive

★ **The Fairmount,** 401 S. Alamo St., San Antonio, TX 78205. ☎ **210/224-8800** or toll free **800/642-3363.** Fax 210/224-2767. 20 rms, 17 suites. A/C TV/VCR TEL

Rates: $165 single; $185 double; $200–$475 suite. Corporate rates, packages available. AE, DC, MC, V. **Parking:** $6 valet.

This lovely boutique hotel, built in an ornate Italianate-Victorian style in 1906, is across the street from HemisFair Park, adjacent to

La Villita, and within walking distance of the King William Historic District—but it wasn't always. In 1985, it was hoisted six blocks across town, earning it a place in the Guinness Book of World Records as the heaviest building ever moved. Excavations of the site on which it now sits uncovered artifacts from the battle at the Alamo; some are showcased in the building's lobby.

The Fairmount once lodged railway travelers, but today's clientele is more likely to jet in; the hotel is sought out by film stars and other celebrities looking for low-key but luxurious digs. The hotel's intimate size, along with richly carpeted corridors and small parlors, make it seem like the home of a rich—and very attentive—friend. The suites are naturally the largest rooms—some have hardwood floors, wet bars, skylights, Jacuzzi tubs, or combinations thereof—but even the so-called standard rooms are outstanding. All are individually decorated in muted southwestern tones, with rich wood furniture (some in Craftsman style), TVs with VCRs, live plants, and original artwork, and all have balconies overlooking either the city or a small central courtyard. Italian marble and brass gleam in the bathrooms, which boast tony Lord & Mayfair toiletries along with makeup mirrors, hair dryers, and monogrammed terry robes.

Dining/Entertainment: You can enjoy the soft strains of a jazz piano at the Polo bar, a cushy, dimly lit room where deals are closed over single-malt scotches and romantic liaisons are celebrated with champagne. Warm smells wafting from the pizza oven may lure folks next door to the elegant Polo's restaurant, which serves some of the most beautifully presented contemporary American food in town (see the "Hotel Dining" section of Chapter 5 for details).

Services: Room service, twice-daily maid service, laundry, dry cleaning, complimentary newspaper, shoe-shine service, concierge, film library.

Facilities: Nonsmoking rooms, wheelchair accessible rooms, complimentary use of nearby Hilton Palacio del Rio health club and swimming pool.

Hilton Palacio del Rio, 200 S. Alamo, San Antonio, TX 78205. ☎ **210/222-1400** or toll free **800/HILTONS.** Fax 210/270-0761. 481 rms, 10 suites. A/C TV TEL

Rates: $175–$195 single ($205 Tower); $195–$215 double ($225 Tower); $375–$550 suites. AE, CB, DC, DISC, MC, V. **Parking:** $7 self, $18 valet.

Although relatively new, the Hilton has already earned a footnote in San Antonio history. To get it finished in time for the 1968 HemisFair, the hotel was built using precast concrete modules: 500 fully furnished, 35-ton rooms were hoisted up into a steel frame. The whole thing was designed, completed, and occupied in a record 202 days.

Inside this miracle of modern construction, the decor is European elegant, with more-than-passing nods to the Southwest: Polished parquet floors, oriental rugs, and a grand piano rub elbows in the hotel lobby with Mexican tile, sink-into-me leather couches, and a beautiful hand-tooled saddle. The guest rooms are not as consistently aesthetic: Those on the Tower Level are done in rich tones and dark woods, but the standard rooms are a bit 1960s, with dusty pink-and-blue decor, including pink leather headboards. All have balconies—half with city views, half with river views—and impressive standard amenities: hair dryers, coffeemakers, and irons and ironing boards. In addition, Tower Level guests get newspapers, mineral water, bathroom scales, and bathrobes in their rooms, and enjoy a continental breakfast, afternoon tea, and evening hors d'oeuvres in a private lounge.

Dining/Entertainment: All of the Hilton's dining and entertainment areas have plum locations either on or overlooking the river. The Rincón Alegre is your standard lobby piano lounge with a twist—the gleaming rosewood instrument plays itself. The music at the casual Cantina del Rio on the River Walk is canned during the week but live on the weekends; sandwiches and snacks are sold here along with drinks. The El Comedor, also on the River Walk, is the hotel's full-service casual restaurant, open for drinks on the patio as well as for breakfast, lunch, or dinner. A loftier vantage point as well as a good regional American menu draws diners to the upscale Stetson (see the "Hotel Dining" section in Chapter 5 for details). Most fun of all is Durty Nelly's Irish Pub, where you can throw your peanut shells on the floor and join in some seriously soppy sing-alongs (see "San Antonio Nights," Chapter 8, for details).

Services: Room service, valet laundry and dry cleaning.

Facilities: Outdoor heated pool, hot tub, fitness room, airlines and car rental desks, complimentary washer/dryer.

Hyatt Regency on the River Walk, 123 Losoya St., San Antonio, TX 78205. ☎ **210/222-1234** or toll free **800/233-1234.** Fax 210/227-4928. 604 rms, 27 suites. A/C MINIBAR TV TEL **Rates:** $205 single; $225 double; $300–$800 suite. AE, CB, DC, DISC, MC, V. **Parking:** $7 self, $12 valet.

There's something stimulating about all the glass and steel rising from this hotel's lobby, where the Hyatt's signature cage elevators can be seen ascending and descending the skylit atrium. Perhaps the quality of openness determines the difference between a hotel that's bustling—and this one is, with families who enjoy its convenience to all the downtown attractions as well as with business travelers—and one that just feels overcrowded. Having an extension of the river running through the lobby also adds dramatic effect.

Guest rooms are unusually attractive, done in Santa Fe–style with light-wood furniture, earth-tone drapes and bedspreads, and live plants. All have excellent standard amenities: hair dryers, ironing boards, and servibars (the latter rather rare in this city). The key to the Gold Passport Floor will get you a slightly larger room with a coffeemaker and a newspaper delivered to your door.

Dining/Entertainment: The casual Chaps Restaurant on the lobby level serves the standard breakfast, lunch, and dinner fare. More interesting is the River Bend Saloon on the River Walk, offering good fajitas and steaks in a shoot-'em-up western-style setting (it would

Downtown San Antonio Accommodations

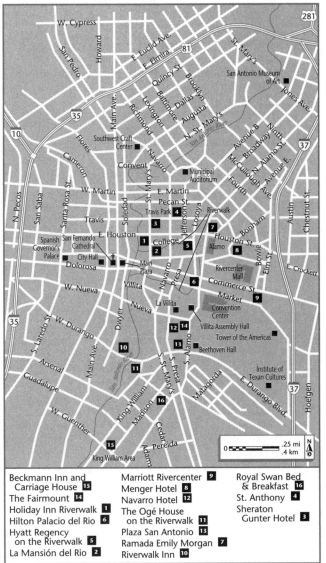

Beckmann Inn and
  Carriage House **15**
The Fairmount **14**
Holiday Inn Riverwalk **1**
Hilton Palacio del Rio **6**
Hyatt Regency
  on the Riverwalk **5**
La Mansión del Rio **2**

Marriott Rivercenter **9**
Menger Hotel **8**
Navarro Hotel **12**
The Ogé House
  on the Riverwalk **11**
Plaza San Antonio **13**
Ramada Emily Morgan **7**
Riverwalk Inn **10**

Royal Swan Bed
  & Breakfast **16**
St. Anthony **4**
Sheraton
  Gunter Hotel **3**

be hard to describe the amusing bar stools tactfully; you'll have to go
see them for yourself). The multileveled atrium River Terrace lounge
has piano music nightly, but the really happening spot is downstairs
at the Landing, where Jim Callum and his band play Dixieland jazz
(see Chapter 8, "San Antonio Nights").

Services: Room service, valet dry cleaning and laundry service, 24-hour currency exchange, express checkout, concierge.

Facilities: Rooftop pool, Jacuzzi, and sundeck; exercise room; river level shopping arcade.

La Mansión del Río, 112 College St., San Antonio, TX 78205.
☎ **210/225-2581** or toll free **800/292-7300** (Texas),
800/531-7208 (U.S., Canada, or Mexico). Fax 210/226-0389.
327 rms, 10 suites. A/C TV TEL

Frommer's Smart Traveler: Hotels

Value-Conscious Travelers Should Take Advantage of the Following:

1. Lower off-season prices (October to mid-April).

2. Chain hotels. The La Quinta chain, headquartered in San Antonio, just underwent a $6 million citywide renovation. These low-end motels offer free continental breakfast and free local calls. And at Holiday Inns, children under 12 eat free.

3. Hotels outside of the downtown area—*if* you drive into town; otherwise the price of renting a car will offset some of the savings.

4. Car-rental and airline packages, AAA discounts.

5. The annual Save San Antonio Vacation promotion. You can pick up a coupon packet, put together by the San Antonio Convention & Visitors Bureau and including some discounts on hotel rooms, at the Visitor Information Center when you get into town or at Southwest Airlines and Alamo-Rent-a-Car ticket counters beforehand.

Questions to Ask If You're on a Budget

1. Is there a parking charge? Most downtown hotels charge at least $6 for self-parking and more for valet (which is sometimes the only kind available).

2. Is there an extra charge for children? Many hotels allow children under 18 to stay free in the same room as their parents, and some extend that policy to children of *any* age (consider that if you're taking your mom on a trip).

3. Is there a lower price for an extended stay? Some bed-and-breakfasts and hotels offer discounts to those who book for at least four days, but generally a week is the minimum.

4. Is there a weekend/during-the-week discount? Some hotels in San Antonio do most of their business with conventions during the week; others cater to tourists who come on the weekend. Ask the hotel you're interested in when they have their lowest rates.

Rates: $190–$260 single or double; $430–$1,500 suite. AE, CB, DC, DISC, MC, V. **Parking:** $5 self, $7 valet.

Everyone from Barbara Bush to ZZ Top has stayed at this Spanish hacienda–style hotel, converted from a 19th-century seminary in 1968 to meet the city's room needs for the HemisFair exposition. The lushly landscaped property fronts the Paseo del Rio and is down the block from the beautifully restored Majestic Theater. Moorish arches, Mexican tile, a central patio, wrought-iron balconies, and antique pieces in every nook and cranny combine to create a low-glitz, high-tone Mediterranean atmosphere. Surprisingly, the public areas aren't as well maintained as one would expect: When I was there, corridor rugs looked worn and elevator panels could have used a fresh coat of paint.

Guest rooms all have rough-hewn beamed ceilings, brick walls, and soothing earth-tone furnishings; luxurious touches include cotton robes and complimentary newspapers. The more expensive quarters boast balconies overlooking the River Walk, but the interior courtyard views are fine, too. Standard rooms have minibars, while suites offer wet bars and dining areas.

Dining/Entertainment: The hotel's upscale dining room, Las Canarias, serves up a terrific river view with its excellent American regional cuisine; cocktails can be enjoyed in an adjoining garden courtyard. The restaurant offers entertainment nightly and a romantic Champagne Sunday Brunch. Capistrano, which looks out on the pool and courtyard, is for those seeking more casual Mexican and American fare. The El Colegio piano bar, located in the lobby, boasts a cozy fireplace.

Services: 24-hour room service, express checkout, concierge.

Facilities: Outdoor pool, gift shop.

Marriott Rivercenter, 101 Bowie St., San Antonio, TX 78205. ☎ **210/223-1000** or toll free **800/228-9290.** Fax 210/223-4092. 1,000 rms, 86 suites. A/C TV TEL

Rates: $165 single; $185 double; $229–$900 suite. AE, DC, DISC, MC, V. **Parking:** $7 self, $10 valet.

Serious retail hounds will find heaven in this glitzy high-rise; they can shop more than 100 Rivercenter emporiums until they're ready to drop and then collapse back into their hotel rooms without ever leaving the mall. Sightseers will be happy here, too; a cruise along the River Walk departs from the mall's downstairs "dock," and the Alamo and HemisFair Park are just a few blocks away.

This hotel has it all—transportation desks, a good range of dining-and-drinking areas, a large indoor/outdoor pool, and an extremely well-equipped exercise center with free weights, weight machines, stair climbers, bicycles, and treadmills. Free washers and dryers on the same floor as the health club and pool let you work out while you're waiting for the rinse cycle to finish. Well-appointed guest rooms are contemporary but elegant in muted pastel tones; many afford spectacular River Walk or city views. Those staying on the concierge level receive upgraded amenities, a free continental breakfast, and afternoon hors d'oeuvres in a concierge lounge.

Note: Built a few years earlier, the Marriott River Walk across the street is a bit smaller (which may appeal to some) and slightly less expensive than the Rivercenter. Its rooms are equally comfortable, and its guests have access to all the facilities of the sister hotel.

Dining/Entertainment: The casual, plant-filled Garden Cafe is open for breakfast (including a buffet), lunch, and dinner; it's adjacent to the River Grill, the hotel's fine dining room, where excellent seafood and steaks are prepared with a southwestern flair (see the "Hotel Dining" section in Chapter 5). The Lobby Bar and the multilevel Atrium Lounge serve drinks and light fare. Guests at the Rivercenter can also charge any meals and drinks they have at the five restaurants and lounges in the Marriott River Walk to their rooms.

Services: Room service, valet laundry service, photocopy service, fax machine, safe-deposit boxes, doctor (24-hour call).

Facilities: Gift shop, airline-reservation desk, car-rental desk, indoor/outdoor pool, health club with separate men's and women's saunas.

Plaza San Antonio, 555 S. Alamo St., San Antonio, TX 78204.
☎ **512/229-1000** or toll free **800/727-3239.** Fax 210/223-6650.
242 rms, 10 suites. A/C TV TEL

Rates: $160 single; $180 double; suites $350 and up. AE, CB, DC, DISC, MC, V. **Parking:** $6 self, $7 valet.

Pheasants stroll the beautifully landscaped grounds of this gracious hotel, located across from HemisFair Park, close to La Villita, and just north of the King William district. Four 19th-century buildings that were saved from HemisFair's bulldozer in 1968 were later incorporated into the Plaza complex. Three are used for intimate conference centers—President Bush, Canadian prime minister Mulrooney, and Mexican president Salinas held the initialing ceremony for the North American Free Trade Agreement in one of them—and the fourth houses the hotel's health club (I'd wager it's the most historic setting for StairMasters anywhere to be found).

Carpeted corridors lead to rooms as elegant as you might expect from this top-notch property; they're decorated in muted colors and floral patterns, with antique-style furnishings that include gleaming cherry headboards. Each accommodation offers a plush terry robe, full-length mirror, snack drawer, and hair dryer. Bottled water and filled ice buckets are left at evening turndown service, and complimentary newspapers are available in the morning. This is one of the few hotels in town that has tennis courts—not to mention a croquet lawn. At the lower end of the "Very Expensive" price range, the Plaza offers a lot of luxury and personal attention for the money.

Dining/Entertainment: You can order drinks or snacks at the pool, or enjoy afternoon tea at the Palm Terrace, overlooking the hotel's lovely gardens (light meals are available here during the entire day). The adjacent Lobby Bar offers cappuccino and espresso in addition to cocktails. The full-service Anaqua restaurant is known for its innovative southwestern cuisine and its international Sunday brunch buffet (see the "Hotel Dining" and "Brunch" sections in Chapter 5 for details).

Services: Twice-daily maid service, 24-hour room service, complimentary shoe shine, complimentary use of bicycles, complimentary limousine to downtown business district Monday to Friday 7:30 to 9:30am, concierge.

Facilities: Health club with men's and women's saunas, swimming pool, Jacuzzi, tennis courts, croquet.

Expensive

Holiday Inn Riverwalk, 217 N. St. Mary's St., San Antonio, TX 78205. ☎ **210/224-2500** or toll free **800/465-4329.** Fax 210/226-0154. 303 rms, 10 suites. A/C TV TEL

Rates: $109–$119 single; $125–$139 double; $175–$275 suite. AE, CB, DISC, DC, MC, V. **Parking:** $5 self, $7 valet.

This luxurious link in the Holiday Inn chain may not have the name-drop cachet of some of the historical hotels nearby, but it does offer a River Walk location and many of the same amenities for a much lower price. The hotel looks out on a quiet stretch of the river, but it's just a few minutes' walk from all the action.

Fairly standard and boxy from the outside, this high-rise opens into a plush lobby with lots of plants, comfortable chairs, and polished tile. Guest rooms are also unexpectedly attractive; the southwestern tones and patterns are tastefully vibrant, and the lamps wouldn't look out of place in a Santa Fe boutique. Almost all of the rooms have balconies; those looking out onto the river are slightly more expensive than those that overlook the city, although the urban vistas can be stunning at night, especially from the higher floors. Suites offer hair dryers, coffeemakers, and minirefrigerators.

Dining/Entertainment: The three-level Fandangos Restaurant serves up a spectacular view of the river with its fairly standard American cuisine; it's open for three meals daily and offers breakfast-and-lunch buffets during the week. Live music—everything from country to classical to pop—fills the Ripples Lounge every evening. A few of the tables peek over onto the river.

Services: Room service, nonsmoking rooms, wheelchair accessible rooms.

Facilities: Outdoor heated pool, whirlpool, exercise room, gift shop.

★ **Menger Hotel,** 204 Alamo Plaza, San Antonio, TX 78205. ☎ **210/223-4361** or toll free **800/345-9285.** Fax 210/223-1328. $ 320 rms, 25 suites. A/C TV TEL

Rates: $102–$122 single; $122–$142 double; $182–$546 suite. AE, CB, DC, DISC, MC, V. **Parking:** $4.95 self, $9.95 valet.

Its location, smack between the Alamo and the Rivercenter Mall and a block from the River Walk, is perfect. Its history is fascinating. Its public areas, particularly the Victorian Lobby, are gorgeous. Its guest rooms are charming. And its rates are reasonable. Why would anyone visiting San Antonio want to stay anywhere else but the Menger?

Indeed, in the late 19th century, no one who was anyone would consider it. A self-guided tour pamphlet of the hotel will take you through halls, ballrooms, and gardens that the likes of Ulysses S. Grant, Sarah Bernhardt, and Oscar Wilde walked—and, in the case of Robert E. Lee, rode his horse through. Established in 1859, the Menger is the only hotel west of the Mississippi that's never closed its doors. It successfully combined the original, restored building with myriad additions (it now takes up an entire city block).

Decor in the guest rooms ranges from ornate 19th-century style to modern, but still characterful—some of the newer rooms have oriental touches, others tasteful western motifs. Those in the rather plain central section built in 1944 offer kitchenettes and balconies. All have modern amenities. If you want to stay in one of the antiques-filled Victorian rooms, specifically request it when you book.

Dining/Entertainment: The Menger Bar is one of San Antonio's great historic taverns; see Chapter 8, "San Antonio Nights", for details. You can also enjoy cocktails in the lobby or at poolside. The pretty Colonial Room Garden Restaurant offers breakfast and lunch buffets and a southwestern-style menu that includes a number of game specials for dinner. Be sure to try the mango ice cream: President Clinton liked it so much, he had hundreds of gallons shipped in for his inauguration. If you don't want a formal breakfast in the morning, nip down the block to the hotel's Blum Street Bake Shop and pick up some coffee and a buttery pecan roll.

Services: 24-hour room service, valet-laundry and dry-cleaning service, limousine service.

Facilities: Heated outdoor pool, hot tub, exercise room, Alamo Plaza Spa (facials, wraps, massage) on premises, shopping arcade, tourist information center, game room, gift shop.

St. Anthony, 300 E. Travis, San Antonio, TX 78204.
☎ **210/227-4392** or toll free **800/338-1338.** Fax 210/227-0915. 308 rms, 42 suites. A/C TV TEL

Rates: $140–$152 single or double; $235–$275 suite. Lower rates on weekends. **Parking:** $6 self, $9 valet.

The place to stay when it opened in 1909, the St. Anthony's retains much of its old polish. The lobby is resplendent with crystal chandeliers, thick area rugs set on gleaming marble floors, and ornate French Provincial–style furnishings. The hotel also has a nice—if no longer quite central—location, just across from pretty Travis Park and only a few blocks from the River Walk. Fully carpeted guest rooms, done in rose or beige tones with floral prints and European dark-wood furnishings, have an old-world appeal.

But the hotel tends to cater more to conventioneers than socialites these days, and the original 1909 tiles in the upstairs hall areas look a little tired. A rooftop pool is enclosed by a chain-link fence, and the exercise room is smaller than most.

Dining/Entertainment: The informal first-floor Cafe serves breakfast, lunch, and dinner; at a lunchtime pasta bar, you can get noodles topped with a variety of cooked-to-order ingredients such as fresh vegetables. Pete's Pub is dark and Victorian style; drinks are also available at the Loggia, a lighter lobby area looking out on Travis Park.

Services: Room service, valet service, laundry service.

Facilities: Pool, sundeck, exercise room, gift shop.

Sheraton Gunther Hotel, 205 E. Houston St., San Antonio, TX 78205. ☎ **210/227-3241** or toll free **800/325-3535.** Fax 210/227-3241. 322 rms, 7 suites. A/C TV TEL

Rates: $130 single; $140 double; $195–$495 suite. AE, CB, DC, DISC, MC, V. **Parking:** $9 valet.

Western stars Will Rogers, John Wayne, and Tom Mix all trod the polished marble halls of this opulent hotel—in dusty, beat-up cowboy boots, no doubt. The first steel structure in San Antonio when it was built in 1909, the Gunther had its posh tone restored in the early 1980s with crystal chandeliers, potted palms, ornate plaster ceiling casts, and rich mahogany fittings. Resting on the site of an even earlier series of hotels and military headquarters, the first one established in 1837 (ask at the front desk for a historical pamphlet), the hotel is a stone's throw from the Majestic Theater and close to the River Walk.

All the guest rooms are done in an updated traditional style, with natural hardwood armoires and tasteful floral bedspreads and drapes. Standard amenities include phones with voice mail, in-room coffeemakers, and bathroom scales (a bit cruel, considering the wonderful pastry shop downstairs). Accommodations on the Executive Level also provide hair dryers and makeup mirrors. Guests on these floors have access to an executive lounge, with a cash bar from 5 to 8pm, a large screen TV, newspapers, a continental breakfast buffet spread, and concierge service.

Dining/Entertainment: Lots of local businessfolk come to the bi-level, glass-and-brass Padre Muldoon's to take advantage of the lunch buffet or to unwind after work in front of the large screen TV. Breakfast, lunch, and dinner are served at the turn-of-the-century–style Houston St. Cafe, but the smell of fresh-baked French and Viennese pastries tempts some diners straight to the award-winning Patisserie Suisse next door.

Services: Room service, valet laundry and dry cleaning.

Facilities: Heated outdoor pool, whirlpool, sundeck, exercise room, gift shop, barber shop, video arcade.

Moderate

Downtown offers only a few convenient chain hotels in the "Moderate" price category. The **La Quinta Convention Center,** 1001 E. Commerce St., 78205 (☎ **210/222-9181** or toll free **800/531-5900**) and the **Days Inn/Downtowner Alamo,** 902 E. Houston St., 78205 (☎ **210/227-6233** or toll free **800/325-2525**), are both close to HemisFair Park and the Rivercenter Mall; **La Quinta Market Square,** 900 Dolorosa, 78207 (☎ 210/271-0001 or toll free 800/531-5900), is near the west-side attractions. The **Alamo TraveLodge,** 405 Broadway, 78205 (☎ 210/222-9401 or toll free 800/578-7878), and **Holiday Inn Downtown/Market Square,** 318 W. Durango, 78204 (☎ 210/225-3211 or toll free 800/422-2419), are a bit farther from the center of things, but both are on the VIA streetcar route.

★ **Ramada Emily Morgan,** 705 E. Houston St., San Antonio, TX 78205. ☎ **210/225-8486** or toll free **800/824-6674.**
$ Fax 210/225-7227. 154 rms, 11 Executive rms, 12 Plaza rms. A/C TV TEL

Rates: $75 single during the week, $85 on weekends; $85 double during the week, $95 on weekends; $129 Executive Rooms; $149 Plaza Rooms. AE, CB, DC, DISC, MC, V. **Parking:** Self parking, $7.

Remodeled and converted to a hotel to the tune of $17.5 million in 1985, the Ramada Emily Morgan is one of downtown's great bargains. Centrally located directly across Alamo Plaza, it's set in a beautiful 1926 Gothic Revival building, the first documented skyscraper built west of the Mississippi. It was originally designed as a medical arts center; be sure to look up at the gargoyles, said to have been placed there to help the doctors ward off disease.

Guest rooms are modern, bright, and immaculate; each has a remote control TV with HBO and pay-for-view movies as well as a hair dryer and coffeemaker—amenities frequently missing from far more expensive accommodations. In addition, pricier Executive and Plaza Rooms offer minirefrigerators and double or single Jacuzzi tubs.

Dining/Entertainment: The lobby hosts the cheerful Yellow Rose Cafe, which features a breakfast-and-lunch buffet and Emily's Oasis Cocktail Lounge, where dinner is served and complimentary hors d'oeuvres are offered during happy hour. In case you were wondering—Emily Morgan, called the "Yellow Rose of Texas," was the mulatto slave mistress of Mexican general Santa Anna; she was reputed to have spied on him for the Texas independence fighters.

Services: Room service.

Facilities: Outdoor pool and whirlpool, exercise room, his-and-her saunas, gift shop.

Inexpensive

Navarro Hotel, 116 Navarro St., San Antonio, TX 78205.
☎ **210/224-0255.** 43 rms. A/C TV

Rates: $25.95–$45 single (including tax); $36.95–$45 double (including tax). DISC, MC, V. **Parking:** Free.

This bare-bones establishment has some ritzy neighbors; it's located just behind the Fairmount and San Antonio Plaza, and is convenient to La Villita, HemisFair Park, and the River Walk. The front desk is friendly and the rooms are basic but clean; some are very large. Covered parking is free, and a 24-hour Mexican restaurant downstairs assures some action on this slightly off-the-beaten-path block, no matter what time you return to your room. For those who can do without air-conditioning, some rooms are available at even lower rates.

Bed & Breakfast

Riverwalk Inn, 329 Old Guilbeau, San Antonio, TX 78204.
☎ **210/212-8300** or toll free **800/254-4440.** Fax 210/229-9422.
10 rms, 1 suite (all with bath). A/C TV TEL
   Rates (including breakfast): $89–$145 single or double; $160 suite. AE, DISC, MC, V.

If you've ever had a hankering to stay in an old log cabin but don't really care to go rustic, consider this unusual bed-and-breakfast. Native Texans Jan and Tracy Hammer had eight 1840s Tennessee cabins taken apart log by log and put back together again near the banks of the San Antonio River, a few blocks south of HemisFair Park and north of the King William area.

   Except for a few details—indoor plumbing, individual air-conditioning and heating units, refrigerators, TVs, phones with voice mail, coffeemakers, and digital alarm clocks—everything is in keeping with the original era of the cabins; each room has a fireplace, quilt, braided rug, and many fascinating primitive antiques. Most rooms also have balconies or porches fronting the river. Fresh-made desserts are served in the parlor every evening, and storytellers come around most weekends to give historical presentations. The wooden plank breakfast table can get a bit crowded on weekend mornings, but that's in keeping with the inn's pioneer spirit—and at least guests don't all have to sleep together in one room.

2   King William Historic District

Bed & Breakfasts

Beckmann Inn and Carriage House, 222 E. Guenther St., San Antonio, TX 78204. ☎ **210/229-1449** or toll free **800/945-1449.** 3 rms, 2 suites (all with bath). A/C TV
   Rates (including breakfast): $90–$100 room; $130 suite. AE, DC, MC, V. **Parking:** Free off street.

Sitting out on the lovely wraparound porch of this 1886 Queen Anne home, you can easily imagine yourself in a kinder, gentler era. You'll be surrounded by quiet, tree-lined streets set along an uncommercialized stretch of the San Antonio River. There's also a view of the flour mill on whose property the Beckmann Inn was originally built. Nor will the illusion of time travel be dispelled when you step through the rare Texas red-pine door into the high-ceiling parlor.

   Innkeepers Betty Jo and Don Schwartz filled the house with antique pieces that do justice to the setting, such as the ornately carved Victorian beds in each of the guest rooms. Two of the rooms have private entrances, as does the separate Carriage House, which is decorated in a somewhat lighter fashion. A full breakfast—perhaps stuffed french toast with light cream cheese and pecans—is served in the formal dining room, but you can enjoy your coffee on a flower-filled sunporch.

★ **The Ogé House on the River Walk,** 209 Washington St., San Antonio, TX 78204. ☎ **210/223-2353** or toll free **800/242-2770.** Fax 210/226-5812. 5 rms, 4 suites (all with bath). A/C TV TEL

Rates (including breakfast): $125–$135 single or double; $165–$195 suite. AE, MC, V. **Parking:** Free.

One of the most glorious of the mansions that grace the King William district, the Greek Revival–style Ogé House is more boutique inn than folksy bed-and-breakfast. You'll still get the personalized attention you would expect from a host home, but it's combined here with the luxury of a sophisticated small hotel. For example, a bountiful continental breakfast is served on individual white-clothed tables set with the finest of crystal and china. Single travelers who don't take to talking to strangers in the morning can bury themselves in one of the daily newspapers laid out on the bureau just beyond the dining room.

More social-minded folks might be seen lounging on the downstairs porch in the late afternoon, perhaps enjoying a drink with hosts Patrick and Sharrie Magatagan; they know all the best places to eat in town and can help you get a reservation. Impeccably decorated in high Victorian style, all the accommodations offer private telephone lines, cable TV, and refrigerators; many have fireplaces and views of the manicured, pecan-shaded grounds, and one looks out on the river from its own wrought-iron balcony. The painstakingly restored home now looks much as it did when it was built in 1867, but if you want to see the carriage house that was originally on the estate, you'll have to visit the Yturri-Edmunds House and Mill (see the "Historic Buildings/Complexes" section of Chapter 6).

Royal Swan Bed & Breakfast, 236 Madison, San Antonio, TX 78204. ☎ **210/223-3776** or toll free **800/368-3073.** 7 rms, 1 suite (all with bath). A/C TV

Rates (including breakfast): $85–$95 room; suites $105 for two guests, $125 for four guests. Discounts Mon–Thurs. AE, DISC, MC, V. **Parking:** Free.

You'll revel in Victoriana at the Royal Swan, which is prettily adorned with flowered rugs, tapestry couches, marble-topped tables, nymph lamps, crystal chandeliers, and lace and fringe galore. The entrance hall to the 1892 house, made of carved aged pine and punctuated by stained-glass windows, is stunning; a beveled balcony at the top of the stairs was designed to provide a stage for a dramatic toss of a bridal bouquet.

Five of the guest rooms are in the main house, the other three in a 1903 Greek Revival–style house across a courtyard (where you'll see the bed-and-breakfast's Jacuzzi). All are beautifully decorated and offer a variety of special touches—some have electric fireplaces, others claw-foot tubs or verandas. One room has a private entrance.

Guests breakfast together in the grand dining room of the main house. During the week a generous continental repast of fresh juice, pastries, muffins, and croissants is served. On the weekends, a hot egg dish is added to the spread.

3 Monte Vista Historic District

Bed & Breakfasts

The Bonner Garden, 145 E. Agarita, San Antonio, TX 78212.
☎ **210/733-4222** or toll free **800/396-4222.** Fax 210/733-6129.
5 rms (all with bath). A/C TV TEL

Rates (including breakfast): $75–$85 double; $95 suite. Weekly and corporate rates available. AE, DISC, MC, V.

Those who like the intimacy of the bed-and-breakfast experience but aren't keen on Victorian froufrou should consider the Bonner Garden, located in the Monte Vista Historic District, about a mile north of downtown. Built for Louisiana artist Mary Bonner in 1910, this large, Italianate villa has a beautiful, classical simplicity *and* lots of gorgeous antiques. Not to mention a 50-foot sunken swimming pool.

The Portico Room, with a private poolside entrance, is the most opulent. Guests can gaze up at a painted blue sky with billowing clouds or look down at an intricate Italian mosaic-tile floor. Most of the rooms have European-type decor, but Mary Bonner's former studio, separate from the main house, is done in tasteful Santa Fe style. In addition to phones and TVs, all the rooms have VCRs— the better to take advantage of the excellent film library the hosts are compiling. By the time you read this, a deck, Jacuzzi, and wet bar are likely to have been installed on the roof, which affords a dazzling view of downtown at night.

Frommer's Cool for Kids: Hotels

Hyatt Regency Hill Country Resort (p. 51) In addition to its many great places for kids to play (including a beach with a shallow swimming area), this hotel has Camp Hyatt, a special program of excursions, sports, and social activities for children 3 to 12. Rates are $17 for the morning program, $18 for the afternoon program, and $27 for a full day (lunch is $7 extra).

Plaza San Antonio (p. 36) A theme-based summer Kid's Club package for children ages 5 to 12 is offered here. In 1994, the hotel's Jurassic Adventure included discount tickets to Sea World of Texas and the Witte Museum (both of which had dinosaur exhibits) and a full roster of supervised activities at the hotel, including a "Dinosaur Dig." All-inclusive rates were $139 for the first night's hotel stay and $120.75 for each additional night.

Sheraton Gunther Hotel (p. 39) You'd never expect it from the staid old boy, but this hotel has a fairly sizable video arcade tucked away on the downstairs level.

Falling Pines, 300 W. French Place, San Antonio, TX 78212.
☎ **210/733-1998** or toll free **800/880-4580.** 3 rms, 1 suite (all with bath). A/C TV TEL

Rates (including breakfast): $100 room; $150 suite. Business rates available. AE, MC, V. **Parking:** Free.

It's not quite as large as Southfork, J. R. Ewing's ranch on *Dallas,* but Falling Pines, the domain of another Texas oilman, is not too shabby, either: The Italianate-Victorian mansion of Bob Daubert and his wife, Grace, measures more than 9,000 square feet. Built in 1911 for a cotton broker married to the granddaughter of Sam Houston, this is the type of place that people gape at in the street. Nor does the inside disappoint; the inn's myriad treasures include a Steinway grand piano, authentic oriental rugs, Baccarat crystal chandeliers, and lots of seriously good antiques.

If you're celebrating a special occasion—or are just feeling like a pasha—book the fabulous 2,000-square-foot Persian Suite, tented from floor to ceiling in white fabric and commanding an inspiring view of downtown. You needn't stay in the suite to feel like royalty, however: fresh flowers, chocolates, and a decanter of brandy await all bed-and-breakfast guests. A full breakfast—perhaps eggs Benedict and one of Bob's home-baked strudels—is served on Royal Doulton china in a lovely tiled solarium.

4 Brackenridge Park Area

$ Park Inn on Broadway, 3617 Broadway, San Antonio, TX 78209. ☎ **210/826-3245.** Fax 210/826-6671. 42 rms. A/C TV TEL

Rates: Nov–Apr $35 single, May–Oct $50; Nov–Apr $45 double, May–Oct $58. DISC, MC, V. **Parking:** Free.

Fronted by a 500-year-old oak tree and a small patio with a stone fountain, the Park Inn stands out from the mostly no-tell motels lining this stretch of Broadway. This was San Antonio's first motel (one section was built in 1935), and a recent renovation spruced up its appealing Spanish colonial–style units with colorful coats of terra-cotta, blue, tan, and green paint. The rooms are nothing fancy, but they're clean and comfortable, and some have delightful details such as the original Mexican-tiled floors. Each unit has its own covered parking space. The motel is within walking distance of many Brackenridge Park attractions, as well as more than 20 restaurants.

5 Fort Sam Houston/Northeast I-35

A number of inexpensive chain hotels along the section of I-35 just northeast of downtown and south of Fort Sam Houston offer rooms in the "Inexpensive" price category. These include **Holiday Inn Northeast,** 3855 I-35, 78219 (☎ **210/226-4361** or toll free **800/ 465-4329**); **Stratford House Inn,** 3911 I-35 north, 78219 (☎ **210/224-4944**); **Days Inn Northeast,** 3443 I-35 north, 78219

(☎ **210/225-4521** or toll free **800/325-2525**); **Economy Inn,** 3645 I-35 north, 78219 (☎ **210/225-8000**); and **Quality Inn & Suites,** 3817 I-35 north, 78219 (☎ **210/224-3030**). All offer swimming pools, and the Holiday Inn and Economy Inn have restaurants and room service in addition. Scenic this area isn't, but the price is right.

Bed & Breakfasts

\$ **Bullis House Inn,** 621 Pierce St., San Antonio, TX 78208. ☎ **210/223-9426.** Fax 210/299-1479. 7 rms (1 with bath, 6 share 3½ baths). A/C TV

Rates (including breakfast): $41–55 single (shared bath), $65 single (private bath); $49–$59 double (shared bath), $69 double (private bath). Weekly rates available. Prices include continental breakfast. AE, DISC, MC, V.

For those who don't mind sharing a bath, this graceful neoclassical mansion is the best bed-and-breakfast bargain in town. Just down the street from the Fort Sam Houston quadrangle, it was built between 1906 and 1909 for General John Lapham Bullis, a frontier Indian fighter who played a key role in capturing Geronimo (some claim the Apache chief's spirit still roams the mansion). More concerned with creature comforts when he retired, the general had oak paneling, parquet floors, crystal chandeliers, and marble fireplaces installed in his home. Beautifully restored in the 1980s, it's often used for wedding receptions these days.

Guest rooms, all with 14-foot ceilings, are furnished with some period antiques along with good reproductions; three of them feature fireplaces. The family room, which sleeps up to six (it's $10 additional for each adult, $6 for each child under 17), has a refrigerator. Near I-35 and Hwy. 281, this bed-and-breakfast is easily accessible to the airport and downtown by car; it's also a short drive from the restaurants and nightlife of the North St. Mary's area.

Services: Movies shown three nights a week, VCR/video rental available.

Facilities: Swimming pool (Apr 15–Oct 15), free off-street parking.

Terrell Castle, 950 E. Grayson St., San Antonio, TX 78208. ☎ **210/271-9145.** For reservations, ☎ **210/824-8036** or toll free **800/356-1605.** 4 rms, 4 suites (all with bath). A/C TV

Rates: $70 single (rooms), $85 single (suites); $85 double (rooms), $100 double (suites). AE, DISC, MC, V.

Unless a trip to Scotland is in the cards, this could be your best chance to spend a night in a castle. Built in 1894 by English-born architect Alfred Giles, this massive limestone structure was commissioned by Edwin Terrell, a statesman who fell in love with the European grand style while serving as U.S. ambassador to Belgium. In 1986, Katherine Poulis and her daughter Nancy Haley decided to buy the place, by this time something of a white elephant in this working-class area near the Fort Sam Houston quadrangle.

The resulting bed-and-breakfast is a bit of a hybrid: Most of the public areas are splendid, but the yard is rather unkempt. And while some of the rooms are tastefully decorated with antiques, others—such as the red, white, and blue Americana room—border on kitsch. That said, this is a unique and refreshingly unintimidating place; you'll find a warm welcome, a big breakfast—and you'll dine out on the experience for years.

Facilities: Fireplaces in two suites and two rooms, wet bar in two suites, free off-street parking.

Youth Hostel

San Antonio International Hostel, 621 Pierce St., San Antonio, TX 78208. ☎ **210/223-9426.** Fax 210/299-1479. 40 beds.

Rates: $12.60 for members, $15.60 for nonmembers. AE, DISC, MC, V.

Right next door to the Bullis House (see above), this youth hostel has a reading room, small kitchen, dining area, and picnic tables, in addition to male and female dorms; hostelers are welcome at the Bullis House on film nights, and the two lodgings share a pool. Day use of the hostel is permitted, and there's no curfew; sheet rentals cost $2, towel rentals 50¢. This pleasant facility is fairly close to downtown, but not especially convenient to it if you're using public transportation.

6 Near the Airport

Expensive

San Antonio Airport Hilton and Conference Center,

611 NW Loop 410, San Antonio, TX 78216. ☎ **210/340-6060** or toll free **800-HILTONS.** Fax 210/377-4646. 376 rms, 11 suites. A/C TV TEL

Rates: $109 single; $124 double; $165 suite. AE, CB, DC, DISC, MC, V. **Parking:** Free (covered).

A $6-million renovation completed in 1994 gave this Hilton's restaurants and downstairs public areas a spiffy new look. In the lobby, a copper-sheeted ceiling, polished Kentucky sandstone floors, and a marble-topped reception desk resembling a saloon bar successfully blend old West themes with contemporary design.

The revamp didn't extend to the guest rooms—which are perfectly comfortable, just not as brand spanking new and stylish as one might have expected after seeing the lobby; furnishings are dark wood, with a Victorian tone. Guests on the 14th-floor Executive Level get bathrobes, coffeemakers, daily newspaper delivery, and free continental breakfast.

Dining/Entertainment: Jock watchers will like the Hilton's new sports bar, with Texas sports memorabilia and enough TVs to let patrons tune into their favorite home games; see Chapter 8, "San Antonio Nights," for details. The adjoining Tex's Grill, serving three meals a day, has country food—chicken-fried steak, catfish, lots of mesquite-grilled things—to match its country decor, including brands, spurs, ropes, hats, boots, and barbed wire.

Services: Room service; valet laundry service (Monday to Friday); complimentary shuttle to airport, North Star Mall, and area restaurants; 24-hour security guards; in-room voice mail and data ports for modems.

Facilities: Outdoor heated pool; men's and women's saunas; exercise room with free weights; video-game room; full-service business center.

Sheraton Fiesta San Antonio, 37 NE Loop 410, San Antonio, TX 78216. ☎ **210/366-2424** or toll free **800/535-1980.** Fax 210/341-0410. 284 rms, 7 suites. A/C TV TEL

Rates: $120–$150 single; $130–$160 double; $225–$295 suite. Various packages available. AE, CB, DC, DISC, MC, V. **Parking:** Free.

The Sheraton Fiesta is five minutes from the airport and in the heart of the busy Loop 410 business district, just across the freeway from two major shopping malls. But when you're lounging at the pool in the hotel's central patio, you'll feel like you're far away from it all.

Developer Patrick J. Kennedy, who converted a downtown seminary into the posh Mansión del Rio hotel (see "Downtown," above), was also responsible for the Sheraton's design. Moorish arches, potted plants, stone fountains, and colorful Mexican tile create a Mediterranean mood in the public areas; intricate wrought-iron elevators descend from the guest floors to the pool patio, eliminating the need to tromp through the lobby in a swimsuit. Guest rooms are equally appealing, with brick walls painted in peach or beige, wood beamed ceilings, draped French doors, and colorful contemporary art. Coffeemakers and fax/modem hookups remind you that the hotel has a large business clientele, much of it from Mexico.

Dining/Entertainment: The hotel's contemporary-style fine dining room, Cascabel, features cutting-edge southwestern cuisine (it's reviewed in Chapter 5). You can enjoy a more casual meal accompanied by the sound of a splashing fountain at the Courtyard Cafe. After dinner, sink down into one of the plush leather chairs of the Spanish colonial–style Cascabel Lounge to hear live music, or visit the Lobby Lounge from 5 to 9pm Monday through Friday; there's always someone there tickling the ivories.

Services: Room service (with complimentary newspapers); concierge staff; secretarial, fax machine, copy service; laundry/valet; safe-deposit boxes; complimentary van service to airport and North Star and Central Malls.

Facilities: Outdoor swimming pool and Jacuzzi; exercise room; sauna.

Moderate

A number of chain properties in the airport area fall into the "Moderate" price range. Almost all offer courtesy van service to the airport; the ones that give you the most facilities for the money include

Accommodations & Dining in
Greater San Antonio

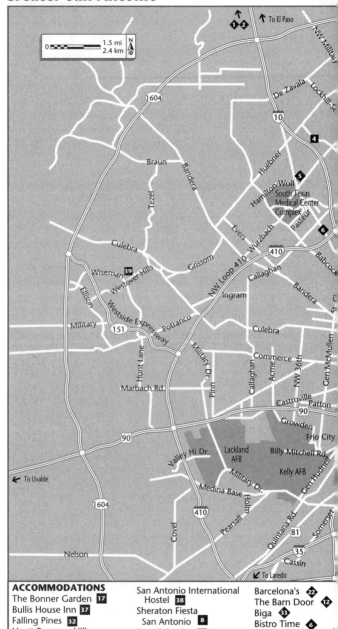

9581

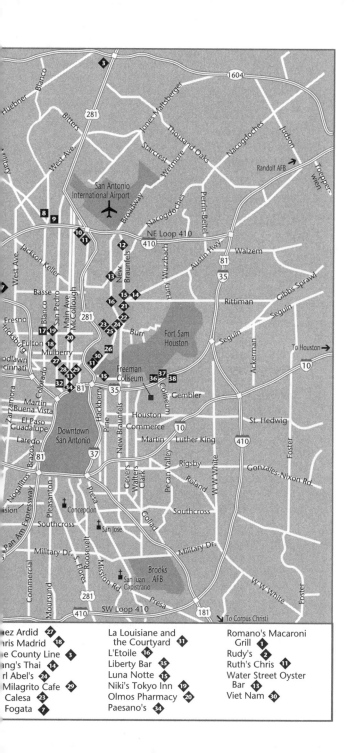

ez Ardid 🔷27
ris Madrid 🔷18
e County Line 🔷3
ng's Thai 🔷14
rl Abel's 🔷24
Milagrito Cafe 🔷29
Calesa 🔷23
Fogata 🔷7

La Louisiane and
  the Courtyard 🔷31
L'Etoile 🔷16
Liberty Bar 🔷35
Luna Notte 🔷15
Niki's Tokyo Inn 🔷19
Olmos Pharmacy 🔷20
Paesano's 🔷34

Romano's Macaroni
  Grill 🔷1
Rudy's 🔷2
Ruth's Chris 🔷11
Water Street Oyster
  Bar 🔷13
Viet Nam 🔷30

AmeriSuites by the Airport, 11221 San Pedro, 78216 (☎ **210/ 342-4800;** exercise room, pool, kitchenettes); **Courtyard by Marriott/Airport,** 8615 Broadway, 78717 (☎ **210/828-7200** or toll free **800/321-2211;** exercise room, pool, restaurant, room service); **Drury Suites/Airport,** 8811 Jones-Maltsberger, 78216 (☎ **210/308-8100** or toll free **800/325-8300;** pool, kitchenettes); **Holiday Inn Airport/North Star Mall,** 77 NE Loop 410, 78216 (☎ **210/349-9900;** exercise room, pool, restaurant, room service); **La Quinta Airport East,** 333 NE Loop 410, 78216 (☎ **210/ 828-0781** or toll free **800/531-5900;** pool, restaurant, room service); and **Ramada Inn Airport,** 1111 NE Loop 410, 78209 (☎ **210/ 828-9031;** pool, restaurant, room service).

Inexpensive

The only lodging near the airport that falls into the "Inexpensive" price range is the **Best Western Town House Motel,** 942 NE Loop 410, 78209 (☎ **210/826-6311** or toll free **800/528-1234;** pool).

7 Medical Center/Northwest

Expensive

Wyndham San Antonio, 9821 Colonnade Blvd., San Antonio, TX 78230. ☎ **210/691-8888** or toll free **800/460-8881, 800/822-4200** (U.S. reservations), **800/631-4200** (Canada reservations). Fax 210/691-1128. 323 rms, 3 suites. A/C TV TEL **Rates:** $150 single; $160 double; $275–$575 suite. AE, CB, DC, DISC, MC, V. **Parking:** Free.

This polished granite high-rise off I.H. 10 west is convenient to both Sea World of Texas and Fiesta Texas as well as to the airport and Hill Country. In addition, a number of the shops and restaurants in the 66-acre Colonnade complex are within easy walking distance.

At the back of the soaring, luxurious lobby, a health complex offers indoor-and-outdoor pools (the latter large enough for laps) and two Jacuzzis, along with a well-equipped exercise room and sauna; racquetball facilities are adjacent to the hotel. Guest rooms are well appointed in a contemporary European style, with rich blues and burgundies and floral patterns. Although the hotel sees a lot of tourist and Medical Center traffic, service here is prompt and courteous.

Dining/Entertainment: At a clubby lobby lounge, you can settle into plush leather chairs and listen to live piano music nightly. Just behind the bar is La Camellia, the hotel's low-lit fine-dining room, which recently shifted its focus from serious steaks to innovative seafood. Lighter meals are available throughout the day at the cheerful, light-filled Park Restaurant. Breakfasts there are fine, but if you're here on Sunday, don't miss the 19th-floor brunch, where wonderful views of Hill Country accompany a copious spread.

Services: Room service, valet laundry/dry cleaning, complimentary airport shuttle.

Facilities: Gift shop, concierge, safe-deposit boxes.

Moderate

The northwest section of San Antonio, home to the huge South Texas Medical Center and the newest part of town to be developed, offers a number of lower-end properties around the area where NW Loop 410 meets I.H. 10 west. The **Embassy Suites Northwest Hotel,** 7750 Briaridge, 78230 (☎ **210/340-5421** or toll free **800/ EMBASSY;** pool, restaurant, room service, kitchenettes), at the high end of the "Moderate" category, has the most spacious rooms and the most facilities of the chain lodgings in this area. **Holiday Inn Northwest,** 3233 NW Loop 410, 78213 (☎ **210/377-3900** or toll free **800/HOLIDAY;** pool, restaurant, room service), is a bit less expensive, but still at the upper end of the "Moderate" range. The cost can drop by some $20 at **the Lexington Hotel Suites,** 4934 NW Loop 410, 78229 (☎ **210/680-3351;** exercise room, kitchenettes, pool), and **Courtyard by Marriott/Medical Center,** 8585 Marriott Dr., 78229 (☎ **210/614-7100** or toll free **800/321-2211;** exercise room, restaurant, pool), and even more at **La Quinta Wurzbach,** 9452 I.H. 10 west, 78230 (☎ **210/593-0338** or toll free **800/531-5900;** pool).

Inexpensive

The lodgings in the area that fall into the "Inexpensive" category include the **Rodeway Inn Crossroads,** 6804 I.H. 10 west, 78201 (☎ **210/734-7111** or toll free **800/228-2000;** pool), and **Motel 6,** 9400 Wurzbach 78219 (☎ **210/333-1850;** pool).

8 West

Very Expensive

★ **Hyatt Regency Hill Country Resort,** 9800 Hyatt Resort Dr., San Antonio, TX 78251. ☎ **210/647-1234** or toll free **800/233-1234.** Fax 210/681-9681. 443 rms, 57 suites, 1 guest house. A/C TV TEL

Rates: $185–$240 single or double, $245–$280 Regency Club; $275–$1,450 suite. AE, CB, DC, DISC, MC, V. **Parking:** Free self, $7 valet.

There's only one problem with this cushy resort on the far west side of town: You might never want to leave it. The setting, on 200 acres of former ranch land, is idyllic. The on-site activities, ranging from golf to tubing on a man-made river, are endless, and Sea World of Texas sits at your doorstep. The restaurants are excellent, the rooms beautifully appointed, and there are even free laundry facilities and a country store for supplies. In short, you'll find something at the Hyatt to fulfill your every need—except the one to make money to pay for all this.

The best of Texas design is showcased here. The resort's low-slung buildings, made of native limestone, are inspired by the architecture of the nearby Hill Country. The light-filled lobby is rustic elegant—sort of Ralph Lauren with antlers—and the guest quarters are done in updated country style: Carved maple beds are topped with quilt-style covers and walls have stenciled borders, but the lines are clean and unfussy. Most rooms feature French doors that open out onto wood-trimmed porches, and all have in-room refrigerators.

The recreation facilities are top-notch. Along with an 18-hole championship golf course, the Hyatt boasts tennis courts; a well-equipped health club (with a Jacuzzi, aerobic-and-weight machines, free weights, and a massage room); two swimming pools (one for adults only); volleyball-and-basketball courts; and jogging-and-bike paths. Above all, there's the 950-foot-long Ramblin' River, a lushly landscaped four-acre park where you can grab an inner tube and float your cares away.

Dining/Entertainment: Sit out on Aunt Mary's Porch and down a good local brew, or stop into Charlie's to see the 56-foot, carved wood-and-copper bar; you might be inspired to shoot a few rounds of pool. Golfers tend to guzzle at the Cactus Oak Tavern, the clubhouse bar and grill with a great view of the course. The Springhouse Cafe, serving three meals a day in the hotel's main building, is country casual, offering both an à la carte menu and buffet service. One way or another, you'll want drop by the hotel's fine-dining room, featuring upscale southwestern cuisine: It boasts the world's largest antler chandelier, nine feet high and made of 506 naturally shed horns.

Services: Room service, shuttle service to airport and to downtown ($10), concierge service, valet-laundry and dry-cleaning service.

Facilities: Gift shop, golf pro shop, car-rental agency, Regency Club lounge, business center, game room, Camp Hyatt (see "Cool for Kids" feature in this chapter for details).

5

San Antonio Dining

IT'S EASY TO EAT WELL IN SAN ANTONIO, ESPECIALLY IF YOU ENJOY MEXICAN food—or are willing to give it a try in a city where it might surprise you with its variety. You can get great Tex-Mex standards here, but you'll find less familiar, often sophisticated, dishes from the interior of Mexico, too. Southwestern cuisine, emphasizing fresh regional ingredients and spices combined in exciting ways, is served in some of the chicest dining rooms in town as well as in some unlikely dives. Then there's great chicken-fried steak, burgers, barbecue . . . in short, something to satisfy every taste and wallet.

The downtown dining scene is burgeoning. By the time you read this, the new South Bank complex, with a Hard Rock Cafe and other popular restaurants, will have opened on the River Walk. But although dining on the river is a unique, not-to-be-missed experience, many of the restaurants that overlook the water are overpriced and overcrowded. In general, even if you're willing to pass up a river view, downtown is not the best place for fine dining. Atypically, the exception to this rule is the hotel restaurants, a number of which have excellent, if sometimes pricey, menus.

Most locals chow down a bit north of downtown. The two closest concentrations of places to eat are the San Antonio College/Monte Vista area, north of I-35 and west of Hwy. 281, and the section around North St. Mary's (the Strip), where you can get live entertainment dished up with your food on the weekends. There are also some good restaurants in Beacon Hill, a working-class neighborhood just northwest of downtown off I-10. But by far the best eating area in San Antonio is on and around Broadway, starting a few blocks south of Hildebrand, extending north to Loop 410, and comprising much of the tony area known as Alamo Heights. Brackenridge Park, the zoo, the botanical gardens, and the Witte and McNay museums are in this part of town, so you can combine your sightseeing with some serious eating.

The price categories into which the restaurants have been divided are only rough approximations; by ordering carefully or by splurging, you can eat more or less expensively at almost any place you choose. In general, **Very Expensive** restaurants will cost you more than $45 per person for dinner with dessert, not including drinks, tax (7³/₄ %), and tip (generally at least 15%). **Expensive** eateries should set you back at least $30. Meals at **Moderate** restaurants are likely to run $20 or less, and you can get by at **Inexpensive** places for under $12.

1 The River Walk & Downtown

Expensive ——————————————————————

Boccacio, 205 N. Presa St. ☎ **225-1500.**

> **Cuisine:** ITALIAN. **Reservations:** Recommended, especially Thurs–Sat.
> **Prices:** Appetizers $5.95–$7.45; main courses $10.95–$21.95. AE, DC, DISC, MC, V.

Open: Lunch Mon–Fri 11am–2:30pm; dinner Mon–Thurs 5:30–10pm, Fri–Sat 5:30–11pm, Sun 5–10pm.

Prepare to feel romantic when you enter Boccacio's pretty, cobble-stoned courtyard through a narrow alleyway. Whether you sit out under an umbrella among the greenery; inside the high-ceiling dining room, all flowing drapes, white columns, classical artwork, and flickering candles; or downstairs in the cozy wine cellar, you'll find it hard to resist falling into an amorous mood. And what food better than Italian to fuel the flames?

The fried calamari appetizer is excellent, but if you don't want to devote yourself to it entirely, consider a sampler plate that will also get you eggplant parmigiana and grilled shrimp with white-wine sauce. Among entrées designed to feed a relationship are the Costoletta alla Val d'Aostano, a 13-ounce veal chop stuffed with prosciutto and fontina cheese, and the frutta di mare—mussels, clams, shrimp, calamari, and crabmeat in marinara sauce on a bed of linguine. You might have a hard time finishing with the triple chocolate cheesecake, but there are things one has to do in the name of love.

⭐ **Boudro's,** 421 E. Commerce St./River Walk. ☎ **224-8484.**
Cuisine: SOUTHWESTERN. **Reservations:** Strongly recommended.
Prices: Appetizers $3.25–$6.75; main courses $12.95–$24.50. AE, CB, DC, MC, V.
Open: Sun–Thurs 11am–11pm, Fri–Sat 11am–midnight.

Locals tend to be critical—okay, downright snooty—about River Walk restaurants; Boudro's is the only one on which almost all heap kudos. And with good reason. The kitchen uses fresh local ingredients—Gulf Coast seafood, Texas beef, Hill Country produce—and the preparations and presentations do them justice. The setting is also out of the ordinary: If you've entered from the river, be sure to turn around and look inside the turn-of-the century limestone building to see its hardwood floors and handmade mesquite bar.

You might start with the guacamole, prepared in front of you at the table and served with tostadas; or the crab quesadillas topped with papaya salsa. The prime rib, blackened on a pecan-wood grill, is deservedly popular, as are the lamb chops with peach chutney and garlic mashed potatoes. The skewered shrimp and scallops with mango sauce and tomatillo cream make a good lighter alternative (the food may be innovative but the portions are not *nouvelle*). For dessert, the whisky-soaked bread pudding is fine, but the lime chess pie with a butter pecan crust—divine. Service is very good, especially considering the volume of business and the fact that the servers spend a good bit of their time mixing up guacamole.

Little Rhein Steak House, 231 S. Alamo. ☎ 225-2111.

Cuisine: AMERICAN. **Reservations:** Recommended.
Prices: Appetizers $5.75–$7.50; main courses $13.75–$29.95. AE, DC, DISC, MC, V.
Open: Sun–Thurs 5–10pm, Fri and Sat 5–11pm.

Built in 1847 in what was then the Rhein district, the oldest two-story structure in San Antonio now houses an elegant steakhouse abutting the river and La Villita. Antique memorabilia decks the indoor main dining room; a miniature train surrounded by historic replicas runs overhead. Leafy branches overhanging the River Walk patio—elevated slightly and railed off for privacy—are draped in little sparkling lights.

Choice steaks from the restaurant's own plant come with salad, baked potato, "Texas Caviar" (deliciously seasoned and baked black-eyed peas), and a small loaf of wheat bread. The most popular plates are the filet mignon, T-bone, and center-cut rib eye. If you're *really* hungry, you might call ahead to see if the 22-ounce porterhouse is available, but keep in mind such homey—and reasonably priced—desserts as cheesecake, vanilla ice cream, and apple pie. Along with the size of each steak, the menu notes its trim-standard number, indicating the amount of surrounding fat; unless you subscribe to the *Meat Purveyor's Guide,* you'll have to ask your server to translate. Less esoteric are the printed suggestions of wines that might complement your entrée.

Moderate/Expensive

Carranza, 701 Austin St. ☎ 223-0903.

Cuisine: ECLECTIC. **Reservations:** Only accepted for large parties.
Prices: Appetizers $2.95–$6.25; main courses $7.50–$28.50. AE.
Open: Lunch Tues–Sat 11am–2pm; dinner Tues–Thurs 5–10pm, Fri–Sat 5–11pm. **Closed:** Sun.

If you and your dining companion can't agree on the type of food you'd like or the amount of money you want to spend for it, you could reconsider the relationship—or come to Carranza. The combined lunch-and-dinner menu is broken down into categories for sandwiches, Italian, Mexican, seafood, and meats: You can get a hearty meatball sandwich on a Mexican roll for $4.25 or a delicious seafood platter, including red snapper, scallops, shrimp, and a soft-shell crab cake, for $28.50. But most people order the succulent mesquite-smoked meats: brisket, chicken, sausage, pork ribs, or chopped barbecue. They're available in reasonably priced combination plates if you don't want to decide between them.

You can also order your barbecue by the pound to go; Carranza has been around as a grocery and market since 1920 and still has a deli counter downstairs. From the upstairs dining room of the restored limestone building, you can watch trains go by during the day or view the city lights at night. Consider combining a meal here with a visit to the nearby San Antonio Museum of Art.

Moderate

La Margarita, 120 Produce Row (Market Square). ☎ 227-7140.

Cuisine: MEXICAN. **Reservations:** Not accepted.
Prices: Appetizers $4.50–$9.75; main courses $5.25–$10.95. AE, DC, MC, V.

Open: Sun–Thurs 11am–10pm, Fri–Sat 11am–midnight.

Worked up an appetite with all that Market Square shopping? There's no better place to satisfy it than La Margarita. This lively restaurant is renowned for its fajitas and for its *parilla* platters: Huge mounds of charbroiled sausage, chicken, and beef accompanied by *queso flameado* (melted cheese), fried potatoes, beans, guacamole, *pico de gallo,* and lots of hot flour tortillas. If you're not quite up to the task, there are many smaller if not exactly lighter dishes to consider—the enchiladas Acapulco filled with seafood stew and topped with shrimp, scallops, and cheese, for example. Or you can just sit outdoors with an order of nachos and sip a margarita; they do credit to the restaurant's name. The people-watching is great and who knows? After a margarita *magnifica,* you might be inspired to invite over one of the strolling mariachis (just don't forget that they expect to be paid).

Zuni Grill, 511 River Walk/223 Losoya St. ☎ 227-0864.

Cuisine: SOUTHWESTERN. **Reservations:** Accepted only for parties of six or more.
Prices: Appetizers $4.95–$7.95; main courses $7.95–$17.95. AE, DC, DISC, MC, V.
Open: Sun–Thurs 8am–11pm, Fri–Sat 8am–midnight.

With its stylized cactuses, metallic hump-backed flute players, and chic southwestern menu, this popular River Walk café is a little bit of Santa Fe-on-the-San Antonio. If you've never had a prickly pear margarita (and who has?), this is the place to try one: Puréed cactus fruit, marinated overnight in tequila and cactus-juice schnapps, turns the potent—and delicious—drink a startling shade of purple. The accompanying tortilla chips, made with achiote seed, also have a kick.

Frommer's Smart Traveler: Restaurants

1. Eat early. Some restaurants have early-bird specials. Also, a number of popular places don't take reservations; if you arrive around 8pm when everyone else does, you can expect to wait up to an hour for a table.

2. Make reservations wherever you can; you'll get to watch the hungry folks who didn't bother wait on line or spend too much money on drinks while you're already enjoying your meal.

3. Eat ethnic—whether you try one of the street vendors near Market Square or dine inside, you'll get a lot of food for your money if you go Mexican.

4. Hit the expensive restaurants at lunch; some of the toniest restaurants in town—including La Louisiane, Chez Ardid, and L'Etoile—have good lunch specials.

The pecan-crusted chicken salad on mixed greens makes a nice, light meal (ideal if you've polished off all those chips). For something more substantial, try the peppered pork chops with whipped sweet potatoes or seared salmon filet with a vegetable quesadilla. You might want to finish with another culinary first, a bourbon pecan crème brûlée that tastes every bit as good as it sounds.

Inexpensive

The Jailhouse Cafe, 1126 W. Commerce St. (under the Commerce Street Bridge at Comal). ☎ **224-5001.**
   Cuisine: AMERICAN. **Reservations:** Not accepted.
   Prices: Appetizers $1.45–$5.95; main courses $4.95–$12.95. AE, CB, DC, DISC, MC, V.
   Open: Mon–Sat 7am–10pm, Sun 9am–8pm.

That big building across the street really is the county jail, and if you eat in this brightly lit café on the far west side of downtown, you'll be joined by detention officers, bail bondsmen, and, at lunchtime during the week, lawyers from the county courthouse. They're all here for the gigantic burgers, heaps of beer-battered onion rings, and huge plates of chicken-fried steak; order anything topped with chili con queso and you'll fill your cholesterol quota for the month. Haute cuisine this ain't, but the food is tasty and the service quick and friendly. Be sure to take away one of the café's enormous cinnamon rolls: For $1.95 you'll have something to dunk in your morning coffee the rest of the week.

Schilo's, 424 E. Commerce St. ☎ **223-6692.**
   Cuisine: GERMAN DELI. **Reservations:** Not accepted.
   Prices: Sandwiches $2.40–$4.95; hot or cold plates $3.85–$4.20; main dishes (served after 5pm) $5.95–$8.95. AE, CB, DC, DISC, MC, V.
   Open: Mon–Sat 7am–8:30pm.

You can't leave town without stopping into this San Antonio institution, if only for a hearty bowl of split-pea soup or a sinful piece of homemade cherry cheesecake. The large, open room with its worn wooden booths gives a glimpse into the city's German past; the waitresses—definitely *not* "servers"—wear dirndl-type outfits and an oompah band plays on Saturday from 5 to 8pm. It's a great place to come for refueling when you're sightseeing near Alamo Plaza; for under $5, a good, greasy Reuben or a Bratwurst plate should keep you going for the rest of the day.

2 King William Historic District

Expensive

Babylon Grill, 910 S. Alamo. ☎ **229-9335.**
   Cuisine: MEDITERRANEAN. **Reservations:** Recommended.
   Prices: Appetizers $4.75–$12; main courses $7.95–$17. AE, DISC, MC, V.
   Open: Mon–Thurs 11am–11pm, Fri–Sat 11am–1am, Sun brunch 10am–3pm.

Downtown San Antonio Dining

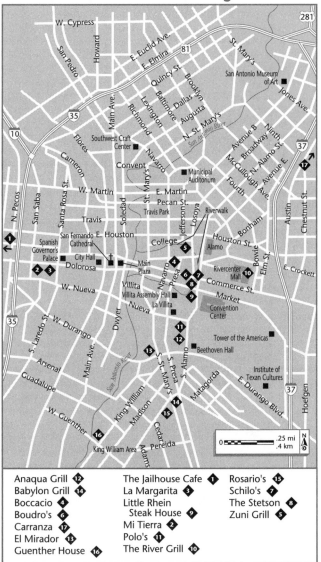

Anaqua Grill ⬧12	The Jailhouse Cafe ◆1	Rosario's ⬧15
Babylon Grill ⬧14	La Margarita ◆3	Schilo's ◆7
Boccacio ◆4	Little Rhein	The Stetson ◆8
Boudro's ◆6	Steak House ◆9	Zuni Grill ◆5
Carranza ⬧17	Mi Tierra ◆2	
El Mirador ⬧13	Polo's ⬧11	
Guenther House ⬧16	The River Grill ⬧10	

With its floor-to-ceiling windows, giant prints and murals, and alternating stark white and brightly colored walls, the Babylon Grill is more art space than dining room. Indeed, this chic restaurant in the King William area also serves as a gallery for local artists. They don't have to pay a commission to the owners, they only have to promise that they'll keep their pieces hanging here for a month after they're sold.

This is a great place to linger over coffee and come up with that great new idea for a film script; you'll even get a free fresh plate of cookies to feed the gray cells. And it's fine for a light lunch—a salad of artichoke hearts, tomato, and basil, say, or a saffron shrimp *focaccia* with sun-dried tomatoes and chèvre—or an after-theater brandy; this is one of the few restaurants in town that stays open past midnight. But the chef hadn't quite hit his stride yet when I visited and the food was uneven. The roast pork loin with spicy potatoes or roast chicken with rosemary are usually reliable choices for dinner.

Moderate

El Mirador, 722 S. St. Mary's St. ☎ 225-9444.

Cuisine: MEXICAN. **Reservations:** Required for five or more only.
Prices: Appetizers $2.50–$5.95; main courses $5.25–$10.95. MC, V.
Open: Breakfast and lunch Mon–Sat 6:30am–3pm; dinner Wed–Sat 5:30–10pm; Sun brunch 9am–3pm.

It's not the decor that draws locals of all stripes to this family-owned restaurant near the King William area, though Saltillo tile floors and a few art prints give a bit of character to two otherwise nondescript rooms. At breakfast, it's the huge plates of eggs scrambled with spicy *machacado* (dried beef) or cooked ranchero style. At lunchtime, it's such specials as enchiladas with chili con carne, rice, refried beans, salad, and two tortillas for $3.95. And at dinner, well, everyone has their favorite. . . .The chicken or beef filet served with spicy *poblano* chile sauce are among mine, and it's hard to go wrong with the shrimp *diablo*—it's not quite as devilishly hot as its name suggests, but it's wonderfully redolent with garlic. The fresh catch of the day is also usually a winner. Save some room for the *nachos de fruta,* sugared cinnamon crisps cut into triangles and served with fresh fruit.

Rosario's, 1014 S. Alamo. ☎ 223-1806.

Cuisine: MEXICAN. **Reservations:** Not accepted.
Prices: Appetizers $3.75–$6.95; dinner $5.25–$12.95. AE, DC, DISC, MC, V.
Open: Lunch Mon–Sat 11am–3pm; dinner Tues–Sat 3–10pm.

No serapes or piñatas for this hip Mexican hangout. Housed in a green-brick building with a pink neon sign, Rosario's is dimly lit, done in turquoise and terra-cotta, and hung with folk art and paintings by local artists. Killer margaritas and huge schooners of beer emerge continuously from a large bar.

You might start with the grilled marinated shrimp, served with a cilantro dipping sauce, or tortilla soup laced with melting mild cheese. But consider that large helpings of such entrées as *carne de puerco en chile Cascabel* (pork tips in a mild, almost nutlike chile sauce) or *enchiladas verde de pollo y helote* (chicken-and-corn-filled enchiladas topped with tomatillo sauce, white cheese, and sour cream) come with rice, refried beans, and tortillas. The bargain weekday lunch specials—perhaps soup, a *chalupa,* and a taco for $4.50—draw a sizable local crowd, but it's on weekend nights, when a live tropical band plays, that the place really sizzles.

Inexpensive

Guenther House, 205 E. Guenther St. ☎ **227-1061.**

> **Cuisine:** AMERICAN. **Reservations:** Not accepted.
> **Prices:** Breakfast $2.50–$5.95; lunch $3.25–$5.95. AE, DISC, MC, V.
> **Open:** Mon–Sat 7am–3pm, Sun 8am–2pm (the house and mill store are open Mon–Sat 9am–5pm, Sun 8am–2pm).

Not only is the food good at the Guenther House, but dining here is a great way to spend some time inside one of King William's historic homes. Hearty breakfasts and light lunches are served indoors in a pretty art nouveau–style dining room added on to the Guenther family residence (built 1860) or outdoors on a trellised patio. The biscuits and gravy are a morning specialty and the pasta salad at lunch is excellent, but you can't go wrong with anything that involves the wonderful baked goods made on the premises. Adjoining the restaurant are a small museum, a Victorian parlor, and a mill store featuring baking-related items. The house fronts a lovely stretch of the San Antonio River; in the back, you can still see the Pioneer Flour Mill that earned the family its fortune.

3 North St. Mary's

Cafe Camile, 517 E. Woodlawn. ☎ 735-2307.

> **Cuisine:** ECLECTIC. **Reservations:** Recommended, especially on weekends.
> **Prices:** Appetizers $4.95–$7.95; main courses $7.95–$13.95. CB, DC, MC, V.
> **Open:** Tues–Fri 11am–11pm, Sun 11am–10pm.

Just off North St. Mary's, behind the Zulu T-Box coffeehouse, a cozy café is tucked away in a former furniture refinishing shop. The back wall of the intimate dining room is covered with an enticing mural; it's dominated by a well-known Manet bar scene, but other French Impressionists also put in an appearance.

The menu is as hard to pin down as the mural, including Mediterranean, continental, Italian, and southwestern dishes. No matter; you'll find the dishes of whatever territory you choose to venture into freshly prepared with great attention to detail. The duck confit crêpe with apple and red onion chutney makes a fine starter, to be followed, perhaps, by the linguine with scallops, shrimp, mussels, tomatoes, and garlic; or the chicken breast rolled in pecans and baked crisp, then topped with a creamy Dijon mustard sauce. Some of the best live jazz in town is played on the restaurant's patio on Friday and Saturday nights, and there's a great Sunday brunch menu.

Liberty Bar, 328 E. Josephine St. ☎ 227-1187.

> **Cuisine:** AMERICAN. **Reservations:** Recommended.
> **Prices:** Appetizers $1.75–$9.95; main courses $5.95–$18.95. AE, MC, V.

Open: Restaurant open Sun–Thurs 11:30am–10:30pm, Fri–Sat 11:30am–midnight; bar open until midnight Sun–Thurs, until 2am Fri–Sat.

You'd be hard-pressed to guess from the outside that this ramshackle former brothel hosts one of the chicest haunts in San Antonio; the area looks unlikely, and the restaurant's name is nowhere to be found (look for the word "Boehlers" on a green-roofed building near the Hwy. 281 underpass).

Don't be put off; it's bright and inviting inside, and you'll find everything here from comfort food (pot roast, say, or a ham-and-swiss sandwich) to cutting-edge cuisine (maybe mesquite-grilled chicken breast with achiote). The toasted French bread with roast garlic spread or eggplant purée goes great with many of the fine—and generally affordable—wines available by the glass; there's a good beer selection, too. And don't worry, even if you've had a few too many, you're not imagining it: The house really *is* leaning.

4   San Antonio College/Monte Vista

Expensive

⭐ **Biga,** 206 E. Locust St. ☎ **225-0722.**
Cuisine: CONTEMPORARY AMERICAN. **Reservations:** Accepted for five or more only.
Prices: Appetizers $6–$10; main courses $12–$24. AE, CB, DC, DISC, MC, V.
Open: Lunch Tues–Fri 11am–2pm, no lunch Sat or Mon; dinner Mon–Thurs 6–10:30pm, Fri–Sat 5:30–11pm. Closed Sun.

Giving the lie to the maxim "Never trust a thin chef," lanky Bruce Auden turns out some of the finest food in San Antonio—and anywhere else for that matter. But while Auden's attention to menu detail is serious and the restaurant is set in a 100-year-old house, Biga is no hushed temple of haute cuisine.

Frommer's Cool for Kids: Restaurants

Chris Madrid (p. 64) If your kids like burgers or even just fries, head to Chris Madrid; there's so much bustle, no one will notice them shouting over the din. Teenagers (and most husbands) will get a charge out of the T-shirts hanging on the walls.

The Jailhouse Cafe (p. 58) This big, clattering place has a menu large enough to satisfy even the pickiest eater. And you can always threaten your darlings with the jail across the street if they don't behave.

La Calesa (p. 67) Here you'll find an inexpensive children's menu ($2.95 to $3.50) and a staff that loves youngsters. It's a great place to introduce your kids to Mexican food.

For one thing, the dining rooms are not overly formal: One is bright with pale yellow walls and lots of windows; the other is masculine cozy, with dark wood and a fireplace. And the menu has a sense of humor. Among the appetizers is one called simply "expensive mushrooms." These—they're shiitakes—are very good, but it's the seared foie gras on a Stilton tart that brought me to raptures, with the radicchio and Bibb packets of game running a close second. Those who want to pace themselves might consider the mildly spicy Thai vegetable salad. (Much of the food—especially the *habanero* ketchup—has a definite kick; if you tend to walk on the mild side, inquire about the heat of the dishes.) Although the menu changes regularly, you can depend on seeing oak-roasted Nilgai antelope and quail or pheasant; the Texas-bred game imported from Africa is remarkably tender. Among the "Desserts to Cheat For" is a spectacular crème brûlée.

The wonderful peasant breads accompanying each meal come from LocuStreet Bakery, the brainchild of Auden's wife, Debra. In addition to an extensive wine list, which thoughtfully groups together the "expensive red wines" and "expensive white wines," Biga also has the best beer selection in town.

Chez Ardid, 1919 San Pedro Ave. ☎ 732-3203.

Cuisine: FRENCH. **Reservations:** Recommended.

Prices: Appetizers $4.75–$9.75; main courses $15–$25. AE, CB, DC, DISC, MC, V.

Open: Lunch Mon–Fri 11:30am–2pm; dinner Mon–Sat 6–10:30pm. Closed Sun.

When Guillermo Ardid retired as chef of this popular French restaurant a few years back, the question around town was whether or not his son Miguel would able to live up to his father's reputation. Most would now agree that, although the style is slightly different, the food here is as good as it ever was. The cuisine is still classic French, but now there are perhaps a few lighter, more nouvelle-type dishes. And like most good chefs these days, Miguel has been using regional ingredients, featuring whatever's freshest and most interesting in his daily specials.

It's hard to choose among the dining rooms in this lovely 1902 home, restored by the Ardid family in the late 1970s; the former central atrium, with its high ceilings and classical columns, has an appealing simplicity, but the Versailles Room behind it retains much of the house's original detail, with a lovely carved oak mantel, oak-and-mahogany parquet floors, and a tinwork ceiling. (Smokers don't have to wrack their brains; they get a smaller, but still attractive dining room off to the side.)

You might start your meal with warm crab "Guillermo" with three sauces—regulars wouldn't let Miguel take his father's signature appetizer off the menu—or a dish of two terrines, one made with deer and rabbit, the other with Muscovy duck. The *filet d'agneau* (in this case, a Texas lamb loin) baked in puffed pastry is an excellent entrée selection, as is the tenderloin médaillon in green peppercorn sauce.

This is one of the few places around that still serves, well, innards: tasty sweetbreads in a Madeira wine sauce, say, or tender veal liver in white wine and shallots. Along with the expected French labels, the wine list includes some good local bottles. Lunch here is a bargain, with daily specials that include soup or salad for around $10.

Paesano's, 1715 McCullough. ☎ **226-9541.**

> **Cuisine:** ITALIAN. **Reservations:** Accepted for lunch only.
> **Prices:** Appetizers $4.25–$4.95; first courses (pasta) $6.95–$11.95; main courses $11.95–$18.50. AE, DC, MC, V.
> **Open:** Lunch Tues–Fri 11am–2pm, no lunch Sat–Sun; dinner Tues–Fri 5–11pm, Sat 5–11:30pm, Sun 5–10pm. Closed Mon.

With its red tablecloths, netted globe candles, and stained-glass panel of the Leaning Tower of Pisa, Paesano's looks like every Italian restaurant I ate while I was growing up in Brooklyn. The large portions of well-prepared northern Italian food also reminded me of home.

Since 1969, devoted locals have been coming to these dimly lit dining rooms for the shrimp Paesano, which is grilled crispy and then dosed with butter, lemon, and garlic. The seafood, flown in fresh every day, is generally a good bet, as is the veal. From Tuesday through Friday, the restaurant has excellent lunch specials; $6.95 might get you osso buco or steak Florentine served with salad and spaghetti.

By the time you read this, another Paesano's will have opened on the River Walk. It remains to be seen whether the volume the place is likely to attract will allow it to keep up the standards of its Monte Vista sister.

---

5   Beacon Hill

Chris Madrid, 1900 Blanco. ☎ **735-3552.**

> **Cuisine:** AMERICAN. **Reservations:** Not accepted.
> **Prices:** $3–$4.35. AE, CB, DC, DISC, MC, V.
> **Open:** Mon–Sat 11am–10pm.

It's hard to drop much money at this funky burger joint, a gas station in an earlier incarnation, but you might lose your shirt here nevertheless; over the years, folks have taken to signing their tees and hanging them on the walls. An even more popular tradition is trying to eat the macho burger, as huge as its name and most often served topped with cheese and jalapeño peppers. The menu is pretty much limited to burgers, nachos, and fries, but the casual atmosphere and down-home cooking keep the large outdoor patio filled.

Niki's Tokyo Inn, 819 W. Hildebrand. ☎ **736-5471.**

> **Cuisine:** JAPANESE. **Reservations:** Recommended only for parties of six or more.
> **Prices:** Appetizers $1–$16; main courses $7–$17. AE, MC, V.
> **Open:** Tues–Thurs 5:30–10:30pm, Fri–Sat 5:30–11pm. Closed Mon.

What this no-frills, wood-paneled restaurant lacks in atmosphere, it more than makes up for in quality and value. Since 1970, Niki's has served San Antonio the largest pieces of fresh sushi for the least amount of money—as our waiter explained, Texans expect their food BIG. A *sunomono* (cucumber) salad, a bowl of steaming miso soup with tofu, and a sizable California maki roll (with rice, avocado, crab, and cucumber) will set you back only around $5. Another delicious bargain is the Temaki Mix; this $12 platter of six huge cone-shaped rolls filled with shrimp, tuna, or salmon skin is plenty large for two. The *anago* (eel in sweet sauce) and the always fresh tuna are among the many sushi bar standouts. The tempura dishes are fine, as are the Chinese-style dinners served with fried rice and egg roll, but delicious raw fish is Niki's biggest draw.

6 Broadway/Alamo Heights

Very Expensive/Moderate

La Louisiane and the Courtyard, 2632 Broadway. ☎ **225-7984** (La Louisiane), **225-7987** (The Courtyard).

Cuisine: FRENCH CREOLE/CONTINENTAL. **Reservations:** Recommended.

Prices: La Louisiane: appetizers $7–25, main courses $19–$52 (all vegetables are à la carte); five-course prix-fixe dinner for two, $190. The Courtyard: appetizers $3.95–$8.75, main courses $7.95–$13.95. AE, CB, DC, DISC, MC, V.

Open: La Louisiane: lunch Mon–Fri 11:30am–2pm, dinner Mon–Thurs 6–10:30pm, Fri–Sat 6–11pm. Closed Sun, no lunch Sat. The Courtyard: Sun–Thurs 11am–midnight, Fri–Sat 11am–2am.

Long the grande dame of San Antonio restaurants, La Lou had acquired a reputation for being a tad stuffy and even down-at-the-heels in recent years. When new owners took over in late 1992, they not only spruced the old place up, but opened a more casual outdoor restaurant next door.

If you want to put on the Ritz, eat inside. La Louisiane is the only place in town where the waiters still wear tuxedos. The setting is regal—all candlelight, sparkling chandeliers, and velvet draping— the service old-world elegant, and the food won't disappoint. Consider going all the way and having something served table side: the tender rack of lamb, perhaps, or the steak Diane in a red-wine sauce. Those who can't bear the stares while their food is being immolated might opt for the more demure filet of snapper à la George, which is topped with mushrooms and sauce meunière.

Then again, attention seekers might also enjoy the pretty, greenery-filled Courtyard, already a place to see and be seen. The menu still keeps company with Louisiana—a fine crab-and-salmon cake appetizer and a fiery gumbo, for example—but it's been flirting with Southwest temptations like duck quesadillas. The parmesan-crusted double pork chop served with orzo and oven-dried tomatoes is a mover, as is the spinach fettuccine in Gorgonzola cream sauce. Sandwiches and salads, especially the huge Caesar, make fine light-dining options, while live jazz and large fans keep things cool even on the steamiest of summer nights.

Expensive

The Barn Door, 8400 N. New Braunfels Ave. ☎ **824-0116.**

Cuisine: AMERICAN. **Reservations:** Recommended for dinner.
Prices: Appetizers $3.25–$12.95; main courses $10–$24.95. AE, DISC, MC, V.
Open: Lunch Mon–Fri 11am–2pm; dinner Mon–Thurs 5–10pm, Fri–Sat 5–10:30pm.

Photographs on the walls of this down-home Texas steakhouse show a San Antonio of 40 years ago, when the restaurant first opened its doors. Hundreds of business cards hanging nearby attest to the number of folks who continue to come here from all around to enjoy excellent cuts of charcoal- and mesquite-grilled beef.

Not all of them down steaks the size of the 24-ounce T-bone in the display case at the entryway; most opt for the 6-, 8-, or 12-ounce filets, all prepared with very little salt. However, if you've been feeling overly underindulgent, consider the chicken-fried steak: the usual versions of this dish use pounded thin, tenderized beef, but here a regular cut gets the Kentucky Colonel treatment.

Call ahead if you're dining here to celebrate an anniversary or a birthday; the event will be announced on a billboard at the front door.

L'Etoile, 6106 Broadway. ☎ **826-4551.**

Cuisine: FRENCH. **Reservations:** Recommended.
Prices: Appetizers $2.95–$9.95; main courses $9.95–$23.95 (lobster may be higher); early-bird menu (daily 5:30–6:30pm) $10.95. AE, CB, DC, DISC, MC, V.
Open: Lunch Mon–Sat 11:30am–2:30pm; dinner Sun–Thurs 5:30–9:30pm, Fri–Sat 5:30–10:30pm.

Knowing some attitude adjustment might be required, the three French owners of this appealing bistro set out to convince a kicked-back Texas town that French dining need not be overly formal. They've managed to combine top-notch service and excellent food with a relaxed atmosphere, and to offer a sufficient number of specials—especially at lunch—to show that you need not spend half the plane fare to France to eat like a Parisian.

Moorish archways, dun-colored brick walls, and an enclosed patio create a Mediterranean mood; upstairs there's an intimate skylit dining nook. The menus change daily, but the focus is always on seafood, as the live-lobster tank attests; you can order your favorite crustacean poached, flamed in cognac, or baked. Or, if it's available, consider the fresh Norwegian salmon Jerez in a white-wine and cherry-vinegar sauce. For dessert, a diet-destroying black-and-white chocolate mousse on a raspberry *coulis* looks almost too gorgeous to eat. Almost. Portions are large, French bread rolls hot and crusty, and a good wine list has some affordable bottles.

It's easy to miss this restaurant, located in a small shopping complex on Albany that turns up suddenly as you round a bend heading north from downtown on Broadway. There's free valet parking once you find it.

Moderate

Barcelona's, 4901 Broadway. ☎ **822-6129.**

> **Cuisine:** MEDITERRANEAN. **Reservations:** Accepted only for parties of six or more.
> **Prices:** Tapas $2–$5; salads $5–7; main courses $8–12. AE, DISC, MC, V.
> **Open:** Daily 11am–11pm.

Stark white walls, wood beam ceilings, Saltillo tile floors, colorful art prints, and opaque blue glassware give Barcelona's an updated Mediterranean look—the perfect setting for its updated Mediterranean menu. The tapas are not the often-heavy appetizers served in Spain but, rather, small portions of such lighter fare as warm Brie, green apples, and rasperry sauce or Tuscany salad with sun-dried tomatoes, olives, and Gorgonzola. For an entrée, try the terrific paella, with seafood, spicy sausage, and saffron rice; or the spicy lamb brochettes with yogurt feta sauce.

The adjoining patio bar offers a small tapas, dessert, and coffee menu; live flamenco music on Friday and Saturday nights helps pass the time during the sometimes-long waits on the weekends, as does the delicious frozen sangría. In addition to a chic young crowd, you'll see lots of dark-haired men in business suits who look like they're cutting important NAFTA-related deals.

Boardwalk Bistro, 4011 Broadway. ☎ **824-0100.**

> **Cuisine:** ECLECTIC. **Reservations:** Required for five or more only.
> **Prices:** Appetizers $3.95–$6.95; main courses $6.95–$12.95. AE, DC, DISC, MC, V.
> **Open:** Mon–Thurs 11am–10:30pm, Fri–Sat 11am–11pm. Closed Sun.

Alamo Heights residents seeking almost anything to eat you can think of head slightly south to this upscale local bistro. Many are drawn by the large vegetarian selection, hard to come by in this beef-oriented town. Among the standouts are the grilled tofu Caesar salad and the paella Gardinera, an all-vegetable version of the Spanish rice dish. An excellent Mediterranean sampler, including hummus, tabbouleh, Greek olives, and dolmas (grape leaves stuffed with herb rice and veggies), is served with warm pita bread.

But between the fine homemade soups and fresh-baked desserts, you'll also find everything from chicken-salad croissants to filet mignon on the huge menu. The cappuccino and espresso are as strong as they should be, as are some of the excellent beers produced by San Antonio's first microbrewery, recently opened next door.

★ **La Calesa,** 2103 E. Hildebrand. ☎ **822-4475.**

💲 **Cuisine:** MEXICAN. **Reservations:** Not accepted.
Prices: Appetizers $1.95–$5.50; main courses $4.95–$11.95.
Open: Mon–Thurs 11am–9:30pm, Fri 11am–10:30pm, Sat 10am–10:30pm, Sun 9am–9:30pm.

Tucked away in an old house just off Broadway—look for Earl Abel's large sign across the street—this family-run restaurant features dishes from the southern Yucatán region, rather than from the northern areas that tend to influence the Tex-Mex style. The difference is mainly in the sauces, and they're done to perfection here. The mole, for example, strikes a fine balance between its rich chocolate base and the picante spices. The enchiladas potosina, topped with potatoes and bits of chorizo, also have a marvelous texture and taste. Rice and black beans—to my mind richer than the usual pintos—accompany many of the meals. Everything is cooked up fresh, including the tortilla chips; even the coffee is good. You can eat indoors in one of three cozy dining rooms, decorated with Diego Rivera prints and Mexican tile work, or outside on the wooden porch.

Cappy's, 5011 Broadway. ☎ 828-9669.

Cuisine: SOUTHWEST. **Reservations:** Recommended.
Prices: Appetizers $2.50–$6; main courses $8.50–$17. AE, DISC, MC, V.
Open: Mon–Thurs 11am–10pm, Fri–Sat 11am–11pm, Sun 10:30am–10pm.

One of the earliest businesses to open up in the now-burgeoning Alamo Heights neighborhood, Cappy's is set in an unusual broken-brick structure dating back to the late 1930s. But there's nothing outdated about this cheerful, light-filled place, with its high, wood beam ceilings, hanging plants, and colorful work by local artists; there's also a romantic, tree-shaded outdoor patio.

As you enter, the enticing smell of the wood-burning grill (no, not mesquite, but the somewhat milder live oak) gives a hint of some of the house specialties: smoked pork tenderloin with a roasted tomatillo sauce, or Cowboy Ribeye steak topped with marinated red onions. Lighter fare includes cappellini with tomato basil salsa and fresh herb pesto, and there's always a Heart Healthy special on offer. When you're trying to find Cappy's, keep an eye out for the Twig Book Store; the restaurant is tucked away behind it.

Dang's Thai, 1146 Austin Hwy. ☎ 829-7345.

Cuisine: THAI. **Reservations:** Required for 10 or more only.
Prices: Appetizers $3–$10; main courses $4.50–$12.50. AE, DC, MC, V.
Open: Mon–Fri 11am–2:30pm and 5:30–10pm, Sat noon–10pm. Closed Sun.

The lush greenery and Thai travel posters in this modest eatery will take you part of the way to Bangkok, but it's the huge menu of Thai seafood, chicken, beef, and noodle dishes that really transports you to Asia. Start with the *pad thai* noodles and *tord mun* (traditional fish cakes)—Dang's versions of both are the best in town—or the *yam woon sen* (a tart and flavorful cold bean-thread salad). The Thai hot pot soups, considered starters, are meals in themselves. Everything here is good, but the seafood dishes such as *haw mok* (fish, scallops, shrimp, and squid in curry and coconut milk) stand out. The Japanese and Thai beers or Thai iced coffee and jasmine ice tea go great with anything you order. If you've got some room left, finish up with fried bananas or sweet rice and mango.

Luna Notte, 6402 N. New Braunfels Ave. ☎ 822-4242.

Cuisine: ITALIAN. **Reservations:** Recommended on weekends.

Prices: Appetizers $3–$6; main courses $7–$14. AE, CB, DC, DISC, MC, V.
Open: Mon–Thurs 11am–10:30pm, Fri 11am–11pm, Sat 5–11pm, Sun 5–10pm.

The high-tech moon hanging above the door of this Sunset Mall restaurant hints at the stylish room inside. An open wood-burning oven imparts some warmth to the industrial-style dining space (not literally—the air-conditioning works just fine), which is all stark grays and blacks and designed down to the last candle holder. It also turns out some mighty tasty pizzas, pastas, and breads. Ingredients are as chic as the setting, but the sauces and portion sizes are nowhere near as pared down.

The pasta topped with peas and prosciutto in cream sauce will leave you very satisfied, as will a vegetarian lasagne, resplendent in green (spinach) and orange (carrots). The pork tenderloin with sun-dried cherries and the hazelnut roasted chicken breast with goat cheese are also excellent. There's a large selection of wines by the glass to wash down whatever you order.

Viet Nam, 3244 Broadway. ☎ 822-7461.

Cuisine: VIETNAMESE/THAI. **Reservations:** Required for five or more only.
Prices: Appetizers $1.35–$11; main courses $4–$8.50. AE, MC, V.
Open: Daily 11am–10pm.

This family-owned restaurant, just south of Alamo Heights, doesn't look like much from the outside—nor from the inside, for that matter: It's dimly lit, with fairly standard Asian decor. What draws the locals in is not the ambience, but a wide-ranging menu that includes everything from well-known Thai favorites such as the crispy noodle and vegetable *pad thai* to more exotic fare like *Banh Xeo*, a Vietnamese crêpe stuffed with pork. The delicate snow rolls with peanut sauce make a fine starter; heartier appetites might consider the pound of crab claws in a spicy butter and lemon sauce. Entrées such as the tasty chicken with lemongrass come with crunchy spring rolls as well as the usual white rice. All the dishes are well complemented by the Vietnamese "fish sauce" found on each table and by supersweet lemon ice tea.

Water Street Oyster Bar, 7500 Broadway. ☎ 829-4853.

Cuisine: SEAFOOD. **Reservations:** Not accepted.
Prices: Appetizers $2.95–$5.50; main courses $7.95–$13.95. AE, DISC, MC, V.
Open: Sun–Thurs 11am–11pm, Fri–Sat 11am–midnight.

For seafood with a Cajun and south-of-the-border flair, come to this open, modern dining room in Alamo Heights' tony Lincoln Heights shopping center. Light meals or reasonably priced full-course plates are available throughout the day. The spicy seafood gumbo is always reliable, as are the New Orleans–style fried oyster sandwiches, but your best bet is the fresh-catch board; whatever comes in that day can be prepared for you blackened or—particularly recommended—*nueces* style (topped with shrimp and crabmeat in a browned butter sauce). Oysters are 25¢ each at happy hour (5 to 7pm every day).

A large mural of a fisherman, along with canvas rigging material on the side of the staircase leading to the upstairs dining area, lend this place an appropriately nautical look. And they run a tight ship here: Service is efficient, even when the room is crowded.

Inexpensive

Earl Abel's, 4200 Broadway. ☎ 822-3358.

> **Cuisine:** AMERICAN. **Reservations:** Accepted for parties of eight or more only.
> **Prices:** Sandwiches $4.25–$6.25; main courses $4.75–$12.95. AE, DC, MC, V.
> **Open:** Daily 6:30am–1am.

Earl Abel opened his first restaurant on Main Street in 1933; an organist for silent-film theaters in the 1920s, he had to find something else to do when the talkies took over. But his old Hollywood chums didn't forget him; Bing Crosby and Gloria Swanson always dropped into Earl's place when they blew through San Antone.

His granddaughter now runs the restaurant, which moved to Broadway in 1940, and the menu is much like it was more than 50 years ago—when what's now called comfort food was simply chow. Neon sign outside notwithstanding, the restaurant is no longer open 24 hours, but you can still come in after midnight for a cup of coffee and a thick slice of lemon-meringue pie. Fried chicken is still the all-time favorite, but lots of folks come around for a hearty breakfast of eggs and biscuits, gravy, and grits.

7   Balcones Heights

La Fogata, 2427 Vance Jackson. ☎ 340-0636.

> **Cuisine:** MEXICAN. **Reservations:** Accepted Mon–Thurs only.
> **Prices:** Appetizers $3–$8.85; main courses $5.50–$9.25. AE, CB, DC, DISC, MC, V.
> **Open:** Tues–Thurs 7:30am–10pm, Fri–Sat 7:30am–11pm, Sun 8am–10pm.

A massive carved wooden door opens into the fountain-splashed courtyard of this northside Mexican restaurant, reminiscent of a sprawling Spanish villa. (If you get lost, as I did, you can also enter through one of the many parking lots). This place is huge: It started out in 1978 as a single dining room and then, like Topsy, just growed. Plant-draped trellises divide off a number of smaller outdoor eating areas, all with Mexican tile floors, wrought-iron tables, and lots of greenery. The newest indoor dining room, done in light wood and hung with Frida Kahlo prints, is the best place to beat the heat.

Many of the dishes served here are from recipes of the owner's mother-in-law, who grew up in Cuernavaca. Along with the more familiar tacos and tamales, you'll find such dishes as *queso flameado* (Mexican sausage mixed with melted Oaxaca cheese and served with tortillas) or *chile poblano al carbon* (pepper stuffed with chicken and cheese and charcoal flamed). The menu is as large as the restaurant and often confusing—some items first listed among the appetizers and soups turn up again among the entrées—but the friendly servers will gladly help you sort it all out. Don't leave without checking out the celebrity photo wall; everyone from President Clinton to Shaquille O'Neil has eaten here.

8 Northwest/Medical Center

Aldo's, 8539 Fredericksburg Rd. ☎ 696-2536.

Cuisine: ITALIAN. **Reservations:** Recommended, especially on weekends.
Prices: Appetizers $6.25–$7.75; main courses $8.95–$19.95. AE, CB, DC, DISC, MC, V.
Open: Mon–Thurs 11am–10pm, Fri 11am–11pm, Sat 5–11pm, Sun 5–10pm.

A northwest San Antonio favorite, Aldo's offers good, old-fashioned Italian food in a pretty, old-fashioned setting. You can enjoy your meal outside on a tree-shaded patio or inside a 100-year-old former ranch house in one of a series of Victorian-style dining rooms.

The scampi Valentino, sautéed shrimp with a basil cream sauce, is a nice starter, as is the lighter steamed mussels in marinara sauce (available seasonally). For an Italian comfort food combo, try the *piatto del capo cuoco:* lasagne, cannelloni, veal parmigiana, and spaghetti. A house specialty, the sautéed snapper di Aldo, comes topped with fresh lump crabmeat, artichoke hearts, mushrooms, and tomatoes in a lemon butter/white-wine sauce. Whatever you order, finish it off with spumoni; I've always held a (widely scoffed at) theory that it makes you feel less full after an Italian dinner.

Bistro Time, 5137 Fredericksburg Rd. ☎ 344-6626.

Cuisine: CONTINENTAL. **Reservations:** Recommended.
Prices: Appetizers $3.25–$5.95; main courses $9.95–$17.95. AE, CB, DC, MC, V.
Open: Lunch Tues–Fri 11am–noon; dinner Tues–Thurs 5–9pm, Fri–Sat 5–10pm. Closed Sun and Mon.

In a nondescript mall in a nondescript northwest neighborhood, a gem of a restaurant hides. This low-key place, with wood-paneling, a wall of mirrors, and floral tablecloths, features classic continental cuisine. The executive chef/owner is from Holland, but the only menu hint is the Matjes herring tucked away among the appetizers.

The menu changes twice weekly, but you can depend on seeing such standards as steak Diane, sautéed with brandy, mushrooms, green onions, and garlic in cream sauce. This is not a place to watch your weight; portions are huge and rich sauces are a specialty (it's easy to catch people surreptitiously mopping their plates with their rolls). And the desserts are especially hard to resist; if you're lucky, a wonderfully chocolatey Sachertorte might be in your stars.

9 The Airport Area

Cascabel, Sheraton Fiesta hotel, 37 NE Loop 410. ☎ **366-2424.**
> **Cuisine:** SOUTHWESTERN. **Reservations:** Recommended at dinner.
> **Prices:** Appetizers $6–$7; main courses $13–$24. AE, CB, DC, DISC, MC, V.
> **Open:** Lunch Mon–Fri 11:30am–2pm, no lunch Sat; dinner Mon–Thurs 5:30–10pm, Fri–Sat 5:30–11pm. Closed Sun.

One of a group of stellar young chefs in San Antonio, Jay McCarty opened his first restaurant at the age of 23. If his menu can seem a bit trendy, perhaps it's excusable, since he's among those in town who sets the trends. A hotel near the airport may appear an unlikely location for his chic eatery—indeed, the ads rarely note the restaurant's address as the Sheraton—but the contemporary-style dining room, with its potted palms, black-lacquer chairs, art deco wall sconces, and marble floors, is easily up to the task of setting an elegant tone.

For an appetizer, consider the pecan-crusted crab cakes with *chipotle* lime aïoli and pineapple jicama salsa, a veritable group marriage of textures and tastes. The crispy roasted duck or the black Angus tenderloin are exciting entrée options. Afterward, convince your companion to share the dessert nachos (it shouldn't be hard)—crunchy sweet chips ready to dip in mounds of ice cream.

Ruth's Chris, 7720 Jones-Maltsberger in Concord Plaza.
☎ **821-5051.**
> **Cuisine:** AMERICAN. **Reservations:** Recommended.
> **Prices:** Appetizers $4–$7.25; main courses $17–$30.
> **Open:** Mon–Sat 5–11pm, Sun 4–10pm.

Ruth's Chris has proved just how serious San Antonio is about steak; of all the franchises of Ruth Fertel's original Louisiana restaurant, this one made the most money in its first year. Considering the steakhouse's high prices and somewhat off-the-beaten-track location—in a high-rise office complex near the airport—this instant success also says a lot about the quality of the food.

The classical columns are a holdover from the Italian restaurant that was here before, but otherwise the elegant room is designed to suggest a south Texas ranch, with stucco walls and a huge walnut wine rack in back. The American standard hit parade—broiled lamb chops, veal chops, and salmon—is covered, but what you come here for are the corn-fed U.S. prime steaks, served sizzling in butter and cooked precisely as you order them. A wonderfully tender filet is the most in demand (it comes in "petite" for smaller appetites), but some customers cut straight to the chase with the huge T-bone. Service is attentive, perhaps to excess; dishes can be whisked off the table a bit too quickly. You'll see mostly suits here, but more casually dressed diners are not turned away.

10 North

The County Line, 607 W. Afton Oaks, off F.M. Rd. 1604.
☎ **496-0011.**
Cuisine: BARBECUE. **Reservations:** Not accepted.
Prices: Platters $8.95–$14.95. AE, CB, DC, DISC, MC, V.
Open: Winter, Mon–Thurs 5:30–9:30pm, Fri–Sat 5–10pm, Sun
11:30am–2:30pm and 5–9pm; summer, Mon–Thurs 5:30–10pm, Fri–
Sat 5–10:30pm, Sun 11:30am–2:30pm and 5–10pm.

There's a country feel to this link in the County Line chain, located
in a quiet area in the far north central part of San Antonio. The main
eating area, wood-slatted with an old-style juke box and neon signs,
is designed to resemble a 1940s roadside diner. There's a full-service
bar on a waiting deck—and wait people do, sometimes up to an hour
or more if they arrive after 6pm on a weekend night, or after 6:30pm
during the week.

Some folks are intent on digging into the fall-off-the-bone beef
ribs, while others are anticipating the tender pork; the restaurant's
claim to fame is that it smokes all its meat for more than 18 hours.
Barbecued chicken, turkey, and even some salads are also available.

Note: A new County Line, just opened on the River Walk next
to the Hard Rock Cafe, is as likely to be as undaunted by crowds as
this location.

11 Leon Springs

Romano's Macaroni Grill, 24116 IH-10 West (Leon Springs/
Boerne Stage Road exit). ☎ **698-0003.**
Cuisine: ITALIAN. **Reservations:** Only accepted weeknights for par-
ties of 15 or more.
Prices: Appetizers $3.95–$6.95; main courses $6.75–$15.95. AE, CB,
DC, DISC, MC, V.
Open: Sun–Thurs 11am–10pm, Fri–Sat 11am–11pm.

Some Saturday nights it seems like everyone's abandoned San Antonio for tiny Leon Springs—a former stagecoach stop some 20 miles
northwest of town—that's how crowded Macaroni's gets. Don't
come here for a quiet, romantic evening; just grab everyone you can
gather for a raucous Italian dinner.

The restaurant tries to hire opera-singing servers, so strains of
Puccini might break out in the room at anytime. Most revelry inspiring, however, are the open gallon jugs of wine from which diners help themselves; at the end of the meal, they simply report how
many glasses they've had—if they can remember. The menu focuses
on northern Italian dishes, particularly grilled seafood and meat; you'll
see the mesquite rotisserie as you enter the large, wood-and-stone
dining room, originally a dance hall. Such standards as chicken sca-
loppine are well prepared, and all the pastas and bread are baked fresh
on the premises.

Rudy's, 24152 I.H.-10 west (Leon Springs/Boerne Stage Road exit).
☎ **698-0418.**
Cuisine: BARBECUE. **Reservations:** Not accepted.
Prices: $4.99/lb–$10.95 rack of ribs.
Open: Sun–Thurs 10am–9pm, Fri–Sat 10am–10pm.

You've got to know the drill at Rudy's. Wait on one line (just follow
the crowd) for the meat—pork ribs, beef short ribs, brisket, sausage,
huge turkey legs, you name it; it'll come wrapped up in butcher paper, with lots and lots of white bread. Then, if you want a side dish—
beans, creamed corn, potato salad, coleslaw—or some peach cobbler,
go next door to the country store. Now plunk it all down on one of
the red-and-white checked vinyl tablecloths or bring it back outside
to the wooden picnic tables; there's barbecue sauce in both places.
Enjoy. You'll be rubbing elbows here with cowboys, bicyclists, and
other city folk who come from miles around for what they insist is
the best barbecue in town.

12 Specialty Dining

Local Favorites

In a city whose population is about half Hispanic, Mexican food is
the indisputable local favorite. Even people who are familiar with
Mexican fare are likely to come across some dishes here that they don't
recognize. At Market Square, you might see vendors selling funnel
cakes—huge, puffy concoctions of fried dough topped with powdered
sugar—so-called because the dough is poured into the hot fat through
a funnel, or *gorditas* (literally, little fat ones)—fried cornmeal cakes
topped with cheese, lettuce, tomatoes, salsa, refried beans, and other
tasty possibilities. At almost every Mexican restaurant, you'll find
some version of *pico de gallo* (chopped tomatoes, onions, and chiles)
on the table; it's usually a bit thicker than salsa (did you know that
more jars of salsa than ketchup are consumed in the United States
today?). In addition to the usual enchiladas, tamales, and quesadillas,
you'll also come across *chalupas,* or open-faced tacos; because the fried
corn tortilla isn't folded over, the usual fillings can be piled high on
top. And though you may already know the joy of huevos rancheros
for breakfast, San Antonio is a great place to be introduced to
chilaquiles—corn tortillas scrambled up with eggs, cheese, and chile
peppers.

Some of the best and most popular places to eat Mexican have
been reviewed above, but you can be sure you'll run into San
Antonians who are passionate about their personal favorite *tacquerias.*

You'll also find emotions rising when the talk runs to barbecue,
with many locals insisting that the place they go to is the best and
most authentic—because the meat has been smoked the longest,
because the place uses the best smoking technique, because the sauce
is the tangiest . . . the criteria are endless and often completely ar-
cane to outsiders. Rudy's in Leon Springs and the County Line in

North Central are reviewed above; a few other possibilities in town for a smoked-meat fix include **Tom's Ribs,** 13323 Nacogoches (☎ **654-7427**); **Bob's Smokehouse,** at 5145 Fredericksburg Rd. (☎ **344-8401**), 3306 Roland Ave. (☎ **333-9338**), and 1219 S. St. Mary's St. (☎ **224-4717**); and **Texas Old Fashioned Bar B Q,** 1023 Austin Hwy. (☎ **826-0800**). Don't despair if you fall in love with one of the barbecue sauces; many places bottle theirs and will mail jars back home.

Lots of folks go to **Billy Blues Barbecue Bar and Grill**, 330 E. Grayson St. (☎ **225-7409**), near The Strip for the music that comes with the ribs. **Bun 'N' Barrel,** 1150 Austin Hwy. (☎ **828-2820**), stands out less for its cooking than for its classic cars; San Antonians have been coming here for 50 years to check out each other's cool Chevys. Hang around on Friday night and you might even see the occasional drag race down Austin Highway. The winner gets the other guy's car.

Dining Areas/Complexes

Los Patios, the self-proclaimed "other River Walk," is a shopping-and-dining complex in northeast San Antonio that sits on the banks of the Salado Creek and is surrounded by 18 wooded acres; you'll see signs for it on Loop 410 between Starcrest and Harry Wurzbach. The food is fine at Los Patios' three restaurants, and the setting is hard to beat. At the Gazebo (open for lunch daily 11:30am to 2:30pm), the specialty is light American and the chicken salad is terrific. The Hacienda (open 11:30am to 2:30pm, except Monday) serves mostly Mexican fare, with some southwestern selections. The Brazier (open 11:30am to 10pm, except Monday) does a lot of mesquite grilling of steaks, chicken, and seafood. All three have outdoor decks or patios shaded by spreading oaks; the Brazier is the only one that actually looks out over the creek. Reservations (☎ **655-6171**) are advised.

Hotel Dining

Anaqua Grill, Plaza San Antonio hotel, 555 S. Alamo. ☎ **229-1000.**
Cuisine: SOUTHWEST. **Reservations:** Recommended.
Prices: Appetizers $2.95–$5.25; main courses $13.95–$17.50. Sun brunch $17.95. AE, CB, DC, DISC, MC, V.
Open: Breakfast Mon–Sat 7:30–10:30am, Sun 7–10am; lunch Mon–Sat 11:30am–2pm, Sun brunch 10am–2pm; dinner Sun–Thurs 6–10pm, Fri–Sat 6–11pm.

The lobby restaurant of the Plaza San Antonio, looking out onto the hotel's beautifully landscaped grounds, dishes up some of the most interesting southwestern cooking in town. The adventurous combinations of local spices and ingredients that characterize this type of cuisine are generally successful here, and the menu is designed to invite diners to try lots of different things.

A sampler plate of cold appetizers might include fresh mozzarella rolled with hazelnuts or roasted pepper; the hot appetizer plate could serve up seared ahi tuna with grilled shiitake mushroom salad. Among the entrées, the stir-fry of shrimp, lobster, and scallops with black-bean sauce and the black-pepper linguine with grilled duck breast are especially good. Or you could skip the lot and go straight for the dessert sampler; my favorite was the chocolate and peanut butter pie (I was always partial to Reese's peanut butter cups). Unfortunately, the service is not as reliable as the cooking: it's sometimes attentive and sometimes nonexistent.

Polo's, The Fairmount hotel, 401 S. Alamo St. ☎ **225-4242.**

Cuisine: REGIONAL AMERICAN. **Reservations:** Recommended.
Prices: Appetizers $7.25–$8.95; main courses $21.95–$27.95. AE, CB, DC, DISC, MC, V.
Open: Breakfast daily 7–10am; lunch Mon–Fri 11:30am–2pm; dinner Mon–Thurs 6–10pm, Fri–Sat 6–10:30pm.

Polo's is known around town as the spawning ground for some of the best chefs in San Antonio; a number have gone on to start successful restaurants of their own. This has meant that the kitchen is sometimes in transition; it remains to be seen whether the Fairmount restaurant's once-solid reputation will be reestablished.

All the portents are good, though. A lovely setting for a special-occasion dinner, the dining rooms are done in muted tones of beige, with etched glass-and-brass partitions and tables adorned with fresh flowers and delicate liquid candles. As you enter, an open wood-burning pizza oven imported from Italy imparts the impression—and the aroma—that some serious cooking is going on.

That oven turns out some very creative pizzas, topped with venison sausage, for example, or Brie and almonds. Combined with a salad, a 12-inch pie makes a nice, light meal. In fact, you could probably get by on just the generous grilled quail salad if you eat enough of the hard-to-resist sourdough rolls that come out hot from the pizza oven. But you're likely to want to try such substantial dishes as the grilled New Zealand lamb or Norwegian salmon, or even one of the menu's low-fat, high-taste entrées. The presentations are astounding; it's an effort not to stare at the artistic mounds emerging from the kitchen and to refrain from asking your fellow diners what they ordered. Service is impeccable, but friendly enough for you to ask your server instead.

The River Grill, Marriott Rivercenter hotel, 101 Bowie St. ☎ **223-1000,** ext. 6804.

Cuisine: SOUTHWESTERN. **Reservations:** Recommended.
Prices: Appetizers $4–$7; main courses $13–$24. AE, CB, DC, DISC, MC, V.
Open: Tues–Sat 6–10pm.

Frenzied Rivercenter shoppers looking for a nice place to unwind over dinner will find one in the Marriott's posh grill. The two-tiered, low-lit room, with draped windows, potted palms, and art nouveau chandeliers, will soothe any nerves the mall may have frazzled.

The food, however, can be stimulating. The grilled chicken salad appetizer has a Thai kick and the tamale with corn, chorizo, beans, and chèvre comes with a chili sauce. "Three from the Sea" piles spicy lobster, scallops, and shrimp atop basmati rice. There are two elk entrées on the menu—one accompanied by Muscovy duck breast with a dried cherry glacé, the other roasted and served with tender, moist Navajo fry bread. Finish off with the pecan fudge cheesecake dipped in white chocolate; hey, you've had a hard day at the mall.

Service is attentive but not hovering, and there's a nice attention to detail; the butter, for example, comes out sculpted in the shape of a cactus.

The Stetson, Hilton Palacio del Rio, 200 S. Alamo. ☎ 222-1400.

Cuisine: AMERICAN. **Reservations:** Recommended.
Prices: Appetizers $4.75–$6.95; main courses $15.25–$25.50. AE, CB, DC, DISC, MC, V.
Open: Dinner daily 5:30–11pm; Sun brunch 11am–2pm.

One floor up from the River Walk, the Stetson is the perfect place to dine overlooking the water without mingling with the hoi polloi. Book a window table in this elegant room and you'll be assured a romantic view in quiet—and temperature controlled—surroundings. The window shades are even programmed to go up and down automatically as the light shifts, so you never have to worry about glare.

Steaks and seafood are prepared with a southwestern touch, but not an overly effete one: You're likely to recognize all the ingredients on the menu. The Texas crab cakes served on mixed greens make a good starter, as do the ravioli stuffed with chorizo. Steak lovers should go straight for the black Angus rib eye served with pecan butter. Seafood fans have a tougher choice: Will it be shrimp Cancún, sautéed in garlic and cilantro and flamed in tequila, or pan-seared sesame-coated salmon? After a satisfying dinner, I found I could still manage the hot apple bread with cinammon ice cream; my companion, who couldn't eat another bite, ploughed through a rich chocolate pecan pie (with whipped cream, yet).

Dining with a View

The vista most people covet in San Antonio is the river; **Boudro's, Zuni Grill,** and **Little Rhein Steak House,** reviewed in the "Downtown" section, sit directly on the River Walk, and the Stetson (see "Hotel Dining") has an excellent view of it. The dining room on the top floor of the **Wyndham Hotel** affords a fine Hill Country panorama, but it's open only for Sunday brunch.

Soda Fountain

Olmos Pharmacy, 3902 McCullough. ☎ 822-3361.

Open: Mon–Fri 7am–7:30pm, Sat 8am–5:30pm, Sun 9am–1:30pm.

When was the last time you had a rich chocolate milk shake served in a large metal container with a glass of whipped cream on the side? Never mind, don't think about it—just grab a stool at the fountain's

Formica counter and enjoy. Open since 1938, Olmos Pharmacy also scoops up old-fashioned ice-cream sodas, Coke or rootbeer floats, sundaes, banana splits . . . if it's cold, sweet, and nostalgia inducing, they've got it. Bring the kids to show them what ice cream is *really* supposed to taste like.

Fast Food

Bright-pink roofs and green neon palm trees have long signaled good fast food to San Antonians: The original **Taco Cabana,** opened in 1973 on 3310 San Pedro Ave., rapidly became a Hill Country chain as word spread of great grilled chicken, freshly made tacos, and other authentic Mexican specialties—not the typical American fast-food versions thereof. You'd be hard-pressed to spend much more than $5 per person for a meal here. There are now 20 Taco Cabanas in San Antonio; the most convenient locations are 101 Alamo Plaza (☎ 224-6158), 2908 Broadway (☎ 829-1616), and the original one on San Pedro Avenue (☎ 733-9332).

Breakfast

El Milagrito Cafe, 521 E. Woodlawn (at North St. Mary's).
☎ 734-8964.
Cuisine: MEXICAN. **Reservations:** Not accepted.
Prices: Tacos 85¢–$1.25; main courses $2.95–$4.25. No credit cards accepted.
Open: Mon–Sat 6am–6pm, Sun 6am–3pm.

After you've spent the night before overindulging on the Strip, come back to this friendly, family-owned restaurant in the morning for a home-style Mexican breakfast; the steaming bowls of *menudo* are reputed to cure even the worst hangovers (just don't ask about the ingredients). Sure, the mariachis that play every Saturday and Sunday morning might not do much for a headache—but everyone else should enjoy the musical accompaniment to tacos *loco* (filled with potato, eggs, beans, and sausage) or huevos rancheros. Owned by the same couple for the last 25 years, El Milagrito is decked with posters and photos of Mexican revolutionary Emiliano Zapata. Much of the one-page photocopied menu is in Spanish only, but the staff is happy to explain anything you don't understand.

BRUNCH

The downtown hotel restaurants are your best bet for Sunday brunch. At the Plaza San Antonio's **Anaqua Grill,** a copious buffet ($19.95 adults, $11.95 for children) gives diners the chance to try different dishes from a single country or region; one week food from Russia might be featured, another week the cuisine of the Yucatán. La Mansión del Río's **Las Canarias** restaurant, overlooking the River Walk, offers a romantic Champagne Brunch ($21.95 for adults, $11.95 children), including huge platters of seafood, salads, cheese, and fruit; Belgian waffle and omelet stations; and a dessert table to die for. The Marriott Rivercenter's Champagne Brunch at the **Garden Cafe** is the most casual of the three; for a bargain $11.95 ($6.50 for children), diners get a choice of breakfast entrées, along with fresh fruit, juice, ice tea, and lots of hot coffee.

24 Hours

Mi Tierra, 281 Produce Row. ☎ 225-1262.

Cuisine: MEXICAN. **Reservations:** Accepted for large groups only.
Prices: Appetizers $4.25–$6.95; main courses $4.75–$10.25. AE, MC, V.
Open: Open 24 hours.

Almost anyone who's ever been within striking distance of San Antonio has heard of this Market Square restaurant, open since 1946. Much expanded and gussied up since then, it still draws a faithful clientele of Latino families and businessmen along with busloads of tourists. Where else could you come at 2am and order anything from chorizo and eggs to an eight-ounce charbroiled rib-eye—and be serenaded by mariachis? A full menu is available all night, but you needn't have anything heavy. Mi Tierra is justly renowned for its *panadería* (bakery), and you can get all kinds of delicious *pan dulces* to go along with a cup of coffee or Mexican hot chocolate.

6

What to See & Do in San Antonio

SAN ANTONIO'S DOGGED PRESERVATION OF ITS PAST AND AVID DEVELOPMENT of its future guarantee that there's something in town to suit every tourist taste. The biggest problem with sightseeing here is figuring out how to get it all in; you can spend days in the downtown area alone and still not cover everything (the itineraries below give some suggestions on how to organize your time). Walkers will love being able to hoof it from one downtown attraction to another, but the sedentary needn't despair—or drive. One of the most visitor-friendly cities imaginable, San Antonio has excellent and inexpensive tourist transportation lines, extending to such far-flung sights as Sea World of Texas and Fiesta Texas.

Before you visit any of the paid attractions, stop in at the San Antonio Visitor Information Center (317 Alamo Plaza, across the street from the Alamo) and ask for their SAVE San Antonio discount book, including everything from the large theme parks to some city tours and museums. Many hotels also have a stash of discount coupons for their guests.

Suggested Itineraries

If You Have 1 Day

If your time is very limited, it makes sense to stay downtown, where many of the prime attractions are concentrated. Start your day at the Alamo, which tends to get more crowded as the day goes on. When you finish touring the complex, take a streetcar from Alamo Square to HemisFair Park; from the observation deck at the Tower of Americas you can literally see everything there is to see in town. Then board the streetcar again and head to the nearby King William Historic District, where you can pick up a self-guided walking tour at the office of the San Antonio Conservation Society. If you're really hungry by now, have lunch at the historic Guenther House; if you can hold out and have a hankering for Mexican food, wait until you get to Market Square (another streetcar will get you there) and eat at Mi Tierra or La Margarita, both owned by the same family. Spend the afternoon poking around the two square blocks of shops and stalls and then head over to the River Walk, where you might catch a riverboat tour before eating at one of the riverside restaurants (I'd vote for Boudro's). Or, if you can manage to get tickets to anything at either the Majestic or the Arneson River theaters, eat early (again, you'll have beaten the crowds) and enjoy the show.

If You Have 2 Days

Day 1   Follow the same itinerary outlined above.

Day 2   See the San Antonio missions in the morning (at the least, Mission San José); if you're traveling with kids, go to Sea World of Texas or Fiesta Texas in the afternoon. If not, tour all four missions and then go to the McNay, Lone Star, or Witte museums (all on the same bus route as the missions) afterward.

If You Have 3 Days

Day 1   Start at the Alamo and then tour the rest of the missions; that way you'll see the military shrine in its historic context. Spend the late afternoon at one of the theme parks or at one of the museums (the San Antonio Art Museum, the McNay, or the Witte).

Day 2   Go to HemisFair Park and visit the Tower of the Americas and the Institute of Texan Cultures or the Mexican Cultural Institute; then stroll around nearby La Villita. Afterward, head down to the King William district and take the tour of the Steves Homestead. In the afternoon, enjoy a riverboat tour and/or visit the Southwest Craft Center.

Day 3   See the Spanish Governor's Palace and the Navarro Cathedral, and then shop and have lunch at Market Square. In the afternoon, go to one of the museums you haven't yet visited.

If You Have 4 Days

Days 1–3   Follow the itinerary outlined in "If You Have 3 Days," but eliminate the attractions in the Brackenridge Park area (the Witte and the McNay museums), substituting another downtown sight or a theme park.

Day 4   Visit the attractions in the Brackenridge Park area, including the Japanese Tea Garden, the Witte Museum, the McNay Museum, the zoo, and the San Antonio Botanical Gardens. Some of the best restaurants in San Antonio are in this part of town.

If You Have 5 Days or More

Days 1–4   Follow the above four-day itinerary, but break it up with:
Day 5   A day trip to Bandera, in scenic ranch country; this sleepy cowboy town will remind you you're in Wild West territory. An afternoon trail ride is great, but if you have more time, book a room at one of Bandera's many dude ranches; a two-night minimum stay is usually required.

1   The Top Attractions

The Alamo, 300 Alamo Plaza. ☎ 225-1391.

Sitting in the heart of downtown San Antonio, the Alamo is the most visited site in Texas, the silhouette of its graceful mission church an instantly recognizable symbol of the state. It was here that 188 Texas volunteers defied the much larger army of Mexican dictator Santa Anna for 13 days in March 1836. Although all the men—among them pioneers Davy Crockett and Jim Bowie—were killed, their death became a rallying cry for Sam Houston, who defeated the Mexican army at the Battle of San Jacinto one month later and secured Texas's independence.

The Daughters of the Republic of Texas, who saved the crumbling complex from being being turned into a hotel by a New York syndicate in 1905, maintain it as a shrine to these fighters. But there are some who would like to see more emphasis placed on the Alamo's other historic roles—including that of being a burial ground for the Native Americans for whom it was founded on a nearby site in 1718 as the Mission San Antonio de Valero. The complex was secularized by the end of the 18th century and leased out to a Spanish cavalry unit; by the time the famous battle took place, it had been abandoned.

Little remains of the original mission today; only the Long Barrack (formerly the *convento,* or living quarters for the missionaries) and the mission church are still here. The former houses a museum detailing the history of Texas in general and the battle in particular; the latter includes artifacts of the Alamo fighters, along with an information desk and small gift shop. A larger museum and gift shop are at the back of the complex; there's also a peaceful garden and an excellent research library on the grounds.

Admission: Free.

Open: Mon–Sat 9am–5:30pm, Sun 10am–5:30pm. **Closed:** Christmas Eve and Christmas. **Streetcar:** All streetcar lines.

Fiesta Texas, 17000 I-10 west (corner of I-10 west and Loop 1604). ☎ 697-5050.

Since south Texas is a bit too large to explore in a single afternoon, this $100 million theme park is a good way to get a taste of the attractions of the state—literally as well as figuratively. A vast variety of food booths share the 200-acre amusement arena with rides, games, and craft demonstrations galore. Dramatic 100-foot cliffs surround the park, which is set in an abandoned limestone quarry on the north end of town.

Did You Know?

- Elmer Doolin, manufacturer of Fritos corn chips, bought the original recipe for $100 from a San Antonio restaurant in 1932. He sold the first batch from the back of his model-T Ford.

- The world's largest bowling-ball manufacturer, Columbia 300 Inc., is in San Antonio.

- Chili con carne originated in San Antonio.

- The first military flight by an American took place at Fort Sam Houston in 1910; in 1915, the United States' entire air force— six reconnaisance planes—resided at the fort.

- *Wings,* a silent World War I epic that won the first Academy Award for best picture in 1927, was filmed in San Antonio. The film also marked the debut of Gary Cooper, who was on screen for a total of 102 seconds.

- Barbed wire was first demonstrated in San Antonio's Military Plaza.

- Lyndon and Lady Bird Johnson were married in San Antonio's St. Mark's Episcopal Church.

The attractions are organized around four themes: Mexican fiesta, German village, country and western, and vintage rock and roll (remember, Buddy Holly was from Texas). There's also a water park—bring your suit—and, the newest feature, a simulated seaside boardwalk with a Ferris wheel, roller-skating rink, and nine-hole miniature golf course. Park highlights include the Rattler, the highest and fastest wooden roller coaster in the world; the Gully Washer, a totally soaking river-rapids ride; and, for the less daring, a variety of professionally presented performances that range from mariachis to oompah bands. Be sure to stay around for the laser-light show put on each evening before the park closes.

Admission: $18.15 adults, $12.85 children 7–11, children 6 and under free. "Come Back Tomorrow" tickets are $5 for all ages. **Parking:** $4 per day.

Open: The schedule varies greatly with the season; the park is generally open weekends or Thurs–Sun from Sept–Nov and Mar–May, open daily from Jun–Aug. Park opening hours are usually 10am; closing 9 or 10pm, depending on the season. Call ahead for current information. **Closed:** Dec–Jan. **Bus:** 94. **Directions:** Take exit 555 on I-10 west.

La Villita National Historic District, bounded by Durango, Navarro, and Alamo St. and the River Walk. ☎ **299-8610.**

Developed by European settlers along the higher east bank of the San Antonio River in the late 18th and early 19th centuries, La Villita (the Little Village) was on the proverbial wrong side of the tracks until flooding of the west bank settlements made it the fashionable place to live. It fell back into poverty by the beginning of the 20th century, only to be revitalized in the late 1930s by artists and craftspeople and by the San Antonio Conservation Society. Now boutiques, craft shops, and restaurants occupy a charming version

Frommer's Favorite San Antonio Experiences

People-Watching at Market Square   After an afternoon of shopping at the square's two lively Mexican markets, take a load off your feet at an outdoor table and sip a margarita or a Coke. Among the colorful crowd, you'll see vendors from Mexico and locals who have been coming here since the days when animals and produce were still being sold in the stalls.

Strolling Along the River   Whether you opt to join the throngs at the restaurants and cafés of the Big Bend portion of the River Walk or get away by yourself to one of its quieter stretches, the green, lush banks of San Antonio's river can match your mood, day or night.

Mariachi Mass at Mission San José   You're welcome to watch members of the congregation of this largest of the mission churches raise their voices in spirited musical prayer every Sunday at noon. Come early; seats are limited, as this is a popular thing to do.

of a Spanish/Mexican–style village, replete with shaded patios, plazas, brick-and-tile streets, and some of the settlement's original adobe structures. You can see (but not enter) the house of General Cós, the Mexican military leader who surrendered to the Texas revolutionary army in 1835, or attend a performance at the Arneson River Theatre (see Chapter 8, "San Antonio Nights").

Admission: Free.

Open: Daily; shop hours 10am–6pm. **Closed:** Thanksgiving Day, Christmas, New Year's Day. **Bus:** 40. **Streetcar:** HemisFair Park/ La Villita/Cattleman Square.

Market Square, between Dolorosa and Commerce Sts. ☎ **299-8600.**

It may not be quite as colorful as it was when big trucks drove up and live chickens squawked around overflowing, makeshift vegetable stands, but Market Square will still transport you south of the border. Stalls in the indoor El Mercado sell everything from onyx chess sets and cheap serapes to beautifully made crafts from the interior of Mexico. More formal shops, some rather pricey, line the outside of the structure. Across the street, the Farmer's Market, which formerly housed the produce market, has carts with more modern goods. If you can tear yourself away from the merchandise, take a look around at the buildings in the complex; some date back to the late 1800s.

Bring your appetite along with your wallet: In addition to two good Mexican restaurants (one open 24 hours a day), almost every weekend sees the emergence of food stalls selling specialties such as *gorditas* (chubby corn cakes topped with a variety of goodies) or funnel cakes (fried dough sprinkled with powdered sugar). Most of the city's Hispanic festivals are held here, and mariachis usually stroll the square.

Admission: Free.

Open: El Mercado and Farmer's Market Plaza open daily Jun– Aug 10am–8pm, Sept–May 10am–6pm; restaurants and some of the shops open later. **Closed:** Thanksgiving Day, Christmas, New Year's Day, and Easter Day. **Streetcar:** St. Paul Square/Market Square; Alamo Plaza/Market Square.

King William Historic District.

San Antonio's first suburb, King William was settled in the late 19th century by prosperous German merchants who displayed their wealth through extravagant homes. They named the 25-block area, located on the east bank of the river just south of downtown, after Kaiser Wilhelm of Prussia.

The neighborhood fell into disrepair for a few decades, but you'd never know it from the pristine condition of most of the houses here today. Before you stroll up and down along tree-shaded King William Street, gawking at the beautifully landscaped, magnificent mansions, stop at the headquarters of the San Antonio Conservation Society (107 King William St.) and pick up a self-guided walking tour booklet outside the gate. Only the Steves Homestead (see "More Attractions," below) and the Guenther House (see Chapter 5, "San Antonio Dining") are open to the public. The neighborhood is within walking distance of the Convention Center and is on the VIA Romana/King William streetcar route.

⭐ **Paseo Del Rio/The River Walk,** downtown from the Municipal Auditorium on the north end to the King William Historic District on the south end.

Just a few steps below the streets of downtown San Antonio lies another world, alternately soothing or exhilarating, depending on where you venture. The quieter areas of the 2^1/$_2$ paved miles of winding river bank, shaded by cypresses, oaks, and willows, exude a tropical, exotic aura; the Big Bend section, filled with sidewalk cafés, tony restaurants, bustling bars, high-rise hotels, and even a huge shopping mall, has a festive, sometimes frenetic feel. Tour boats, water taxis, and floating picnic barges regularly ply the river, and local parades and festivals fill its banks with revelers.

Although plans to cement over the river, inspired by a disastrous flood in 1921, were stymied, it wasn't until the late 1930s that the federal Works Project Administration (WPA) carried out architect Robert Hugman's designs for the waterway, installing cobblestone walks, arched bridges, and entrance steps from various street-level locations. And it wasn't until the late 1960s, when the River Walk proved to be one of the most popular attractions of the HemisFair exposition, that its commercial development began in earnest.

There's a real danger of the River Walk becoming overdeveloped—new restaurants are opening at an alarming pace, and the crush of bodies along the busiest sections can be claustrophobic in the summer heat—but plenty of quieter spots still exist. And if you're caught up in the sparkling lights reflected on the water on a breeze-swept night, you might forget there was ever anyone else around.

⭐ **San Antonio Missions National Historic Park.**

It's impossible *not* to remember the Alamo when you're in San Antonio; more difficult to recall is that it was originally just the first of five missions established by the Franciscans along the San Antonio River to Christianize the native population. The four missions that now fall under the aegis of the National Parks Department are still active parishes, run in cooperation with the Archdiocese of San Antonio.

The missions were complex communities, not only churches, and the Parks Department has assigned each of the four an interpretive theme to educate visitors about the roles they played in early San Antonio society. They may be visited separately, but if you have the time, see all of them—they were built uncharacteristically close to one another and the cumulative experience is hard to match. Signs direct visitors from the Alamo to the 5^1/$_2$-mile mission trail that begins at Mission Concepción and winds its way south through the city streets to Mission Espada. Some $14 million in federal funds were recently allocated to create a more cohesive connecting trail, but for the time being pay close attention to the brown directional signs or to the National Parks map. Or take the bus, which runs frequently and stops at each of the missions.

Attractions & Shopping in
Downtown San Antonio

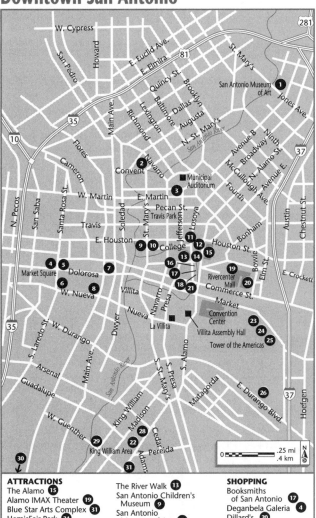

ATTRACTIONS

The Alamo **15**
Alamo IMAX Theater **19**
Blue Star Arts Complex **31**
HemisFair Park **24**
Hertzberg Circus Collection and Museum **21**
Institute of Texan Cultures **26**
Jose Antonio Navarro State Historical Park **6**
King William Historic District **22**
Majestic Theater **10**
Mexican Cultural Institute **23**
Ripley's Believe It or Not **14**

The River Walk **13**
San Antonio Children's Museum **9**
San Antonio Museum of Art **1**
San Fernando Cathedral **7**
Southwest Craft Center **2**
Spanish Governor's Palace **5**
Steves Homestead **29**
The Texas Adventure **12**
Tower of the Americas **25**
Vietnam Veteran's Memorial **3**

SHOPPING

Booksmiths of San Antonio **17**
Deganbela Galeria **4**
Dillard's **20**
Kallison's Western Wear **8**
Keene Gallery **18**
Market Square **4**
Papa Jim's Botanica **30**
Paris Hatters **11**
Recuerdos De Mi Madre **16**
Rivercenter Mall **20**
Southwestern Craft Center **2**
Tequila Tree **4**
Tienda Guadalupe Folk Art & Gifts **28**

9583

Concepción, 807 Mission Rd. at Felisa (☎ **229-5732**), was built in 1731. The oldest unrestored Texas mission, Concepción looks much as it did 200 years ago. Many of us tend to think of religious sites as somber and austere, but traces of color on the facade and restored wall paintings inside show how cheerful this one originally was.

San José, 6539 San José Dr. at Mission Road (☎ **229-4770** or **229-4771**), established in 1720, was the largest, best-known, and most beautiful of the Texas missions. It was reconstructed to give visitors a complete picture of life in a mission community—right down to the granary, mill, and Indian pueblo. Popular mariachi masses are held here every Sunday at noon (come early if you want a seat), and pageants and plays are put on at an outdoor arena.

Moved from an earlier site in east Texas to its present location in 1731, **San Juan Capistrano,** 9102 Graf at Ashley (☎ **229-5734**), doesn't have the grandeur of the missions to the north—the larger church intended for it was never completed—but the original simple chapel and the wilder setting give it a peaceful, spiritual aura. A short (three-tenths of a mile) interpretative trail, with a number of overlook platforms, winds through the woods to the banks of the old river channel.

The southernmost mission in the San Antonio chain, **San Francisco de la Espada,** 10040 Espada Rd. (☎ **627-2021**), also has an ancient, isolated feel, although the beautifully kept up church shows just how vital it still is to the local community. Be sure to visit the **Espada Aqueduct,** part of the mission's original *acequia* (irrigation ditch) system, about one mile to the north of the mission; dating from 1740, it's one of the oldest Spanish aqueducts in the United States.

Admission: Free, donations accepted.

Open: All the missions are open daily 8am–5pm; during daylight saving time, 9am–6pm. **Closed:** Christmas, New Year's Day. Call ahead to inquire about National Park Ranger tours. **Bus:** 40.

Sea World of Texas, 10500 Sea World Dr. ☎ 523-3611.

Leave it to Texas to provide Shamu, the performing killer whale, with his most spacious digs: At 250 acres, this $140-million Sea World is not only the largest of the Anheuser Busch–owned marine theme parks, but also the largest in the world. The walk-through habitats where you can watch penguins, sea lions, sharks, tropical fish, and flamingos do their thing are endlessly fascinating, but for my money, the aquatic acrobatics at the stadium shows are the most fun. The humans hold their own with an impressive water-skiing exhibition on a 12$^{1}/_{2}$-acre lake.

But one needn't get frustrated by just looking at all that water: there are lots of places here to get wet. The Lost Lagoon has a huge wave pool and water slides aplenty, and the Texas Splashdown flume ride and the Rio Loco river rapids ride also offer splashy fun; younger children can cavort in Shamu's Happy Harbor. Lockers and changing areas let you dry off and stay around for the regular summer-night multimedia laser shows or one of the special high-season concerts, which showcase big names like the Beach Boys and country stars Vince Gill and Alan Jackson.

Admission: One-day pass $24.95 adults, $16.95 children 3–11, children 2 and under free. Two-day pass (valid only for visits on consecutive days) $30.95 adults, $22.95 children 3–11. **Parking:** $3 per day.

Open: The schedule varies greatly with the season; the park is generally open weekends and some holidays in spring and fall, daily during summer. Opening hours are 10am, closing hours 6, 8, or 10pm, depending on the season. Call ahead for current information. **Closed:** Nov to mid-March. **Bus:** 63. **Directions:** From Loop 410 or from Hwy. 90 west, exit Hwy. 151 west to the park.

2   More Attractions

Churches

San Fernando Cathedral, 115 Main Plaza. ☎ 227-1297.

Construction of a church on this site, overlooking what was once the town's central plaza, was begun in 1738 by San Antonio's original Canary Island settlers and completed in 1749. Part of the early structure—the oldest cathedral sanctuary in the United States and the oldest parish church in Texas—is incorporated into the magnificent Gothic Revival–style cathedral built in 1868. Jim Bowie got married here and General Santa Anna raised the flag of "no quarter" from the roof during the siege of the Alamo in 1836. A bronze plaque outside directs visitors to the chapel where, it says, the bones of the Alamo heroes are entombed, but that claim is widely disputed.

Admission: Free.

Open: Daily 6am–6pm. **Streetcar:** Alamo Plaza/Market Square; Romana Plaza/King William.

Historic Buildings/Complexes

Fort Sam Houston, about 2¹/₂ miles northeast of downtown.

Since 1718, when the armed Presidio de Béxar was established to defend the Spanish missions, the military has played a key role in San Antonio's development; it remains the number one employer in town today. The 3,434-acre Fort Sam Houston affords visitors an unusual opportunity to view the city's military past in the context of its military present. Most of its historic buildings are still in use and thus off limits, but three are open to the public. The **Fort Sam Houston Museum** (open 10am to 4pm on Wednesday to Sunday, free admission; ☎ 221-1886) details the history of the armed forces in Texas, with a focus on San Antonio, while the **U.S. Army Medical Department Museum** (open 10am to 4pm on Wednesday to Saturday, free admission; ☎ 221-6277) includes displays of army medical equipment and American prisoner-of-war memorabilia. Free self-guided tour maps of the historic sites are available at the gift shop in the **Quadrangle** (New Braunfels Avenue, between Grayson Street and Wilson Road; gift shop open daily 9am to 5pm). This impressive 1876 limestone structure, the oldest on the post, is centered by a brick clock tower and encloses a grassy square where peacocks, deer, and rabbits roam freely; the Apache chief Geronimo was held captive here for 40 days in 1886.

José Antonio Navarro State Historical Park, 228 S. Laredo St. ☎ **226-4801.**

A key player in the transition of Texas from Spanish territory to American state, José Antonio Navarro was a Mexican mayor of San Antonio in 1821; a signer of the 1836 declaration of Texas independence; and the only native Texan to take part in the convention that ratified the annexation of Texas to the United States in 1845. His former living quarters, built around 1850, are an interesting amalgam of the architectural fashions of his time: A restored office, house, and separate kitchen, constructed of adobe and limestone, blend elements from Mexican, French, German, and pioneer styles. Guided tours and demonstrations are available; call ahead to inquire.

Admission: $2 adults, $1 children 6–12.

Open: Wed–Thurs 1–4pm, Fri–Sat 10am–4pm. **Closed:** Sun–Tues and Federal holidays. **Streetcar:** HemisFair Park/Cattleman Square; Romano Plaza/Blue Star Arts Complex.

Majestic Theatre, 230 E. Houston St. ☎ **226-3333.**

Everyone from Jack Benny to Mae West played this opulent vaudeville and film palace, designed in baroque Moorish/Spanish Revival style by John Eberson in 1929 and magnificently restored in 1989. One of the last "atmospheric" theaters to be built—the stock market crashed four months after it opened and no one could afford such elaborate showplaces again—it's also one of the few such theaters remaining in the United States, and was recently designated a National Historic Landmark. The Majestic is not generally open to the public during the day, but you may be able to get on a group guided tour; call Las Casas, ☎ **223-4343,** to find out. If not, book a seat for whatever's on at the theater at night (see "San Antonio Nights," Chapter 8, for details); a glimpse at the fabulous overhead dome, with its simulated stars and clouds, is alone worth the price of admission.

Spanish Governor's Palace, 105 Plaza de Armas. ☎ **224-0601.**

Never actually a palace, this building formerly served as the residence and headquarters for the captain of the Spanish presidio. This 1749 adobe structure, its high ceilings crossed by protruding *viga* beams, is beautiful in its simplicity, and the 10 rooms crowded with period furnishings paint a vivid portrait of upper-class life in a rough-hewn society. Consider taking a picnic lunch to eat on the tree-shaded, cobblestoned patio, overlooking a flowing stone fountain.

Admission: $1 adults, 50¢ children 7–13, children 6 and under free.

Open: Mon–Sat 9am–5pm, Sun 10am–5pm. **Closed:** Christmas, New Year's Day, and Fiesta week. **Streetcar:** Romana Plaza/King William.

Steves Homestead, 509 King William St. ☎ **225-5924.**
Built in 1876 for lumber magnate Edward Steves by prominent San Antonio architect Alfred Giles, this Victorian mansion was restored by the San Antonio Conservation Society, to whom it was willed by Steves's granddaughter. One of the only houses in the King William Historic District open to the public, it gives a fascinating glimpse into the lifestyle of the rich and locally famous of the late 19th century. You can't enter without taking a docent-led tour, which is fine: You wouldn't want to miss the great gossip—um, historical information—about the Steves family that the society's very knowledgeable volunteers pass along.

Admission: $2.

Open: Daily 10am–4:15pm (hours subject to change); tours, lasting 30 to 45 minutes, given every half hour. **Streetcar:** Romana Plaza/King William.

Yturri-Edmunds House and Mill, 257 Yellowstone.
☎ **534-8237.**
More than 150 years of the city's architecture are spanned by the exhibits on this site. Acquired in 1824 by Manuel Yturri-Castillo, a native of Spain, the property formerly belonged to Mission Concepción and included a gristmill that may have been built as early as 1720, as well as one of the mission's irrigation ditches. A six-room adobe house, one of the few that still exists in San Antonio, was constructed between 1840 and 1860. Also here are an 1881 carriage house from the King William Historic District and an 1855 block-and-rubble house that was originally located downtown; both were moved here by the San Antonio Conservation Society, which now owns the property. A tour guide is always on hand to take visitors around.

Admission: $2 adults, children under 12 free.

Open: Mon–Sat 10am–4pm, Sun noon–4pm. **Bus:** No. 40.

Museums & Galleries

Blue Star Arts Complex, 1400 S. Alamo. ☎ **227-6960.**
At the (cutting) edge of the King William neighborhood, this huge former warehouse hosts a collection of working studios and galleries, along with a performance space for the Jump-Start theater company; the artist-run, 11,000-square-foot Contemporary Art Museum is its anchor. The style of work varies from gallery to gallery—you'll see everything from Latin American folk art to feminist photography—but the level of professionalism is uniformly high.

Admission: Free.

Open: Hours vary from gallery to gallery; most are open Wed–Sun noon–6pm. **Streetcar:** Romano Plaza/Blue Star.

Hertzberg Circus Collection and Museum, 210 Market St.
☎ **299-7810.**
Sober or not, you'll be seeing pink elephants when you visit this nostalgia-inducing museum; they're posted as sentries on the side of

the front steps. Displays chosen from the massive collection of "circusana" that Harry Hertzberg bequeathed to the San Antonio Public Library (of which this is a branch) include Tom Thumb's carriage, a flea circus, and photographs of Buffalo Bill's Wild West show. Some things here will appeal to kids—including pictures of the sideshow freaks, likely to evoke memories of mixed fascination and horror in older visitors—but when there are no special children's shows on, adults will probably get the most out of this history-oriented place.

Admission: $2 adults, $1 children 3–12; free Tues.

Open: Mon–Sat 9am–5pm and (May–Sept only) Sun and holidays 1–5pm. **Streetcar:** Near all four streetcar lines.

Institute of Texan Cultures, 801 S. Bowie St., in HemisFair Park. ☎ 558-2300.

It's the rare visitor who won't discover here that his or her ethnic group has contributed to the history of Texas: 28 different cultures are represented in the imaginative, hands-on displays of this educational center, part of the University of Texas at San Antonio. Outbuildings include a one-room schoolhouse and a windmill, and the multimedia Dome Theater presents images of Texas on 36 screens. Volunteer docents frequently put on puppet shows; call ahead to see if one is scheduled for the day you plan to visit.

Admission: Free, donation accepted; $2 parking.

Open: Tues–Sun 9am–5pm. Dome shows presented at 10:15am, noon, 2 and 3:30pm. **Closed:** Mon, Thanksgiving Day, and Christmas. **Streetcar:** HemisFair Park/La Villita/Cattleman Square.

Lone Star Buckhorn Museums, 600 Lone Star Blvd. ☎ 270-9467.

If you like your educational experiences accompanied by a cold one, this is the place to come. With its huge stuffed animals, mounted fish, and Lone Star memorabeeria, this complex on the grounds of an active brewery fulfills every out-of-stater's stereotype of what a Texas museum might be like. In addition to the Hall of Horns, Hall of Feathers, Hall of Fins, and the Texas History Wax Museum, there's a small office that was once occupied by the short story writer O. Henry; outside are a lake and picnic grounds. Regardless of what you might think of great white hunters, it's hard to resist pictures made out of beer-can tabs or designed from rattlesnake rattles. A free beer or soft drink is included in the price of admission.

Admission: $3.50 adults, $3 senior citizens, $1.50 children 6–11, children under age 6 free.

Open: Daily 9:30am–5pm. **Bus:** 40.

Mexican Cultural Institute, 600 HemisFair Park. ☎ 227-0123.

Sponsored by the Mexican Ministry of Foreign Affairs, the institute hosts shifting displays of art and artifacts relating to Mexican history and culture, from Pre-Columbian to contemporary. Latin American film series, conferences, performances, contests, and workshops—including ones on language, literature, and folklore as well as art—are also held here.

Admission: Free, donations accepted.

Open: Tues–Fri 10am–5pm, Sat–Sun 11am–5pm. **Streetcar:** HemisFair Park/Cattleman Square.

⭐ **Marion Koogler McNay Art Museum,** 6000 N. New Braunfels Ave. ☎ **824-5368.**

Set on a hill north of Brackenridge Park with a striking view of downtown, the sprawling Spanish Mediterranean–style mansion of oil-heiress and artist Marion Koogler McNay has been an art museum since 1954. Its main strength is French postimpressionist and early 20th-century European painting, but there's also a fine collection of theater arts (costumes, set designs, etc.) and some excellent special exhibits (for example, a Rodin show in 1994). A well-stocked gift shop adjoins a shaded central patio. The graciousness of the setting, used for numerous weddings and photo shoots, combined with the intimacy of the collection, make this a most appealing place to look at art.

Admission: Free. Fee for special exhibits.

Open: Tues–Sat 10am–5pm, Sun noon–5pm. Docent tours given Sun at 2pm. **Closed:** Mon, New Years Day, Fourth of July, Thanksgiving Day, Christmas. **Bus:** 7.

San Antonio Museum of Art, 200 W. Jones Ave. ☎ **829-7262.**

A number of the castlelike buildings of the 1904 Lone Star Brewery were gutted, connected, and turned into a visually exciting exhibition space in 1981. The spare and, in some sections, skylit interiors of the structures contrast strikingly with the more intricately detailed brick exterior; the multiwindowed crosswalk between the two buildings affords fine views of downtown. The Latin American folk art collection is outstanding, and there are some good pieces in the other collections, ranging from early Egyptian, Greek, and Asian to 19th- and 20th-century American.

Admission: $4 adults, $2 senior citizens and students with ID, $1.75 children 4–11, children 3 and under free. Free on Tues from 3–9pm.

Open: Mon and Wed–Sat 10am–5pm, Tues 10am–9pm, Sun noon–5pm (6pm Jun–Aug). **Bus:** 7.

Southwest Craft Center, 300 Augusta. ☎ **224-1848.**

A stroll along the River Walk to the northern corner of downtown will bring you to another world—or two: A rare French-designed cloister where contemporary crafts are now being created. Two exhibition galleries and artist studios-cum-classrooms occupy the garden-filled grounds of the first girl's school in San Antonio, established by the Ursuline order in the mid-19th century. Take a look around—note the First Academy Building, made by an unusual rammed-earth process, and the wood-and-native limestone Gothic church—and then relax in one of many oak-shaded nooks. The Ursuline Gallery's gift shop carries unique craft items, and you can enjoy a nice, light lunch in the Copper Kitchen Restaurant.

Greater San Antonio Attractions & Shopping

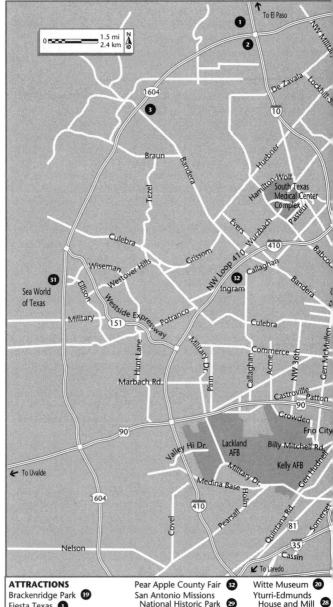

ATTRACTIONS
Brackenridge Park ⑲
Fiesta Texas ①
Fort Sam Houston ㉕
Japanese Tea Garden ⑱
Lone Star Buckhorn
  Museums ㉗
Marion Koogler
  McNay Art Museum ⑫

Pear Apple County Fair ㉜
San Antonio Missions
  National Historic Park ㉙
San Antonio
  Botanical Gardens ㉓
San Antonio Zoological
  Gardens and Aquarium ⑯
Sea World of Texas ㉛
Splashtown ㉖

Witte Museum ⑳
Yturri-Edmunds
  House and Mill ㉘

SHOPPING
Adelante Boutique
Austin Highway
  Flea Market ⑭
Bussey's Flea Market
Central Park Mall ⑥

9484

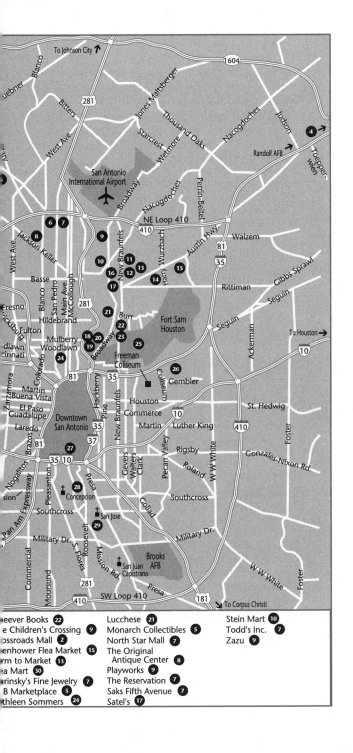

Admission: Free.

Open: Galleries, Mon–Sat 10am–4pm; restaurant, Mon–Fri 11:30am–2pm. **Streetcar:** Romana Plaza/King William.

⭐ **Witte Museum,** 3810 Broadway, at the edge of Brackenridge Park. ☎ **829-7262.**

A family museum that adults will enjoy as much as children, the Witte focusses on Texas history, natural science, and anthropology, but often ranges far afield—to the Berlin Wall, say, or the history of American advertising. Your senses will be engaged along with your intellect: You might hear animal cries as you crouch through south Texas thorn brush, or feel rough-hewn stone carved with Native American pictographs under your feet. An EcoLab is home to live Texas critters ranging from tarantulas to tortoises. Visitors can also explore a butterfly and hummingbird garden, a log cabin, and three restored historic homes outdoors. Excellent film, concert, and performing arts series draw folks back here on weekend afternoons and weekday evenings.

Admission: $4 adults, $2 senior citizens and students with ID, $1.75 children 4–11, children 3 and under free. Free on Tues from 3–9pm.

Open: Mon and Wed–Sat 10am–5pm, Tues 10am–9pm, Sun noon–5pm (6pm Jun–Aug). **Closed:** Thanksgiving Day and Christmas. **Bus:** 7.

Outdoor Art

Vietnam Veteran's Memorial, one block north of Travis Park at E. Martin and Jefferson Sts.

"Hill 881 S," a moving bronze monument created by combat artist Austin Deuel and dedicated to the Vietnam War veterans, depicts a marine holding a wounded comrade while looking skyward for an Evac helicopter.

Panorama

Tower of the Americas, 600 HemisFair Park. ☎ **299-8617.**

If you want to get the lay of the land—and don't have a fear of heights—circle the eight panoramic panels on the observation level of the 750-foot-high tower built for the HemisFair in 1968; the deck sits at the equivalent of 59 stories and is lit for spectacular night viewing. The tower also hosts a revolving restaurant and a cocktail lounge that sits still.

Admission: $2.50 adults, $1.25 senior citizens, $1 children 4–12, children under 4 free.

Open: Daily 8am–11pm. **Streetcar:** HemisFair Park/Cattleman Square.

Parks & Gardens

Brackenridge Park, main entrance 2800 block of N. Broadway.

With its rustic stone bridges and winding walkways, the city's main park, opened in 1899, has a charming, old-fashioned quality; it also serves as a popular center for recreational activities including golf, polo, biking, picnicking, horseback riding, and paddleboating. Just opposite the zoo entrance are a cable-car sky ride, a miniature railway, and a carousel (☎ **734-5401** for information on all three). See also entries for the San Antonio Zoo and the Japanese Tea Garden in this section, and for "Horseback Riding" and "Paddleboats" in "Recreation," below.

Admission: The sky ride, railway, and carousel each cost $2.15 adults, $1.60 children 1–11.

Open: The park is open daily from 8am–dusk. The sky ride operates Mon–Fri 9:30am–5:30pm, Sat–Sun 9:30am–6:30pm; the railway runs daily 9:30am–6pm; the carousel is open daily 9:30am–6pm. **Bus:** 7.

HemisFair Park, 200 S. Alamo. ☎ 299-8572.

Built for the 1968 HemisFair, an exposition celebrating the 250th anniversary of the founding of San Antonio, this urban oasis boasts water gardens, a wood-and-sand playground constructed by children, and a group of historic houses slated to become a German heritage park. Among its indoor diversions are the Institute of Texan Cultures, the Tower of the Americas (already described in this section), and the Mexican Cultural Institute (see above). Be sure to walk over to the Henry B. Gonzales Convention Center and take a look at the striking mosaic mural by Mexican artist Juan O'Gorman.

Bus: 40. **Streetcar:** HemisFair Park/Cattleman Square.

Japanese Tea Garden, Brackenridge Park, next to the zoo.
☎ 735-0663.

In 1917, the Japanese Tea Garden—also called the Japanese Sunken Garden—was created by prison labor to beautify an abandoned cement quarry, one of the largest in the world in the 1880s and 1890s; cement rock taken from it helped create the state capitol in Austin. You can still glimpse a brick smokestack and a number of the old lime kilns among the beautiful flower arrangements, which are less austere than those in many Japanese gardens. After Pearl Harbor, the site was officially renamed the Chinese Sunken Garden and a Chinese-style entryway added on; not until 1983 was the original name restored. Just to the southwest, a bowl of limestone cliffs found to have natural acoustic properties was turned into the Sunken Garden Theater (see Chapter 8, "San Antonio Nights," for details).

Admission: Free.

Open: Daily 8am–dusk. **Bus:** 7.

San Antonio Botanical Gardens, 555 Funston. ☎ 821-5115.

Take a horticultural tour of Texas at this gracious 38-acre garden, encompassing everything from south Texas scrub to Hill Country wildflowers and east Texas formal rose gardens. Fountains, pools, paved paths, and examples of Texas architecture—including the 1896 Sullivan Carriage House, moved stone-by-stone from downtown—provide visual contrast. There's also a garden for the blind, an herb garden, and a children's garden. Perhaps most outstanding is the $6.5-million Lucile Halsell Conservatory complex, a bermed, below-ground greenhouse replicating a variety of tropical-and-desert environments.

Admission: $3 adults, $1.50 seniors, $1 children 3–13, children under 3 free.

Open: Tues–Sun and holidays 9am–6pm. **Closed:** Mon, Christmas, New Year's Day. **Bus:** 7.

Zoo

San Antonio Zoological Gardens and Aquarium, 3903 N. St. Mary's St. in Brackenridge Park. ☎ **734-7183.**

Home to more than 700 different species, this zoo in Brackenridge Park hosts the third largest animal collection in North America. Considered one of the top zoos in the country, with excellent success in breeding and conservation programs, it may nevertheless strike those familiar with more modern facilities as a bit old-fashioned: It has expanded and upgraded most of its exhibits since it opened in 1914, but a number of rather small and/or spare cages still remain.

Admission: $6 adults, $4 children 4–11 and seniors over 62, children 3 and under free. Boat rides $1.25, camel rides $1.50.

Open: Summer, daily 9am–10pm; winter, 9am–6pm. **Bus:** 7.

Walking Tour
Downtown

One of downtown San Antonio's great gifts to visitors on foot is its wonderfully meandering early pathways—not laid out by drunken cattle drivers as has been wryly suggested, but formed by the course of the San Antonio River and the various settlements that grew up around it. Turn any corner in this area and you'll come across some fascinating testament to the city's historically rich past.

Note: Stops 1, 5, 6, 7, 9, 11, 13, and 14 are described earlier in this chapter; entrance hours and admission fees (if applicable) are listed there. See Chapter 4 for additional information on stop no. 2.

Start The Alamo.
Finish Market Square.
Time Approximately 1¹/₂ hours, not including stops at shops, eateries, or attractions.
Best Times Early morning during the week, when the streets and attractions are less crowded. If you're willing to tour the Alamo museums and shrine another time, consider starting out before they open (9am).
Worst Times Weekend afternoons, especially in summer, when the crowds and the heat render this long stroll rather uncomfortable (if you do get tired, you can always pick up a streetcar within a block or two of most parts of this route).

Built to be within easy reach of one another, San Antonio's earliest military, religious, and civil settlements are concentrated in the downtown area. The city spread out quite a bit in the next two-and-a-half centuries, but downtown still functions as the seat of the municipal-and-county government, as well as the hub of tourist activities.

Start your tour at Alamo Plaza (bounded by East Houston Street on the north); at the plaza's northeast corner you'll come to the entrance for:

1. **The Alamo,** originally established in 1718 as the Mission San Antonio de Valero; the first of the city's five missions, it was moved twice before settling into this site. The heavy limestone walls of the church and its adjacent compound were later discovered to make an excellent fortress; in 1836, the fighters for Texas's independence from Mexico took a heroic, if ultimately unsuccessful, stand against Mexican general Santa Anna here.

When you leave the walled complex, walk south along the plaza to reach:

2. **The Menger Hotel,** built by William Menger in 1859 on the site of his earlier brewery; legend has it that he wanted a place to lodge hard-drinking friends who used to spend the night sleeping on his long bar. Far more prestigious guests—presidents, Civil War generals, writers, stage actors, you name it—stayed here over the years; the hotel turns up in several short stories by frequent guest William Sidney Porter (O. Henry). The Menger has been much expanded since it first opened, but retains its gorgeous, three-tiered Victorian lobby.

On the Blum Street (south) side of the hotel, Alamo Plaza turns back into North Alamo Street. Take it south one block until you reach Commerce Street, where you'll see:

3. **Joske's** (now Dillard's), San Antonio's oldest department store. The more modest retail emporium opened by the Joske Brothers in 1889 was swallowed up in 1939 by the huge modernist building you see now, distinctive for its intricate Spanish Renaissance–style details; look for the miniaturized versions of Mission San José's sacristy window on the building's ground floor shadow boxes.

Walk a short way along the Commerce Street side of the building to come to:

4. **St. Joseph's Catholic Church,** built for San Antonio's German community in 1876. This Gothic Revival–style house of worship is as notable for the intransigence of its congregation as it is for its beautiful stained-glass windows. The worshipers' refusal to move from the site when Joske's department store was rising up all around it earned the church the affectionate moniker "St. Joske's."

Head back to Alamo Street and continue south two blocks past the San Antonio Convention Center to reach:

5. **La Villita,** once the site of a Coahuiltecan Indian village. It was settled over the centuries by Spanish, Germans, and, in the thirties and forties, a community of artists; a number of buildings here have been continuously occupied for more than 200 years. The "Little Village" on the river was restored by a joint effort of the city and the San Antonio Conservation Society in 1939 and now hosts a number of crafts shops and two upscale restaurants in addition to the historic General Cós House and the Arneson River Theatre.

Just south of La Villita you'll see HemisFair Way and the large iron gates of:

6. **HemisFair Plaza,** built for the 1968 exposition held to celebrate the 250th anniversary of San Antonio's founding. The expansive former fairgrounds are home to two museums and a number of historic houses, as well as to an observation tower—the tallest structure in the city and a great reference point if you get lost downtown. The plaza is too large to explore even superficially on this tour; come back another time.

Retrace your steps to Paseo de la Villita and walk one block west to Presa Street. Take it north for about half a block until you see the Presa Street Bridge and descend from it to:

7. **The River Walk.** You'll find yourself on a quiet section of the 2.8-mile paved walkway that lines the banks of the San Antonio River through a large part of downtown and the King William Historic District. The bustling café, restaurant, and hotel action is all just behind you, on the stretch of the river that winds north of La Villita.

Stroll down this tree-shaded thoroughfare until you reach the St. Mary's Street Bridge (you'll pass only one other bridge, the Navarro Street Bridge, along the way) and ascend here. Then walk north half a block until you come to Market Street. Take it west one long block, where you'll find:

8. **Main Plaza** (Plaza de Las Islas), the heart of the town established in 1731 by 15 Canary Island families sent by King Philip V of Spain to settle his remote New World outpost. Much of the history of San Antonio—and of Texas—unfolded on this modest square. A peace treaty with the Apaches was signed (and later broken) on the plaza in 1749; in 1835, freedom fighters battled Santa Anna's troops here before barricading themselves in the Alamo across the river. Much calmer these days, the plaza still sees some action as home to the

Walking Tour: Downtown San Antonio

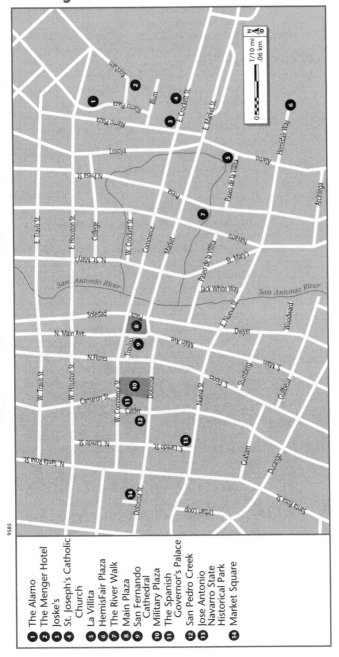

1. The Alamo
2. The Menger Hotel
3. Joske's
4. St. Joseph's Catholic Church
5. La Villita
6. HemisFair Plaza
7. The River Walk
8. Main Plaza
9. San Fernando Cathedral
10. Military Plaza
11. The Spanish Governor's Palace
12. San Pedro Creek
13. Jose Antonio Navarro State Historical Park
14. Market Square

Romanesque-style Béxar County Courthouse, built out of native Texas granite and sandstone in 1892.

Walk along the south side of Main Plaza to the corner of Main Avenue. Across the street and just to the north you'll see:

9. **San Fernando Cathedral,** the oldest parish church building in Texas and site of the earliest marked graves in San Antonio. Three walls of the original church started by the Canary Island settlers in 1738 can still be seen in the rear of the 1868 Gothic Revival cathedral. Among those buried within the sanctuary walls are Eugenio Navarro, brother of José Antonio Navarro (see below) and Don Manuel Muñoz, first governor of Texas when it was a province of a newly independent Mexico.

On the north side of the cathedral is Trevino Street; take it west to the next corner and cross the street to reach:

10. **Military Plaza** (Plaza de Armas), once the drill ground for the Presidio San Antonio de Béxar; the garrison, established in 1718 to protect the San Antonio de Valero mission, was moved to this nearby site four years later. Military Plaza was one of the liveliest spots in Texas for the 50 years after Texas won its independence. In the 1860s, it was the site of vigilante lynchings, and after the Civil War it hosted a bustling outdoor market; at night the townsfolk would come to its open-air booths to buy chili con carne from their favorite chili queen. The plaza remained completely open until 1889, when the ornate City Hall was built at its center.

The one-story white building you'll see directly across the street from the west side of the plaza is:

11. **The Spanish Governor's Palace,** former residence and headquarters of the captain of the Presidio de Béxar (but not of any Spanish governors); from here, the commander could watch his troops going through their drills across the street. The source of the house's misnomer is not entirely clear; as the home of the highest local authority and thus the nicest digs in the area, the "palace" probably hosted any important Spanish officials who came through town.

From the front of the Governor's Palace, walk south until you come to the crosswalk; just west across Dolorosa Street you'll see a drainage ditch, the sad remains of:

12. **San Pedro Creek.** The west bank of this body of water, once lovely and full flowing, was the original site of both the Mission San Antonio de Valero and the Presidio de Béxar. At the creek's former headwaters, approximately two miles north of here, San Pedro Park was established

in 1729 by a grant from the king of Spain; it's the second-oldest municipal park in the United States (the oldest is the Boston Common).

Continue west along Dolorosa Street to Laredo Street and take it south about three-quarters of a block until you come to:

13. José Antonio Navarro State Historical Park. Navarro's career as a statesman traces the history of Texas itself: He was born in Spanish territory, fought for Mexico's independence from Spain, then worked to achieve Texas's freedom from Mexico (he was one of only two native-born Texans to sign the 1836 Declaration of Independence). In 1845, he voted for Texas's annexation to the United States, and a year later became a senator in the new Texas State Legislature. Navarro died here in 1871 at the age of 76.

Trace your steps back to Laredo and Dolorosa, and go west on Dolorosa Street; when you reach Santa Rosa you'll be facing:

14. Market Square, home to the city's Market House at the turn of the century; when the low, arcaded structure was converted to El Mercado in 1973, it switched from selling household goods and personal items to crafts, clothing, and other more tourist-oriented Mexican wares. Directly behind and west of this lively square, the former Haymarket Plaza has become the Farmer's Market, and now sells souvenirs instead of produce.

Refueling Stops

Fortify yourself at the beginning of this walk with coffee and a pecan roll at the **Blum Street Bake Shop** (on the Dillard's side of the Menger Hotel); it opens at 7am. Then try to hold out until you get to Market Square, where you can take a load off your feet at **Mi Tierra** or **La Margarita**—or, if you still have the energy, graze your way through the Mexican goodies at the outdoor stalls.

3 Cool for Kids

Prime spots for kids are **Sea World** and **Fiesta Texas.** They'll also like the hands-on, interactive **Witte Museum** and the **miniature train ride** and **carousel** at Brackenridge Park. There's a children's area in the **zoo,** which vends food packets throughout so people of all ages can feed the animals. Youngsters will also get a kick out of petting the critters roaming around the **Quadrangle at Fort Sam Houston.** In addition to these sights, detailed in "The Top Attractions" and "More Attractions" sections, above, the following should also appeal to the sandbox set and up.

Alamo Imax Theater, 849 B. Crockett, in the Rivercenter Mall. ☎ **225-4629** (recording schedule information) or **225-5624.**

Having them view the "Alamo: Price of Freedom" on a six-story-high screen with a stereo sound system is a good way to get kids psyched for the historical battle site (which, though it's across the street, can't be reached without wending your way past lots and lots of Rivercenter shops). The theater also shows nature movies produced especially for the large screen, and, occasionally, commercial films such as *Jurassic Park*.

Admission: $6.25 adults, $3.95 children 3–11.

Open: Daily 10am–10pm. **Streetcar:** All four streetcar lines.

Pear Apple County Fair, 5820 NW Loop 410. ☎ **521-9500.**

Miniature golf, an indoor Ferris wheel, bumper cars, and go-carts are among the attractions at this completely kid-oriented amusement park. Some of these might even lure your children away from the fair's huge video arcade.

Admission: Free; prices on individual games and attractions vary.

Open: Memorial Day until start of school, daily 11am–11pm; rest of the year open Wed–Thurs 4–10pm, Fri 4–11pm, Sat 11am–11pm, Sun 11am–10pm; closed Mon–Tues. **Directions:** Exit Loop 410 on Bandera Road and drive south on access road.

Ripley's Believe It or Not & Plaza Theater of Wax, 301 Alamo Plaza. ☎ **224-9299.**

Adults may get the bigger charge out of the waxy silent-film stars and some of the oddities collected by the globe-trotting Mr. Ripley, but there's plenty for kids to enjoy at this twofer attraction. Although tame compared to Jason's *Halloween* adventures, the walk-through wax Theater of Horrors should elicit some pleasant shudders. At Believe It or Not, children will like learning about people around the world whose habits—such as sticking nails through their noses—are even weirder than their own.

Admission: Single attraction ticket $6.95 adults, $3.95 children 4–12. Both attractions ticket $9.95 adults, $6.95 children 4–12.

Open: Memorial Day to Labor Day, daily 9am–10pm; remainder of the year, Mon–Thurs 10am–7pm, Fri–Sun 9am–10pm (ticket office closes an hour before listed closing times). **Streetcar:** All four streetcar lines.

The San Antonio Children's Museum, 305 E. Houston St. ☎ **21-CHILD.**

Opening in summer 1995, San Antonio's new children's museum will feature interactive exhibits that focus on both the city's past and present. For example, kids will be able to grind corn in an old Spanish marketplace and then "shop" at a modern supermarket. At a sophisticated global village communication station, older children can teleconference and exchange E-mail with their counterparts in Mexico City's Papalote Museum.

Admission: $3.50 adults, $1.50 children.

Open: Tues–Sat 9am–6pm, Sun 1–6pm. **Streetcar:** All four streetcar lines. **Bus:** 7/40.

Splashtown, 3600 North Pan Am Expressway. ☎ **227-1100.**

Cool off at this 15-acre water recreation park, which includes the largest wave pool in Texas; hydro tubes nearly 300 feet long; more than a dozen water slides; and a two-story playhouse for the smaller children. A variety of concerts, contests, and special events are held here.

Admission: $13.95 adults, $10.95 children under four-feet tall, seniors over 65 and children under 2 free.

Open: Most weekends in May, daily late May to late Aug, weekends in early Sept (call ahead for exact schedule). Open 11am–6pm or 9pm, depending on the date. **Closed:** Mid-Sept to Apr. **Directions:** Get off I-35 at exit 160.

The Texas Adventure, 307 Alamo Plaza. ☎ **227-0388.**

San Antonio's latest foray into the high-tech history field, the world's first Encountarium F·X Theatre re-creates the battle at the Alamo with dazzling special effects, including life-size holographic images of the Alamo heroes and cannon fire roaring through a sophisticated stereo sound system. The theater's courtyard hosts live entertainment and historical displays.

Admission: $6.25 adults, $4.25 children ages 3–11.

Open: Winter, daily 9am–6pm; Summer, daily 9am–10pm. **Streetcar:** All four streetcar lines.

---

4   Special-Interest Tours

Ghost Tour

If you enjoy things that go bump in the night, the **Spirits of San Antonio Tour** (☎ **210/493-2454**) is right up your dark alley. Docia Williams, author of two historical guides to haunts around Texas, will take you to hotels, homes, and other spook-ridden spots in town. Your guide can't guarantee a ghost—apparently they're not big on command performances—but she will guarantee a good time. Tours (conducted at night, naturally) last around three hours and include dinner at a haunted restaurant. A minimum of six are required for each outing; if you can't get that number of specter lovers together, you might be able to squeeze in on another group's tour (they're especially popular around Halloween).

Prices: $32 per person (dinner included), less for larger groups.

Stadium/Arena Tour

Alamodome, 100 Montana St. ☎ **207-3652.**

You don't have to be a sports nut to want to see San Antonio's new state-of-the-art, $186-million athletic arena, even when there's no team playing here. It does help to be in good shape, however, because the 45-minute tour involves lots of walking and some stair climbing (consider that each of the two locker rooms alone measures nearly 5,000 square feet). The Alamodome has the world's largest retractable seating system, and its roof encompasses nine acres.

Tours: Tues–Sat 10am, 1pm, 3pm (disabled guests can call to arrange private tours by appointment).

Prices: $3 adults, $1.50 senior citizens and children 4–12, children under 4 free. Parking is free in the south (Durango Boulevard) lot on days that no events are scheduled.

The Mission Trail

If you want a personal tour guide to the San Antonio missions but don't like to crowd your car, consider picking up a copy of *On The Mission Trail*, an audio travel tape produced by **Miles To Go,** P.O. Box 43391, Austin, TX 78745 (☎ **512/441-7940**). Starting with the Alamo, the tape gives background information and interesting historical tidbits about the five missions along the trail. It's available for $9.95 at such downtown retail outlets as Booksmiths and La Tienda on Alamo Plaza; you can also order it directly from the company.

5 Organized Tours

Bus Tours

Gray Line, 217 Alamo Plaza. ☎ **210/226-1706** or toll free **800/472-9546.**

Gray Line serves up a large menu of guided bus tours, everything from the Mission Trail or Romantic San Antonio to forays south of the border or to the Hill Country. The company even offers some combination plates—morning tours from column A plus afternoon excursions from column B. Call for details.

Prices: Tours range from $18 adults and $9 children under 12 (three hours) to $38 adults, $19 children (full day). Unless tours include lunch, children under 5 ride free.

Tours: Earliest tours depart at 8am, latest return at 7pm; tours run daily except Thanksgiving Day, Christmas, New Year's Day.

Trolley Tours

Lone Star Trolley, 301 Alamo Plaza (Ripley's Believe It or Not & Plaza Theater of Wax). ☎ **224-9299.**

Lots of people confuse the red-and-green Lone Star Trolleys with the plain green (and unguided) city-run streetcars. Boarding these will cost you a bit more—but you'll also be learning a lot about what you're looking at. Hour-long tours touch on all the downtown highlights, taking you to the King William Historic District, Market Square, and more. Lone Star's are the only handicapped-accessible trolleys in town.

Prices: $6 adults, $4 children 4–12.

Tours: Daily 10am–6:15pm.

River Cruises

Paseo del Rio Boats, 430 E. Commerce St. ☎ **222-1701.**

Maybe you've sat in a River Walk café looking out at people riding back and forth in open, flat-bottom barges. Go ahead, give in, join 'em. An amusing, informative tour, lasting from 30 to 45 minutes, will take you 1¼ miles down the most built-up sections of the Paseo del Rio, pointing out interesting sights along the way. You'll learn a lot about the river—and find out what all those folks you watched were laughing about.

Prices: $3 adults, $1 children 48 inches and under.

Tours: Apr 1 to Oct 31, daily 9am–11:30pm (Sun–Thurs 10:30pm closing when school is in session); Nov 1 to March 31, daily 10am–8pm (weather permitting).

 # 6 Sports & Recreation

Spectator Sports

AUTO RACING   The best local drag-race action is at the **San Antonio Speedway** (four miles south of Loop 410 on Texas Hwy. 16 south), where an average of 3,500 fans turn up every Saturday from April through September to watch three NASCAR classes compete in eight-lap heat races and 40-lap feature races on a high-banked, half-mile paved oval. Gates open at 4pm and racing starts at 7pm.

Prices: $10 adults, $8 senior and military, $3 children 6–12.

BASEBALL   In the 1994 season (mid-April through the end of August), the minor league **San Antonio Missions** began batting at the new Municipal Stadium at 5757 Hwy 90 west. All home games start at 7:05pm except Sunday games, which start at 6:05pm. Double-headers also begin at 6:05pm. Tickets range from $4 for adult general admission to $7 for seats in the Executive Box. Call **675-7275** for schedules and tickets.

BASKETBALL   Spur madness hits San Antonio every year from mid-October through May, when the city's only major-league franchise, the **San Antonio Spurs,** shoot hoops at the huge new Alamodome (see "Stadium/Arena Tour," above). For most games, tickets are sold only for the dome's lower level, where prices range from $10 for seats behind the basket end zones to $45 for seats on the corners of the court. Nosebleed-level upper-tier seats, running from $5 to $8, open up for the most popular games. Tickets are available at the Spurs Ticket Office (south end of the Alamodome) or by phoning Rainbow Ticketmaster (☎ **224-9600**).

GOLF   The **Dominion Senior PGA Tournament** is held each May at the Dominion Country Club, 1 Dominion Dr. (☎ **698-1146**). The **Texas Open,** the oldest golf tournament on the winter tour, hosts the most famous professional players every fall at the Oak Hills Country Club, 5403 Fredericksburg Rd. (☎ **349-6354**).

HORSE RACING   Right now San Antonians' favorite place to play the ponies—quarter horse, thoroughbred, or Arabian—is **Bandera Downs,** about 30 minutes northwest of town on Hwy. 16 (☎ **210/796-7781** or toll free **800/572-2332**) in Hill Country; the track offers pari-mutuel betting on all its live events as well as on simulcast satellite races. By the time you read this, the brand-new $79-million **Retama Park** thoroughbred and quarter-horse track should be open in northeast San Antonio, near the intersection of I-35 and Loop 1604. Call **651-7000** for current information.

ICE HOCKEY   The first hockey team in city history, the Central Hockey League's **San Antonio Iguanas** dropped their first puck at the Freeman Coliseum (3201 E. Houston St.) in November 1994. CHL adult tickets cost $8, $10, or $12 (☎ **327-4449**).

RODEO   If you're in town in early February, don't miss the chance to see two weeks of Wild West events like calf roping, steer wrestling, and bull riding at the annual **San Antonio Stock Show and Rodeo.** (You'll also enjoy live country and western bands, and you're likely to find something to add to your luggage at an exposition hall packed with Texas handcrafts.) Tickets run $10 for bleacher rows, $15 for the balcony. Write San Antonio Livestock Exposition Inc. (P.O. Box 200230, San Antonio, TX 78220) for additional information in advance, or call **225-4237** or **225-5851** in San Antonio. **Smaller rodeos** are held throughout the year in nearby Bandera County, the self-proclaimed "Cowboy Capital of the World"; call the Bandera County Convention and Visitors Bureau (☎ **210/796-3045** or toll free **800/364-3833**) for details.

SOCCER   The **San Antonio Pumas,** members of the United States Interregional Soccer League, try to get their goals at the Blossom Athletic Center (Bitters Road and Jones-Maltsberger) from mid-April through the end of July. Adult tickets cost $7, and it's $4 for children 5 to 12. Call **223-KICK** or Ticketmaster (☎ **224-3000**) for tickets and schedules.

Recreation

Most San Antonians head to the hills—that is, nearby Hill Country—for outdoor recreation. Some suggestions of sports in or around town follow; see Chapter 17, "Easy Excursions from San Antonio & Austin," for more.

BICYCLING   There aren't many scenic cycling trails within San Antonio itself—locals tend to ride in Brackenridge Park; in McAllister Park on the city's north side, 13102 Jones-Maltsberger (☎ **210/821-3120**); and around the area near Sea World of Texas—but there are a number of appealing places to bike in the vicinity. Phone **San Antonio Wheelmen** (☎ **210/826-5015** [recorded ride information hot line] or **659-3806**) for details on organized rides in the area.

FISHING Closest to town for good angling are Braunig Lake, a 1,350-acre, city-owned reservoir, a few miles southeast of San Antonio off I-37, and Calaveras Lake, one of Texas's great bass lakes, a few miles southeast of San Antonio off U.S. 181 south and Loop 1604. A bit farther afield (astream?) but still easy to reach from San Antonio are Canyon Lake, about 20 miles north of New Braunfels, and Medina Lake, some 23 miles southeast of Bandera. Fishing licenses, sold at most sporting goods and tackle stores, county courthouses, and Parks & Wildlife Department offices, are required for all nonresidents; for current information call **512/389-4800** or toll free **800/792-1112** (in Texas only).

GOLF Visitors are welcome at San Antonio's eight municipal golf courses. One of the most notable is **Brackenridge,** 2315 Ave. B (☎ **226-5612**), the oldest public course in Texas, built in 1915. Oaks and pecans shade its fairways and greens fees are very reasonable. Another municipal course, the $4.3-million **Cedar Creek,** 8250 Vista Colina (☎ **695-5050**), in northwest San Antonio, offers three-tiered greens and scenic Hill Country views. Also open to the public and getting rave reviews is the high-end **Quarry,** 444 E. Basse Rd. (☎ **824-4500**), San Antonio's newest 18-hole golf course; as its name suggests, it's located on the site of a former quarry (about 10 minutes from downtown). Unaffiliated golfers can also tee-off at the 200-acre **Pecan Valley,** 4700 Pecan Valley Dr. (☎ **333-9018**), site of the 50th PGA Championship; it crosses the Salado Creek seven times and has an 800-year-old oak near its 13th hole.

HIKING Friedrich Wilderness Park, 21480 Milsa (☎ **698-1057**), operated by the city of San Antonio as a nature preserve, is crisscrossed by five miles of trails that attract bird-watchers as well as hikers. Enchanted Rock State Park near Fredericksburg is the most popular spot for trekking out of town.

HORSEBACK RIDING In town, **Brackenridge Stables,** 840 E. Mulberry Ave. (☎ **732-8881**), offers year-round rides through wooded trails in Brackenridge Park; rates are $20 per hour for riding on your own, $12.50 for a 20- to 30-minute guided trail ride, and $17.50 for a 45-minute ride. Hours change seasonally; call ahead to check the schedule. If you have the time, take an hour's drive out to Bandera County and saddle up in some of the prettiest country you could hope to find. Riders of all levels of experience are welcome at **Running-R Ranch,** Rte. 1, Bandera (☎ **210/796-3968**); **Lightning Ranch,** Rte. 1, Pipe Creek (☎ **210/535-4096**); and **Heartland Stables,** Medina (☎ **210/589-2587**).

PADDLEBOATS To paddle around the lake at Brackenridge Park ($8 an hour, $5 for a half hour), go to the boat rental office at 3910 St. Mary's St. (☎ **734-5401**), across the street from the main entrance to the San Antonio Zoo.

RIVER SPORTS Tubing, Rafting, Canoeing: The nearby Guadalupe and Comal Rivers are favorites for San Antonio river rats.

You can rent tubes and canoes at a number of places on Hwy. 46 just outside **Guadalupe River State Park,** 3350 Park Rd. 31 (☎ **210/438-2656**), 2,000 acres of cypress-lined river some 35 miles northwest of downtown. In the same area, at the **Bergheim Campground,** F.M. 3351 in Bergheim (☎ **210/336-2235**), you can get tubes for $6 per person (ask for one with a bottom for your cooler), rafts for $15 per person (children 12 and under half-price), and canoes for $25 per day. See also the New Braunfels section of Chapter 17 for equipment rental suggestions.

SWIMMING/WATER PARKS   Most hotels have swimming pools but if yours doesn't, call the Parks and Recreation Department (☎ **299-8480**) to find the nearest municipal one. Splashtown water recreation park is described in the "Cool for Kids" section, above. Many San Antonians head out to New Braunfels to get wet at the **Schlitterbahn,** 400 N. Liberty (☎ **210/625-2351**), the largest water park in Texas.

TENNIS   You can play at the lighted courts at the **Fairchild Tennis Center,** 1214 E. Crockett (☎ **226-6912**), and **McFarlin Tennis Center,** 1503 San Pedro Ave. (☎ **732-1223**), both municipal facilities, for $1.50 per hour per person, $2.50 after 5pm.

7

San Antonio Shopping

Sᴀɴ Aɴᴛoɴɪo oꜰꜰᴇʀs ᴛʜᴇ ʀᴇᴛᴀɪʟ-ʙoᴜɴᴅ ᴀ ɴɪᴄᴇ ʙᴀʟᴀɴᴄᴇ oꜰ ʟᴀʀɢᴇ ᴍᴀʟʟs and little enclaves of specialized shops. You'll find everything here from the utilitarian to the unusual: huge Sears and K-Mart department stores, along with a Saks Fifth Avenue fronted by a 40-foot pair of cowboy boots, a mall with a river running through it, and some of the best Mexican markets north of the border.

1 The Shopping Scene

Most out-of-town shoppers will find all they need downtown. In this area are concentrated the large **Rivercenter Mall**; the boutiques and crafts shops of **La Villita**; the colorful Mexican wares of **Market Square;** the **Southwest Craft Center**; and assorted retailers and galleries on and around Alamo Plaza.

San Antonians also tend to shop the **Loop 410 malls**, especially North Star and Central Park near the airport, and cruise the upscale **strip centers along Broadway** in Alamo Heights (the posh Collection and Lincoln Heights are particularly noteworthy). Weekends might see locals poking around a number of terrific **flea markets**. For serious bargains on brand labels, they head out to New Braunfels and San Marcos, home to three large **factory outlet malls** (see Chapter 17 for details).

Two off-the-beaten-path shopping areas are also worth mentioning. **Los Patios,** 2015 NE Loop 410 at the Starcrest exit (☎ 655-6171), features 10 upscale specialty shops—selling, among other things, imported clothing, crafts, jewelry, and antique furniture—in an 18-acre wooded setting. **Artisans Alley,** 555 Bitters Rd. (☎ 494-3226), packs a lot of charm under one large, wooden roof: folk art, ethnic clothing, pottery-and-sculpture studios, even a tearoom.

You can count on most shops around town being open from 9 or 10am until 5:30 or 6pm Monday through Saturday, with shorter hours on Sunday. In the downtown area, many shops don't close their doors until dark (or after) during the busy summer tourist season. Malls are generally open Monday through Saturday 10am to 9pm, Sunday from noon until 6pm.

2 Shopping A to Z

Antiques

In addition to the places that follow, a number of antiques shops line Hildebrand between Blanco and San Pedro; one fun store is the bluntly named **Dead People's Stuff,** 726 W. Hildebrand (☎ 735-2448).

The Original Antique Center, 5525 Blanco. ☎ 344-4131.

In this air-conditioned antiques mall, the focus is on expensive, hand-selected furniture, as well as on fine crystal, glass, and silverware. But you can find fun and funky items here, too: jukeboxes, Coke machines, old advertising signs, costume jewelry, and more.

Center for Antiques, 8505 Broadway. ☎ 804-6300.

About 25 different vendors ply their goods at this huge, open warehouse near the airport, making the Center for Antiques an eclectic and interesting place to shop. There are booths specializing in knick-knacks, others in old records, jewelry, or clothes, and still others in good-quality furniture for serious collectors. Some contemporary southwestern crafts are sold here, too.

Art Galleries

In the King William neighborhood, the **Blue Star Arts Complex,** 1400 S. Alamo (☎ 227-6960), a growing collection of contemporary galleries, is the up-and-coming place to buy art. Downtown is also beginning to hold its own in the art world, as more and more galleries enter the area.

DeganBela Galeria, 102 Concho (in Market Square). ☎ 225-0731.

If a big-name artist is represented or temporarily shown in town, it'll be at DeganBela, San Antonio's premier southwestern gallery. The work, much of it by Native American and New Mexican painters, is more Santa Fe than San Antonio—and so are the prices. Even if you can't afford to buy, stop in to check out the commercial art world's flavor of the month.

Keene Gallery, 242 Losoya St. ☎ 299-1999.

Just off Alamo Plaza, this gallery has three rooms full of work by contemporary local and regional artists: fine pottery, sculpture, paintings, jewelry, even furniture. Prices are relatively reasonable for art of this quality, especially for downtown where they're often jacked up for tourists; consider investing in some of the lesser-known artists who show here.

Books

Booksmiths of San Antonio, 209 Alamo Plaza. ☎ 271-9177.

You'll find a wide-ranging selection at this friendly downtown bookstore; it's particularly strong on Texas and regional volumes, carrying everything from southwestern cookbooks to San Antonio ghost guides. It also often hosts book signings by local authors. Kiddie lit is the focus of the adjoining **Red Balloon** (☎ 271-9461), owned by the same family. Both stores deliver free to any of the downtown hotels.

Cheever Books, 140 Carnahan. ☎ 824-2665.

Come to Cheever's, across the street from the Witte Museum, for good-quality used books; there are more than 30,000 of them in stock. You'll find lots of rare volumes, as well as many recent history and art books.

Crafts

See also Recuerdos de Mi Madre and Tienda Guadalupe in "Gifts/ Souvenirs," below.

Southwest Craft Center, 300 Augusta. ☎ **224-1848.**

The gift shop at the restored Ursuline Academy for girls (see the "More Attractions" section in Chapter 6 for details) sells handcrafted pottery, jewelry, clothing, and carryalls, most made by local artisans, and none of it run-of-the mill.

Tequila Tree, 202 Produce Row (in Market Square). ☎ **224-6202.**

I had a hard time deciding whether to put the Tequila Tree into the "gifts," "clothing," "jewelry," or "crafts" category: This lively three-level shop at El Mercado carries large quantities of all four. Thirty-eight countries, many in Africa and Asia, are represented by wall-hangings, rugs, religious figurines, and much more. Prices can run a bit high, but, if nothing else, come here to comparison shop; you may see some of the pottery and other crafts from Mexico sold for less elsewhere in the market.

DO-IT-YOURSELF

Garden Ridge Pottery, 17975 I-35 north. ☎ **599-7500.**

As its name suggests, this huge store once sold only unglazed outdoor pottery, from teacup-size to practically large enough to fill half a yard. Now San Antonio crafters of every kind drive out to Schertz (about half an hour north of downtown) every weekend to buy embroidery kits, appliqués, beads, candles, baskets, and dried flowers, along with paving stones and other garden decorations: If an indoor or outdoor artisan needs it, they've got it here.

Department Stores

Dillard's, 102 Alamo Plaza/Rivercenter Mall. ☎ **227-4343.**

You'll find links in this Arkansas-based chain in many Southwest cities and in a number of San Antonio malls; they all offer nice mid- to upper-range clothing and housewares, but the Dillard's in the Rivercenter Mall also has a section specializing in stylish western fashions. Enter or exit on Alamo Plaza so you can get a look at the historic building's ornate facade (see the "Joske's" entry in Chapter 6 for details).

Saks Fifth Avenue, North Star Mall. ☎ **341-4111.**

Forget low-key and unobtrusive; this is Texas. Sure this department store has the high-quality, upscale wares and attentive service one would expect from a Saks Fifth Avenue, but it also has something more: a 40-foot-high pair of cowboy boots in front. You can't miss this tony retail emporium from the highway.

Discount Shopping

Burlington Coat Factory, Crosslands Mall. ☎ **735-9595.**

As anyone who's ever shopped at—or listened to a TV ad for—one of these outlets knows, Burlington Coat Factory sells much more than just coats, and almost all at significant discounts. Like most bargain stores, this one is hit-and-miss; some days you'll find terrific styles in just your size, and other days it'll seem like there's nothing but schlock—usually in just your size, too.

Marshall's, 8505 Blanco. ☎ **340-9576.**

You can also catch Marshall's on a bad day (or two), but usually this is a good bet for fashionable, up-to-date clothing at cut-rate prices. Nice, inexpensive jewelry, especially silver, is also available here.

Fashions

The following stores offer clothing in a variety of styles; if you're keen on the cowpuncher look, see "Western Wear," below.

MEN'S FASHION

Satel's, 5100 Broadway. ☎ **822-3376.**

This family-run Alamo Heights store has been *the* place to shop for menswear in San Antonio for 44 years; classic, high-quality clothing and personal service make it a standout. There have been sightings here of the neighborhood's most famous resident, Tommy Lee Jones.

Todd's Inc., North Star Mall. ☎ **349-6464.**

Mexico's elite come to Todd's to buy their suits, casual wear, and accessories. Fine style doesn't come cheap, however; shop here only if you're prepared to part with some big bucks.

WOMEN'S FASHION

Adelante Boutique, 6414 N. Braunfels Ave. (in Sunset Ridge). ☎ **826-6770.**

Years back, this store was a hybrid: part women's clothing store, part Mexican restaurant. The Mexican restaurant—one of San Antonio's few health-oriented ones—moved down the block, giving Adelante more room for its stylish fashions, which focus on the ethnic and the handmade. The store also offers a nice selection of leather belts and whimsical jewelry and gifts.

Kathleen Sommers, 2417 N. Main. ☎ **732-8437.**

This small shop on the corner of Main and Woodlawn has been setting trends for San Antonio women for years. Kathleen Sommers, who works mainly in linen and other natural fabrics, designs all the clothes herself and they bear her label. The store also carries great jewelry, bath items, and a selection of unusual gifts.

CHILDREN'S FASHION

The Children's Crossing, 7979 Broadway (in the Collection). ☎ **828-1388.**

The well-dressed child—or the dresser thereof—will find out-of-the-ordinary items here for anything from slumber parties to special occasions. Smaller manufacturers from California are featured. As parents are all too aware, pint-sized clothing doesn't mean pint-sized prices; stores in the upscale Collection retail center tend toward the expensive, and this one is no exception.

Stein Mart, 999 E. Basse (in Lincoln Heights). ☎ **829-7198.**

Although the Lincoln Heights shopping center can go head-to-head with the Collection for pricey items, its kiddie clothing store offers bargains galore: Stein Mart carries high-quality goods at prices 25%

to 50% lower than those in the department stores. Infants as well as older children can be stylishly outfitted here for less. There's another Stein Mart in the Crossroads Mall (☎ 732-7012).

Food

Farm to Market, 1133 Austin Hwy. ☎ 822-4450.

Consider bringing back jars of salsa, *nopalitos* (tender marinated cactus strips), and other southwestern treats from this small Alamo Heights market, also a good place to shop for fruits and vegetables, pâtés, fresh pasta, homemade sausage, and other gourmet goodies. The ready-to-eat entrées are excellent, too. Saturday is samples day; keep coming back for tastes of the cilantro bread or other delicious baked goods and you might not have to buy lunch.

HEB Marketplace, 5601 Bandera Rd. at Loop 410. ☎ 647-2400.

The HEB grocery chain, headquartered in San Antonio, runs this huge marketplace; it's a bit out of the way (about 20 to 25 minutes from downtown), but an impressive array of edibles makes it worth the trip. Along with packaged grocery items—among them many Mexican, Asian, and Middle Eastern foods—are fresh goods from a bakery; deli; butcher shop (pick up your rattlesnake and buffalo steaks here); tortilla factory; and ice creamery. There's also a terrific flower section. Shipping is available.

Gifts/Souvenirs

Recuerdos de Mi Madre, 214 Losoya St. ☎ 227-9001.

Just up from the River Walk and near Alamo Square, this delightful gallery and gift shop emphasizes paintings and crafts from Mexico; the owners often go south of the border to buy directly from the artists. You'll find everything here from *cascarones*—confetti-filled eggs broken open during Fiesta—to colorful Mayan-design T-shirts and painted wooden animals from Oaxaca. Prices are very reasonable for work of this high quality.

Tienda Guadalupe Folk Art & Gifts, 1001 S. Alamo. ☎ 226-5873.

This incense-scented shop in the King William area, just across the street from Rosario's restaurant, also focuses on things Hispanic: artwork from Latin America, Day of the Dead T-shirts, woven belts and clothing, and many other interesting crafts.

Zazu, 7959 Broadway (in the Collection). ☎ 828-9838.

Come to this tony boutique for gifts you won't find anywhere else in San Antonio: one-of-a-kind coffee mugs, T-shirts, picture frames, jewelry, and things you'd never think of. The bath shop sells luscious shower gels, silky oils, and all-natural soap for dogs. Even if you can't afford to buy anything—keep in mind that the Alamo Heights crowd who shops here *will* shell out to buy Spot those organic suds—this is a fun place to browse.

Jewelry

For more casual jewelry, see also "Crafts" and "Gifts/Souvenirs."

Gurinsky's Fine Jewelry, North Star Mall, ☎ **524-9999;**
Central Park Mall, ☎ **349-2446;** 7900 I-35 north, ☎ **599-0116;**
6301 NW Loop 410, ☎ **647-0073.**

The Gurinsky family has decked San Antonio in diamonds for
years—also in pearls, gold, and other precious stones and metals. This
is a trusted name in high-quality jewelry.

The Reservation, North Star Mall. ☎ **341-7805.**

Gorgeous but pricey southwestern jewelry is this store's draw: silver
earrings, bracelets, rings, chokers, and watchbands intricately inlaid
with turquoise and other semiprecious stones. The store's name is
meant to allude to the Native American designs used, but it's also
what you're likely to have when you contemplate getting the bill for
anything you buy here.

Magic Potions

Papa Jim's Botanica, 5630 S. Flores. ☎ **922-6665.**

San Antonio is home to countless small *botanicas.* They specialize in
articles used in the practice of *curandera,* a Mexican version of
voodoo; Papa Jim's is the best known among them. Along with standard religious artifacts, you'll find magic floor washes; candles
designed to keep the law off your back; wolf skulls; amulets; herbal
remedies; and, of course, love potions. For a bit extra, Papa Jim will
bless almost any item you buy. Not to worry in case of an emergency
down the road—Papa Jim also runs a mail-order business.

Malls/Shopping Centers

Central Park Mall, Loop 410 and Blanco. ☎ **344-2236.**

Lots of shoppers start out by ogling the goods at North Star Mall
and then head next door to Central Park, where they can actually
afford to buy something. Anchored by Bealls, Dillard's, and Sears
department stores, this mall has lots of popular chains—the Gap,
Lane Bryant, the Foot Locker, Radio Shack, and B. Dalton—among
its 90 plus stores, and many reasonably priced places to eat in its food
court.

Crossroads Mall, 4522 Fredericksburg Rd. (off Loop 410 and I-10).
☎ **735-9137.**

Located near the South Texas Medical Center, this is San Antonio's
bargain mall, featuring Burlington Coat Factory, Montgomery Ward,
and Woolworth department stores along with smaller discount shops.

North Star Mall, Loop 410 at McCullough. ☎ **342-2325.**

Starring Saks Fifth Avenue and upscale boutiques like Adrienne
Vittadini, Gucci, Crabtree & Evelyn, Laura Ashley, and
Williams-Sonoma, this is the crème de la crème of the San Antonio
malls. But there are many sensible shops here, too, including a

Mervyn's department store. Food choices also climb up and down the class scale, ranging from a Godiva Chocolatier to a Luby's Cafeteria.

Rivercenter Mall, between Alamo Plaza, and Bowie, Crockett, and Commerce. ☎ **225-0000.**

There's a festive atmosphere at this bustling, light-filled mall, created, among other things, by its location on an extension of the San Antonio River: You can pick up a ferry from a downstairs dock or listen to bands play on a stage surrounded by water. The shops—more than 135 of them—run the price gamut, but tend toward the upscale, including the first Lord & Taylor in south Texas. If nothing catches your fancy at the regular mall restaurants or snack shops, you can also consider the eateries at the huge Rivercenter Marriott.

Markets

Market Square, between Dolorosa and Commerce Sts. ☎ **299-8600.**

Two large indoor markets, El Mercado and the Farmer's Market, occupy adjacent blocks on Market Square, sharing the space with other shops, restaurants, and food stalls; the whole complex is often just called the Mexican market. Come here for local Hispanic handcrafts and south-of-the-border imports, as well as for a good time; you'll often find yourself buying to the beat of a mariachi band.

FLEA MARKETS

Austin Highway Flea Market, 1428 Austin Hwy. ☎ **828-1488.**

This open-air flea market sells used and vintage clothing (the line between these categories drawn according to one's age), plants, toys, jewelry, coins, birds and small animals, among other things. You can find some real furniture bargains here.

Bussey's Flea Market, 18738 I-35 north. ☎ **651-6830.**

Unless you're heading to New Braunfels or Austin, Bussey's is a bit out of the way. But these 20 acres of indoor-and-outdoor vendors selling goods from as far afield as Asia and Africa are definitely worth the drive (about half hour north of downtown). Crafts, jewelry, antiques, incense, fruits and vegetables—it's hard to imagine what you *couldn't* find in this market. There's even a botanica (see "Magic Potions," above) here.

Eisenhower Flea Market, 3903 Eisenhower Rd. ☎ **653-7592.**

The all-indoors, all-air-conditioned Eisenhower, replete with snack bar and Old West–style saloon, is a good flea market to hit in the height of summer. You'll see lots of new stuff here—purses, jewelry, furniture, toys, shoes—and everything from houseplants to kinky leatherwear; you can even get a tattoo to go along with the latter.

Flea Mart, 12280 Hwy. 16 south (about one mile south of Loop 410). ☎ **624-2666.**

For a bit of Mexico that hasn't been gussied up for the tourists, this is the place to come. On weekends, Mexican-American families make a day of this huge market, bringing the entire family to exchange gossip, listen to live bands, and eat freshly made tamales and tacos. There are always fruits and vegetables, electronics, crafts, and new-and-used clothing—and you never know what else you might find.

Toys

The following stores carry unusual, but often pricey toys. If your child is especially hard on playthings or your cash supply is running low, consider buying used toys at **Kids Junction Resale Station,** 2267 NW Military Hwy. (☎ 340-5532), or **Too Good to Be Threw,** 7115 Blanco (☎ 340-2422).

Monarch Collectibles, 2012 NW Military Hwy. ☎ 341-3655.

Welcome to doll heaven. Many of the models that fill Monarch's four rooms—about 3,000 dolls in all—are collectible and made from delicate materials like porcelain and baked clay, but others are cute and cuddly; some come with real hair and eyelashes, and some, like a three-feet-high Lillie Langtry, are literally one of a kind. Doll furniture is also sold here, along with plates and a few stuffed animals.

Playworks, 7959 Broadway (in the Collection). ☎ 828-3400.

It's a toss-up who's going to spend more time oohing and aahing their way through this store, children or their parents. Along with the detailed Playmobil universe, imported from Germany, Playworks carries all kinds of life-science projects: ant farms, Grow-A-Frog, butterfly gardens . . . you'd be amazed at the creatures that are sent through the mail. Adults will have trouble keeping away from the nostalgia toys: pogo sticks, stilts, and puppet theaters. A second Playworks store is located at 1931 NW Military Hwy. (☎ 340-2328).

Western Wear

GENERAL
Kallison's Western Wear, 123 S. Flores. ☎ 222-1364.

When this place opened down the road from the county courthouse in 1899, the idea of anyone wearing blue jeans who wasn't prepared to handle a horse would have been peculiar, to say the least. Real ranch hands still shop at Kallison's, but these days so do urban cowboys and cowgirls. They get outfitted here from their Stetson hats right down to their Justin boots. There's a newer Kallison's across from Sears in Shopper City Mall, 616A SW Military Dr. (☎ 924-9441).

BOOTS
⭐ **Lucchese,** 4025 Broadway (in the Boardwalk). ☎ 828-9419.

If it once crawled, ran, hopped, or swam, Lucchese can probably put it on your feet: This store has got boots made of alligator, antelope, ostrich, shark, stingray, lizard, and snake. Come here for everything from executive to special-occasion boots—all handmade and expensive, all serious Texas status symbols. Lucchese also carries jackets, belts, and sterling silver belt buckles.

HATS

Paris Hatters, 119 Broadway. ☎ **223-3453.**

Anyone who was anyone sent to Paris for material to make fine hats in 1917, the year this store opened. The fabric may no longer come from France, but Paris Hatters still sells only high-quality headgear, whether Stetsons, coonskin caps, or fedoras. Hats are literally piled to the ceiling in the small downtown space.

Wines

Gabriel's, 837 Hildebrand. ☎ **735-8329.**

A large, warehouse-style store, Gabriel's combines a good selection with good prices. A recorded specials hot line (☎ **599-7700**) will clue you in to the bargains of the day for whatever spirits you're seeking. The Hildebrand store is slightly north of downtown; there's also another location near the airport, 7233 Blanco (☎ **349-7472**).

The Wine Shop, 4011 Broadway (in the Boardwalk). ☎ **822-6220.**

The Wine Shop covers the full price spectrum, but specializes in good, affordable bottles ($7 to $14). The store offers a nice array of Texas wines and has a staff qualified to give advice on those that might suit your particular taste in the grape.

8

San Antonio Nights

Sᴀɴ Aɴᴛᴏɴɪᴏ ʜᴀs ɪᴛs sʏᴍᴘʜᴏɴʏ ᴀɴᴅ ɪᴛs Bʀᴏᴀᴅᴡᴀʏ sʜᴏᴡs, ᴀɴᴅ ʏᴏᴜ ᴄᴀɴ see both at one of the most beautiful old movie palaces in the country. But much of what the city has to offer is less mainstream. A Latin flavor lends spice to some of the best local nightlife: San Antonio is America's capital for Tejano music, a unique blend of German polka and northern Mexico ranchero sounds, with a touch of pop for good measure. It's also a town where you can sit on one side of a river and watch colorful dance troupes like Ballet Folklórico perform on the other. Keep in mind, too, that the Fiesta City throws big public parties year-round; check the papers for ethnic events of all kinds.

For the most complete listings of what's on while you're visiting, pick up a free copy of the weekly alternative newspaper, the *Current,* or the Friday "Weekender" section of the *San Antonio-Express.* There is no central office in town for tickets, discounted or otherwise. You'll need to reserve seats directly through the theaters or clubs, or, in the case of large events, through Ticketmaster (☎ **224-9600**).

1 The Performing Arts

The San Antonio Symphony is the city's only resident performing arts company of national stature, but smaller, less professional groups keep the local arts scene lively, and cultural organizations draw world-renowned artists. The city provides them with some unique venues for their work—everything from standout historic stuctures like the Majestic, Arneson, and Sunken Garden theaters to the brand-new, high-tech Alamodome.

Major Performing Arts Companies

CLASSICAL MUSIC

San Antonio Symphony, 222 E. Houston St. ☎ **554-1010.**

Winner of the Creative Programming Award by the American Society of Composers, Authors, and Publishers (ASCAP) in 1994, San Antonio's symphony is one of the finest in the United States. Founded in 1939, the orchestra celebrated its 50th anniversary by

---

Major Concert & Performance Halls

Alamodome. ☎ **207-3663.**

Arneson River Theatre. ☎ **299-8610.**

Beethoven Hall. ☎ **222-1521.**

Carver Community Cultural Theater. ☎ **299-7211.**

Convention Center Arena. ☎ **299-8500.**

Guadalupe Cultural Arts Center. ☎ **271-3151.**

Laurie Auditorium. ☎ **736-8119.**

The Majestic Theatre. ☎ **226-3333.**

Sunken Garden Theater. ☎ **735-0663.**

being installed in the stunning Majestic Theatre, whose reopening was planned to coincide with the event. The symphony offers two annual series, a standard classical one and a pops. The former showcases the talents of music director Christopher Wilkens and resident conductor David Mairs; for the latter, the orchestra plays second fiddle to such artists as Bobby McFerrin, Emmylou Harris, and Tejano star Emilio Navaira.

THEATER

Actors Theater of San Antonio, 1608 N. Main. ☎ 227-2872.

Established in the early 1980s, the Actors Theater uses local talent for its productions, which tend to be in the off-Broadway tradition. Dramatic performances have included *Suddenly Last Summer, Bent,* and *Someone to Watch Over Me; The Fantasticks* and *Chicago* were among the musicals. The company divides its time between the small (80-seat) Main Avenue Studio and the upstairs stage of the Alamo Street Theater & Restaurant (see below).

Alamo City Theater (ACT) at the Josephine Street Theater, 339 W. Josephine St. ☎ 733-6363.

The community-based Alamo City Theater puts on an average of five productions a year at the art deco–style Josephine Street Theater, built in 1945. The award-winning group does mostly musicals—*Godspell, Evita,* and *How to Succeed in Business Without Really Trying* among them—but it also performs dramatic classics such as *Of Mice and Men* and *The Diary of Anne Frank.* The Josephine Street Theater is only five minutes from downtown and around the corner from several restaurants and nightclubs.

Jump-Start Performance Company, 108 Blue Star Arts Complex, 1400 S. Alamo. ☎ 227-JUMP.

Whether it's an original piece by a member of the company or a work by a guest artist, anything you see at Jump-Start is bound to be unconventional. This is the place to find the big-name performance artists like Karen Finley or Holly Hughes who tour San Antonio, and also to discover what's happening on the cutting edge in town. In addition to its theatrical events, Jump-Start hosts a dance series by the New Moves ensemble, and holds poetry readings on alternate Monday nights.

San Antonio Little Theatre (SALT), 800 W. Ashby (at San Pedro Ave.). ☎ 733-SALT.

This local troupe presents a wide range of plays in a neoclassical-style performance hall built in 1930. Currently being renovated, it was the first public theater to open in San Antonio. SALT's season might open with a blockbuster musical like *Guys and Dolls,* include a family show such as *Peter Pan* at Christmastime, and move on to something a bit more offbeat—say, *Sweeney Todd*—later in the year. Original work by San Antonio playrights sometimes shakes the audience at the smaller SALT Cellar Theatre downstairs. Naturally, the children's division of the group is called the Saltines.

Major Concert Halls & All-Purpose Auditoriums ──────

Alamodome, 100 Montana St. ☎ 207-3663.

In May 1993, Paul McCartney kicked off the Alamodome's first megaconcert. Since then, the Eagles, Pink Floyd, George Strait, Rod Stewart, Elton John, and Billy Joel have all played the state-of-the-art sports and music stadium. A giant retractable curtain can transform the 70,000-plus-capacity dome into a somewhat more intimate arena.

⭐ **Arneson River Theatre,** La Villita. ☎ 299-8610.

If you're visiting San Antonio in the summer, be sure to see something at the Arneson. Built by the Works Project Administration in 1939 as part of architect Robert Hugman's design for the River Walk, this unique theater stages shows on one side of the river while the audience watches from an amphitheater on the other. Most of the year performance schedules are erratic and include everything from opera to Tejano, but June through August run on a strict calendar: The Fiesta Flamenca on Sunday, Monday, and Tuesday; Fiesta Rio del Noche on Thursday, Friday, and Saturday; and the Fandango folkloric troupe every Wednesday. All offer lively music and dance with a south-of-the-border flair.

Beethoven Hall, 422 Pereida. ☎ 222-1521.

San Antonio's German heritage is celebrated at Beethoven Hall, a converted 1894 Victorian mansion in the King William area. The season starts in April with music-and-dance performances for the citywide Fiesta. After that, monthly concerts with a choir and brass band are held in a lovely pecan-shaded garden. The Beethoven folk dancers entertain here, too. Traditional German food, drink, and revelry make Oktoberfest an autumn high point. The hall closes down after November, when a Kristkindle Markt welcomes the holiday season with an old country–style arts-and-crafts fair.

Carver Community Cultural Center, 226 N. Hackberry.
☎ 225-6516.

Located near the Alamodome on the east edge of downtown, the Carver's Theater was built for the city's African American community in 1928 and continues to serve that group while providing a widely popular venue for an international array of performers. Roughly 20 seasonal events include drama, music, and dance. In 1993–1994 the theater hosted ensembles as diverse as Kodo, a Japanese Taiko drum troupe, and DanceBrazil. Each year, the Carver Jazz Festival draws top-notch artists from all over.

⭐ **Guadalupe Cultural Arts Center,** 1300 Guadalupe.
☎ 271-3151.

There's always something happening at the Guadalupe Center, the main locus for Latino cultural activity in San Antonio. Visiting or local directors put on six or seven plays a year; the resident Guadalupe Dance Company might collaborate with the city's symphony or invite modern masters up from Mexico City; the Xicano Music Program celebrates such popular local forms as conjunto and Tejano; an annual book fair brings in Spanish-language literature from around the world; and the CineFestival, now in its 16th year, is one of the town's major film events. And then there are always the parties thrown to celebrate new installations at the theater's art gallery and its annex.

Laurie Auditorium, Trinity University, 715 Stadium Dr.
☎ **736-8119.**

Some pretty high-powered people turn up at the Laurie Auditorium, on the Trinity University campus in the north-central part of town. Everyone from Margaret Thatcher to Colin Powell has taken part in the university's Distinguished Lecture Series, subsidized by grants and open to the public for free. The recently refurbished 2,700-seat hall also hosts major players in the performing arts: Classical pianist Victor Borge has tickled the ivories here and Hal Holbrook donned his Mark Twain mask. Dance recitals, jazz concerts, and plays, many including internationally renowned artists, are held here, too.

★ **Majestic Theatre,** 230 E. Houston. ☎ **226-3333.**

The Majestic hosts much of the best entertainment in town—the symphony, major Broadway productions, big-name solo performers—but it's also a show unto itself. John Eberson, the prolific architect who built it, introduced the concept of the "atmospheric" theater to the United States. While you wait for the feature to begin, a three-dimensional Moorish-Italian village, replete with cypresses, palm trees, trailing vines, peacocks, and fountains, slowly darkens as stars begin to twinkle and clouds drift in shifting patterns overhead. Because the Majestic brought air-conditioning to San Antonio for the first time—the hall was billed beforehand as "an acre of cool, comfortable seats"—society women wore fur coats to its opening, held on a warm June night in 1929. Thanks to a wonderful restoration of this fabulous showplace, coming here is still a major event.

Sunken Garden Theater, Brackenridge Park, North St. Mary's St./Mulberry Ave. entrance. ☎ **735-0663.**

Built by the WPA in 1936 in a natural acoustic bowl in Brackenridge Park, the Sunken Garden Theater boasts an open-air stage set against a wooded hillside; cut-limestone buildings in Greek Revival style hold the wings and the dressing rooms. Known mostly as a venue for big names in rock like Bob Dylan, Crosby, Stills, & Nash, Santana, Megadeth, and Mötley Crüe, this appealing outdoor arena offers a little bit of everything—country, hip-hop, rap, jazz, Tejano, Cajun, sometimes even the San Antonio Symphony. The bard has been coming around every summer since 1990 for a week and a half of Shakespeare in the Park.

Dinner Theater

Alamo Street Theatre & Restaurant, 1150 S. Alamo.
☎ **271-7791.**

You're bound to have a good time at the King William district's Alamo Street Theatre, no matter which of its two shows you decide to attend. Interactive murder mysteries take place in the dining room, where meals are buffet style; entrées change depending on the accompanying comedy-thriller, but there are always soups, salads, veggies, and desserts to die for (as it were). Upstairs it's straight comedy—everything from local plays like *Ladies at the Alamo* to Neil Simon's *Biloxi Blues*. The church now occupied by the Alamo Street Theater was built in 1912 and is on the National Register of Historic Places; the mysteries play in what were once choir rooms, the comedies in the old sanctuary.

2 The Club & Music Scene

The closest San Antonio comes to having a club district is the stretch of North St. Mary's between Josephine and Magnolia—just north of downtown and south of Brackenridge Park—known as the Strip. This area was hotter—or is that cooler?—four or five years ago, but it still draws locals to its restaurants and lounges on the weekend.

Comedy Club

Rivercenter Comedy Club, 849 E. Commerce St./Rivercenter Mall, third level. ☎ 229-1420.

This club books the big names in stand-up like Dennis Miller and Garry Shandling, but it also takes advantage of local talent. On Mondays, two ComedySportz teams improvise on athletic themes suggested by the audience; every third Thursday, Latino comics provide the yuks for Ha!Lapeno Comedy night.

Country & Western

Leon Springs Dancehall, 24135 I.H. 10 (Boerne Stage Road exit). ☎ 698-7072.

This lively 1880s-style dance hall can pack about 1,200 people into its 7,000 square feet—and often does. Don't fret if you can't two-step: There are free dance lessons Wednesday, Thursday, and Saturday nights. Lots of people come with their kids when the place opens at 6pm, though the crowd turns older (but not that much) after the lessons start. Some of the best local country and western talent is showcased here.

Cibolo Creek Country Club, 8640 Evans Rd. (one mile north of 1604). ☎ 651-6652.

For a taste of down-home Texas, come to this friendly honky-tonk in the northeast part of town. There's always a couple of dogs running around the large outdoor patio and a couple of people hanging out on the porch swing. Inside, you can flop down on one of the old couches next to the bar, sit at a table that has legs wearing blue jeans and boots, or stand around and shoot pool. Live bands play alternative Texas music, from rockabilly and updated country and western to rock, zydeco, and blues.

★ **Floore Country Store,** 14664 Bandera Rd./Hwy. 16, Helote (two miles north of Loop 1604). ☎ 695-8827.

The first manager of the Majestic Theatre and an unsuccessful candidate for mayor of San Antonio, John P. Floore opened up his country store in 1942. A couple of years later, he added a café and a dance floor—at half an acre, the largest in south Texas. The café is closed now, but otherwise nothing much else has changed. Boots, hats, and antique farm equipment hang from the ceiling of this typical Texas roadhouse; pictures of Willie Nelson, Hank Williams, Sr., Conway Twitty, Ernest Tubb, and other country greats who have played here line the walls. There's always live music on weekends—Willie still performs now and then, as does his friend Jerry Jeff Walker. The café still serves homemade bread, homemade tamales, and old-fashioned sausage.

Jazz & Blues

In addition to the clubs listed below, you might also try Camille's and the Courtyard at La Louisiane, both reviewed in "San Antonio Dining," Chapter 5, and both offering cool outdoor jazz on hot nights.

★ **The Landing,** Hyatt Regency hotel, River Walk. ☎ **223-7266.**

You might have heard cornetist Jim Cullum on the airwaves: His American Public Radio program, "Riverwalk, Live from the Landing," is broadcast on more than 150 stations nationwide. The Landing is one of the best traditional jazz clubs in the country; if you like big bands and Dixieland, there's no better place to listen to music downtown. Jim Cullum and his band have backed some of the finest jazz artists of our time.

Billy Blues, 330 E. Grayson St. ☎ **225-7409.**

Sit out back under the Billy Dome, a temperature-controlled covered patio, and enjoy some barbecue, beer, and blues. This laid-back venue gets good local bands and sometimes books nationally known acts, too. The dance floor is small, but the stage is larger than most in San Antonio.

Tycoon Flats, 2926 N. St. Mary's St. ☎ **737-1929.**

Another friendly music garden, Tycoon Flats is a fun place to kick back and listen to some blues, rock, acoustic, or jazz; the burgers are good, too. Bring the kids; an outdoor sandbox is larger than the dance floor. There's no cover for the almost-nightly live music except on some Thursdays, when bigger name bands are co-sponsored by local radio stations.

Nona's, 2809 N. St. Mary's St. ☎ **732-6662.**

What with the brightly painted cherubs peeking out from behind the stage; the Italian menu; live music ranging from rock and jazz to marimba; and the owner's belly dancing on the weekends, Nona's is a real trip. It's worth dropping by to check out the action; if it doesn't appeal, Tycoon Flats, Salute, and Camille are right nearby.

Salute, 2801 N. St. Mary's St. ☎ **732-5307.**

The live jazz at Salute's tends to have a Latin base, but you never know what you're going to find here. I came one time to hear a conjunto band and ended up (briefly) listening to synthesized 1970s sounds. This tiny place has a reputation for drawing the best local talent; it was probably just an off night.

Rock

Beauregard, 320 Beauregard. ☎ 227-2328.

Recently redone in drop-dead black-and-white, this King William area club serves up live rock from mainstream to alternative, along with some reggae, jazz, and rhythm and blues. The indoor room where the bands play is pretty small, but there's a large outdoor patio with picnic tables. If you're hungry, go for the quesadillas.

Doza's Ice House, 3306 N. St. Mary's St. ☎ 733-6027.

Derived from the days when live bands played outside neighborhood stores selling fresh tacos, beer, and ice, the term "icehouse" is generic in San Antonio for an informal club. One of the few college bars in town that focuses on alternative rock, Doza's mainly attracts a crowd from nearby Trinity, but older folks (maybe 30?) also come to hear bands that are more than a few steps up from garage grunge.

Sneakers, 11431 Perrin Beitel. ☎ 653-9176.

Fans of Fog Hat and Blue Oyster Cult turn out for these bands in droves when they play Sneakers, in the far northeast part of town. Heavy rock and metal dominate at this huge club, but you can also find some blues and alternative rock here.

Taco Land, 103 W. Grayson St. ☎ 223-8406.

Loud and not much to look at—low ceilings, red vinyl booths, garage pin-up calendars stapled to the ceiling—tiny Taco Land is the hottest alternative music club in San Antonio, showcasing everything from mainstream rock to surf punk. Some of the bands that turn up may seem less than impressive, but, hey, you never know; Nirvana played here before they hit the big time. College kids mingle at this club with the crew from the nearby Pearl Brewery. Name notwithstanding, Taco Land only recently began selling tacos.

Specialty Clubs

GAY

The Bonham Exchange, 411 Bonham. ☎ 271-3811.

Tina Turner, Deborah Harry, and Latoya Jackson have all played this high-tech dance club near the Alamo—the real stars, not drag impersonators. While you may find an occasional cross-dressing show here, the mixed crowd of gays and straights, young and old, come mainly to move to the beat under wildly flashing lights. All the action takes place in a restored German-style building dating back to the 1880s. Roll over, Beethoven.

Industria, 450 Soledad. ☎ 227-0484.

A view of the river from the windows of this old printing building, about eight blocks south of the Alamo, is one of the attractions of this popular gay bar; an upbeat, cheerful atmosphere is another. A fairly young and preppie crowd dances to high-energy popular music upstairs or stands and chats around the ground floor video bar. Both levels are decorated in light colors with a postmodern industrial flair.

Nexus, 8021 Pine Brook Dr. (near I-10 and Callahan). ☎ **341-2818.**

If you don't find your friend out on the floor dancing to a country and western or Top 40 beat, she might be out back playing volleyball or, on Thursday night, enjoying a barbecue; bring your own meat, and the owner will cook it for you and supply the trimmings. This clean, friendly club in the northwest attracts mostly professional women, who tend to get dressed up on Friday and Saturday nights.

Tejano/Conjunto

Tejano (Spanish for Texas) is the 20th-century offspring of conjunto music, the late 19th-century marriage of the polka-based sounds of Texas's German settlers and the Latin rhythms of northern Mexico. The two most prominent instruments in Tejano remain the accordian and the 12-string guitar, but the music incorporates more modern forms, including pop, jazz, and country and western, into the traditional conjunto repertoire. At clubs not exclusively devoted to Latino sounds, what you're likely to hear is Tejano.

T-Town, 7011 San Pedro Ave. ☎ **340-8026.**

Of the many nightspots that focus on conjunto and Tejano music in San Antonio, T-Town is probably the most visitor friendly. It's the place to hear the top Tejano acts, including Mazz, Ram Herrera, and David Lee Garza. You'll see a big sign for the club as you drive up San Pedro Avenue; it's on top of a hill, behind a shopping center.

3 The Bar Scene

Brew Pubs

Because of a law on the Texas books that required separate manufacturers, wholesalers, and retailers to be involved in any sale of alcoholic beverages, brew pubs, which combine these functions, had long been barred from operating in the state. Largely because Anheuser-Busch lobbied hard for the right to sell its beer at San Antonio's Sea World of Texas—which the company also owns—this law was repealed in late 1993, and brew pubs are now beginning to crop up all over the state. Most of those in San Antonio were too new to review for this edition.

Boardwalk Bistro and Brewery, 4011 Broadway. ☎ **824-0100.**

Opened in April 1994, San Antonio's first brew pub is the newest addition to Boardwalk Bistro, a restaurant with an eclectic menu (see Chapter 5, "San Antonio Dining") and live music ranging from Celtic to jazz. There are three constants among a shifting variety of home brews: the slightly smoky Bistro Bock; light and flavorful Barb Lager; and Smithson Stout, a meal unto itself.

Specialty Bars

Cadillac Bar & Restaurant, 212 S. Flores. ☎ **223-5533.**

During the week, lawyers and judges come to unwind at the Cadillac Bar, set in a historic stucco building near the Béxar County

Courthouse and City Hall; on the weekends, singles take the stand. Live bands, mostly Tejano, entertain on Wednesdays and Thursdays; Friday nights, a DJ is on music duty. Full dinners are served in a patio out back.

Dick's Last Resort, 406 Navarro St., River Walk. ☎ **224-0026.**

The self-proclaimed "shame of the river," Dick's Last Resort is the place to come if you're feeling especially obnoxious or are in the mood to embarrass someone. Food is served in buckets by a waitstaff who get paid to do what most only fantasize about—insult the clientele. As you might have guessed, Dick's attracts a raucous college crowd.

Durty Nellie's Irish Pub, 715 River Walk (Hilton Palacio del Rio Hotel). ☎ **222-1400.**

Chug a lager & lime, toss your peanut shells on the floor, and sing along with the piano player at this wonderfully corny version of an Irish pub. You've forgotten the words to "Danny Boy"? Not to worry—18 old-time favorite songs are printed on the back of the menu. After a couple of Guinnesses, you'll be bellowing "H-A-, double R-I, G-A-N spells Harrigan," loud as the rest of 'em.

La Tuna, 100 Probant. ☎ **224-8862.**

Gallery groupies tend to gather at this bar in the King William area's Blue Star Arts district—look for the brightly colored sign on a tiny concrete-and-corrugated aluminum building—but lots of nonartsy types drop by for a beer, too. You can sit out on the patio and watch the trains roll slowly by a block away; after downtown parades, the floats cruise past on their way back to the warehouses. There's music on Saturday nights, weather permitting, year-round; in winter, a bonfire blazes from a pit built into the patio.

The Menger Bar, Menger Hotel, 204 Alamo Plaza. ☎ **223-4361.**

More than 100 years ago, Teddy Roosevelt recruited men for his Rough Riders unit at this dark, wooded bar; they were outfitted for the Spanish-American War at nearby Fort Sam Houston. William Menger built his landmark hotel in 1859 on the site of his earlier, successful brewery and saloon, and it's still a good spot to toss back a few.

Polo's, Fairmount Hotel, 40 S. Alamo St. ☎ **224-8800.**

For piano music in a high-tone atmosphere, come to Polo's Thursday through Saturday night; you can sink down into a plush green leather couch or perch on a stool at the marble bar and enjoy some jazz or Broadway sounds. This romantic spot tends to draw an older crowd, who can afford the price of the drinks.

Tex's, San Antonio Airport Hilton and Conference Center, 611 NW Loop 410. ☎ **340-6060.**

If you want to hang with the Spurs, come to Tex's, voted San Antonio's best sports bar in a 1994 *Current* reader's poll. Three satellite dishes, two large-screen TVs and 17 smaller sets, along with killer margaritas and giant burgers, keep the bleachers happy. Among Tex's major array of exclusively Texas sports memorabilia are a signed

Nolan Ryan jersey; a football used by the champion Dallas Cowboys in the 1977 Super Bowl; and a pair of George Gervin's basketball shoes.

Tower of the Americas, 600 HemisFair Park. ☎ **223-3101.**

No matter what, or how much, you have to drink, you'll get higher here than anywhere else in San Antonio—more than 700 feet high, in fact. Just below the observation-deck level, the bar at the Tower of the Americas Restaurant affords dazzling views of the city at night.

4 More Entertainment

Movies

There's not much of a cinema scene in San Antonio—art-and-foreign movies turn up primarily at the **Crossroads Theater,** Crossroads Mall, No. 14 Loop 410 at Frederickburg Rd. (☎ 524-4600)—but the **Guadalupe Cultural Arts Center** and the **McNay** and **Witte museums** often have interesting film series. In addition to "Alamo, the Price of Freedom," **IMAX,** Rivercenter Mall, 849 E. Crockett (☎ 225-4629), shows nature films designed for the theater's huge screen.

Poetry

Shades of Jack Kerouac: In recent years, coffeehouse poetry readings have been cropping up all over San Antonio. **Zoey's,** 3610 Ave. B, just off Broadway (☎ 805-0901), **Espuma,** 928 South Alamo (☎ 226-1912), and **Coffee Book,** 1615 McCullough (☎ 224-BOOK), are among the most popular of the eight or so java huts hosting blossoming bards. The **Jump-Start Performance Company** also runs a poetry series; see the "Theater" section, above.

9

Introducing Austin

Aaah, Austin, that laid-back city in the lake-laced hills, home to cyberpunks and environmentalists, high culture and haute cuisine. A leafy intellectual enclave lying well outside the realm of Lone Star stereotypes, Austin has been compared to Berkeley and Seattle, but it is at once its own place and entirely of Texas.

Born on the frontier out of the grandiose dreams of a man whose middle name was Buonaparte, the town spent its formative years fighting to maintain its status as capital. Texan hubris and feistiness remain key to Austin's character today—from state legislators who descend, squabbling, on the town every other year, to the locals fighting to save the golden-cheeked warbler from the developer's bulldozer.

The resident symphony is well attended, but the town's very borders are synonymous with country-and-western music: Who hasn't heard of *Austin City Limits,* PBS's longest-running show? Local theaters may screen the most foreign films in the state, but the first TV program to air in Austin, on Thanksgiving Day 1952, was the University of Texas–Texas A&M football game. And the source of much of the city's culture is literally crude: When an oil well on land belonging to the University of Texas system blew in a gusher in 1923, money for the arts was assured.

Many Texans who live in faster-paced places like Dallas or Houston dream of someday escaping to Austin, which, though pushing the half-million population mark, still has a leisurely, small-town feel. Meanwhile, they smile upon the city as they would on a beloved but eccentric younger sister; whenever an especially contrary story about her is told, they shrug and shake their heads and fondly say, "Well, that's Austin."

1   Geography & History

Geography

If you look up as you pass along Austin's Balcones Drive, you can glimpse a portion of the Balcones Escarpment, a fault zone that marks the boundary between the rich Blacklands Prairie to the east and the hilly Edwards Plateau to the west. The limestone comprising the plateau, uplifted millions of years ago from the bottom of the shallow sea that covered most of Texas, renders the underground water that rises at such pools as Austin's Barton Springs remarkably clear. It also acts as a filter for the waters of the Highland Lakes, a sparkling, 150-mile-long chain, created by a series of dams, which spreads northwest from the city in an ever-widening pattern.

History

A VAST TERRITORY THAT THREW off foreign rule to become an independent nation—remember the Alamo?—Texas has always played a starring role in the romance of the American West. So it is only fitting

Dateline

- **1730** Franciscans build a mission at Barton Springs, but abandon it within a year.

➤

What's Special About Austin

Natural Spectacles
- The Highland Lakes, a sparkling recreational mecca, stretch 150 miles northwest from Austin.
- Hill Country, one of Texas's loveliest regions, begins in Austin's backyard.

Swimming Hole
- Barton Springs Pool, at a constant 68 degrees, draws Austin's bathers year-round.

Buildings
- The State Capitol of Texas (1888) is second only in size to that of the United States.
- The Governor's Mansion (1856) hosts the chief executive in gracious old-world style.

University
- The University of Texas, home to the LBJ Library and other excellent museums, is also the city's sports and performing arts center.

Panorama
- Mt. Bonnell, the highest overlook of the city, is shrouded with romantic legends.

Gardens
- Zilker Botanical Gardens boast a beautiful range of blossoms, from cactus flowers to water lilies.

Natural Phenomenon
- Bats—more than hang out in Carlsbad Caverns—roost under the Congress Avenue Bridge; their nightly flight is an amazing sight.

Festival
- The music industry meets at the huge SXSW conference, which fans out into hundreds of concerts around town.

Activities
- Austin's lakes inspire water sports galore—jetskiing, canoeing, and fishing, among others.
- Hikers and bikers enjoy thousands of acres of green space that the city has set aside for them.

Entertainment
- The self-styled Live Music Capital of the World keeps the beat going at more than 100 local venues.

Regional Food & Drink
- Tex-Mex and barbecue are enjoyed in some of Austin's most funky, laid-back restaurants.

Dateline

- **1836** Texas wins independence from Mexico; Republic of Texas established.
- **1838** Jacob Harrell sets up camp on the Colorado River, calls the settlement Waterloo; Mirabeau B. Lamar succeeds Sam Houston as president of Texas.
- **1839** Congressional commission recommends Waterloo as site for new capital of the republic.
- **1842** Sam Houston succeeds Lamar as president, reestablishes Houston as Texas's capital, and orders nation's archives moved there. Austinites resist.
- **1844** Anson Jones succeeds Houston as president, returns capital to Austin.
- **1845** Constitutional convention in Austin approves annexation of Texas by the United States.
- **1850s** Austin undergoes a building boom; construction includes limestone capitol (1853), Governor's Mansion (1856), and General Land Office (1857).
- **1861** At Austin convention, Texas votes to secede from the Union (Travis County, which includes Austin, votes against secession). ➤

that Texas's capital should spring, full-blown, from the imagination of a man on a buffalo hunt.

A CAPITAL DILEMMA

The man was Mirabeau Buonaparte Lamar, who had earned a reputation for bravery in Texas's struggle for independence from Mexico. In 1838, when our story begins, Lamar was vice president of the two-year-old Republic of Texas; Sam Houston, the even more renowned hero of the Battle of San Jacinto, was president. Though they had a strong will in common, the two men had very different ideas about the future of the nation whose reins they held: Houston tended to look eastward, toward union with the United States, while Lamar saw independence as the first step to establishing an empire that would stretch to the Pacific.

That year, an adventurer named Jacob Harrell set up a camp called Waterloo at the western edge of the frontier; lying on the northern banks of Texas's Colorado River (not to be confused with the larger waterway up north), it was nestled against a series of gentle hills. Some 100 years earlier, the Franciscans had established a temporary mission here; in the 1820s, Stephen F. Austin, Texas's earliest and greatest land developer, had the area surveyed for the smaller of the two colonies he was to establish on Mexican territory.

But the place had otherwise seen few Anglos before Harrell arrived; for thousands of years it had been visited mainly by nomadic Indian tribes, including the Comanches, Lipan Apaches, and Tonkawas. Thus it was to a rather pristine spot that, in the autumn of 1838, Harrell invited his friend Mirabeau Lamar to take part in a shooting expedition. The buffalo hunt proved extremely successful, and when Lamar gazed at the rolling, wooded land surrounding Waterloo, he saw that it was good.

In December of the same year, Lamar became president. He ordered the congressional commission that had been charged with the task of selecting a site for a permanent capital, to be named after Stephen F.

Austin, to check out Waterloo. Much to the horror of those who lived in Houston, home to the temporary capital, and in east Texas, which considered Waterloo a dangerous wilderness outpost, the commission recommended Lamar's pet site.

In early 1839, Lamar's friend Edwin Waller was dispatched to plan a city—the only one in the United States besides Washington, D.C., designed to be an independent nation's capital. The first public lots went on sale on August 1, 1839; by November of that year, Austin was ready to host its first session of Congress.

Austin's position as capital was far from entrenched, however. Attacks on the republic by Mexico in 1842 gave Sam Houston, now president again, sufficient excuse to order the national archives relocated from remote Austin for security reasons. Resistant Austinites greeted with a cannon the 26 armed men who came to repossess the historic papers. After a struggle, the men returned empty-handed and Houston abandoned his plan, thus ceding Austin the victory in what came to be called the Archive War.

Although Austin won this skirmish, it was losing a larger battle for existence. Houston refused to convene Congress in town; by 1843, Austin's population had dropped down to 200 and its buildings lay in disrepair. Help came in the person of Anson Jones, who succeeded to the presidency in 1844. The constitutional convention that he called in 1845 not only approved Texas's annexation to the United States, but also named Austin capital until 1850, when voters of what was now the state of Texas would choose their governmental seat for the next 20 years. In 1850, Austin campaigned hard for the position, and won by a landslide.

A CAPITAL SOLUTION

Under the protection of the U.S. Army, Austin thrived. The first permanent buildings to go up during the 1850s construction boom following statehood included an impressive limestone capitol; two of the

Dateline

- **1865** General Custer is among those who come to restore order in Austin during Reconstruction.
- **1871** First rail line to Austin completed.
- **1883** University of Texas opens.
- **1923** Santa Rita No. 1, an oil well on University of Texas land, strikes a gusher.
- **1937** Lyndon Johnson elected U.S. representative from Tenth Congressional District, which includes Austin.
- **Late 1930s to early 1950s** Six dams built on the Colorado River by the Lower Colorado River Authority, resulting in formation of Highland Lakes chain.
- **1960s** High-tech firms, including IBM, move to Austin.
- **1972** Willie Nelson moves to Austin from Nashville, helps spur live-music scene on Sixth Street.
- **1980s** Booming real-estate market goes bust.
- **1995** Capitol, including new annex, reopens after massive refurbishing.

buildings in its complex, the General Land Office and the Governor's Mansion, are still in use today.

The boom was short-lived, however: Although Austin's Travis County voted against secession, Texas decided to put in its lot with the Confederacy in 1861. By 1865, Union army units—including one led by General George Armstrong Custer—were sent to restore order to a defeated and looted Austin after the Civil War.

But Austin once again rebounded: With the arrival of the railroad in 1871, the city's recovery was sealed. By the following year, when Austin won the final general election to choose the state's capital, it was delivered.

Still, there were more battles for status to be fought. Back in 1839, the Republic of Texas had declared that a "university of the first class" was to be built; in 1876, a new state constitution mandated its establishment. Through yet another bout of heavy electioneering, Austin won the right to have the flagship of Texas's higher educational system on its soil. In 1883, their classrooms not yet completed, the first 221 members of what is now a student body of 50,000 met the eight instructors of the University of Texas for the first time.

In that year, the university wasn't the only Austin institution without permanent quarters: The old limestone capitol had burned in 1881, and a new, much larger home for the legislature was being built. In 1888, after a series of mishaps—the need to construct a railroad branch to transport the donated building materials, among them—the current capitol was completed. The grand red-granite edifice looking down upon the city proclaimed that Austin had arrived at last.

DAMS, OIL & MICROCHIPS

This symbol of prosperity notwithstanding, the city was once again in a slump. Although some believed that quality of life would be sacrificed to growth—a view still strongly argued today—most townspeople embraced the idea of harnessing the fast-flowing waters of the Colorado River as the solution to Austin's economic woes. A dam, they thought, would not only provide a cheap source of electricity for residents, but also supply power for irrigation and new factories. Dedicated in 1893, the Austin Dam did indeed fulfill these goals—but only temporarily. The energy source proved to be limited, and when torrential rains pelted the city in April 1900, Austin's dreams came crashing down with its dam.

Another dam, attempted in 1915, was never finished. It wasn't until the late 1930s that a permanent solution to the water-power problem was found. The successful plea of young Lyndon Johnson, the newly elected representative from Austin's Tenth Congressional District, to President Roosevelt for federal funds was crucial to the construction of six dams along the lower Colorado River. In conjunction with each other, these dams not only afforded Austin and central Texas all the hydroelectric power and drinking water they needed, but also created the seven Highland Lakes—aesthetically appealing, and a great source of recreational revenues.

Still, Austin might have remained a backwater capital seat abutting a beautiful lake had it not been for the discovery of oil on University of Texas (U.T.) land in 1923. The huge amounts of money that subsequently flowed into the Permanent University Fund—worth some $4 billion today—enabled Austin's campus to become truly first-class. While most of the country was cutting back during the Depression, U.T. went on a building binge and began hiring faculty as impressive as the new halls of academe in which they were to hold forth.

The indirect effects of the oil bonus reached far beyond College Hill. Tracor, the first of Austin's more than 250 high-tech companies, was founded by U.T. scientists and engineers in 1955. Lured by the city's natural attractions and its access to a growing bank of young brainpower, many outside companies soon arrived: IBM (1967), Texas Instruments (1968), and Motorola's Semiconductor Products Section (1974). In the 1980s, two huge computer consortiums, MCC and SEMATECH, opted to make Austin their home.

Willie Nelson's move to Austin from Nashville in 1972 didn't have quite as profound an effect on the economy, but it had one on the city's live-music scene. Hippies and country-and-western fans now found common ground at the many clubs that began to sprout up along downtown's Sixth Street, which had largely been abandoned. Combined with the construction that followed in the wake of the city's high-tech success, these music venues helped spur downtown's resurgence. True, the oil and savings-and-loan crashes of the mid-1980s left many of the new office towers partially empty, but given its record as the comeback kid of cities, who can doubt Austin's complete recovery?

2 Recommended Books, Films & Recordings

Books

The foibles of the Texas "lege"—along with those of Congress and the rest of Washington—are hilariously pilloried by Molly Ivins, Austin's resident scourge, in two collections of her syndicated newspaper columns: *Molly Ivins Can't Say That, Can She?* and *Nothing But Good Times Ahead.* For background into the city's unique music scene, try Jan Reid's *The Improbable Rise of Red Neck Rock.* Serious history buffs might want to dip into Robert Caro's excellent multivolume biography of Lyndon Baines Johnson, the consummate Texas politician who had a profound effect on the Austin area.

William Syndey Porter, better known as O. Henry, published a satirical newspaper in Austin in the late 19th century. Among the many short tales he wrote about the area—collected in *O. Henry's Texas Stories*—are four inspired by his stint as a draftsman in the General Land Office. Set largely in Austin, Billy Lee Brammer's *The Gay Place*—the title adjective meant only "lively" when the book was published (1961)—is a fictional portrait of a political figure loosely based on LBJ. Austin is also the locus for the more recent *Zero at the Bone,* an acclaimed mystery by Mary Willis Walker, and *The Boyfriend School,* a humorous novel by Sarah Bird. The city's most famous scribe, James Michener, placed his historical epic, *Texas,* in the frame of a governor's task force operating out of Austin.

Films

If you don't recognize Austin in many of the Hollywood films that were shot here—more than 65 in the last two decades—it's because the area offers such a wide range of landscapes, filling in for locations as far afield as Vietnam. But Texas does feature prominently in a number of the following famous Austin area productions: *Texas Chainsaw Massacre* (1972); *Honeysuckle Rose* (1980, Willie Nelson and Dyann Cannon); *The Best Little Whorehouse in Texas* (1982, Burt Reynolds and Dolly Parton); the Coen brothers' *Blood Simple* (1984); *Songwriter* (1984, Willie Nelson and Kris Kristofferson); *Nadine* (1987, Jeff Bridges and Kim Basinger); *D.O.A.* (1988, Meg Ryan and Dennis Quaid); *The Ballad of the Sad Cafe* (1991, Vanessa Redgrave and Keith Carradine); *What's Eating Gilbert Grape* (1993, Johnny Depp and Juliette Lewis); and *A Perfect World* (1993, Kevin Costner and Clint Eastwood).

Low-budget movies have also put Austin on the cinematic map. University of Texas graduate Richard Linklater captured some of the loopier members of his alma mater in *Slackers;* his similarly acclaimed follow-up, *Dazed and Confused,* turns to high school for its satire of school days. Another U.T. student, Richard Rodriguez, grabbed national attention, not only because he got a Hollywood contract for a film school project, *El Mariachi,* but because he raised much of the money for it by serving as a guinea pig for medical experiments.

Austin has also been showcased on the tube. *Lonesome Dove,* featuring Robert Duvall, Tommy Lee Jones, and Anjelica Houston, is the most famous of many miniseries shot in the area. And the Public Broadcasting Service has kept the city consistently on the small screen since 1975, when the network first began taping concerts by renowned country-and-western performers for *Austin City Limits.*

Recordings

Janis Joplin, who attended U.T. for a time, played local gigs around town for years; many other famous musicians such as the late Stevie Ray Vaughan also got their start in Austin clubs. Since 1980, the list of artists who signed on to major record labels while living in Austin includes Timbuk 3, Asleep at the Wheel, Lucinda Williams, Lee Roy Parnell, Joe Ely, Jerry Jeff Walker, Hal Ketchum, and Jimmie Dale Gilmore. Willie Nelson has his own recording studio on the outskirts of town.

10

Planning a Trip to Austin

PLANNING A TRIP IS NOT ONLY HALF THE FUN OF GETTING THERE, BUT A WAY to help ensure your enjoyment when you arrive. If you're inclined to using your own sports gear, for example, you'll want to check out Austin's many outdoor options (see Chapter 14) so you'll know just what to bring.

Because Austin doesn't have an overabundance of hotel rooms, it's always important to book ahead of time. Summer season is typically busy, but legislative sessions (the first half of odd-numbered years) and University of Texas events (graduation, say, or home-team games) can also help fill up the town's lodgings.

---

1   Information

Call the **Austin Convention and Visitors Bureau,** 201 E. Second St., 78701 (☎ toll free **800/926-2282**), to receive a general information packet in the mail; the same toll-free number will connect you to a menu with recorded data on everything from the city's current events to its outdoor recreation and tour possibilities, or to a representative who can answer any of your specific questions.

If you'd like the comprehensive *Texas State Travel Guide,* Texas highway maps, an accommodations listing, and other general information about the state, phone the **Texas Highway Department**

What Things Cost in Austin	U.S.$
Taxi from the airport to the city center	$7.00–$10.00
Bus ride between any two downtown points	Free
Local telephone call	.25
Double at the Four Seasons (very expensive)	$175.00
Double at Radisson Hotel on Town Lake (moderate)	$105.00
Double at Days Inn North (inexpensive)	$50.00
Lunch for one at the Shoreline Grill (expensive)	$12.00
Lunch for one at Las Manitas (inexpensive)	$6.00
Dinner for one, without wine, at Jeffrey's (expensive)	$30.00
Dinner for one, without wine, at Manuel's (moderate)	$15.00
Dinner for one, without beer, at The Iron Works (inexpensive)	$7.00
Pint of beer at brew pub	$2.50
Coca-Cola	$1.00
Cup of espresso	$1.50
Admission to Laguna Gloria Art Museum	$2.00
Roll of ASA 100 Kodacolor film, 36 exposures	$5.25
Movie ticket	$1.50–$6.50
Austin Symphony ticket	$8.00–$22.00

(☎ 800/452-9292); its representatives can also advise you about current road conditions, fall foliage or spring wildflower sites, and other topical travel details.

2 When to Go

Climate

May showers follow April flowers in the Austin/Texas Hill Country area; by the time the late spring rains set in, the bluebonnets and most of the other wildflowers have already peaked. Mother Nature thoughtfully arranges mild, generally dry weather in which to enjoy her glorious floral arrangements in early spring—an ideal and deservedly popular time to visit. Summers can be steamy, but Austin offers plenty of great places to cool off, among them the Highland Lakes and Barton Springs. Fall foliage in this leafy area is another treat, and it's hard to beat a Texas evening by a cozy fireplace—admittedly more for show than for warmth in Austin, which generally enjoys mild winters.

Austin's Average Monthly Temperature & Rainfall

	Jan	Feb	Mar	Apr	May	June	July	Aug	Sept	Oct	Nov	Dec
Average	52.0	54.5	60.8	68.2	75.3	81.9	84.0	83.8	79.3	70.5	59.7	53.2
Rainfall	1.66	2.06	1.54	2.54	3.07	2.79	1.69	2.41	3.71	2.84	1.77	1.46

Celebrating Austin

A party for a fictional donkey and a tribute to canned meat? Austin wouldn't be Austin if some of its festivals weren't offbeat. Other events are more traditional; many capitalize on the great outdoors and the large community of local musicians. The major annual events are listed below; see also Chapter 16 for information on the various free concerts and other cultural events held every summer.

Austin Calendar of Events

January

- **Red Eye Regatta,** Austin Yacht Club, Lake Travis. The bracing lake air at this New Year's Day keelboat race should help cure what ails you from the night before. ☎ 512/266-1336.

February

- **Carnival Brasileiro,** City Coliseum. Conga lines, elaborate costumes, samba bands, and confetti are all part of this sizzling event, started by homesick Brazilian University of Texas students in 1975. ☎ 512 /452-6832.

March

- **Austin/Travis County Livestock Show and Rodeo,** Texas Exposition Center. This 10-day Wild West extravaganza features rodeos, cattle auctions, a youth fair, and lots of live country music. ☎ 512/467-9811.
- **Jerry Jeff Walker's Birthday Weekend,** various locations. Three days of country music, dancing, and golf culminate in a performance by the legendary singer/ songwriter at the Paramount Theatre. ☎ 512/288-1695.

★ South by Southwest (SXSW) Music & Media Conference

The Austin Music Awards kick off this huge conference, which organizes hundreds of concerts at more than two dozen city venues. Aspiring music industry professionals sign up months in advance; keynote speakers have included Johnny Cash.

Where: Austin Convention Center, all around town. **When:** Four days in mid-March. **How:** ☎ 512/ 467-7979 for conference and concert schedules.

March–April

- **Texas Hill Country Wine and Food Festival** (most events at the Four Seasons Hotel). Book a month in advance for the cooking demonstrations, beer, wine, and food tastings, and celebrity chef dinners; for the food fair, just turn up with an appetite. ☎ 512/329-0770.

April

- **Eeyore's Birthday Party,** Pease Park. Costume contests, face painting, and live music celebrate A. A. Milne's donkey at this huge rites-of-spring fest. ☎ 512/467-8633.
- **Spamarama,** La Zona Rosa. The awards for creative cooking with Spam are the highlight of this hilarious event, judged by Texas celebrities; there's also a live music Spam Jam. ☎ 512/416-9307.

April–May

- **Flora Rama,** Zilker Botanical Gardens. There's plenty of flower power at this huge gathering—sales booths, gardening demonstrations, and a variety of entertainment. ☎ 512/477-8672.

May

- **O. Henry Pun-Off,** O. Henry Museum. One of the punniest events around, this annual battle of the wits is for a wordy cause—the upkeep of the O. Henry Museum. ☎ 512/472-1903 or 453-4431.
- **Old Pecan Street Spring Arts and Crafts Festival,** Sixth Street. Eat and shop your way along Austin's restored Victorian main street while bands play in the background. ☎ 512/448-1797.

- **Cinco de Mayo,** Fiesta Gardens. Mariachis, flamenco dancers, Tejano music, tacos, and tamales are all part of the traditional May 5 Mexican freedom celebration. ☎ **512/499-2264** or **322-2703.**
- **Fiesta Laguna Gloria,** Laguna Gloria Art Museum. Set on the shores of Lake Austin, the museum's major fundraiser features a juried art show, an auction, and lots of kids' activities. ☎ **512/458-6073.**

June

★ Juneteenth Freedom Festival

This huge celebration of African American emancipation features parades, a jazz and blues festival, gospel singing, a rap competition, and a children's rodeo and carnival. **Where:** Travis County Exposition Center and east Austin. **When:** Five days surrounding June 15. **How:** ☎ **512/933-9501** for details on tickets and events.

- **Hyde Park Historic Homes Tour.** The Victorian and early 20th-century homes of Austin's first residential suburb are open to the public every Father's Day weekend. ☎ **512/452-4139.**

July

- **Freedom Festival and Fireworks,** Zilker Park. Top rock and country entertainers draw huge crowds for this outdoor event, which ends with the traditional pyrotechnics. ☎ **512/448-1797.**
- **Governor's Cup Sailing Regatta,** Austin Yacht Club, Lake Travis. Bring along a picnic and cheer on your favorite keelboat at this Independence Day event. ☎ **512/266-1336.**

August

- **Austin Aqua Festival,** at Town Lake and throughout the city. Nine days of sporting events, feasting, and especially music are played out on the land as well as on the lake. ☎ **512/472-5664.**
- **Fall Creek Vineyards Celebration & Grape Stomp,** Lake Buchanan. Grape squishing, footprint T-shirts, and wine tastings are all part of the fun on the last two Saturdays in August. ☎ **512/476-4477.**
- **Hot Sauce Festival,** Travis County Farmer's Market. It's the largest event of its kind in the world, with more than 400 entries judged by celebrity chefs and food editors. ☎ **512/454-1002.**

September

★ Diez y Seis de Septiembre

Mariachis and folk dancers, Tex-Mex conjunto and Tejano music, as well as fajitas, piñatas, and clowns help celebrate Mexico's independence from Spain. The highlight: The crowning of the Fiestas Patrias Queen. **Where:** Fiesta Gardens. **When:** Six days, starting September 16. **How:** ☎ **512/499-2264** or **322-2703** for information.

* **Fall Jazz Festival,** Zilker Hillside Theater. Zilker Park swings on the third weekend of September, when top local jazz acts turn out for two days of free concerts. ☎ **512/440-1414.**

October

* **Halloween,** Sixth Street. Seven blocks of historic Sixth Street are barricaded off for Texas's kookiest spook parade. ☎ **512/478-0098.**

November

* **Dia de los Muertos** (Day of the Dead), Congress Avenue. Death is embraced as part of the life cycle in this Halloween-like Hispanic festival, involving Latino music, a parade, and, of course, food. ☎ **512/480-9373.**
* **Victorian Christmas on Sixth St.** Downtown's former main drag takes on a turn-of-the-century aura on Thanksgiving weekend, with five blocks of crafts booths kicking off the holiday shopping season. ☎ **512/448-1797.**

December

* **Christmas Open House,** French Legation. Père Nöel (the French Santa Claus) and costumed guides help host this lively gift bazaar, held in an 1840 historic house. ☎ **512/472-8180.**
* **West End Christmas Walk,** 1100 and 1200 blocks of West Sixth Street. Madrigal and gospel singers greet shoppers at galleries, boutiques, and bakeries, open late for the occasion. ☎ **512/472-9696** or **473-8334.**
* **Armadillo Christmas Bazaar,** Austin Opera House at the Terrace. Revel in Tex-Mex food, live music, and a full bar at this high-quality art, craft, and gift show, starting around two weeks before Christmas. ☎ **512/447-1605.**

---

3 Tips for Special Travelers

FOR THE DISABLED   For information on local resources in Austin, travelers with any type of disability can contact **Travelin' Talk,** Box 3534, Clarksville, TN 37043 (☎ **615/552-6670,** fax 615/552-1182). The organization also publishes a huge directory including travel agents and tour operators who specialize in working with the disabled.

FOR SENIORS   Those over age 50 are eligible to join the influential **American Association of Retired Persons** (**AARP**) 601 E St. NW, Washington, DC 20049 (☎ **202/434-2277**), which can help you get good rates on lodging, transportation, and attractions; trip-routing information and emergency road service are also available through the organization.

The study programs offered by **Elderhostel,** 75 Federal St., third floor, Boston, MA 02110 (☎ **617/426-7788**), for those age 60 and older are becoming increasingly popular; room and board are included in these inexpensive, educational packages. Among the many classes offered in Austin in 1994 were "Traveling to the Future? Take the Information Highway" and "Texas Wines: Hear It Through the Grapevine."

FOR FAMILIES   The *Family Travel Times* newsletter, Travel With Your Children, 45 W. 18th St., Seventh floor, New York, NY 10011 (☎ **212/206-0688**), is a good resource for information about vacationing with kids. You can get an annual subscription (10 issues) for $55; a sample issue costs $2.

The free monthly *Austin Child Magazine* includes a calendar of events and suggestions for family fun; it's available at libraries, YMCAs, schools, and retail outlets in town, or from the publisher, 4125 Keller Springs Rd., Suite 146, Dallas, TX 75244 (☎ **214/447-9188**); enclose $2 for postage.

FOR STUDENTS   To find out about the discounts on airfares, rail fares, and lodgings offered by the **Council on International Educational Exchange** (**CIEE**), 205 E. 42nd St., New York, NY 10017 (☎ **212/661-1414**), send for the organization's *Student Travels* magazine. A Council travel office in Austin, 2000 Guadalupe St., 78705 (☎ **512/472-4932**), can arrange tour bookings. If you join **Hostelling International-American Youth Hostels** (**HI-AYH**), Box 37613, Washington, DC 20013-7613 (☎ **202/783-6161**), open to all ages, you'll be eligible for discounts at the organization's many dorm-style accommodations; and on rail and bus travel in many places.

4   Getting There

By Plane

Robert Mueller Municipal Airport (☎ **512/495-7600**) is approximately two miles north of downtown.

THE MAJOR AIRLINES   America West (☎ **512/479-8765** or toll free **800/235-9292**), **American** (☎ toll free **800/433-7300**), **Continental** (☎ **512/477-6716** or toll free **800/525-0280**), **Delta** (☎ toll free **800/221-1212**), **Northwest** (☎ toll free **800/225-2525**), **Southwest** (☎ toll free **800/435-9792**), **TWA** (☎ **512/454-8900** or toll free **800/221-2000**), **United** (☎ toll free **800/241-6522**), and **USAir** (☎ toll free **800/428-4322**) all fly into Austin. **Conquest** (☎ toll free **800/722-0860**) is Austin's short-hop commuter airline. There is no direct international service to the city.

All the airlines run seasonal specials that can lower fares considerably. If your dates of travel don't coincide with these promotions, however, the least expensive way to travel is to purchase tickets at least 14 days in advance, stay over Saturday night, and travel during the week. Within these parameters, Delta, Northwest, TWA, and USAir offer the best round-trip fares from **New York** to Austin (from around $318 to $324, not including tax); Continental's fares are slightly higher (around $350). Those flying from **Chicago** to Austin will get the lowest rates on Delta, Northwest, Southwest, TWA, and United (from $262 to $278). From **Los Angeles,** America West's fares ($198) are the most economical; next in line are Delta, Northwest, Southwest, TWA, and United (between $258 and $288).

By Train

To get to points east or west of Austin via **Amtrak,** 250 N. Lamar Blvd. (☎ toll free **800/872-7245**), you'll have to go to San Antonio (see the "By Train" section of Chapter 2); trains depart from Austin to San Antonio on Monday, Wednesday, and Saturday mornings, and rates range from $16 one-way to $18 to $32 round-trip, depending on dates of travel and length of advance reservations. The Texas Eagle departs from Austin to Chicago three times a week; round-trip fares range from $178 to $350. The train station is on the western edge of downtown, near the Seton Medical Center.

By Bus

You'll also be going through San Antonio if you're traveling from the east or west to Austin via **Greyhound,** 916 E. Koenig Lane (☎ toll free **800/231-2222**); see Chapter 2 for details. There are approximately nine buses between the two cities each day, with one-way fares running around $10. To get from Austin to Chicago, the rate is $139 each way; you can sometimes cut that price in half by taking advantage of advance-purchase programs. The bus terminal is about 10 minutes north of downtown, near Highland Mall.

By Car

I-35 runs through Austin in a north-south direction; U.S. Hwy. 290 leads east to Dallas/Forth Worth, about four hours away, and goes west via a scenic Hill Country route to I-10, the main east-west throughfare. I-10 can also be picked up by heading south to San Antonio, some 80 miles away on I-35.

In case you're planning a state capital tour, it's 896 miles from Austin to Atlanta; 1,911 miles to Boston; 921 miles to Springfield, Illinois; 671 miles to Santa Fe; 963 miles to Phoenix; and 1,745 miles to Sacramento, California.

11

Getting to Know Austin

THOUSANDS OF ACRES OF PARKS, PRESERVES, AND LAKES HAVE BEEN SET ASIDE for public enjoyment in Austin, making it an unusually people-friendly city. But if you spend a lot of time negotiating I-35 between the airport motels and the downtown business and historical district, it would be easy to get the wrong impression. Be sure to go just a few blocks past the office towers to the green shores of Town Lake, where you'll begin to see what Austin is all about.

Central Austin is, very roughly, bounded by Town Lake to the south, Hwy. 290 to the north, I-35 to the east, and Mo-Pac (Loop 1) to the west. South Austin, east of Mopac, tends to be blue collar residential, though the northern sections have been gentrified; the volume of high-tech companies moving into this area is likely to be turned up when the city's new international airport is built in this area. High-tech development is also proceeding apace in north Austin, which is seeing a good deal of residential growth, too. The flat former farmland of older east Austin is largely Hispanic and black, while the lakeshores and hills of west Austin host some of the most opulent mansions in town.

1 Orientation

Arriving

BY PLANE Small and easy to negotiate, Robert Mueller Municipal Airport, 3600 Manor Rd. (☎ 512/495-7600), is located about two miles from downtown, near I-35. Although this single-terminal airport has been slated to be replaced by a larger one at the former Bergstrom Air Force Base on the south side, nothing is likely to happen until 1997. See the "Getting There" section of Chapter 10 for information about airlines serving Austin.

Just outside the terminal is posted a list of hotels that offer shuttle service from the airport. The service is complimentary in many cases, but some hotels tack on a charge to your bill after the fact. Inquire when you make reservations whether or not your hotel sends out a van—and whether or not it's free for guests.

Taxis from the major companies in town form a queue across the street from the terminal. The cab line sometimes thins between 8:45 and 10:15pm, when most flights arrive in Austin; if you don't see a taxi or if you need special service, call one of the companies whose numbers are posted on the door leading out to the ground transportation area. To ensure off-hour pick up in advance, phone Yellow Checker Cab (☎ toll free **800/749-3450**) or American Cab (☎ toll free **800/456-TAXI**) before you leave home. The ride between the airport and downtown generally costs between $7 and $10. The flag-drop charge is $1.25, and it's 25¢ for every fifth of a mile after that.

It's approximately 20 minutes from the airport to downtown via bus no. 20 on Capital Metro Transit (☎ **512/574-1200,** TDD ☎ **512/385-5872**); detailed schedules are available inside the terminal. The fare is 50¢ for adults; see the "By Bus" section in "By Public Transportation," below, for additional information.

Most of the major car-rental companies—Advantage, Alamo, Avis, Budget, Hertz, National, and Thrifty—have outlets at the airport; see "Car Rentals" in the "Getting Around" section of this chapter for details. The trip from the airport to downtown by car or taxi isn't likely to take more than 15 minutes at any time of the day.

BY TRAIN The Amtrak station is in the southwest corner of downtown, at Lamar and West First Street, 250 N. Lamar Blvd. (☎ **512/476-5684** or toll free **800/872-7245**). There are generally a few cabs around to meet the trains, but if you don't see one, a list of phone numbers of taxi companies is posted near the pay phones. Some of the downtown hotels offer courtesy pick up from the train station. A cab ride shouldn't run more than $4 or $5 (there's a $3 minimum charge).

BY BUS The Greyhound station, 916 E. Koenig Lane (☎ **512/454-9686** or toll free **800/231-2222**), is located behind Highland Mall, just south of the I-35 motel zone. Some places to sleep are within walking distance, and many others are a short cab ride away; a few taxis usually wait outside the station. If you want to go downtown, you can catch either bus no. 7 (Duval) or no. 15 (Red River) from the stop across the street. A cab ride downtown—about 10 minutes away on the freeway—should cost from $6 to $8.

BY CAR I-35 is the north-south approach to Austin; it intersects with Hwy. 290, a major east-west throughoughfare, and Hwy. 183, which also runs roughly north-south through town. If you're staying on the west side of Austin, hook up with Loop 1, almost always called Mo-Pac by locals.

Tourist Information

The **Austin Convention and Visitors Bureau,** 201 E. Second St. (☎ toll free **800/926-2282**), across the street from the Convention Center in the southeast section of downtown, is open Monday to Friday 8:30am to 5pm, Saturday 9am to 5pm, and Sunday noon to 5pm (except Thanksgiving Day and Christmas). A branch of the ACVB is supposed to be open at the airport Monday to Friday 9am to 8pm, Saturday 9am to 5pm, and Sunday 10am to 4pm or 1 to 6pm, but it is staffed solely by volunteers and is frequently left unattended. You can pick up tourist information pamphlets downtown at the **Old Bakery and Emporium,** 1006 Congress Ave. (☎ **512/477-5961**), open June to August and December (before Christmas) Monday to Friday, 9am to 4pm, Saturday, 10am to 3pm, closed Saturday and Sunday the rest of the year. Those particularly interested in Austin's African American community might contact the **Capital City Chamber of Commerce,** 5407 I-35 North, Suite 304 (☎ **512/459-1181**).

The free alternative newspaper, the *Chronicle,* is the best source of information about Austin events; it's distributed to stores, hotels, and restaurants around town every Thursday. The various weekend editions of the *Austin-American Statesman* also list local happenings.

City Layout

In 1839, Austin was laid out on in a grid on the northern shore of the Colorado River, bounded by Shoal Creek to the west and Waller Creek to the east. The section of the river abutting the original settlement is now known as Town Lake, and the city has spread far beyond its original borders in all directions. The land to the east is flat Texas plain; the rolling Hill Country begins on the west side of town.

MAIN ARTERIES & STREETS I-35, comprising the border between central and east Austin, is the main north-south thoroughfare; Loop 1, usually called Mo-Pac, is its more scenic west-side equivalent. Hwy. 290, which frequently changes its name on the north end of town (to 2222, Northland, and Koenig) runs east and west, as does 183, also called Research Boulevard. Ben White Boulevard, a major east-west road to the south of town, is another incarnation of Hwy. 290, connecting with Hwy. 71 east of I-35. Important north-south city streets include Lamar, Guadalupe, and Burnet; if you want to get across town north of the river, use First Street (sometimes called Cesar Chavez); 12th Street (which turns into Enfield west of Lamar); Martin Luther King, Jr., Blvd. (the equivalent of 19th Street); 38th Street; and 45th Street.

FINDING AN ADDRESS Congress Avenue was the earliest dividing line between east and west, while the Colorado River marks the north and south border of the city. This system of determining addresses works reasonably well in the older sections of town, but breaks down where the neat street grid does (look at a street map to see where the right angles end). All the east-west streets were originally named after trees native to the city (for example, Sixth Street was once Pecan Street); many that run north and south, such as San Jacinto, Lavaca, and Guadalupe, retain their original Texas river monickers.

STREET MAPS A number of the car-rental companies give out surprisingly detailed street maps of central Austin. If you're going farther afield, I'd recommend the Gousha city maps, available at most convenience stores, drugstores, newsstands, and bookstores.

Neighborhoods in Brief

With a few exceptions, locals tend to speak in terms of landmarks (the University of Texas) or geographical sections (east Austin) rather than neighborhoods. In recent years, booming bedroom communities like Round Rock have grown up to the north of Austin; the west, in the direction of Hill Country, has seen such affluent residential developments as the separately incorporated West Lake Hills. Following are descriptions of some of the city's older and closer-knit areas.

Downtown The original city, laid out by Edwin Waller in 1839, runs roughly north-south from the river (First Street) to the capitol (15th Street), and east-west between I-35 and Lamar. This prime sightseeing and hotel area has seen a resurgence in the last two decades, with more and more music clubs, restaurants, shops, and galleries moving onto and around Sixth Street. Businesses are also coming back to the beautiful old office buildings that line Sixth Street and Congress Avenue as well as to the newer towers that lay partially abandoned after the savings-and-loan and oil crashes of the 1980s.

Fairview Park & Travis Heights These adjoining neighborhoods between Congress and I-35 from Town Lake to Oltdorf Street were Austin's first settlements south of the river. At the end of the 19th century, the bluffs here became desirable as Austin residents realized they were not as likely to be flooded as the lower-ground residents north of the Colorado. Many mansions in what had become a working-class district have lately been reclaimed and antiques shops have begun springing up all over.

East Austin The section east of I-35 between First Street and Martin Luther King, Jr., Boulevard is home to many of Austin's Latino and black residents. Mexican restaurants and markets dot the area, which also hosts a number of African American heritage sites, including Huston Tillotson College, Metropolitan African Methodist Episcopal Church, and Madison Cabin. Hispanic festivals are often held at Parque Zaragosa.

Old West Austin Of the neighborhoods that developed as downtown Austin expanded beyond Shoal Creek, Clarksville, just east of Mo-Pac, is among the most interesting: Founded by a former slave in 1871 as a utopian community for freed blacks, it's now an artist's enclave. Directly to the north, from about West 15th to West 24th Streets, Enfield boasts a number of beautiful homes and upscale restaurants. Larger mansions line the northern shores of Lake Austin, in the section known as Tarrytown; it's just south of Mt. Bonnell and a beautiful stretch of land where, some historians say, Stephen F. Austin himself planned to retire.

The University of Texas The original 40 acres that were alloted to build an institution of higher education just north of the capitol have expanded to 357 since the 19th century, and Guadalupe Street, along the west side of the campus, is now the popular shopping strip known as the Drag. Many of the large old houses in the area have been converted to student apartments, but the trend has turned toward restoring them to family residences.

Hyde Park North of the University between 38th and 45th Streets, Hyde Park got its start in 1891 as one of Austin's first planned suburbs; its Victorian and early Craftsman houses began to be renovated in the 1970s. There's a real neighborhood feel about this pretty area, where children ride tricycles and people walk their dogs along quiet, tree-lined streets.

2 Getting Around

By Public Transportation

BY BUS   Austin's public transportation system, Capital Metropolitan Transportation Authority, is excellent, including more than 50 bus lines and a variety of pay strata. The regular adult one-way fare on Metro routes is 50¢; express service from various Park & Ride lots costs $1; four 'Dillo routes—Downtown Austin, the Capitol Complex, the University of Texas campus, and the Convention Center—are free. You'll need exact change or fare tickets (see below) to board the bus; free transfers are good for three hours. Call **474-1200** (TDD **385-5872**) for point-to-point routing information; you can also pick up a schedule booklet at any HEB, Fiesta, and Albertson grocery store or at the Capital Metro Information Center on Fifth Street and Congress Avenue.

Discount Fares   With the exception of Special Transit Service and Public Event shuttles, passengers 65 and older or those with mobility impairments may ride all fixed bus routes for free upon presenting a Capital Metro ID card to the driver; these cards are available for a $3 charge from Passport Express, 1107 Rio Grande (open Monday to Friday 9am to 5pm, Saturday 11am to 2pm), or from Capital Metro's administration office, 2910 W. Fifth St. (open Monday to Friday 9am to 1pm and 2 to 5pm). University of Texas students also ride for free upon presentation of a U.T. ID card; all other students who get a Capital Metro ID card pay half-price. If you buy a Ticket Book, available at the same places as schedule booklets (see above), you can get 20 50¢ tickets for only $5—a 50% savings. Children five years or younger ride free when accompanied by adults.

By Other Transportation

BY TAXI   Among the major cab companies in Austin are American Cab (☎ **452-9999**), Austin Cab (☎ **478-2222**), Roy's Taxi (☎ **482-0000**), and Yellow-Checker Cab (☎ **472-1111**). Rates are regulated by the city: It's $1.25 for the first fifth of a mile, $1.25 for each additional mile.

BY CAR   It's not a good idea to fall into a driver's daze in Austin: Those unfamiliar with the local turf need to be vigilant on the city streets as well as the highways. The former are rife with signs that suddenly insist "Left lane must turn left" or "Right lane must turn right"—positioned so they're most noticeable when it's too late to switch. I-35 is mined with tricky on-and-off ramps and, around downtown, a confusing complex of upper-and-lower levels; it's easy to miss your exit or to find yourself exiting where you don't want to. If you possibly can, avoid Hwy. 183, which connects I-35 with Mo-Pac and the Capital of Texas Hwy. to the west: Perpetually under construction, the road is rife with narrowing lane mergings and sudden, precipitous turnoffs. You can still see bumper stickers around town proclaiming, "Pray for me, I drive 183."

Car Rentals   If you're planning to travel at a popular time, it's a good idea to book as far in advance as you can, both to secure the quoted rates and to ensure that you get a car. Some of the companies I phoned in early October to inquire about the winter holiday season were already filled up for Christmas.

Advantage (☎ **512/388-3377** or toll free **800/777-5500**), Alamo (☎ **512/474-2922** or toll free **800/327-9633**), Avis (toll free **800/831-2847**), Budget (☎ **512/478-6437** or toll free **800/527-0700**), Dollar (☎ **512/322-9081** or toll free **800/800-4000**), Hertz (☎ **512/478-9321** or toll free **800/654-3131**), National Interrent (☎ **512/476-6189** or toll free **800/227-7368**), and Thrifty (☎ **512/469-0270** or toll free **800/367-2277**) all have representatives at the airport. A comparative price check for the Christmas season gave a range of $133 (Alamo) to $166 (Thrifty) for a two-door subcompact with unlimited mileage for a week. Additional days cost anywhere from $29.50 (Budget) to $37 (Thrifty). Cars rented from Enterprise (☎ toll free **800/325-8007**), another reliable company, run $125 per week, $25 per extra day; they'll send a van to pick you up at the airport or at your hotel.

Note: the rates quoted above were all undiscounted. Lower prices are often available for those who are flexible about dates of travel or who are members of frequent-flyer or frequent hotel stay programs or of organizations such as AAA or AARP. It can't hurt to mention every travel-related program you belong to when you're calling to reserve a car; you'd be surprised at the bargains you might turn up.

Parking   Unless you have congressional plates, you're likely to find the selection of parking spots downtown and near the capitol extremely limited during the week. Bring pocketfuls of quarters and prepare to feed the meter at intervals that can be as short as 15 minutes. There are a number of lots around the area, costing anywhere from $2.50 to $4, but the most convenient ones tend to fill up quickly. The university area is similarly congested during the week; trying to find a spot near the shopping strip known as the Drag can be just that. Cruise the side streets; you're eventually bound to find a lot that's not filled. The two on-campus parking garages are near San Jacinto and E. 26th streets and off 25th Street between San Antonio and Nueces; there are also parking lots near the visitors centers at the LBJ Library and the Arno Nowotny Building.

Driving Rules   Unless specifically forbidden, right turns are permitted on red after coming to a full stop. Seat belts and child-restraint seats are mandatory in Texas.

BY BICYCLE   It would be hard to find a city more accommodating to two-wheelers than Austin. Many city streets have separate bicycle lanes and lots of scenic areas have been set aside for hiking and biking or for biking alone; see the "Recreation" section of Chapter 14 for details.

ON FOOT   Crossing wide avenues such as Congress is not as easy as it might be because lights tend to be geared toward motorists rather than pedestrians, but downtown Austin and the other older sections of the city are generally very walkable. And Austin is dotted with lovely, tree-shaded spots for everything from strolling to roller-blading. The jaywalking laws are not generally enforced, except downtown.

Fast Facts: Austin

Airport   See "Orientation" in this chapter.

American Express   2943 W. Anderson Lane (☎ 452-8166).

Area Code   The telephone area code in Austin is **512.**

Babysitters   Grandparents Unlimited (☎ **280-5108**) and Austin's Capital Grannies (☎ **371-3402**) are licensed and bonded child-care providers that use seniors or older reliable people. If it's boundless energy you're after, Career Services at the University of Texas (☎ **471-1217**) can refer you to a college student.

Business Hours   Banks and office hours are generally Monday through Friday from 8 or 9am to 5pm. Some banks offer drive-through service on Saturday from 9am to noon or 1pm. Specialty shops and malls tend to open around 9 or 10am, Monday through Saturday; the former close at about 5 or 6pm, the latter at around 9 or 10pm. You can also shop at most malls and boutiques on Sunday from noon until 6pm. Bars and clubs don't tend to close until midnight during the week, 2am on weekends.

Car Rentals   See "Getting Around" in this chapter.

Climate   See "When to Go" in Chapter 10.

Currency & Exchange   See "Fast Facts: For the Foreign Traveler" in the Appendix.

Dentists   Both the Dentist Information Service (☎ **323-2332**) and the Medical Service Bureau (☎ **458-1121**) can recommend local dentists.

Doctors   Brackenridge (☎ **480-1122**), Seton (☎ **338-5065**), and Children's (☎ **800/542-1522**) hospitals have physician referral services.

Documents Required   See "Preparing for Your Trip" in the Appendix.

Driving Rules   See "Getting Around" in this chapter.

Drugstores   You'll find many Walgreens and Eckerd drugstores around the city; most HEB grocery stores also have pharmacies. The Walgreens at Airport and North Lamar Boulevards (☎ **458-4269**), the Eckerd at 2301A S. Congress Ave. (☎ **444-3671**), and the HEB at 9414 N. Lamar Blvd. are all open 24 hours.

Embassies/Consulates   See "Fast Facts: For the Foreign Traveler" in the Appendix.

Emergencies   Call **911** if you need the police, fire department, or an ambulance.

Eyeglasses   TSO and Lenscrafters are two fast, dependable chains with many convenient locations around town.

Hairdressers/Barbers   For an easy, inexpensive trim, try one of the Supercuts or Command Performance salons. Maximum FX, on the Drag, 2326 Guadalupe St. (☎ **472-3331**), can be relied on not to give you a bad hair day.

Holidays   See "Calendar of Events" in Chapter 10, and "Holidays" in "Fast Facts: For the Foreign Traveler" in the Appendix.

Hospitals   Brackenridge, 601 E. 15th St. (☎ **476-6461**), and St. David's (I.H.-35 at 32nd Street) (☎ **397-4240**), have good and convenient emergency-care facilities.

Hot Lines   Inside Line (☎ **512/416-5700**) can clue you in on Austin information from the essential to the esoteric—everything from weather forecasts (ext. 7034) and restaurant reviews (ext. 3663) to comedy (ext. 5233) and bat viewing (ext. 1630). Other possibilities include nightclub updates (ext. 2582), movie reviews (ext. 3465), theater reviews (ext. 7439), traveler's forecasts (ext. 6849), world-news updates (ext. 6700), and current events (ext. 5463). Punch extension 6955 for instructions on how to use the system.

Information   See "Tourist Information" in this chapter.

Laundry/Dry Cleaning   Voted best in town by readers of *The Austin Chronicle,* members of the long-established Jack Brown dry-cleaning chain offer friendly, one-day service.

Libraries   The downtown Austin Public Library and adjoining Austin History Center, 810 Guadalupe St. (☎ **499-7480**), are excellent information resources.

Liquor Laws   You have to be 21 to drink in Texas. It's illegal to have an open container in your car, and liquor cannot be served before noon on Sunday except at brunches.

Lost Property   You can phone the police at **480-5028** to check if something you've lost has been turned in. If you leave something on a city bus, call **389-7454;** on a train heading for Austin or at the Amtrak station, ☎ **476-5684;** on a Greyhound bus or at the station, ☎ **458-4463;** at the airport, ☎ **495-7600.**

Luggage Storage/Lockers   Coin-operated storage lockers in the airport cost from 50¢ to $1, depending on the size. At the Greyhound station, there's only one size locker; the price is $1 per 24 hours. You can check your luggage at the Amtrak station for $1.50 per bag per 24 hours.

Maps   See "City Layout" in this chapter.

Newspapers/Magazines   The daily *Austin American-Statesman* is the only large-circulation, mainstream newspaper in town. *The Austin Chronicle,* a free alternative weekly, focuses on the arts, entertainment, and politics. Monday through Thursday, the University of Texas publishes the surprisingly sophisticated *Daily Texan* newspaper, covering everything from on-campus to international events.

Photographic Needs   Back in a Flash, Fox Photo, and HEB Food Stores all offer reliable one-hour photo processing at convenient locations around the city. For repairs, try Precision Camera & Video, 3810 N. Lamar Blvd. (☎ **467-7676**).

Police   The 24-hour nonemergency number for the Austin Police Department is ☎ **480-5000.**

Post Office   The city's main post office is at 8225 Cross Park Dr. (☎ **929-1253**); more convenient to tourist sights are the Capitol Station, in the LBJ Building (☎ **477-3903**), and the Downtown Station, 217 W. Ninth St. (☎ **477-7907**).

Radio/TV   On the FM dial, turn to KMFA (89.5) for classical music; KUT (90.5) for National Public Radio; KASE (100.7) for country; KUTZ (98.9) for contemporary rock; KGSR (107.1) for folk, reggae, rock, blues, and jazz. AM stations include KVET (1300) for news and talk and KJCE (1300) for soul and Motown oldies.

If you want to tune into your favorite noncable TV shows, you'll find CBS (KTBC) on Channel 2; ABC (KVUE) on Channel 3; NBC (KXAN) on Channel 4; Fox (KBVO) on Channel 5; and PBS (KLRU) on Channel 9.

Religious Services   You'll find a list of places of worship under "Churches" and "Synagogues" in the Yellow Pages. Austin Metropolitan Ministries (☎ **512/472-7627**) also provides information about church services around town.

Restrooms   Good luck finding a restroom downtown on Sunday morning when most of the stores and restaurants are closed; the capitol complex and hotels are your best bet. Malls and parks are well provided with public bathrooms.

Safety   Austin has the third-lowest crime rate of America's major cities, but that doesn't mean you should throw common sense to the winds. It's never a good idea to walk down dark streets alone at night, and major tourist areas always attract pickpockets; keep your purse or wallet in a safe place.

Shoe Repairs   Drop off your injured footwear at one of Austin Shoe Hospital's many drive-through facilities (they took over a former photo-processing chain). They'll even phone you and remind you to pick up your shoes.

Taxes   The tax on hotel rooms is 13%. Sales tax, added to restaurant bills as well as to other purchases, is 8%.

Taxis See "Getting Around" in this chapter.

Time Austin is on central daylight time and observes daylight saving time.

Tipping Gratuities are still contingent on good service in Austin. If you get it, a 15% to 20% tip is standard in restaurants; at least 10% is expected by taxi drivers. Bellhops and valets should get from $1 to $2 per bag, depending on the size of your luggage and the quality of the hotel. Tip chambermaids anywhere from $1 to $5 per person per night.

Transit Information Capital Metro Transit (☎ **474-1200** or TDD **385-5872**).

Useful Telephone Numbers Time and temperature (☎ **973-3555**).

Weather ☎ **476-7736.**

---

3 Networks & Resources

For Students

There are endless resources for students in this university town. Persons of the college persuasion need only go over to the University of Texas Student Union Building (see map in Chapter 14) to find out what they need to know—or where they can go to find out. Austin's oldest institution of higher learning, Huston Tillotson College, 600 Chicon St. (☎ **505-3000**), in east Austin, is especially helpful for getting African American students oriented. The AYH Hostel (see "Youth Hostel," Chapter 12) is another great repository of information for students.

For Gay Men & Lesbians

Book Woman (see "For Women," below) and **Liberty Books,** 1014 N. Lamar Blvd. (☎ **495-9737**), are the best places to find gay and lesbian books and magazines; they also carry the local gay newspapers, the weekly *Texas Triangle,* and the bimonthly *Fag Rag.* At **Lobo,** 3204-A Guadalupe St. (☎ **454-5406**), the focus is on videos and magazines for gay men. The *Austin Gay-Friendly Resource Directory,* published by Austin Media Visions ($4.95) and available at Book Woman and Liberty, has more than 800 listings. A number of gay bars and dance clubs are listed in Chapter 16, "Austin Nights." Hippie Hollow, near Lake Travis, is a popular daytime gathering spot for gays.

For Women

In addition to being an excellent resource for publications by and about women, **Book Woman,** 325 E. Sixth St. (☎ **472-2785**), is the closest thing Austin has to a women's information center. The rape crisis center number is **440-7273.**

For Seniors

The Old Bakery and Emporium, 1006 Congress Ave. (☎ **477-5961**), not only sells crafts and baked goods made by senior citizens, but also serves as a volunteer center for people over 50. It's a good place to find out about any senior activities in town. Another excellent resource is the monthly *Senior Advocate* newspaper, P.O. Box 4806, 78765 (☎ **451-7433**), available for free at Food Land and Albertson's supermarkets, bingo halls, libraries, and many other places. You can also call or write in advance for a subscription, which costs $8 a year.

12

Austin Accommodations

Eɴᴅʟᴇss ᴄʜᴀɪɴ ᴍᴏᴛᴇʟs sᴛʀᴜɴɢ ᴀʟᴏɴɢ I-35 ɴᴏʀᴛʜ ᴏF ᴛʜᴇ ᴀɪʀᴘᴏʀᴛ
notwithstanding, Austin has a room shortage. Resistance to development, strict residential zoning laws, and uncertainty about the
opening date—and, for a long time, the location—of a new airport
have all added to the pinch. Sometimes it's a cinch to find a place to
stay; other times those needing to attend an event in Austin can find
themselves lodged almost as far away as San Antonio.

If you can't guess when major microchip conventions are going
to come to town, you can make some sense out of what might seem
like random runs on hotel space by keeping two things in mind: the
state legislature and the University of Texas (enrollment nearly
50,000). Lawmakers and lobbyists converge on the capital for
140-day sessions at the start of odd-numbered years, so you can expect fewer free rooms in the first half of 1995 and 1997. And figure
that the beginning of fall term, graduation week, and important home
games of the Longhorns football team—U.T.'s Memorial Stadium
has nearly 80,000 seats—are going to draw parents and sports fans
into town en masse. It's always a good idea to book as far in advance
as possible; it's essential if you're planning to come in around these
times.

Along with airport proximity, low cost and quick downtown freeway access help fill the I-35 motels. But you'll get a far better feel for
what makes Austin special if you stay in the verdant Town Lake area;
closer than any others to the major sights, the hotels here are also on
or near a 10-mile hike-and-bike trail. Farther afield but convenient
to various high-tech complexes are the accommodation clusters to
the south and northwest of town. Those with a penchant for playing on the water or putting should consider staying out near the lakes
and golf courses to the west.

Austin offers some glitzy high-rises but only one historic hotel;
if it's character you're after, you might opt for one of the
bed-and-breakfasts beginning to crop up around town. The phenomenon is so new that no bed-and-breakfast reservation agency exists
yet, but a group of innkeepers has recently formed a quality-screening
association; for information, call the **Woodburn House**
(☎ **512/458-4335**). Some of the member inns also belong to the
Historic Hotel Association of Texas, 231 W. Main, Fredericksburg,
TX 78624 (☎ **210/997-3980**); write or phone for a pamphlet listing bed-and-breakfasts in the Austin area.

In the reviews that follow, the **Very Expensive** category covers
hotels that charge over $160 for a double room, not including tax
(13%); **Expensive** means you'll pay from $110 to $160; **Moderate**
rooms run from $60 to $110; and you'll get away for under $60 if
you stay in an **Inexpensive** place.

1 Downtown

Very Expensive

Four Seasons Austin, 98 San Jacinto Blvd., Austin, TX 78701.
☎ **512/478-4500** or toll free **800/332-3442.** Fax 512/478-3117.
251 rms, 28 suites. A/C TV TEL

Rates: $145–$178 single; $167–$203 double ($122–$170 single or
double on weekends); $198–$1,100 suite. Packages available. AE, CB,
DC, DISC, MC, V. **Parking:** $3 self, $8 valet.

Queen Elizabeth, Prince Charles, and King Philip of Spain have all
bedded down—at different times—at this, the most luxe of the luxe
hotels on Town Lake, but you don't have to be royalty to be treated
that way at the Four Seasons. Can't be parted from your pooch? Bring
him along; you can treat him to German Shepherds Pie from a special room service menu for pets and get a bellman to trot him around
the grounds after dinner. Your taste in animals runs to the more
exotic? Still no sweat. A group of Busch Gardens penguins were given
their own room, its bathtub constantly replenished with ice.

But while you revel in posh European-type treatment, you won't
forget you're in Texas: Polished sandstone floors, a cowhide sofa, horn
lamps, and an elk head hanging over the fireplace lend the lobby a
Hill Country ranch-house look. Elegant guest rooms also have southwestern touches, with Native American patterned bedspreads,
leatherette headboards, and light-wood furnishings. Not all are as
enormous as the Presidential Suite where the queen slept, but you'll
have plenty of space to stretch out. The city views are fine, but the
ones of the lake are prime.

Those inclined toward self-punishment can indulge at one
of the best health clubs in town, gratis (you can't use the old
"I-forgot-my-workout-clothes" excuse here; the hotel will lend guests
shorts and T-shirts). More sybaritic types might depart the premises
with that polished, pampered glow brought on by one of the myriad
masks, massages, and wraps on offer at the spa.

Dining/Entertainment: Order snacks and drinks by the pool or
gaze out at the lake over cocktails in the Lobby Lounge, which serves
hors d'oeuvres from midday until the wee hours. You'll get the same
idyllic vista from the windows or patio of the excellent Café (see the
"Hotel Dining" section of Chapter 13); some of the best bat watching in the city draws diners to vie for seating at dusk.

Services: 24-hour room service and concierge service, 24-hour
security rounds, valet laundry/dry cleaning (including emergency
two-hour service), physician on call.

Facilities: Health club/spa, Jacuzzi, saunas, pool, gift shop.

Guest Quarters Suite Hotel, 303 W. 15th St., Austin, TX 78701.
☎ **512/478-4000** or toll free **800/424-2900.** Fax 512/478-5103.
189 suites, including 14 2-bedroom suites. A/C TV TEL

Rates: $145 single; $165 double; $235 two-bedroom suite. Corporate rates, extended-stay rates available. AE, DC, DISC, MC, V. **Parking:** $6 self or valet.

Lobbyists sock in for winter legislative sessions at this tony all-suites high-rise, a stone's throw from the State Capitol; in summer, the Dallas Cowboys, in town for training camp at St. Edward's University, touch down in some of the rooms. It would be hard to find more comfortable temporary quarters: At 625 square feet, the standard one-bedroom suites are larger than many New York apartments.

All are decorated in tasteful contemporary style, with blue or gray carpets, floral bedspreads, rattan-style chairs, cushy sofas, and large mirrored closets; baths are spacious, too. Many rooms have balconies with capitol views. Full-sized refrigerators, toasters, stoves, coffeemakers, and cookware allow guests to prepare meals in comfort; unlike kitchens in many all-suite hotels, those here are separate, so you don't have to stare at dirty dishes—washed by the maid every day—after you eat. For folks who don't like to cook on vacation (or ever), there's also 24-hour room service. You'll get a fresh supply of coffee every day and, if you request it, a newspaper delivered to your door during the week.

Dining/Entertainment: For hearty seafood, Tex-Mex, or steak, dine indoors or out at the white tableclothed 15th Street Cafe, serving three meals a day. You can sink your teeth (and your diet) in a Texas Reuben—the usual, plus jalepeños—at the more casual adjoining lounge.

Services: Valet laundry/dry cleaning, safe-deposit boxes, complimentary hotel shuttle within two-mile radius, pets allowed in some suites, secretarial services and babysitting available.

Facilities: Heated outdoor pool, sundeck, whirlpool, saunas, exercise room, coin-operated laundry, guest library.

Hyatt Regency Austin on Town Lake, 208 Barton Springs Rd., Austin TX 78704. ☎ **512/477-1234** or toll free **800/233-1234.** Fax 512/480-2069. 429 rms, 17 suites. A/C TV TEL

Rates: $135–$160 single; $160–$185 double; $250–$650 suite. Weekend specials, corporate and state-government rates available. AE, CB, DC, DISC, MC, V. **Parking:** Free self, $5 valet.

Austin's Hyatt Regency brings the outdoors in—its signature atrium lobby is anchored by a Hill Country–type tableau of limestone-banked flowing stream, waterfalls, and oak trees. It's impressive all right, but the genuine item outside is more striking still: Because the hotel sits on Town Lake's south shore, its watery vistas have stunning city backdrops.

Although the Hyatt is just minutes from downtown, outdoor recreation makes the hotel tick. Bat tours depart from a private dock, which also rents paddleboats and canoes. Guests can borrow mountain bikes to ride on the hike-and-bike trail, right outside the door. To add to the family appeal, the Hyatt has set aside various play areas for children and offers supervised camp activities; see the "Cool for Kids" insert, below, for details.

All the accommodations, newly redecorated in western denims, plaids, and oak, have desks, hair dryers, ironing boards, and irons; special business plan rooms offer fax machines and two-line phones, along with access to computer printers, copy machines, and office supplies. Gold Passport Floors for frequent travelers provide coffee and tea areas and newspaper delivery to rooms.

Dining/Entertainment: Townies as well as hotel guests come to the casual La Vista restaurant for its great fajitas; see the "Hotel Dining" section in Chapter 13 for details. The atrium's Branchwater Lounge was recently hooked up to La Vista's kitchen, so you can order from its menu or, in the evening, just enjoy a drink to the accompaniment of country-and-western music. Lots of photographers take their best shot from the Foothills Restaurant, a romantic lounge with a focus on steak and a forever view of Town Lake and the downtown Austin skyline.

Services: Room service, laundry/valet, concierge, staff fluency in French, German, Spanish.

Facilities: Fitness room, outdoor pool, whirlpool, newsstand, drugstore, gift shop.

Frommer's Smart Traveler: Hotels

Value-Conscious Travelers Should Take Advantage of the Following:

1. Substantially lower prices on the weekends at most hotels, and lower prices Sunday through Thursday at most bed-and-breakfasts. If you don't mind changing rooms once, you can get the best of both discount worlds.

2. Chain hotels. Austin has a lot of low-end properties running along I-35; many offer free continental breakfasts, free local phone calls, and other money-saving extras.

3. Car-rental and airline packages, AAA and AARP discounts.

Questions to Ask if You're on a Budget:

1. Is there a parking charge? Though prices for leaving your car in Austin are not as high as they are in some cities, fees can still add up here.

2. Is there an extra cost for children? Some chains, such as Hilton, don't charge for offspring, no matter what age. Others allow children under 18 or 12 to stay free in the same room as their parents.

3. Is there a lower price for an extended stay? Some bed-and-breakfasts offer discounts to those who book for at least four days.

Downtown Austin Accommodations

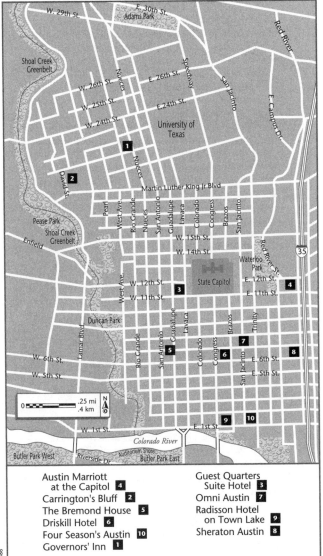

Austin Marriott at the Capitol **4**	Guest Quarters Suite Hotel **3**
Carrington's Bluff **2**	Omni Austin **7**
The Bremond House **5**	Radisson Hotel on Town Lake **9**
Driskill Hotel **6**	Sheraton Austin **8**
Four Season's Austin **10**	
Governors' Inn **1**	

9586

Omni Austin, 700 San Jacinto Blvd., Austin, TX 78701.
☎ **512/476-3700** or toll free **800/THE-OMNI.** Fax 512/320-5882. 304 rms, 26 suites. A/C TV TEL
Rates: $155 single; $175 double; $180–$230 suite. Weekend and summer specials available. AE, CB, DC, DISC, MC, V. **Parking:** Free self, $8 valet.

Stay at the Omni and you can have a suit custom-made or rent a tuxedo without stepping outdoors: The hotel shares space with tony shops and offices at the ultramodern Austin Center complex, including a jeweler, art gallery, travel agent, and hairdresser.

The lobby's spectacular 200-foot rise of sunstruck glass and steel makes one feel simultaneously dwarfed and exhilarated. Brass elevators ascend to extra-large guest quarters with Louis XV- and Empire-style furnishings and polished parquet floors; warm wine tones predominate. Each room has a sitting area, marble desk, and spacious bath with a full-length mirror. Omni Club rooms on the 13th and 14th floors offer such upgraded amenities as terry-cloth robes, scales, hair dryers, and makeup mirrors. The complimentary continental breakfast and afternoon hors d'oeuvres and cocktails are all par for an executive-level course, but you're also treated here to the ultimate bedtime comfort snack: fresh-baked cookies and milk.

It'd be tough to beat the views from the Omni's rooftop pool, perched 20 stories high. You can also bask on the adjoining sundeck or soak in the Jacuzzi while gazing out over the city.

Dining/Entertainment: An outdoor menu lets you order snacks upstairs by the pool, but the rest of the hotel's eating and entertainment are grounded on the lobby level. You can listen to piano music nightly at the Atrium Lounge, or throw darts in Billiards, which is part English pub, part American sports bar. New Texas cuisine is featured at the hotel's full service restaurant, Anchos. It's pretty posh for a public place.

Services: Room service, valet/laundry service, business center services available, complimentary airport van.

Facilities: Pool, sundeck, Jacuzzi, exercise room, sauna, shops, car-rental agency.

Sheraton Austin, I.H. 35 and Sixth Street, Austin TX 78701. ☎ **512/480-8181** or toll free **800/325-3535.** Fax 512/462-0660. 242 rms, 7 suites. A/C TV TEL

Rates: $149 single; $169 double; $325 suite. Weekend specials, summer specials, holiday-saver rates available. AE, CB, DC, DISC, MC, V. **Parking:** Free.

Austin's Sheraton, although well located near the convention center and the Sixth Street entertainment district, suffers from multiple personalities. A marble-and-brass lobby, bustling with activity, is separated from a hushed skylit atrium rising from the 10th floor. The latter, done in Roman neoclassical style with a central fountain, is attractive, and the arrangement blocks entry-level noise from the guest rooms, but there's something about the soaring space that doesn't invite lingering. The area can be disconcertingly deserted during the day.

Then there are the English/European–style rooms, beautifully furnished with Queen Anne and Chippendale Drexel Heritage pieces—and southwestern touches. Deluxe suites are similarly decked out, but enjoy an extra bedroom and a Jacuzzi in each bath. Windows look out onto the atrium or the exterior, which could mean the highway, unless you specify otherwise. It's back to ancient Rome at the health club, where a 25-person hot tub needs only toga-clad attendants to complete the hedonistic picture.

Dining/Entertainment: This aspect of the hotel is similarly schizy: The lobby bar is appropriately cushy, but you'd expect an ITT Sheraton to have a fine-dining room, and this one doesn't. The romantic city views afforded by the 18th-floor, full-service restaurant aren't as well served as they could be by the casual, collegiate-type fare.

Services: Room service, valet laundry/dry cleaning.

Facilities: Outdoor pool, exercise room, steam bath, massage room.

Expensive

Austin Marriott at the Capitol, 701 E. 11th St., Austin, TX 78701. ☎ **512/478-1111** or toll free **800/228-9290.** Fax 512/478-3700. 365 rms, 12 suites. A/C TV TEL

Rates: $145 single; $155 double; $180 suite. Weekend packages available. AE, CB, DC, DISC, MC, V. **Parking:** Free, covered.

There are advantages to staying at any Marriott: frequent-flyer miles for each visit, upgraded rooms for repeat guests, and a guarantee that you'll be checked in within 10 minutes. The advantages to staying at the Marriott in Austin include a convenient downtown location and such perks as complimentary parking and airport shuttle, half-price meals at the restaurant for kids under 12 (3 and under eat free), and an iron in every room. Three-day advance booking and weekend deals lower the rates here considerably.

The walls of windows on the atrium levels of the blocky 16-story building lend the public areas an open, airy look. Rooms, done in light green and burgundy with standard hotel florals, also feel unconfined; the ones on the higher floors have terrific city views and those on the west side all look out on the State Capitol, four blocks away. Booking a room on the concierge floor will get you mineral water, plants, and an electric shoe-shine machine in your room, along with newspaper delivery and access to a lounge where a continental breakfast and afternoon hors d'oeuvres are on the house.

Dining/Entertainment: Come to the casual Cafe Caribbean for suds, sandwiches, and satellite dishes; the Marriott's sports lounge boasts two pool tables and TVs that broadcast games from around the world. In the evening, you can also drink in the lobby lounge. The skylit Cafe Veranda is the hotel's main restaurant, serving somewhat southwestern American and continental fare indoors and out.

Services: Room service, valet/laundry service.

Facilities: Indoor/outdoor pool, Jacuzzi, sauna, exercise room, gift shop, guest washer and dryer, video arcade.

⭐ **Driskill Hotel,** 604 Brazos St., Austin TX 78701.
☎ **512/474-5911** or toll free **800/527-2008** (U.S.) or **800/252-9367** (Texas only). Fax 512/474-2214. 160 rms, 15 suites. A/C TV TEL

Rates: $109–$119 single; $119–$129 double; suites $200 and up. Corporate and weekend rates and various packages available. AE, CB, DC, DISC, MC, V. **Parking:** $4 self, $6 valet.

Lyndon Johnson holed up here during the final days of his presidential campaign, anxiously awaiting the election results. Texas governor Ann Richards held her inaugural ball at the Driskill, and the hotel hosted Tommy Lee Jones's wedding reception. The Daughters of the Republic of Texas gathered here to decide the fate of the Alamo, and Texas lawmen met to set an ambush for Bonnie and Clyde. Since 1886, cattle baron Jesse Driskill has perched on a column atop his grand hotel, literally stone-faced, surveying it all.

Never mind that the magnificent halls of Austin's only historic hotel are a tad shabby: When you travel back through Texas's bygone eras on one of the hotel's free guided tours, you'll forget about any peeling paint. Moreover, the guest rooms—100 of them in a 1930s addition, the rest in the original structure—are beautifully maintained; some boast the original 19th-century furnishings, others have lovely 1930s reproductions. All have modern amenities, including large working desks and phones with modem capability, and are conveniently arranged with sinks and mirrors outside the bathroom area.

Dining/Entertainment: Adjoining the hotel's cushy piano bar (see Chapter 16, "Austin Nights"), the Driskill Bar and Grill looks like a ladies' tearoom; one would expect to find watercress sandwiches here, not chicken-fried steak and other southwestern grill fare (lighter meals like salad and pasta are also available). If you want your meals served up with murder, book a place at the hotel's Mystery Dinner Theater, held every alternating weekend. A dine-around arrangement with five local restaurants lets you eat out and bill the meals to your room.

Services: Room service, valet dry-cleaning/laundry service; Gold's Gym privileges for $5.

Facilities: Florist, men's clothing boutique, hairdresser, airlines ticket office in lobby.

Embassy Suites Downtown Austin, 300 S. Congress Ave., Austin, TX 78704. ☎ **512/469-9000** or toll free **800/EMBASSY.** Fax 512/480-9164. 261 suites. A/C TV TEL

Rates: $129 single or double during the week, $105 weekends. AE, CB, DC, DISC, MC, V. **Parking:** Free.

Spacious, well-equipped Embassy Suites are generally a good deal for those traveling on business or with families, and this link in the national chain has a great location to boot. It's a straight shot north from the property to the State Capitol, and only a few blocks west to the row of restaurants on Barton Springs Road. And when you step outside the hotel's door, you're only a few minutes on foot from the Town Lake hike-and-bike trail (you can rent a bike from the front desk for $5 a day).

All the attractive, modern accommodations have two TVs, two telephones, a microwave, refrigerator, wet bar, coffeemaker and coffee supplies, full-size ironing boards and irons, and hair dryers; living rooms feature queen-size sleeper sofas along with well-lighted work areas. About a third of the suites look out on downtown, the lake, and the hills. The open atrium arrangement of the rooms is its own security system, but the hotel also offers 24-hour security escort service around the grounds. On top of all this, Embassy Suites has a hard-to-beat guarantee policy: You don't pay if you're not satisfied. Chances are they don't lose any money on the deal at this property.

Dining/Entertainment: The free full breakfast is one of the hotel's draws: Cooked-to-order eggs, pancakes, and other griddle fare go along with a fresh fruit, cereal, and baked-goods buffet in the morning. From 5:30 to 7:30pm, it's complimentary cocktails and wine or beer with unlimited popcorn and chips. If you don't want to drink your dinner, drop in at the Capital City Bistro, where you can order from a limited Pizza Hut menu.

Services: Room service, complimentary transportation to the airport and the downtown business district, complimentary newspapers.

Facilities: Pool, whirlpool, sauna, exercise room, guest laundry, gift shop, video-game room.

Moderate

Holiday Inn Austin Town Lake, 200 N. I.H.-35, Austin, TX 78701. ☎ **512/472-8211** or toll free **800/HOLIDAY.** Fax 512/472-4636. 319 rms. A/C TV TEL
Rates: $89–$109 single; $99–$119 double. Weekend and holiday rates available. AE, CB, DC, DISC, MC, V. **Parking:** Free.

The most upscale Holiday Inn in Austin, this high-rise is also the best situated: it's on the north shore of Town Lake, at the edge of downtown and just off I-35. Guest rooms underwent a major renovation in 1994 and appear spanking new and stylish, with simulated brick walls, light-wood furniture, and southwestern patterns; the ones looking out on Town Lake are the most expensive. Fifty of the accommodations have additional sofa sleepers; since children under 18 are free, that can translate into real family savings. Rooms on the executive level offer robes, hair dryers, and coffeemakers. A rooftop pool large enough for laps affords fine lake views.

Dining/Entertainment: Pistachio's sports bar and lounge holds its happy-hour specials from 5 to 7pm; you can watch the games here or shoot some pool. Monday through Friday, breakfast and lunch at the Pecan Tree Restaurant are all-you-can eat bargains; dinner is served here, too.

Services: Room service, valet dry cleaning during the week, complimentary airport transportation.

Facilities: Exercise room, outdoor heated pool, sundeck, sauna, whirlpool, gift shop, coin-operated guest laundry.

$ **Radisson Hotel on Town Lake,** 11 E. First St., Austin, TX 78701. ☎ **512/478-9611** or toll free **800/333-3333.** Fax 512/478-3227. 259 rms, 24 suites. A/C TV TEL

Rates: $95 single; $105 double; $125 suite. Corporate, family, and weekend rates available. AE, CB, DC, DISC, MC, V. **Parking:** Free.

A lower-priced alternative to the downtown luxury high-rises, the Radisson offers its guests a prime Town Lake location along with many of the perks of the pricier properties (among them, free newspaper delivery and coffeemakers in all the rooms). "Shades of summer" and supersaver rates can bring prices down as low as $69. From the airy, open lobby, with its potted palms and patterned rug, to pleasant rooms decorated in shades of turquoise or peach, the ambience is light and cheery. The lakeside views are the most sought after, but the ones of the capitol are not to be scoffed at.

Dining/Entertainment: One of Austin's favorite bat-watching venues, TGIF's upholds the tradition of the national chain for hearty collegiate food—chicken wings, burgers, pizza—and general rowdiness. A cozy dark-wood lounge is a bit quieter, but the Radisson caters to conventioneers, so don't expect a romantic getaway.

Services: Room service, valet laundry/dry cleaning, complimentary airport transfers and transportation within four-mile radius of hotel.

Facilities: Outdoor pool, exercise room, gift shop.

Youth Hostel

Austin International AYH Hostel, 2200 S. Lakeshore Blvd., Austin, TX 78741. ☎ **512/444-2294.** 40 beds in 3 dorms and 1 private rm.

Rates: $12 dorm for AYH members, $3 additional for nonmembers; $26 double private room for members, $3 additional for nonmembers. MC, V.

Youth- and nature-oriented Austin goes all out for its hostelers at this winning facility, located on the hike-and-bike trail, with a glass-fronted common room overlooking Town Lake. The hostel organizes inexpensive day trips (one to New Braunfels for rafting, for example) and drops visitors off in the downtown area at night; by summer 1995, a van for airport and train station pick ups should be in place. Facilities include a TV room, laundry room, kitchen, and a small store selling such things as sleep sacks and hosteling books. The building, which once served as a boathouse, is solar paneled and—shades of the 1960s—the dorms offer waterbeds (solid mattresses are available, too).

Bed & Breakfasts

The Bremond House, 404 W. Seventh St., Austin, TX 78701. ☎ 512/482-0411. 2 rms with private bath, 2 rms share 1 bath, 2 suites with private bath. A/C TV TEL

Rates (including breakfast): $104 room with private bath, $94 shared bath; $110–$135 suite, $5 less for single occupancy. Business rates available during the week. AE, MC, V.

A black wrought-iron fence guards the grand Italianate home built by financier Eugene Bremond in 1873; guests staying at what is now a bed-and-breakfast can step beyond it to see how the other half lived in the late 19th century. This was one of the first houses in Austin to install indoor plumbing; the pipes have been replaced, but a number of the original claw-foot tubs remain.

Owners David and Vicki Bell put their own imprint on this beautifully maintained place by bringing in original artwork and fine European antiques—all the guest rooms boast beautiful four-poster beds, for example—but this is no hands-off shrine to the past; guests might wander into the kitchen and chat with Vicki while she prepares fresh-baked biscuits, sausage, and french toast for breakfast (she's also happy to accommodate special dietary needs). Weather permitting, the morning repast may be taken on a lovely covered porch looking out on ancient live oak trees. A separate carriage house offers two spacious suites, one with a kitchen and both with private entrances.

Fairview, 1304 Newning Ave., Austin, TX 78704. ☎ **512/444-4746** or toll free **800/310-4746.** 3 rms, 1 suite, 2 suites with kitchen (all with private bath). A/C TV TEL

Rates (including breakfast-and-afternoon refreshments): $89–$99 single or double; $109–$129 suite. Discounts for stays of four nights or longer available. AE, CB, DC, MC, V.

In 1886, Fairview Park was developed as a posh residential subdivision, its bluffs less susceptible to flooding than the lower ground north of the river. Such stately homes as Duke and Nancy Waggoner's Colonial Revival mansion, only minutes from downtown by car, attest to the area's cachet.

After buying it in 1991, the Waggoners spent a year refurbishing the place, and the results are impressive, indeed; the house received an award from the Austin Heritage Society for its impeccable preservation. The furnishings the couple brought into it are equally outstanding; serious antiques freaks, the Waggoners can tell you the provenance of every item in their gracious guest accommodations—four of them in the main house, two in a carriage house set off from a rose arbor out back. Breakfast here is an elaborate affair that might include stuffed french toast garnished with fresh fruit. Local Texas wines are brought out to accompany afternoon snacks. The imperious Sasha, a long-haired, domesticated alley cat, entertains guests throughout the day.

Ziller House, 800 Edgecliff Terrace, Austin, TX 78704. ☎ **512/462-0100** or toll free **800/949-5446.** Fax 512/462-9166. 3 rms, 1 suite (all with private bath). A/C TV TEL

Rates (including breakfast): $110 single, double, or suite. AE, MC, V.

Ziller House could bill itself as "Bed-and-Breakfast to the Stars," but it's far too discreet to do anything of the sort. Which is why this wooded retreat on a rise overlooking the south shore of Town Lake has hosted the likes of Lyle Lovett and Julia Roberts—yes, at the same time—Clint Eastwood, Walter Cronkite, and Al Gore. Although you might bump into them in the hallways, don't expect to rub elbows with the celebs around a cozy breakfast table: quiches, frittatas, and other gourmet goodies cooked up in the afternoon are placed in an in-room refrigerator, to be heated in an accompanying microwave the next morning.

Originally the headquarters for Austin's Humane Society, which was founded by the somewhat eccentric Zillers, this 1928 Italianate mansion was built without doors so animals could roam through it freely. Now only Alexander Magnus, a lion-faced Shar Pei dog belonging to Sam Kindred and Wendy Sandberg, holds sway here, and the house has come under his owners' civilizing influence. A rustic stone-and-fossil fireplace in the living room is set off by a meltingly supple green leather sofa, jade miniature peach tree, and intricately carved emperor's chairs. Guest rooms, many with the original art deco fixtures, are individually decorated in the best of eclectic taste right down to the last detail without being overly fussy; original artwork from local galleries is rotated every six months.

2 North University/Hyde Park

Bed & Breakfasts

⭐ **The Brook House,** 609 W. 33rd St., Austin, TX 78705. ☎ **512/459-0534.** 2 rms, cottage and carriage house (all with private bath). A/C TV TEL

Rates (including breakfast): $69 single or double (rooms); $79 (cottage and carriage house). Lower weekday rates available Sun–Thurs. AE, CB, DC, DISC, MC, V.

Colorado-born Barbara Love has a smile as wide as the river that runs through her home state; she and her Labrador Ernie extend a warm welcome to guests at this comfortable bed-and-breakfast. The 1922 colonial revival–style home near the university used to be a crash pad; chances are that Janis Joplin, who lived in the area in the 1960s, dropped in now and then. Although it's been a respectable bed-and-breakfast since 1985, the Brook House has still got good vibes.

The main house contains the romantic Rose Room, with lace curtains and a claw-foot tub, as well as the sunny Blue Room, featuring a mahogany four-poster and a private screened porch. The separate cottage and carriage house, both offering kitchen facilities, private entrances, and TVs, are roomy, antiques-filled bargains. On nice days, a full breakfast—lots of fresh-baked goods, fruit, juices, and a hot dish—is served outside on the peaceful covered patio.

Carrington's Bluff, 1900 David St., Austin, TX 78705. ☎ and fax **512/479-0638.** 6 rms with private baths, 2 rms share 1 bath. A/C TV TEL

Rates (including breakfast): $55–$80 single; $60–$85 double. $10 less Sun–Thurs, except holidays. AE, CB, DC, DISC, MC, V.

The acreage of the lot on which this 1877 farmhouse stands may have dwindled from 22 down to one over the years, but Carrington's Bluff still has a bucolic atmosphere. A manicured front lawn, shade trees, a rambling 35-foot porch, and a pretty gazebo all add to the sense of one's having entered a more leisurely, genteel world.

Hosts Gwen and David Fullbrook help sustain the impression, she with her native Texas hospitality, he with his native English civility and wit. The house itself is decorated in a pleasing mix of contemporary country patterns and dark-wood antiques; florals predominate, but this place feels relaxed rather than precious. After breakfast—a spread of fresh fruit, low-fat yogurt, homemade granola, and an egg dish if desired—guests are welcome to use the kitchen anytime. Convenient to the university and the Capitol, Carrington's Bluff draws a lot of satisfied repeat visitors, including the various wordsmiths who have had rooms in the separate Writer's Cottage named after them.

Governors' Inn, 611 W. 22nd St., Austin, TX 78705.

☎ **512/477-0711.** 10 rms (one a single), all with private bath. A/C TEL

Rates (including breakfast): $55 single room; $69–$99 other rooms. $10 less Sun–Thurs, except holidays, $5 less for single occupancy of double rooms. AE, CB, DC, DISC, MC, V.

The Fullbrooks, who own Carrington's Bluff (see above), more recently acquired the Governors' Inn. Although the two properties share a spirit of hospitality—maintained here by a personable resident manager—they have distinct personalities. This 1897 neo-classical residence is more spacious but feels citified, in part because it's only two blocks from the busy U.T. campus.

Guest rooms, named for long dead and thus noncontroversial governors of Texas, are a bit more formal, too, decorated in Laura Ashley or Ralph Lauren prints and boasting good antique pieces. Rooms vary quite a bit in size and layout; most are reasonably large, but this bed-and-breakfast also harbors that rarity, a real single. It's little but not claustrophic; in fact, all the accommodations are nice and light. Three rooms open directly onto a covered porch, and the rest have access to it. Breakfast, which might include pancakes or eggs Benedict, is served on lace-clothed tables in two sunny breakfast chambers.

The McCallum House, 613 W. 32nd St., Austin, TX 78705.

☎ and fax **512/451-6744.** 3 rms, 2 suites (all with private bath). A/C TV TEL

Rates (including breakfast): $65 single room, $75 double room weekends and holidays; $85 single suite, $95 double suite weekends and holidays. All rooms and suites $10 less Sun–Thurs; extended-stay discounts during the week, monthly rates available. MC, V.

In 1907, Jane Y. McCallum took time out from tending five children and leading the Texas Women's Suffrage Movement to design this appealingly eclectic house—part Queen Anne, part early Craftsman. Nancy and Roger Danley didn't have quite so much on their plates when they bought and refurbished the place, but they did make modest history by opening it up to the public in 1983 as the first bed-and-breakfast in Austin. They also achieved recognition for their fine restoration.

As befits a home intended for a large family, the McCallum House is comfortable and unpretentious, with wall-to-wall carpeting in the guest quarters. The accommodations seem more like intimate apartments than temporary lodgings:Each room has its own kitchen, telephone with answering machine, desk, clock radio, and color TV; four out of five also have private porches that look out onto a front lawn graced by old pecans, oaks, and elms. These amenities, along with the peaceful residential setting and proximity to the university, make this inn especially popular with visiting academics.

Woodburn House, 4401 Ave. D, Austin, TX 78705.
☎ **512/458-4335.** 4 rms with private bath. A/C TEL

Rates (including breakfast): $55–$65 single; $68–$78 double. Corporate and monthly rates available. No credit cards.

Herb and Sandra Dickson's late Victorian home couldn't look more firmly rooted; one would be hard-pressed to guess that, in danger of being bulldozed in 1980, it was jacked up, loaded on a flatbed trailer, and shifted from its original location six blocks away. Now settled in as the only bed-and-breakfast in Hyde Park, the Woodburn House is not only a delightful place to stay, but also a prime source of information about the historic neighborhood.

The inn itself speaks volumes about the first decade of the 20th century, the era in which it was built: Lustrous moldings made of Louisiana long-leaf pine, hardwood floors, and a built-in corner cabinet recall an age of meticulous attention to detail. Such original attributes are complemented throughout by American period antiques handed down over the years by the Dickson family. Breakfasts are designed to be heart healthy, though you'd never know it: Strawberry-filled crêpes topped with yogurt, apple-cinnamon pancakes, or a Mexican casserole might turn up on any given morning, along with delicious home-baked bread.

3 The Airport Area

Expensive

Austin North Hilton and Towers, 6000 Middle Fiskville Rd., Austin, TX 78752. ☎ **512/451-5757** or toll free **800/347-0330** or **800/HILTONS** (reservations). Fax 512/467-7644. 237 rms, 3 suites. A/C TV TEL

Rates: $109–$129 single; $119–$139 double; $235–$290 suite. Weekend specials available. AE, CB, DC, DISC, MC, V. **Parking:** Free.

This airport-area property, Austin's first convention hotel, is a bit of a surprise: A blocky, nondescript exterior gives no hint of the gracious public areas inside. The lobby was recently redone in a rustic, elegant Hill Country style, including hardwood floors, leather chairs, an antler chandelier, and a native-limestone reception desk. The pool area is a tree-shaded oasis in a concrete desert—but one where you can drop a lot of dough. The Hilton adjoins the shops, restaurants, and movie theaters of the Highland Mall, and is within walking distance of the tonier Lincoln Village.

Rooms have been beautifully redecorated with plush teal or mint rugs, delicately striped bedspreads, and tastefully contrasting floral drapes and chairs; all are large and some have vaulted ceilings. Designed for business travelers, they also have oversized desks and two telephones. A concierge-key level offers the usual amenities—continental breakfast, evening hors d'oeuvres, and an honor bar—in an unusually homey lounge.

Dining/Entertainment: The Sausalito Lounge is the hotel's casual sports bar, offering different hot appetizers each night—nachos, potato skins, you name it. For more substantial fare, the Baja Grille offers breakfast-and-lunch buffets and dinners with a southwestern theme.

Services: Room service, valet laundry/dry cleaning, complimentary airport transfers, World Gym privileges for $5.

Facilities: Exercise room, outdoor pool, gift shop.

Doubletree Hotel Austin, 6505 N. I.H.-35, Austin, TX 78752.
☎ **512/454-3737** or toll free **800/222-TREE.** Fax 512/454-6915. 330 rms, 20 suites. A/C TV TEL

Rates: $139 single; $159 double; $170–$230 suite. Corporate, weekend rates; romance package available. AE, CB, DC, DISC, MC, V. **Parking:** Free.

Leisure travelers should take advantage of the fact that prices plummet on weekends at Austin's Doubletree, another tony business-oriented hotel near the airport. Once you step inside, you'll feel as though you're in a private luxury property rather than a chain lodging just off the freeway. The reception lobby has polished Mexican-tile floors and carved-wood ceiling beams; an adjoining colonnade boasts a massive cherry hutch and other antiques from Mexico, along with 19th-century English wall tapestries. There's even a first-floor gallery featuring local artists.

In keeping with the hacienda theme, rooms are arranged around a lushly landscaped courtyard, dotted with umbrella-shaded tables. Writing desks and separate sitting areas allow business to be conducted comfortably in the spacious guest quarters, which are decorated in earth tones and feature French doors, floral tapestry chairs, and stenciled borders. An upgrade to the concierge floor will get you extra room amenities, as well as free continental breakfast and afternoon hors d'oeuvres. Wherever you stay, you needn't walk very far to reach your car; all the sleeping floors have direct access, via room key, to the parking garage.

Dining/Entertainment: Resembling the library of a large estate, the Courtyard Lounge sports a fireplace, large-screen TV, and pool table. Breakfast, lunch, and dinner are served at the Courtyard Cafe, overlooking multilevel waterscapes and profuse greenery; the evening menu is continental with a Texas flair. Incidentally, if you've never checked into a Doubletree, you're in for a treat: two large, chewy chocolate-chip cookies greet you upon arrival.

Services: Room service, same-day laundry and dry cleaning, complimentary shuttle within two-mile radius, including airport and Highland Mall, World Gym privileges for $5.

Facilities: Outdoor pool, whirlpool, volleyball court, exercise room, sauna, gift shop, art gallery.

Red Lion Hotel Austin Airport, 6121 N. I.H.-35, Austin, TX 78752. ☎ **512/323-5466** or toll free **800/547-8010.** Fax 512/453-1945. 300 rms, 4 suites. A/C TV TEL

Rates: $109 single; $119 double; $225–$300 suite. Spring value specials available. AE, CB, DC, DISC, MC, V. **Parking:** Free.

The West Coast–based Red Lion chain is known for its high-tone properties, and this one is no exception. A low-lit, carpeted lobby is decked out with large chandeliers, potted plants, and classical columns (though the elegant mood is somewhat broken by the presence of a large-screen TV).

Red Lions are also known for their roomy rooms, and the Austin hotel doesn't disappoint in that area, either. They're decorated in deep greens, burgundies, and beiges, with dark-wood furniture and framed oriental prints on the walls; each has an executive-size desk and conference table. One caveat: Corridors are creepily dim, even during the day.

Dining/Entertainment: You'll be reminded of the 1970s at Club Max, a popular disco replete with dance floor and DJ booth. That decade still give you the shudders? Just come in for happy hour; there's a copious complimentary hors d'oeuvres buffet for guests Wednesday to Friday. There are also buffets—though not free—at the lobby's Garden Terrace restaurant; if you don't feel like helping yourself, full à la carte menus are available for breakfast, lunch, and dinner.

Services: Room service, valet laundry/dry cleaning, complimentary airport and Highland Mall shuttle, World Gym privileges for $5.

Facilities: Exercise room, outdoor swimming pool, whirlpool, sauna, airline-ticket desk, gift shop.

Moderate

Courtyard by Marriott, 5660 N. I.H.-35, Austin, TX 78751. ☎ **512/458-2340** or toll free **800/321-2211.** Fax 512/458-8535. 186 rms, 12 suites. A/C TV TEL

Rates: $89 single; $99 double; $109 suite. Weekend and corporate rates available. AE, CB, DC, DISC, MC, V. **Parking:** Free.

A $2-million renovation in 1994 gave this Marriott a fresh, clean look, evident as soon as you enter the cheery, plant-filled lobby. Guest rooms are also light and attractive, with dusty rose decor, silk-flower arrangements, and silk ivy twining along the walls. They're comfortable and utilitarian, too: Each has a coffeemaker, iron and ironing board, hair dryer, nice-sized desk, cushy chairs or couch, and phone with an extra-long cord. Refrigerators are available upon request. An outdoor heated pool in the courtyard is surprisingly quiet, considering the hotel's off-highway location.

Dining/Entertainment: There's a breakfast buffet and evening cocktails with complimentary snacks (Monday to Saturday), but no full-service restaurant at this Marriott. However, a large number of eateries in the area will deliver directly to your room; the hotel can provide you with their menus.

Services: Free airport transfers.

Facilities: Exercise room, pool, complimentary guest laundry.

A number of chain hotels along the freeway north of the airport fall into the low end of the moderate price range. These include: **Drury Inn North,** 6511 N. I.H.-35, 78751 (☎ **512/467-9500** or toll free **800/325-8300;** pool); **Hampton Inn North,** 7619 N. I.H.-35, 78752 (☎ **512/452-3300;** pool); **Howard Johnson Plaza North,** 7800 N. I.H.-35, 78753 (☎ **512/836-8520;** pool, exercise room, restaurant, cocktail lounge, room service); **Holiday Inn Airport,** 6911 N. I.H.-35, 78752 (☎ **512/459-4251** or toll free **800/HOLIDAY;** pool, exercise room, restaurant, cocktail lounge, room service); **Holiday Inn Express,** 7622 N. I.H.-35, 78752 (☎ **512/467-1701** or toll free **800/HOLIDAY;** pool, cocktail lounge); **La Quinta Inn Highland Mall,** 5812 N. I.H.-35, 78751 (☎ **512/459-4381** or toll free **800/531-5900;** pool, restaurant, cocktail lounge); and **La Quinta Inn North,** 7100 N. I.H.-35, 78752 (☎ **512/452-9401** or toll free **800/531-5900;** pool).

Inexpensive

The following familiar names along I-35 offer rooms for under $60: **Best Western Chariot Inn,** 7300 N. I.H.-35, 78752 (☎ **512/452-9371** or toll free **800/228-9290;** pool, restaurant, cocktail lounge, room service); **Comfort Inn,** 7928 Gessner Dr., 78753 (☎ **512/339-7311;** pool, restaurant); **Days Inn North,** 8210 N. I.H.-35, 78753 (☎ **512/835-2200** or toll free **800/325-2525;** pool, restaurant, kitchenettes); **Drury Inn Highland Mall,** 919 Koenig Lane, 78751 (☎ **512/454-1144** or toll free **800/325-8300;** pool); **Econolodge,** 820 E. Anderson Lane, 78752 (☎ **512/835-4311;** pool); **Motel 6 Airport,** 5330 N. I.H.-35, 78751 (☎ **512/467-9111;** pool); **Motel 6 Central,** 8010 N. I.H.-35, 78753 (☎ **512/837-9890;** pool); **Motel 6 North,** 9420 N. I.H.-35, 78753 (☎ **512/339-6161;** pool); **Quality Inn Airport,** 909 E. Koenig Lane, 78751 (☎ **512/452-4200** or toll free **800/228-5151;** pool, cocktail lounge, exercise room); **Ramada North at Rundberg,** 9220 N. I.H.-35, 78752 (☎ **512/323-5466** or toll free **800/766-7060;** pool, restaurant, cocktail lounge); **Rodeway Inn Airport,** 5526 N. I.H.-35, 78751 (☎ **512/451-7001** or toll free **800/880-0709;** pool); **Super 8 Motel,** 6000 Middle Fiskville Rd., 78752 (☎ **512/467-8163** or toll free **800/800-8000;** pool, restaurant, room service); **Travelodge,** 8300 N. I.H.-35 (☎ **512/835-5050** or toll free **800/255-3050;** pool, kitchens).

4   South Austin

Expensive

Wyndham Austin Hotel at Southpark, 4140 Governor's Row, Austin, TX 78744. ☎ **512/448-2222** or toll free **800/433-2241** (U.S.) or **800/631-4200** (Canada). Fax 512/448-4744. 307 rms, 7 suites. A/C TV TEL

Rates: $119 single; $139 double; $79 single or double weekends; $239–$250 suite. AE, CB, DC, DISC, MC, V. **Parking:** Free.

Rising above the industrial sprawl south of Austin, the Wyndham primarily attracts a high-tech business trade. But you never know what unbuttoned types might turn up at this executive-style hotel; actor Dennis Hopper, rocker Ted Nugent, *L.A. Law*'s Jill Eikenberry, and baseball's Nolan Ryan have all stayed here at one time or another. Whoever you are, you can expect friendly and efficient service from a staff who actually seem happy you're here.

    Sleeping quarters are the picture of updated traditional taste, their dark-wood furnishings complemented by the deep blues, roses, and burgundies of the bedspreads and carpeting; all come with coffeemakers and desks and many offer comfortable ottomans. Open long hours, the Wyndham's health club stands out in a town where many hotels have only minimal exercise facilities; it includes a lap-length pool that's half in-, half out-of-doors, a whirlpool, a sauna, and an exercise room with a full array of aerobic equipment and weight machines.

Frommer's Cool for Kids: Hotels

Four Seasons Austin   (p. 162) Tell the reservations clerk that you're traveling with kids when you book a room here and you'll be automatically enrolled in the free amenities program: Age-appropriate snacks—cookies and milk for children under 10, popcorn and soda for those older than 10—along with various toys and games will be waiting for you when you arrive.

Hyatt Regency Austin on Town Lake   (p. 163) Probably the kid-friendliest place to stay in town, this hotel offers a playscape, including a jungle gym and a sandbox, near the pool, along with a variety of board games that can be checked out from the front desk. But the biggest small-fry benefit at the hotel is Camp Hyatt, a program of supervised activities geared for children three and up. Rates are $6.50 per hour for the first child, and only $1 more per hour for each additional child.

Embassy Suites Downtown Austin   (p. 168) Large quarters give children enough space to play at Embassy Suites, and the hotel's Town Lake location allows for lots of running around outside; there's also a video-game room on the first floor.

Dining/Entertainment: Everyone looks like they're having fun sitting around the sunken bar in the Lobby Lounge, chatting animatedly to the backdrop of an automatic piano. A more pensive mood might prevail at Sweetwater's Lounge on Tuesday through Thursday, when a blues singer often wails heartbreak songs. The skylit Onion Creek Grille, the hotel's full-service restaurant, serves breakfast and lunch in a casual setting that turns more formal when the candles and white tablecloths come out at night.

Services: Room service, valet laundry/dry cleaning, complimentary shoe-shine service, complimentary area transportation.

Facilities: Indoor/outdoor pool, exercise room, whirlpool, sauna, basketball court, newsstand/gift shop.

Moderate

Hawthorne Suites South, 4020 I.H.-35 South, Austin, TX 78704. ☎ 512/440-7722 or toll free **800/527-1133.** Fax 512/440-4815. 95 standard suites, 32 penthouse suites. A/C TV TEL

Rates: $99–$109 standard suites, single or double occupancy; $119 penthouse suites. Weekend specials, corporate rates available. **Parking:** Free.

If you want to settle in for a spell and get someone else to do your grocery shopping, Hawthorne Suites is a good way to go. Accommodations are set up like small studio apartments, with separate kitchens; penthouse suites offer bedrooms on two levels. Done in your basic southwestern pastels—peaches, teals, and beiges—accommodations are fairly generic, but pleasant enough all the same; many have fireplaces. Out-of-the-ordinary extras, including a tennis court and video rentals for in-room VCRs, also recommend this business-oriented chain; there are two additional properties in Austin, one near the airport, one in the northwest.

Dining/Entertainment: A complimentary continental breakfast buffet is laid out in the lobby every morning; the free drinks and light hors d'oeuvres are restricted to Monday through Thursday (5 to 7 pm).

Services: Valet laundry/dry cleaning, airport shuttle, business services, free newspaper.

Facilities: Pool, hot tub, sports court, Laundromat.

Inexpensive

A number of low-end chains have properties on I-35 south in the vicinity of Ben White Boulevard; more are likely to join them when a new airport is built in the area. For the time being, you can find cut-rate lodgings at: Best Western Seville Plaza Inn, 4323 S. I.H.-35, 78744 (☎ 512/447-5511 or toll free **800/528-1234;** pool, restaurant, cocktail lounge, room service); Best Western South, 3909 S. I.H.-35, 78741 (☎ **512/444-0531** or toll free **800/528-1234;** pool, restaurant); Days Inn South, 4420 S. I.H.-35, 78745 (☎ **512/441-9242** or toll free **800/325-2525;** pool, restaurant); La Quinta

Greater Austin Accommodations & Dining

ACCOMMODATIONS

Austin International
AYH Hostel **25**

Austin North Hilton
and Towers **4**

Barton Creek
Conference Resort **33**

The Brook House **12**

Courtyard by Marriott **8**

Doubletree Hotel Austin **6**

Embassy Suites
Downtown Austin **23**

Fairview **29**

Hawthorne Suites South **32**

Holiday Inn Austin
Town Lake **22**

Hyatt Regency Austin
on Town Lake **19**

The McCallum House **13**

Red Lion Hotel
Austin Airport **7**

Stouffer Austin Hotel **1**

Woodburn House **10**

Wyndham Austin Hotel
at Southpark **31**

Ziller House **24**

DINING

Chuy's **17**

Eastside Cafe **14**

Fonda San Miguel **9**

Green Pastures **27**

Güero's **30**

The Hula Hut **15**

Kim Phung **2**

La Vista **20** **4**

Magnolia Cafe **28**

Matt's El Rancho **26**

Mexico Tipico **21**

Mother's Cafe
& Garden **11**

Pappadeux **5**

Shady Grove **18**

Taj Palace **3**

Trattoria Grande **1**

Zoot **16**

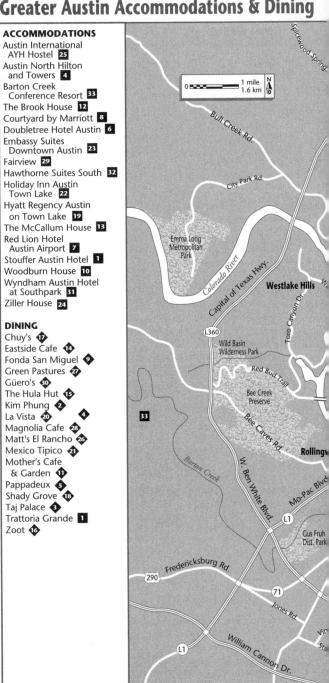

9587

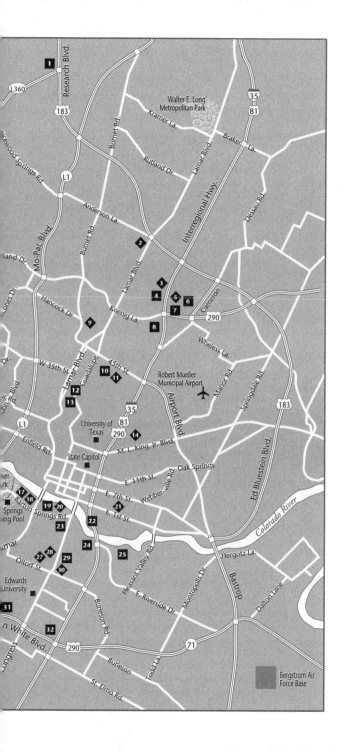

Inn Ben White, 4200 S. I.H.-35, 78745 (☎ **512/443-1774** or toll free **800/531-5900;** pool, restaurant); and Hotel 6 South, 2704 S. I.H.-35, 78741 (☎ **512/444-5882**; pool, restaurant).

5 Northwest Austin

Very Expensive

Stouffer Austin Hotel, 9721 Arboretum Blvd., Austin, TX 78759. ☎ **512/343-2626** or toll free **800/HOTELS-1.** Fax 512/346-7953. 467 rms, 99 suites. A/C TV TEL

Rates: $147–$167 single; $167–$187 double; $195–$275 suite. Weekend packages available. AE, CB, DC, DISC, MC, V. **Parking:** Free self, $7 valet.

Anchoring the upscale Arboretum mall on Austin's northwest side, the luxurious Stouffer caters to executives visiting the nearby computer firms. But on weekends, when rates are slashed nearly in half, even underlings can afford to take advantage of the hotel's many amenities, including an excellent health club and direct access to the myriad allures of the mall (movie theaters among them). Guests buzz around the eateries, elevator banks, and lounges of a nine-story-high atrium lobby, but the dramatic space is sufficiently large to avoid even the slightest sense of crowding.

Soothing shades of pale green, tan, and peach add to the understated elegance of oversized guest rooms, all with comfortable sitting areas: Silk wallpaper, lacquer chests, and Japanese-design draperies and bedspreads add an oriental flavor. Many of the suites offer refrigerators, wet bars, and electric shoe buffers. Rooms on the Club Floor include bathrobes and extended services such as express checkout; a concierge; and free continental breakfast and afternoon hors d'oeuvres. No matter where you stay, tell housekeeping what time you want to get up and a complimentary carafe of coffee and a newspaper will appear at your door immediately following your wake-up call.

Dining/Entertainment: Who knows what wheels of high-tech intrigue have been oiled in the hotel's clubby Lobby Bar, where cocktails are expertly mixed to the tunes of a live piano. Discussions can be fueled all night long at the nearby Pavillion, with a 24-hour menu of deli sandwiches, snacks, and desserts. Another place to chow down in the lobby is the Garden Cafe, offering a full breakfast-and-lunch menu. Upstairs, the northern Italian Trattoria Grande doubles as a power-lunch spot and a romantic evening retreat; see "Hotel Dining" in Chapter 13 for details. Business and leisure travelers alike are drawn to the happy hour and complimentary buffet at Tangerine's nightclub; many linger on to dance to music that spans the decades.

Services: 24-hour room service, same-day laundry Monday to Saturday, valet dry cleaning, complimentary shoe shine.

Facilities: Indoor-and-outdoor pools, exercise room, whirlpool, sauna, game room, access to jogging-and-walking trail, gift shop.

6 West Austin

Very Expensive

⭐ **Barton Creek Conference Resort,** 8212 Barton Club Dr., Austin, TX 78735. ☎ **512/329-4000** or toll free **800/336-6158.** Fax 512/329-4597. 147 rms, 4 suites. A/C TV TEL

Rates: $165 single; $180 double; $305–$680 suite. AE, CB, DC, DISC, MC, V. **Parking:** Free self or valet.

Sure it's a conference resort—the name even says so—but with three 18-hole championship golf courses, 12 outdoor tennis courts, and a state-of-the-art spa and fitness center, just how much work do you suppose actually gets done here, anyway? If you don't happen to be employed by a company that plans to send you, go ahead and book a room on your own; Barton Creek has put together a variety of golf-and-spa packages designed to draw individual travelers.

This place is gorgeous. Spread out over 4,000 gently rolling and wooded acres in west Austin, the hotel complex includes two main buildings resembling European châteaus. Both host accommodations as large and as high-toned as one might expect, with 10-foot ceilings, custom-made Drexel Heritage pieces, marble-topped sinks and vanities, and—that rarity in Texas—minibars. Some have balconies; rooms in the back offer superb views of the Texas Hill Country.

The resort's three courses were designed by a trinity of golf greats—Tom Fazio, Ben Crenshaw, and Arnold Palmer. The first two greens are on the premises, the latter on the stunning Lakeside satellite facility. Don't worry if your drive is not up to par; a Golf Advantage School can help set it straight. And although aromatherapy is among the featured treatments, Barton Creek's spa is nothing to sneeze at. You can get buffed, pummeled, and wrapped to your heart's content, or indulge in a one-hour pedicure.

Dining/Entertainment: Aside from the resorts two clubhouses, the Grille is the most relaxed place to replenish your fluids after a hard day of teeing off; it offers light meals, a large-screen TV, billiard table, and a liquor list as long as a pool cue. Generous breakfast-and-lunch buffets are laid on in the light-wood Terrace. The Tejas Room, serving southwestern cuisine, is the more informal of the two dinner restaurants; it's open for lunch, too. You'll dine to the dulcet tones of two harps at the ultraposh Palm Court, probably the only place in Austin that requires men to wear jackets; lots of table-side tossing and flambéing add drama to an otherwise staid atmosphere.

Services: Room service, same-day dry cleaning and pressing, complimentary newspaper delivery.

Facilities: Tennis clinic, indoor-and-outdoor pool, spa, hair salon, indoor track, steam room, Jacuzzi, weight room, aerobics, sauna, sporting clays, Ping-Pong, volleyball, jogging course.

Lakeway Inn, 101 Lakeway Dr., Austin, TX 78734.

☎ **512/261-6600** or toll free **800/LAKEWAY.** Fax 512/261-7322. 115 rms, 22 suites. A/C TV TEL

Rates: $160 rooms, double or single occupancy; $170 suites. Golf-packages available. AE, CB, DC, DISC, MC, V. **Parking:** Free.

Older and less glitzy than Barton Creek (see above), this golf-and-conference resort 18 miles northwest of Austin has two things its rival doesn't: a full-service marina and magnificent views of Lake Travis. The rooms may not be exciting—they're comfortably and predictably Southwest contemporary—but they all have balconies overlooking either the lake or the marina. Many folks bring their families; Lakeway is casual and has lots of room for kids to run around.

If it's water play you're after, this is the place to come: You can rent pontoons, runabouts, ski boats, wave-runners, fishing gear and guides—just about everything but sailboats and fish that promise to bite. Tennis buffs won't be disappointed either; Lakeway's 32-court complex, designed for indoor or outdoor, day or night games, was ranked among the top-25 facilities by *World Tennis* magazine; it has a pro shop with trainers and even a racquet-shaped swimming pool. Nor will golfers find anything to complain about: Two 18-hole championship courses dotted with oaks and junipers, creeks and canyons, provide challenging play for all levels. If you're up for instruction, the Jack Nicklaus–designed Academy of Golf can help you take your best shot.

Dining/Entertainment: Take some indoor R and R at Legends, a pub and a billiards room with a grill menu of burgers and sandwiches. The Travis Room, looking out on the lake and offering a rotating continental menu, is a bit more formal; you'll want to don your best shorts for dinner.

Services: Room service, valet laundry and dry cleaning; sunset cruises on weekends.

Facilities: Two outdoor pools, exercise room, spa, jogging-and-walking trails, shuffleboard, two golf pro shops, gift shop.

Bed & Breakfast

⭐ **Lake Travis B&B,** 4446 Bok Lane, Austin, TX 78734.

☎ and fax **512/266-3386** or toll free **800/484-9095.** 3 rms with private bath. A/C TV TEL

Rates (including breakfast and afternoon snacks): $95 single; $110 double. AE, MC, V.

Best described as a destination bed-and-breakfast, this inn gives its guests only two reasons to leave the premises: lunch and dinner. A former travel agent, host Judy Dwyer, and her husband, Vic, have designed a bed-and-breakfast that offers the advantages of a resort hotel in an intimate and dramatic setting. The limestone in the cliffs on which their seven-level property sits acts as a filter, rendering the water of Lake Travis directly off their private dock unusually transparent.

Rooms are romantic to the max: Each has a private lake-view deck and contains plush robes, fluffy comforters, and a marble tub, along with a welcome basket of fruit, Perrier, and nuts. A teddy bear holding a poem—a slightly over-the-top touch—announces that a tray with breakfast will arrive outside the door in the morning. But the best part of a stay here lies outdoors. Guests can play board games on a raised table in the pool, or descend to a floating dock with a kitchen, bar, and sundeck. Fishing, swimming, and snorkeling are all options, but if you want to sail, it's strictly BYOB (bring your own boat). Oh yes, there is one other incentive to stray from paradise: The Slaughter Leftwich Winery is just down the road, within easy staggering distance back after a wine tasting.

Services: Nightly chocolate-truffle turndown service.

Facilities: Fireplace, pool table, library with VCR and movies, hot tub, steam bath, massage available.

13

Austin Dining

YOU MIGHT EXPECT TO EAT WELL IN A TOWN WHERE LAWMAKERS SCHMOOZE power brokers, lobbyists try to oil squeaky legislative wheels, and academics can be tough culinary graders. With more restaurants per capita than any other city in the United States, Austin doesn't disappoint. Chic industrial spaces vie for diners' dollars with gracious 100-year-old houses and plant-filled hippie shacks. Inside, the food ranges from the stylish but reasonably priced cuisine dubbed "Nouveau Grub" by *Texas Monthly* magazine to tofu burgers, barbecue, and Mexican.

Many hip new restaurants are opening up downtown, where you can also enjoy a meal with a view of Town Lake. Fast-food and chain eateries are concentrated to the north off I-35, near the strip of airport hotels; to the east of the highway, in the vicinity of downtown, are many authentic Mexican places. Barton Springs Road, near Zilker Park; the Enfield area around Mo-Pac; Lake Austin, near the Tom Miller dam; and the tiny town of Bee Cave to the far west are also popular dining enclaves, but there's good food to be found in almost every part of town. Wherever you eat, think casual. The Palm Court at the Barton Creek Resort aside, there isn't a restaurant in town that requires men to put on a tie and jacket.

In the reviews that follow, dinner at a restaurant in the **Very Expensive** price category will run more than $40 per person, including dessert but not drinks, tax (8%), and tip (around 15%); at an **Expensive** eatery, an evening meal should cost up to $25. **Moderate** restaurant dinners will run $17.50 or under, while **Inexpensive** places shouldn't set you back more than $10.

1   Downtown

Expensive ───────────────────────────

Dan McKlusky's, 301 E. Sixth St. ☎ 473-8924.

> **Cuisine:** STEAK. **Reservations:** Accepted for six or more only.
> **Prices:** Appetizers $3.75–$6.25; main courses $10.75–$29.95. AE, DC, DISC, MC, V.
> **Open:** Lunch Mon–Fri 11:30am–2pm; dinner Mon–Thurs 5–10:30pm, Fri–Sat 5–11pm. Closed Sun.

A bastion of traditionalism in an area fast turning trendy, Dan McKlusky's offers sanctuary to folks tempted to say "gesundheit" when they hear the word "achiote." Good, old-fashioned surf and turf—especially turf—draws people into these dimly lit dining rooms with exposed-brick walls.

An on-premises butcher cuts fresh, corn-fed beef to your specifications, so you can adjust the size and price of your steak to your appetite; you can also order as many chops or chicken breasts as you like, or customize an entire dinner, combining six fried shrimp, say, with an eight-ounce rib eye. A choice of comforting desserts such as cheesecake and hot apple pie ensures that you'll waddle out of here completely satisfied.

Kyoto, 315 Congress Ave., upstairs. ☎ 482-9010.

> **Cuisine:** JAPANESE. **Reservations:** Accepted for parties over six only.
> **Prices:** Appetizers $3–$7; sushi 50¢–$9.50; main courses $9–$26. AE, MC, V.
> **Open:** Lunch Tues–Fri 11:30am–2pm; dinner Mon–Thurs 5:30–10pm, Fri–Sat 5:30–11pm.

Dine at the sushi bar or one of the two small dining rooms of this attractive Japanese restaurant, and you can keep your shoes on; opt for the cushioned and bamboo-matted tatami room, and you'll have to remove them. Shod or unshod, you'll enjoy Kyoto's well-prepared specialties, especially the sushi. Along with the standard tuna, salmon, and mackerel, all flown in fresh, are rarer delicacies such as fresh and saltwater eel, salmon skin, and sea urchin; the Texas rolls with jalapeños are a tasty nod to local culture.

There are plenty of choices for those who prefer their food cooked—the soft, pork-filled gyoza dumplings, for starters. The Seafood Delight platter lays on crab claws, teriyaki salmon, and shrimp and scallop shish kebabs, among other delights; the beef teriyaki and deep-fried chicken *karaage* are very satisfying, too. Sweet ginger or green-tea ice cream make clean, light finishes to the meal.

Shoreline Grill, 98 San Jacinto Blvd. ☎ 477-3300.

> **Cuisine:** SEAFOOD/AMERICAN REGIONAL. **Reservations:** Recommended for lunch and dinner (patio is first-come, first-served).
> **Prices:** Appetizers $5.95–$7.95; main courses $10.95–$24.95. AE, CB, DC, DISC, MC, V.
> **Open:** Lunch Mon–Fri 11am–2pm; dinner Sun–Thurs 5–10pm, Fri–Sat 5–10:30pm.

Fish is the prime bait at this tony grill, which looks out over Town Lake and the Congress Avenue Bridge, but in late spring through

---

Frommer's Smart Traveler: Restaurants

1. Eat at off-hours, either early or late, especially if the restaurant you're interested in doesn't take reservations (many don't). If you arrive at a popular place at prime time—around 8pm—you may find yourself waiting an hour or more for a table.

2. Make reservations whenever you can, and make them as far in advance as possible; dining out can be a competitive business in Austin.

3. Take advantage of Austin's budget gourmet trend; if the chic new downtown restaurants aren't exactly cheap, they offer innovative, high-quality food for considerably less than equivalent eateries in other cities.

4. Eat ethnic—there are many inexpensive Mexican restaurants around town, especially in east Austin—or eat vegetarian; lots of places in Austin that eschew meat are good and reasonably priced.

early fall, bats run a close second. During this period, when thousands of Mexican free-tailed bats emerge in unison from under the bridge at dusk, patio tables for viewing the phenomenon are at a premium.

When they're not going batty, diners focus on such starters as oysters on the half shell with red-pepper salsa or plump Chinese dumplings with ginger sauce. Menus change seasonally; in summer, lots of entrée-sized salads are offered. Drum, a moist, meaty fish from the Gulf, is worth trying, however it's prepared; the swordfish, which I had grilled in gazpacho butter, was excellent, too. Among the options for those who don't like food that has spent its life wet are medallions of pork with a cornmeal crust; braised lamb shanks in red-wine broth; or any of the pasta dishes (a vegetarian one is always included). The wine list covers a nice range, with bottles ranging from $12 to $135, and service is prompt and cheerful.

Moderate/Expensive

Basil's, 900 W. 10th St. ☎ 477-7497.

Cuisine: ITALIAN. **Reservations:** Advised, especially on weekends.
Prices: Appetizers $5.25–$5.95; main courses $8.25–$16.95. AE, CB, DC, DISC, MC, V.
Open: Sun–Thurs 6–10pm, Fri–Sat 6–10:30pm.

Pretty in pink, with lace curtains, oak trim, and lazily swirling ceiling fans, Basil's dining room is a romantic backdrop for fine northern Italian cuisine. You'll find the traditional dishes here, but turned out with innovative touches. For example, the pasta primavera is heaped with vegetables served al dente, not soggy or overcooked, and many of the preparations include colorful carrot or spinach noodles.

Consider starting with a half order of the primavera instead of a salad; it's a delicious way to get your greens in for the day. You might follow it with one of the restaurant's specialty fish dishes: the Pesce Angelica, sautéed with crab and artichokes in a mustard cream sauce, or the shrimp in white-wine and garlic sauce. Amy's ice cream, a popular local brand, makes a sweet successor to the meal.

★ **The Bitter End,** 311 Colorado St. ☎ 478-2337.

Cuisine: REGIONAL AMERICAN. **Reservations:** Accepted for five or more only.
Prices: Appetizers $3.25–$7.50; pizzas $5.50–$6.50; main courses $9.50–$17.50. AE, DC, DISC, MC, V.
Open: Mon–Thurs 11:30am–1am, Fri–Sat 11:30am–2am, Sun 11:30am–midnight.

The food is as good as the beer at this new brew pub—and the beer is very good indeed (my favorites were the smooth, light E-Z Wheat and the toasty Uptown Brown). One of the downtown warehouses that have recently been renovated, the Bitter End is all tall windows, brick walls, and galvanized metal light fixtures. But such touches as a rustic wood bar and large, comfy booths keep the atmosphere from being too austere.

Seared yellowfin tuna, semolina-fried calamari, or a refreshing salade niçoise are all auspicious ways to begin. Perfectly cooked entrées have included a wood-roasted flounder baked in herb-infused oil; a rosemary-crusted beef tenderloin; and a vegetable risotto with corn, asparagus, and spinach. Pizzas, topped with chicken, sweet peppers, and provolone, for example, are deliciously imaginative, too. Try to save room for desserts like warm Concord grape cobbler (Texas BlueBell ice cream optional) or nutmeg carrot cake.

$ **Chez Nous,** 510 Neches St. ☎ 473-2413.

Cuisine: FRENCH. **Reservations:** Only accepted for five or more.
Prices: Appetizers $4.50–$8.50; main courses $12.50–$18.50; menu du jour $15.50. AE, DC, MC, V.
Open: Lunch Tues–Sun 11:45am–2pm; dinner Tues–Sun 6–10:30pm. Closed Mon.

Just around the corner from the Sixth Street action, this intimate little restaurant feels as far away as Paris; lace curtains, fresh flowers in anisette bottles, and Folies-Bergère posters create a casual Left-Bank atmosphere. Since the early 1980s, Chez Nous's friendly French owners have been offering Austin fine bistro fare.

Items on the à la carte dinner menu are reasonably priced, but the real bargain is the Menu du Jour: $15.50 gets you a choice of soup, salad, or pâté; one of three designated entrées; and either crème caramel, chocolate mousse, or Brie for dessert. The main courses might include an excellent *poisson poivre vert* (fresh fish of the day with a green-peppercorn sauce) or a simple but delicious roast chicken. Lunch is even more of a steal, with its $7.50 daily special, and crêpes that run no higher than $5.50. Everything from the pâtés to the profiterolles (puff pastry filled with ice cream and dripping with warm chocolate) is made on the premises.

Louie's 106, 106 E. Sixth St. ☎ 476-1997.

Cuisine: MEDITERRANEAN. **Reservations:** Recommended for lunch, accepted only for six or more at dinner.
Prices: Appetizers $3.95–$5 (tapas $1.50–$5); main courses $8.50–$16.50. AE, CB, DC, DISC, MC, V.
Open: Lunch Mon–Fri 11:15am–5pm; dinner Mon–Thurs 5–10:30pm, Fri–Sat 5–11pm, Sun 5:30–10pm.

Looking for a place to cut a serious deal? Louie's has all the requisites: a location in the historic Littlefield office building; the tony atmosphere of a private club; and even a separate cigar room for puffing expensive stogies. But this is not to suggest it doesn't double as a pleasure palace, especially on the weekends when a flamenco guitarist entertains waiting diners in the glossy outside corridor.

You can enjoy Louie's updated versions of the traditional Spanish tapas—for example, grilled portabello mushrooms or crostini with pesto and smoked shrimp—at the bar of the large, high-ceilinged dining room, or at one of the downstairs or mezzanine-level tables; larger portions of similar appetizers are also available on the regular lunch-and-dinner menus. A classic paella Valenciana (saffron rice

Downtown Austin Dining

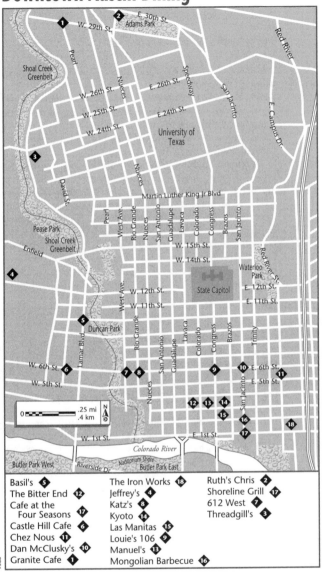

Basil's **5**
The Bitter End **12**
Cafe at the
 Four Seasons **17**
Castle Hill Cafe **6**
Chez Nous **11**
Dan McClusky's **10**
Granite Cafe **1**

The Iron Works **18**
Jeffrey's **4**
Katz's **8**
Kyoto **14**
Las Manitas **15**
Louie's 106 **9**
Manuel's **13**
Mongolian Barbecue **16**

Ruth's Chris **2**
Shoreline Grill **17**
612 West **7**
Threadgill's **3**

with seafood and sausage) makes a good, hearty entrée, as does the oven-baked moussaka, layered with lamb, potatoes, and eggplant. Portions are more substantial than the prices.

612 West, 612 W. Sixth St. ☎ 476-0612.

 Cuisine: SOUTHWESTERN. **Reservations:** Accepted for parties of six or more only.

Prices: Appetizers $4.95–$6.95; main courses $10.75–$18.95. AE, DC, MC, V.

Open: Lunch Mon–Fri 11am–2pm; dinner Sun–Thurs 5–10pm, Fri–Sat 5–11pm.

Soho meets Southfork at 612 West, a sleek downtown industrial space with such western motifs as a huge stone fire pit and desert-toned booths. The menu is equally eclectic, and equally successful, at blending diverse elements—primarily from Mexico, Asia, and the American South. By carefully balancing cuisine and setting to create an experience, not just a meal, 612 and other like-minded restaurants have raised dining out in Austin to an art.

Of course attitude is part of the package, but luckily here it's far more Texas than New York: The staff is as unfailingly nice as it is hip. But if you're feeling overwhelmed by all the chicness, consider starting with a frosty 612 cocktail, which is spiked with vodka, rum, and fruit liqueurs; it'll quickly put you at ease. For the first course, crawfish tamales with cascabel (pepper) cream sauce or cabrito *flautas* are both winners; the fish is flown in daily from the Gulf and West Coast. An on-premises smokehouse turns out succulent duck with Chinese barbecue sauce and moist pork tenderloin accompanied by corn cakes.

Moderate

Manuel's, 310 Congress Ave. ☎ 472-7555.

Cuisine: MEXICAN. **Reservations:** Not accepted.
Prices: Appetizers $3–$9; main courses $5–$13. AE, DC, MC, V.
Open: Daily 6:30am–10:30pm.

The setting—black-leather booths, floor-to-ceiling mirrors, a neon-backed bar—says upscale, but the prices and the atmosphere both say have a good time. Downtown executives are among the many who come to relax during Manuel's weekday happy hour (4 to 7 pm), animatedly downing hors d'oeuvres to a salsa music backdrop.

The food, which includes dishes from the interior of Mexico, is a creative cut above many Tex-Mex places. You can get well-prepared versions of the standards, but Manuel's also offers unusual variations on the theme—blue-crab nachos, for example, or a chicken with cheese and piquant mole appetizer. The excellent *enchiladas banderas* come topped with the colors of the Mexican flag: a green tomatillo *verde* sauce; a white sour-creamy *suiza;* and a red *adobada,* made with ancho chiles. At a sizzling Sunday Jazz Brunch, eggs with venison chorizo or spicy *chili con queso* (cheese and peppers) are accompanied by live music.

Inexpensive

The Iron Works, Red River and E. First Sts. ☎ 478-2272 or toll free 800/669-3602. Fax 512/478-2272.

Cuisine: BARBECUE. **Reservations:** Not accepted.
Prices: Sandwiches $1.85–$3.80; plates $4.90–$10.95; by the pound $3–$8.50. AE, MC, V.
Open: Mon–Fri 11am–9pm. Closed Sat and Sun.

Some of the best barbecue in Austin is served in one of the most unusual settings: Until 1977 this building housed the ironworks of the Weigl family, who came over from Germany in 1913. You can see their ornamental craft all around town, including at the State Capitol; cattle brands created for Jack Benny (Lasting 39), Lucille Ball, and Bob Hope are displayed in front of the restaurant. The fall-off-the-bones-tender beef ribs are the most popular order, with the brisket running a close second; lean turkey breast and juicy chicken are also smoked to perfection.

Mongolian Barbecue, 117 San Jacinto Blvd. ☎ **476-3938.**
Cuisine: CHINESE. **Reservations:** Weekends only.
Prices: Side dishes $2; lunch $5; dinner $7. AE, MC, V.
Open: Lunch Mon–Sat 11am–3pm; dinner Mon–Thurs 5–9:30pm, Fri–Sat 5–11pm.

Across the street from the Convention Center, this all-you-can-eat Chinese stir-fry buffet is a great place to grab a quick, delicious lunch or a casual dinner. Equipped with a bowl, you'll work your way through a long bar containing a wealth of uncooked vegetables and meats—bell peppers, zucchini, mushrooms, beef, pork, and chicken—to a section displaying such sauces and ingredients as soy, ginger, sesame, peanuts, and pineapple; recipes are posted to guide those seeking traditional tastes like sweet-and-sour or hot garlic Szechuan. Once you've made your final selections, hand them to the nimble chef, who presides over a huge grill. Although he may cook up to 10 dishes at once, he somehow manages to get all of them right all of the time.

2 Near West Side

Expensive

⭐ **Jeffrey's,** 1204 W. Lynn. ☎ **477-5584.**
Cuisine: SOUTHWESTERN. **Reservations:** Advised on weekends.
Prices: Appetizers $6.95–$9.25; main courses $19.75–$26.75 (bistro menu $11.75–$15.75). AE, CB, DISC, MC, V.
Open: Mon–Thurs 6–10pm, Fri–Sat 6–10:30pm. **Closed** Sun.

David Garrido, Jeffrey's boyish executive chef, exudes culinary passion; you might catch him excitedly explaining to an admiring patron how he went out at dawn to buy just the right mushrooms for one of his daily specials. While his innovative Texas fare is dazzling, the setting for his performance is low-key; people walk into this three-room former storefront, in the artsy Clarksville neighborhood, wearing anything from a T-shirt to a tux.

You can't tell who'll turn up on the ever-changing menu, but you can depend on flavors and textures to dance wildly together without falling down. Among the appetizers I tried were a wonderful goose liver pâté served with mustard and raspberries and crispy oysters topped with a five-alarm honey garlic butter. The aforementioned mushroom search resulted in the stellar morel cream sauce that topped a succulent duck with wild rice. Jeffrey's lower-priced bistro menu might include such lighter and smaller entrées as an arugula/tuna salad with saffron vinaigrette. The wine list, cited by *Wine Spectator* magazine as one of the most outstanding in the world, has more than 150 domestic and European items, 20 of which are available by the glass. Desserts such as Chocolate Intemperance live up to their diet-destroying promise.

Moderate/Expensive

Castle Hill Cafe, 1101 W. Fifth St. ☎ 476-0728.

Cuisine: NEW TEXAS. **Reservations:** Accepted for eight or more only.
Prices: Appetizers $2–$5; main courses $9–$14. AE, MC, V.
Open: Lunch Mon–Fri 11:30am–2pm; dinner Mon–Sat 6–10pm.

Surrounded on three sides by trees, Castle Hill gives the illusion of being tucked away somewhere remote, but it's just a block beyond downtown's western border, near two major throughfares. From the one open side, the view of the Austin skyline is magical at sunset. With its dark-wood, muted southwestern tones, and abundant folk art, this favored yuppie haunt strikes a casual but elegant note.

A panoply of exciting flavors emerges from the kitchen, which is far less subdued than the dining room. The empanadas filled with curried lamb and raisins and topped with a cilantro yogurt sauce make a superb appetizer, perhaps followed by one of the entrée salads such as the Szechuan hacked chicken with cream cheese–stuffed dumplings. Imaginatively conceived and beautifully arranged dinners include beef tenderloin marinated in herbs and served with fried cassava and guava banana ketchup; and shrimp-and-crab enchiladas, splashed with colorful marigold salsa.

★ **Zoot,** 509 Hearn. ☎ 477-6535.

Cuisine: AMERICAN REGIONAL. **Reservations:** Advised, especially on weekends.
Prices: Appetizers $5.95–$8.95; main courses $9.95–$17.95. AE, CB, DC, DISC, MC, V.
Open: Daily 5:30–10:30pm.

Texas chauvinism, eco-consciousness, and 1990s belt-tightening have come together in a number of dining rooms around the state to produce a cuisine that's delicious, fresh, and affordable. Zoot is a prime example of this propitious trend. This cozy Enfield restaurant, set in a 1920s cottage, uses only organic vegetables, and designs its dishes around ingredients grown in the area.

There's not a leaf of iceberg lettuce in the house salad, a delightful mix of mustard greens, arugula, and radicchio. And the wonderful pan-seared oysters, served on rigatoni as an appetizer, come straight from the Gulf. The menu changes seasonally, but you'll be sure to encounter roast chicken with smoked corn custard and grilled beef tenderloin with horseradish cream among the entrées; regulars complained too loudly when those items were rotated off. Vegetarians will be thrilled to find something to eat besides pasta—maybe marinated tofu tempura in a spicy peanut sauce. Zoot also appeals to other senses besides taste: Presentations are gorgeous and soft jazz plays in the background.

Moderate

Shady Grove, 1624 Barton Springs Rd. ☎ 474-9991.

   Cuisine: TEX-AMERICAN. **Reservations:** Taken weekends only, as needed.
   Prices: Appetizers $2–$5; main courses $7–$10. AE, DISC, MC, V.
   Open: Sun–Thurs 11am–11pm, Fri–Sat 11am–midnight.

If your idea of comfort food involves chile peppers, don't pass up Shady Grove. The restaurant takes its early Texas nostalgia theme to the point of kitsch with cowboy paintings, rattlesnake skins, and wagon-wheel chandeliers, but creates a homey, roadhouse atmosphere nevertheless. There's a good "unplugged" music series on the large, tree-shaded patio on Thursday nights, and other live bands on the weekend.

   After a day of fresh air at nearby Barton Springs, Freddie's Airstream chili, cooked with 10 different peppers, might be just the thing. All the burgers are made with high-grade ground sirloin, and if you've never had a frito pie (chili in a corn-chip bowl), this is a good place to try one. Or pull out all the stops and go for the huge portions of chicken-fried steak, Cajun meat loaf, or barbecued turkey breast. Good salads—among them, noodles with snow peas— or the Hippie sandwich (grilled eggplant, veggies, and cheese) will satisfy less hearty appetites.

Inexpensive

Chuy's, 1728 Barton Springs Rd. ☎ 474-4452.

   Cuisine: TEX-MEX. **Reservations:** Accepted for parties over 12 only.
   Prices: Appetizers $2.75–$5.95; main courses $5.75–$7.95. AE, CB, DC, DISC, MC, V.
   Open: Sun–Thurs 11am–10:30pm, Fri–Sat 11am–midnight.

One of the row of low-priced, friendly restaurants that line Barton Springs Road just east of Zilker Park, Chuy's stands out for its determinedly wacky decor—hubcaps lining the ceiling, Elvis memorabilia galore—and its sauce-smothered Tex-Mex fare. You're not likely to leave hungry after scarfing specials such as Southwestern Enchiladas, piled high with smoked chicken and topped with a fried egg; or a huge sopaipilla stuffed with grilled sirloin, among other things. Chuy's happy-hour food topped the *Chronicle*'s "Best of" reader's poll in 1994. The margaritas are good and the T-shirts, designed by local artists, even better.

   There's another Chuy's in north Austin, 10520 N. Lamar Blvd. (☎ 836-3218).

3 University/North Central

Very Expensive

Ruth's Chris, 3010 Guadalupe St. ☎ 477-RUTH.

Cuisine: AMERICAN. **Reservations:** Recommended.
Prices: Appetizers $4–$7.25; main courses $16.95–$30. AE, CB, DC, MC, V.
Open: Mon–Thurs 5:30–10:30pm, Fri–Sat 5:30–11pm, Sun 5:30–10pm.

It's been said that dressing up in Austin means ironing creases in your jeans, and that the town's upscale restaurants serve chicken-fried chateaubriand. The steaks at Ruth's Chris are sizzled in butter, not batter; many of the diners show up in suits; and there are even white cloths on the tables. Still, with its wooden booths and wide screen TV in back, this could well be the most casual of Ruth Fartel's franchises. Housed in a former stagecoach stop that dates back more than 100 years, it could also be one of the most fitting settings for consuming large quantities of beef.

If the food here is expensive—mainly because everything, including vegetables, is à la carte—the quality is consistently high. Thick cuts of New York strip, filet, rib eye, and porterhouse steaks are unwaveringly tender, the taste seared in by extra-high cooking temperatures. Like the panoramic photographs on the walls, side dishes such as fried onion rings and asparagus with hollandaise hearken back to the days before anyone ever heard of cholesterol. Service is superb, but, as you might have surmised, not stiflingly formal.

Moderate/Expensive

Granite Cafe, 2905 San Gabriel St. ☎ 472-6483.

Cuisine: SOUTHWEST. **Reservations:** Recommended on weekends.
Prices: Appetizers $5–$8; main courses $9–$16. AE, CB, DC, DISC, MC, V.
Open: Lunch Mon–Sat 11:30am–3pm; salads and pizzas 3–6pm; dinner 6–10 or 11pm; Sun brunch 11am–3pm.

Frommer's Cool for Kids: Restaurants

Chuy's (see p. 195) Teens and aspiring teens will enjoy this colorful, inexpensive restaurant with its cool T-shirts, Elvis kitsch, and green iguanas crawling up the walls.

Threadgill's (see p.197) This bustling, cheerful diner has an impressive music history (surely you've told your kids about Janis Joplin?) and an inexpensive ($2.45 to $3.45) "miniature" menu for ages 12 and under.

Mongolian Barbecue (see p. 193) Children are bound to find something they like among the many mix-and-match ingredients here. They'll also be fascinated by the whirling dervish of a chef. Best yet, kids' dinners cost only $4.

With its dusty tones, diffused lighting, and global-consciousness-with-money folk art, the Granite Cafe brings the sophistication of downtown up to the west U.T. campus area. One of the hip new restaurants around Austin that tend to play musical chefs, this place can be a bit uneven, but it's definitely worth a shot.

Warm sourdough bread with garlic herb butter arrives immediately after you're seated. The stylish menu changes daily, but you'll always find creative appetizers like lobster and portabello mushrooms over wild greens. An array of wood oven–baked pizzas play variations on classic topping themes; one comes with mushrooms and almond pesto, Bermuda onions, and smoked bacon. If you're lucky, tomato-basil fondue with grilled shrimp over cappellini or grilled yellowfin tuna served on couscous might appear among the entrées. The wine list is extensive and, generally, expensive; two wine-tasting dinners are available.

Moderate

Eastside Cafe, 2113 Manor Rd. ☎ 476-5858.

> **Cuisine:** AMERICAN. **Reservations:** Advised for weekend evenings and Sunday brunch.
> **Prices:** Appetizers $2.95–$5.50; main courses $5.25–$14.95. AE, CB, DC, DISC, MC, V.
> **Open:** Mon–Thurs 11am–10pm, Sat 10am–11pm, Sun 10am–10pm (brunch 10am–3pm).

Located in a nondescript neighborhood not far from the airport, the East Side Cafe is nonetheless popular with locals; it's just east of the university and northeast of the capitol. Diners enjoy eating on a tree-shaded patio or in one of a series of cheery, intimate rooms in a classic turn-of-the-century bungalow.

This restaurant gears its menu to the size of its patrons' appetites; you can get half orders of all the pasta dishes, including an excellent artichoke manicotti, and of some salads, such as the mixed field greens with goat-cheese rounds. The main course emphasis is on light meats and fish—sesame-breaded catfish, say, or chicken—but unrepentant carnivores can always tuck into eight ounces of beef tenderloin. Each morning, the gardener informs the head chef which of the vegetables in the restaurant's large organic garden are ready to be pulled up into service.

Inexpensive/Moderate

★ **Threadgill's,** 6416 N. Lamar Blvd. ☎ 451-5440.

> **Cuisine:** AMERICAN/SOUTHERN. **Reservations:** Not accepted.
> **$ Prices:** Sandwiches and specials $3.95–$5.45; main courses $4.95–$16.95. MC, V.
> **Open:** Daily 10am–11pm.

When Kenneth Threadgill got Travis County's first legal liquor license after the repeal of Prohibition in 1933, he turned his Gulf gas station into a club. His Wednesday night hootenannies became legendary in the 1960s, with performers like Janis Joplin turning up regularly. The southern-style diner added on in 1980 continues in the tradition of the adjoining club—it's down-home casual and good.

If Threadgill's is famous for its $4.95 blue-plate specials and its huge chicken-fried steaks, it's also renowned for its vegetables: You can get jalapeño jambalaya, squash casserole, and Cajun Italian eggplant in combination plates or as sides to the other dishes (seconds are free). Listed under the same menu category, the garlic cheese grits might not come under the National Health Department's definition of a vegetable, but they're delicious.

Inexpensive

Mother's Cafe & Garden, 4215 Duval St. ☎ 451-3994.

Cuisine: VEGETARIAN. **Reservations:** Taken for parties of six or more only.

Prices: Soups and salads $2.50–$4.95; main courses $4.75–$6.95. CB, DC, DISC, MC, V.

Open: Mon–Fri 11:15am–10pm, Sat–Sun 10am–10pm.

If you want your body to think you're treating it right, but don't want to risk a revolt from your taste buds, head over to Mother's. The Save the Earth crowd that frequents this Hyde Park eatery enjoys an international array of veggie dishes, but the inspiration for most of the mainstays comes from south of the border: You'll find classic chili rellenos, burritos, and nachos, along with the more unusual tofu enchiladas. A three-cheese spinach lasagne is especially popular. The tropical shack-style back garden is appealing; the young staff is friendly, but not nauseatingly so; and there's a good, inexpensive selection of local beers and wines.

4 South Austin

Expensive

Green Pastures, 811 W. Live Oak Rd. ☎ 444-4747.

Cuisine: CONTINENTAL. **Reservations:** Advised for lunch and dinner Thurs–Sat.

Prices: Appetizers $4.50–$6.75; main courses $10.75–$22.95. AE, DC, MC, V.

Open: Mon–Sat 11:30am–2pm and 6–10pm; Sun brunch 11am–2pm.

Peacocks strut their stuff among the 225 live oaks surrounding this mansion, which was built in 1894 and has remained in the hands of the same renowned Austin family since 1916; the current owner's mother turned it into a restaurant in 1945. You'll find southern comfort in the gracious setting and polite service, as well as in a continental menu that nods only gently toward current culinary trends. The lunch crowd may be a bit blue haired, but nighttime draws in Austinites of all stripes; everyone from Van Cliburn to James Michener has dined here.

The creamy lobster crêpes or baked Brie in puff pastry go far to enhance the feeling of well-being brought on by the lovely surroundings. Although the menu changes seasonally, you'll always find two popular dishes on it: duck Texana, wrapped in bacon and served with black-currant sauce, and snapper Florentine, topped with hollandaise and shrimp. The Texas pecan ball (vanilla ice cream rolled in nuts and dripping fudge) is enough to weaken the strongest resolve, but you may want to go for baroque—flaming Bananas Foster for two.

Moderate

Matt's El Rancho, 2613 S. Lamar Blvd. ☎ 462-9333.

Cuisine: TEX-MEX. **Reservations:** Not accepted after 5pm on weekends, except for large groups.

Prices: Appetizers $4–$6; main courses $6–$9. AE, CB, DC, DISC, MC, V.

Open: Mon, Wed–Thurs, and Sun 11am–10pm; Fri–Sat 11am–11pm. Closed Tues.

Lyndon Johnson hadn't been serving in the U.S. Senate very long when Matt's El Rancho first opened its doors. Although owner Matt Martinez outlived LBJ and other early customers, plenty of his original patrons followed when he moved his restaurant south of downtown in 1986. They came not out of habit, but because Matt has been dishing up consistently good food since 1952.

Some of the items show the regulars' influence; you can thank former land commissioner Bob Armstrong for the tasty cheese, guacamole, and spiced-meat dip that bears his name. Chile rellenos and grilled shrimp seasoned with garlic and soy are among everyone's perennial favorites. Although the place can seat almost 500, you might still have to wait for an hour on weekend nights. Just sit out on the terrace, sip a fresh-lime margarita, and chill.

Inexpensive

Güero's, 614 E. Oltdorf. ☎ 447-7688.

Cuisine: MEXICAN. **Reservations:** Not accepted.

Prices: Appetizers $1.50–$4.95; main courses $5.75–$9.95. DISC, MC, V.

Open: Mon–Fri 7am–10pm, Sat–Sun 8am–10pm.

With its Pepto Bismol–pink walls, Formica tables, and tongue-in-cheek menu listings—the entry for one pork dish describes it as being the same as the beef version "except piggish"—Güero's is geared toward a hip gringo crowd. It's a casual, fun place to enjoy health-conscious versions of Tex-Mex standards as well as of some dishes from the interior of Mexico: snapper *a la veracruzano* (with tomatoes, green olives, and jalapeños), say, or Michoacán-style tamales. Lots of plates come topped with cheese, guacamole, and sour cream, but you can also get delicious, low-fat entrées like the chicken *al carbon* (breast meat grilled in achiote, a Yucatán spice), served with whole-wheat tortillas and nonrefried beans.

5 East Austin

Moderate

Mexico Tipico, 1707 E. Sixth St. ☎ 472-3222.
   Cuisine: TEX-MEX. **Reservations:** Not accepted.
   Prices: Appetizers $1.50–$6.25; main courses $6–$14. AE, MC, V.
   Open: Tues–Wed 9am–3pm, Thurs–Sun 8am–10pm (lunch menu Tues–
   Fri 11am–3pm). Closed Mon.

Owned by the friendly Valero family, Mexico Tipico is among the
most popular of the informal restaurants dotting the residential neighborhood east of I-35, the unofficial dividing line between Anglo and
Hispanic Austin. Set back from the street and boasting a delightful
rose- and magnolia-filled patio, this modest place is decorated with
folk art, tinwork mirrors, and niches holding pictures of the Virgin
of Gaudalupe.

   Diners from both sides of the divide pile in for authentic versions
of such specialties as *caldo,* hearty beef soup heaped with potatoes
and vegetables, or *rojas con queso,* a dip of poblano peppers, ham,
onions, and cheese served with hot corn tortillas. It's hard to decide
among the chile rellenos, enchiladas verdes, or a quarter of
a flame-roasted chicken; to avoid the "I-shoulda" syndrome, consider one of the combinations. Huge inexpensive margaritas in
cactus-shaped glasses will complement whatever you order.

6 North/Airport

Moderate/Expensive

⭐ **Fonda San Miguel,** 2330 W. North Loop. ☎ 459-4121.
   Cuisine: MEXICAN REGIONAL. **Reservations:** Accepted for eight or
   more only for dinner, four or more for brunch.
   Prices: Appetizers $5.50–$6.95; main courses $7.95–$15.95. AE, CB,
   DISC, MC, V.
   Open: Sun–Thurs 5:30–9:30pm, Fri–Sat 5:30–10:30pm; Sun brunch
   11:30am–2pm.

Like American Southwest chefs who look to Native American staples
such as blue corn for inspiration, Mexico City chefs have had their
own back-to-the-roots movement, which might involve including
ancient Aztec ingredients in their dishes. Such trends are carefully
tracked and artfully translated by Miguel Ravago at Fonda San
Miguel, the best place in town for Mexican regional cuisine. You'll
discover that food from the northern Mexico state of Sonora, on
which most Tex-Mex fare is based, represents Mexico in the same
way that hearty midwestern cooking represents the United States—
in a very limited fashion.

   The huge dining room, with its carved wooden doors, colorful
paintings, and live ficus tree, is a gorgeous backdrop to such appetizers as Veracruz-style ceviche or quesadillas with *huitacoche,* a corn

fungus as rare as French truffles. *Conchinita pibil,* pork baked in banana leaves, is one of the Yucatán offerings; hearty appetites will also enjoy the grilled beef tenderloin from the Tampico region. Familiar northern Mexican fare, extremely well-prepared, is offered, too.

Pappadeaux, 6319 N. I.H.-35. ☎ **452-9363.**

> **Cuisine:** SEAFOOD/CAJUN. **Reservations:** Not accepted.
> **Prices:** Appetizers $3.40–$6.80; main courses $9.25–$17.95 (lunch and dinner). AE, MC, V.
> **Open:** Sun–Thurs 11am–10pm, Fri–Sat 11am–11pm.

In spite of the huge dining room of this popular chain seafood restaurant—semi-Victorian, semi-nautical, and totally casual—its first-come, first-served policy usually means a long line. This place fills up with tourists staying on the hotel strip north of the airport, as well as with locals who drop by for lunch or maybe a singles mingle after work.

Still, it's worth waiting for the large portions of shrimp, crab, catfish, and other denizens of the deep cooked up with a Cajun accent. You might start with the spicy seafood gumbo or some fresh Gulf oysters, followed by shrimp étouffé or soft-shell crab over dirty rice. There's a fried-fish selection—served with french fries, natch—but you can get almost anything on the menu either blackened, pan broiled, or charbroiled. That way you can justify trying the bread pudding with bourbon sauce or, perhaps, the sweet-potato pecan pie.

Moderate

Taj Palace, 6700 Middle Fiskville Rd. ☎ **452-9959.**

> **Cuisine:** INDIAN. **Reservations:** Advised on weekends.
> **Prices:** Appetizers $2.95–$4.95; main courses $5.95–$11.95. AE, DC, DISC, MC, V.
> **Open:** Lunch Mon–Fri 11am–2pm, Sat–Sun 11:30am–2:30pm; dinner Sun–Thurs 5:30–10pm, Fri–Sat 5:30–10:30pm.

An exotic experience awaits in a strip center off I-35, just north of Highland Mall: Statues of Ganesh, Krishna, and other Hindu deities preside over dining rooms decorated with colorful masks and Japoori-style wall hangings. If you're not familiar with Indian food, you might consider sampling some at Taj Palace's all-you-can-eat luncheon buffet, which costs $5.95 during the week, $7.95 on the weekend. In any case, servers are happy to answer any questions you might have about the menu.

Ordering a bread basket is a good way to try such treats as naan or *aloo paratha,* baked in a tandoor oven. The oven also produces such low-fat specialties as fish *tikka,* which is skewered into kabobs. Dishes like *malai kofta,* cheese and vegetable dumplings in a cream and almond sauce, or *murg tikka makhni,* chicken in an herb and tomato sauce with a bit of butter, are richly delicious. This restaurant has another location in south Austin, Brodie Oaks Center, 4141 Capital of Texas Hwy. (☎ **447-1997**).

Inexpensive

★ **Kim Phung,** 7601 N. Lamar Blvd., No. 1. ☎ 451-2464.
$ **Cuisine:** VIETNAMESE/CHINESE. **Reservations:** Accepted but not required.
Prices: Appetizers $1–$3; lunch special $3.25–$4.25; main courses $4.25–$8.50. DISC, MC, V.
Open: Mon–Thurs 10am–9pm, Fri–Sun 10am–10pm.

The rest of Austin has lately caught on to what the Asian community to the north has known for some time: That Kim Phung is one of the best, most efficient, and least expensive restaurants in town. The low-key strip mall setting doesn't detract from the main draw: huge portions of terrific Vietnamese and Chinese food. Perfectly crisp spring rolls come topped with a thick peanut sauce that's hard to stop sampling. Entrées such as kung pao shrimp or rice with shredded pork skin and crab cakes are good, but most outstanding are the noodle dishes. Particularly recommended are those heaped with chicken, garlic, and hot peppers; grilled tofu; and charbroiled shrimp. The house specialty *pho* noodle soup allows you to tailor your dinner: You choose the main ingredients and then add cilantro, basil, jalapeño, lime, or sprouts to taste. Thai-style coffee, served thick and dark over ice and a dollop of condensed milk, ends the meal with a delicious caffeine jolt.

7 Far West Side

Very Expensive

Emerald Cafe, 13614 Hwy. 71 West, Bee Cave. ☎ 263-2147.
Cuisine: IRISH/CONTINENTAL. **Reservations:** Recommended.
Prices: Appetizers $6.95; main courses $14.50–$24.50. MC, V.
Open: Daily 5–11pm.

There's a wee bit o' the blarney about this Bee Cave restaurant, what with its green rugs, green-stemmed glasses, green tablecloths, and shamrock with a calendar countdown to St. Patrick's Day, but it's come by honestly: Hostess and co-owner Marge Kinsella hails from County Mayo, Ireland. With the help of traditional family recipes, her husband, Paul, the kitchen manager, and their son Paul John, the chef, turn out excellent versions of old-fashioned Irish and European favorites.

Wear something with an elastic waist; there isn't a light item in the bunch. A hearty potato soup makes a good starter, especially accompanied by fresh-baked Irish soda bread. The Emerald Cafe is rightly renowned for its stuffed roast duck in a brandied cherry sauce, but the red snapper with crab and shrimp in cream is no slouch, either. The restaurant maintains a custom from the days when the man always paid and it was considered crass for his sweetheart to know just how much he was shelling out for her: Unless two members of the same sex are dining together, a menu without prices is always handed to the woman.

Hudson's on the Bend, 3509 R.R. 620 North. ☎ **266-1369.**

> **Cuisine:** SOUTHWEST. **Reservations:** Accepted, required on Sat.
> **Prices:** Appetizers $7.25–$7.75; main courses $18.95–$26. AE, DC, MC, V.
> **Open:** Mon–Thurs 6–10pm, Fri–Sat 5:30–10pm, Sun 6–9pm (closing times may be earlier in winter; call ahead).

If you're game for things that once roamed the wild, served in a very civilized setting, come to Hudson's. Soft candlelight, fresh flowers, fine china, and attentive service combine with out-of-the-ordinary cuisine to make this worth a special-occasion splurge. Sparkling lights draped over a cluster of oak trees draw you into the romantic dining room, set in an old house some 1¹/₂ miles southwest of the Mansfield Dam, near Lake Travis.

The *chipotle* cream sauce on top was sufficiently spicy that I couldn't tell whether or not Omar's rattlesnake cakes tasted like chicken, but they were very good, as were the black-bean ravioli and smoked-shrimp quesadilla appetizers. Javelina stuffed with boar and pecans and a mixed grill of venison, quail, and pheasant sausage were available when I visited, but I opted for a superb trout served with tangy mango chili butter. Although portions are more than generous, finishing a slice of key lime pie with graham-cracker crust posed no problem.

One caveat: Its popularity and its charming but acoustically poor setting can make Hudson's very noisy on weekends; instead of the sweet nothings of your dining companion, you might find yourself listening to a marital spat at the next table.

Moderate

County Line on the Hill, 6500 W. Bee Cave Rd. ☎ **327-1742.**

> **Cuisine:** BARBECUE. **Reservations:** Not accepted.
> **Prices:** Plates $7.95–$16.95. AE, CB, DC, DISC, MC, V.
> **Open:** Summer, Sun–Thurs 5–9:30pm, Fri–Sat 5–10pm; call for winter hours.

Some critics deride the County Line chain for its "suburban" barbecue, but Austinites have voted with their feet (or, rather, their cars); if you don't get here before 6pm, you can expect to wait as long as an hour and a half to eat. Should this happen, sit out on the deck and soak in the views of Hill Country, or look at the old advertising signs hung on the knotty-pine planks of this 1920s roadhouse, formerly a speakeasy and a brothel. In addition to the barbecue—oh-so-slowly-smoked ribs, brisket, chicken, or sausage—skewered meat or vegetables plates are available. County Line on the Lake, near Lake Austin, 5204 F.M. 2222 (☎ **346-3664**), offering the same menu, is open for lunch as well as dinner.

Inexpensive/Moderate

 The Salt Lick, F.M. 1826, Driftwood, TX. ☎ 858-4959.
Cuisine: BARBECUE. **Reservations:** Only for large occasions.
Prices: $7–$15, depending on nightly menu. Cash only.
Open: Tues–Sun noon–10pm.

It's 11½ miles from the junction of 290 west and F.M. 1826 (turn right) to the Salt Lick, but you'll start smelling the smoke during the last five. Moist chicken, beef, and pork, as well as terrific homemade pickles, more than justify the drive. You're faced with a tough decision here: If you have the all-you-can-eat platter of brisket, sausage, and ribs, you might have to pass on the fresh-baked peach or blackberry cobbler, which would be a pity. In warm weather, seating is outside at picnic tables under live oak trees; in winter, the tables are set down near blazing fireplaces inside. Whatever the season, this is one of the best, real Texas dining experiences you could hope to have.

Inexpensive

Rosie's Tamale House, 13436 Hwy. 71, Bee Cave. ☎ 263-5245.
Cuisine: TEX-MEX. **Reservations:** Not accepted.
Prices: Appetizers $2.70–$5.25; main courses $4.45–$9.15. No credit cards.
Open: Sun–Mon, Wed–Thurs 11am–10pm, Tues 5–10pm, Fri–Sat 11am–10:30pm.

When Willie Nelson first started coming to Rosie's in 1973, he always asked for a taco, a beef enchilada, chile con queso, and guacamole. Rosie has moved to a larger place, down the road from her original converted gas station, and Nelson's standing order is now enshrined on the menu as Willie's Plate, but the singer still drops by and Rosie is still here to greet him—and everyone else who comes in. The food's not fancy, but it's filling and good. Before you leave, take out a dozen fresh tamales ($4.50) for a midnight snack and check out the back wall, lined with photos of famous and not-so-famous regular customers. The two other Austin restaurants that bear Rosie's name are run by family members.

8 Specialty Dining

Local Favorites

Back East, when it comes to barbecue, sauce is everything; in Texas, quality is judged by the method and length of smoking the meat. Locals care deeply, even obsessively, about the issue; some of their favorites, Iron Works, the County Line restaurants, and the Salt Lick, are described above. You can get live music with your ribs at **Green Mesquite,** 1400 Barton Springs Rd. (☎ 479-0485), and **Arz Rib House,** 2330 S. Lamar Blvd. (☎ 442-8283); **Ruby's BBQ,** 512 W. 29th St. (☎ 477-1651), is known for its all-natural, hormone-free meat.

If coffee is your speed, you'll appreciate the many cafés that have been cropping up around town. I recommend **Little City,** 916 Congress Ave. (☎ 476-2489), for its ultrachic design and its proximity to the downtown tourist sights—it's the only place where you can get a java fix near the capitol on Sunday; **Mozart's,** 3825 Lake Austin Blvd. (☎ 477-2900), for its terrific views of Lake Austin and its white-chocolate almond croissants; and **Ruta Maya,** 218 W. Fourth St. (☎ 472-9637), for its funky atmosphere, live Latin music (four nights a week), and perfectly brewed coffee.

Hotel Dining

 The Cafe at the Four Seasons, Four Seasons hotel, 98 San Jacinto Blvd. ☎ 478-4500.

Cuisine: AMERICAN/CONTINENTAL. **Reservations:** Suggested for brunch and dinner.

Prices: Appetizers $7.50–$8.50; main courses $14.50–$26. AE, CB, DC, DISC, MC, V.

Open: Breakfast Mon–Fri 6:30am–11am, Sat–Sun 7am–11am; lunch daily 11am–2pm; dinner daily 6–11pm; Sun brunch 10:30am–2pm.

Maybe one shouldn't judge a restaurant by its bread basket, but I often do; a place that doesn't do right by its rolls has got to spend the rest of the evening proving to me it cares. So when warm sun-dried tomato brioches and other fresh-baked delights were set down on the table, the Cafe at the Four Seasons had me in the palm of its able, culinary hands.

Things only got better at this hotel dining room, reminiscent of an informal Roman villa; if you sit window side or on the outdoor patio, you can see the swans glide across Town Lake. The crab quesadillas, topped with guacamole and *pico de gallo,* make a delicious starter, as does the sea scallop and wild-mushroom lasagne; you'd be hard-pressed to guess that the latter is among the "alternative cuisine" selections, reduced in everything except taste. Entrées are by no means behind the times—a side of trendy polenta comes with the veal osso buco, for example, and the pork tenderloin is covered with a focaccia Dijon crust—but you can also enjoy such comforting standards as New England lobster or barbecued shrimp with home-style biscuits.

Trattoria Grande, Stouffer Austin Hotel, 9721 Arboretum Blvd. ☎ 343-2626.

Cuisine: NORTHERN ITALIAN. **Reservations:** Strongly advised on weekends.

Prices: Appetizers $5.75–$6.95; main courses $9.95–$18.75. AE, CB, DC, DISC, MC, V.

Open: Lunch Mon–Fri 11:30am–2pm; dinner Sun–Thurs 6–10pm, Fri–Sat 6–11pm.

At midday, the striking Hill Country views from the Trattoria Grande's arched windows may distract power lunchers from serious discussions. In the evening, when the lights of the sophisticated black-and-brass room are dimmed, the diner's gaze tends to be drawn toward the flickering candles on the table—and one's dining companion.

The fine northern Italian cuisine is attention grabbing, too. Fried calamari (served hot with marinara sauce or tossed cold in a salad) and ravioli stuffed with duck and mushrooms are among the interesting array of appetizers. If you go for one of the reduced-calorie pastas such as spaghetti with fresh basil, you might be able to move on to the *secondi piatti* (main course) section of the menu. Tender veal, sautéed with artichokes and peppers or prepared with mushrooms in a red-wine sauce, is a specialty. Avert your eyes from the dessert tray if you don't want to be tempted by the creamy cannoli drizzled with chocolate.

La Vista, Hyatt Regency on Town Lake, 208 Barton Springs Rd. ☎ 477-1234.

Cuisine: AMERICAN. **Reservations:** For six or more only.
Prices: Appetizers $3.25–$5.95; main courses $7.25–$15.95. AE, CB, DC, DISC, MC, V.
Open: Breakfast daily 6:30am–11am; lunch and dinner 11am–11:30pm.

La Vista's spicy fajitas consistently top the local readers polls, but the 385-calorie chicken quesadillas—one of the items on the spa-style "cuisine naturalle" menu—are surprisingly tasty, too. One comprehensive menu for both lunch and dinner means you can get a burger, salad, or sandwich at night, or enjoy a more substantial meal—maybe baby-back ribs or fried catfish—during the day. The Hyatt's laid-back, casual restaurant also offers a full array of tropical drinks, many of them nonalcoholic. Go at off-hours if you want a Town Lake view; you can only reserve one if you're with a party of six or more.

Dining with a View

The Hula Hut, 3826 Lake Austin Blvd. ☎ 476-4852.

Cuisine: MEXICAN/POLYNESIAN/HAWAIIAN. **Reservations:** Not accepted.
Prices: Appetizers $4–$7; main courses $7–$17. AE, CB, DC, DISC, MC, V.
Open: Sun–Thurs 11am–11pm, Fri–Sat 11am–midnight.

The Hula Hut has perfected the technique of cross-Polynesation: It's mixed Mexican and Pacific Island cooking, added decks reaching out over Lake Austin, and arrived at the formula for fun. This place is especially cheerful if you come with a group ready to experiment with different platters. The Huli Huli Luau Mexicano includes generous portions of smoked ribs, grilled chicken nachos, chicken tacos, garlic roasted potatoes, and an array of delicious sauces such as ranch with jalapeños. The Cancún Pu-Pu offers lots of fresh fish and vegetables. At $19.95, these platters easily satisfy two for lunch or dinner; four could—and often do—enjoy them as appetizers.

The Oasis, 6550 Comanche Trail, near Lake Travis. ☎ 266-2441.

Cuisine: TEX-MEX. **Reservations:** Not accepted.
Prices: Appetizers $4.95–$8.95; main courses $7.95–$13.95. AE, CB, DC, DISC, MC, V.
Open: Daily 11am until 9, 10, or 11pm, depending on the weather.

This is the Austinite's premier place to take out-of-town guests to at sunset; no one ever leaves unimpressed with the sight of the Lake Travis/Texas Hill Country backdrop set against the descent of the fiery orb. The Oasis's Tex-Mex fare is not nearly as inspiring, although the quesadillas are pretty good. If you're not starving after a day of water sports on the lake, consider just sitting out on one of the 28 decks and having a margarita, and maybe some chips and salsa. It doesn't get much mellower.

Bat-Side Dining

In late March through mid-November, when thousands of bats fly out from under the Congress Avenue Bridge to seek a hearty bug dinner, the most coveted seats in town are the ones with a view of the amazing phenomenon. The **Shoreline Grill,** the **Cafe at the Four Seasons,** and **La Vista** are reviewed above; in addition, **TGIF's,** Radisson Hotel on Town Lake, 11 E. First St. (☎ **478-9611**), offers a casual, collegial roost from which to observe the bats depart for their sunset food forage.

Fast Food

Stop in at a **Taco Cabana** for some inexpensive Tex-Mex food and you'll see why these San Antonio–based restaurants are spreading all over central Texas. Tasty standards such as tacos and fajitas, along with authentic local favorites like *menudo* (spicy tripe stew), are served in a cheerful, pleasant atmosphere; the charcoal-grilled chicken is especially good. Of the eight Austin locations, the ones on 517 W. Martin Luther King, Jr., Blvd. (☎ **478-0875**) and 211 S. Lamar Blvd. (☎ **472-8098**) are the most central.

Breakfast

Las Manitas, 211 Congress Ave. ☎ 472-9357.

> **Cuisine:** TEX-MEX. **Reservations:** Not accepted.
> **Prices:** Breakfast $1.75–$4.50; lunch $2.55–$5.95. MC, V.
> **Open:** Breakfast Mon–Fri 7:30am–11:30am, Sat–Sun 8am–2:30pm; lunch Mon–Fri 11:30am–4pm, Sat–Sun 11:30am–2:30pm.

It's hard to leave town without at least hearing about this funky Mexican diner, decked out with local artwork and colorful tables and chairs. A rack of alternative newspapers at the door sets the political tone, but businesspeople and slackers alike pile into this small place for breakfasts of *migas con queso* (eggs scrambled with corn tortillas, white cheese, and ranchero sauce) or *chilaquiles verdes* (tortilla strips topped with green tomatillo sauce, Jack cheese, and onions). Not all the staff of this family-owned and -operated café speak English, but don't worry; if you don't get exactly what you like, you'll like whatever you get.

Brunch

The Sunday buffet brunch ($19) at **Green Pastures** (see the "South Austin" section, above) is an Austin institution. One of the biggest draws is the milk punch, liberally dosed with bourbon, rum, brandy, ice cream, and nutmeg, but the spread of salads, seafood dishes, pâtés, and baked goods is pretty impressive, too. Live piano music enhances an already elegant atmosphere.

Another of Austin's most popular brunches is the buffet ($18.95) at **Fonda San Miguel** (see the "North/Airport" section, above), which runs a delicious Mexican geographical gamut. Resident chef Miguel Ravago is often joined by other stellar cooks, who pull out all creative stops for the occasion. The gracious hacienda-style restaurant is the perfect setting for this movable feast.

24 Hours

Katz's, 618 W. Sixth St. ☎ 472-2037.

> **Cuisine:** DELI. **Reservations:** Not accepted downstairs, recommended on weekends at Top of the Marc.
> **Prices:** Appetizers $3.95–$6.50; sandwiches $3.95–$8.25; dinner $5.95–$8.95. AE, DC, DISC, MC, V.
> **Open:** Downstairs, 24 hours; Top of the Marc, Tues–Sat 5pm–2am.

If it doesn't quite achieve New York–deli status—for one thing, the staff is not nearly rude enough—Katz's is as close as you'll come in Austin. The matzoh balls are as light and the cheesecake as dense as they're supposed to be, and the corned-beef sandwiches come in the requisite gargantuan portions. Offering the same menu, the popular Top of the Marc club upstairs gives this deli the jump on its East Coast rivals in at least one significant aspect: Where else can you enjoy good jazz *and* good blueberry blintzes?

Magnolia Cafe, 1920 S. Congress Ave. ☎ 445-0000.

> **Cuisine:** AMERICAN/HEALTH. **Reservations:** Not accepted.
> **Prices:** Appetizers $1–$5; main courses $4–$7. AE, DISC, MC, V.
> **Open:** 24 hours every day except Christmas.

Local musicians finishing up a gig at the nearby Continental Club often drop into "the Mag"—not just because it's the only place in the area open at that hour, but because the food is inexpensive and good. You can get anything from buckwheat pancakes and steroid-free burgers to black-bean tacos around-the-clock; there are also special breakfast, dinner, and late-night menus. The LOVE veggies sautéed in garlic butter and the Deep Eddy omelet with a spicy carrot-haberno pepper sauce are popular choices. A pleasant new patio out back has almost doubled the size of this place.

The original Magnolia Cafe, 2304 Lake Austin Blvd. (☎ 478-8645), offers the same food and the same colorful crowd.

14

What to See & Do in Austin

Sᴛʀᴏʟʟ ᴜᴘ Cᴏɴɢʀᴇss Aᴠᴇɴᴜᴇ, ᴀɴᴅ ʏᴏᴜ'ʟʟ sᴇᴇ ᴍᴜᴄʜ ᴛʜᴇ sᴀᴍᴇ sɪɢʜᴛ ᴀs visitors to Austin did more than 100 years ago: a broad thoroughfare gently rising to the grandest of all state capitols. Obsessed from early on with its place in history, the city is not neglecting it now, either. The capitol just underwent a complete overhaul and presents a better face than ever to the public, while downtown's historic Sixth Street is continually turning back the clock with ongoing restorations.

But it is Austin's myriad natural attractions that put the city on all the "most-livable" lists. From bats and birds to Barton Springs, from the Highland Lakes to the hike-and-bike trails, Austin lays out the green carpet for its visitors. You'd be hard-pressed to find a town that has more to offer fresh-air enthusiasts.

Bicycling is not the only free ride in Austin; there's no charge for transportation on the city's three 'Dillo lines, which cover most of the downtown tourist sites as well as the University of Texas. Other freebies include the Convention and Visitors Bureau's excellent guided walks and the state-sponsored tours of the Governor's Mansion and the State Capitol.

Suggested Itineraries

If You Have 1 Day

You'll see much of what makes Austin unique if you spend a day downtown. You might start out with a cup of coffee and croissant at the Little City Cafe or a heartier breakfast at Las Manitas; if you opt for the Mexican meal, you'll also have the longer walk to work it off. Head over to the Old Land Office Building, interesting in itself and, as an information center, the ideal place to begin your tour of the Capitol Complex. The capitol itself and its new extension are next; you'll be impressed by results of the costly restoration. After that it's on to the Governor's Mansion; keep in mind that the last tour is at 11:40am. If you still have the strength and want to see how the other half lived in the late 19th century, walk west to the nearby historic Bremond Block; otherwise, head south toward Sixth Street and some lunch (perhaps Louie's 106 or Dan McKlusky's). Thus fortified, stroll along historic Sixth Street. Still south but not very far is the north shore of Town Lake; you can rest here under the shade of a cherry tree or join the athletic hordes in perpetual motion on the hike-and-bike trail. If you're in town from late March through October, book a table at the Shoreline Grill and watch the bats take off at dusk from under the Congress Avenue Bridge. Devote any energy you have left to the live music scene back on Sixth Street, which takes on an entirely new character at night.

If You Have 2 Days

Day 1 Scope out the cityscape at Mt. Bonnell, the highest point in Austin; then head down to the Laguna Gloria Art Museum, at the foot of the mount. If the weather is nice, have lunch at one of the restaurants along Barton Springs Road and then spend the afternoon in Zilker Park: Go for a stroll at the lovely Botanical Gardens and afterward dip into the Barton Springs pool. If it's cool or rainy, go to the LBJ Library, Texas Memorial Museum, and the Huntington Art collection on the University of Texas campus (if you're traveling with youngsters, substitute the excellent Children's Museum or the Jourdan Bachman Pioneer Farm).

Day 2 Follow the itinerary outlined in "If You Have 1 Day," above.

If You Have 3 Days

Days 1–2 Same as Days 1 and 2 in "If You Have 2 Days."

Day 3 Visit the LBJ Library and other museums on the U.T. campus if you haven't already been there on Day 2. In the afternoon, tour the sights on Austin's east side—the George Washington Carver Museum, the State Cemetery, and the French Legation; there are a number of good, inexpensive Mexican restaurants in the area.

If You Have 4 Days

Days 1–3 Same as Days 1–3 in "If You Have 3 Days."

Day 4 Take a day trip to Fredericksburg or New Braunfels in the Hill Country, both appealing old German towns. Fredericksburg lays on the charm a bit more; New Braunfels competes with a discount mall and lots of river-rafting options.

If You Have 5 Days or More

Days 1–3 Follow the strategy in "If You Have 3 Days," above.

Days 4–5 Stay overnight at a bed-and-breakfast in Fredericksburg, and visit the LBJ Ranch, Enchanted Rock State Park, and some nearby Hill Country towns (see Chapter 17).

1 The Top Attractions

⭐ **Barton Springs Pool,** Zilker Park, 2201 Barton Springs Rd. ☎ **476-9044.**

If the University of Texas is the seat of Austin's intellect and the State Capitol its political pulse, Barton Springs is the city's soul. The Native Americans who settled near these waters believed they had spiritual powers; today's residents still place their faith in the abilities of the spring-fed pool to soothe them as well as cool them.

Each day, approximately 32-million gallons of water from the underground Edwards Aquifer bubble to the surface here; at one time, this force powered several Austin mills. Although the original limestone bottom remains, concrete was added to the banks to form uniform sides to what is now a swimming pool of about 1,000 feet by 125 feet. Maintaining a constant 68-degree temperature, the amazingly clear water is bracing in summer and warming in winter, when many hearty souls brave the cold for a dip. Lifeguards are on duty for most of the day, and a large bathhouse operated by the Parks and Recreation Department offers changing facilities and an information center/gift shop.

Admission: $2 adults Mon–Fri, $2.50 Sat–Sun; 50¢ children 12–17, 25¢ children 11 and under; free (no lifeguards present) 5am–9am Memorial Day–Labor Day, off-season 5am–9am and dusk–10pm.

Open: Tues–Wed, and Fri–Sun 5am–10pm, Mon and Thurs 5am–7:30pm; gift shop and information center open Mon–Fri noon–6pm, Sat–Sun 10am–6pm. **Bus:** 30 (Barton Creek Square).

Bats, Congress Avenue Bridge across Town Lake.

Austin loves its bats, and you'll no doubt take to them, too. If nothing else, it's impossible not to be impressed by the sight of 1 1/2 million emerging en masse from under the Congress Avenue Bridge.

Each March, free-tailed bats migrate from central Mexico to various roost sites in the Southwest. In 1980, when a deck reconstruction of Austin's bridge created an ideal environment for bringing up babies, some 750,000 pregnant females began settling in every year. Each bat gives birth to a single pup; by August, these offspring can take part in nightly forays west for bugs, usually around dusk. Depending on the group's size, the bats might munch on anywhere from 10,000 to 30,000 pounds of insects a night—one of the things that makes them so popular with Austinites. By November, they're old enough to hitch a ride back south with the group on the winds of an early cold front.

When the bats are in town, an educational kiosk designed to dispel some of the more popular myths about them is set up each evening on the north bank of the river, just east of the bridge. You'll learn, for example, that bats are not rodents, but mammals, and that they're not in the least interested in getting in anyone's hair.

Did You Know?

- Austin has the largest urban bat population in North America.
- Austin is the only city in the world to preserve its first public electric lights; 17 of the original 31 Moonlight Towers are still operating around the city.
- Sixty-nine percent of Austinites use computers, making Austin the most computer-literate city in the United States.
- The University of Texas's Buford H. Jester Center, which hosts the college dormitories, has the largest kitchen in Texas, capable of serving more than 13,000 students a day.
- The world's first photograph, created by Joseph Nicèphore Nièpce in 1826, is at U.T.'s Harry Ransom Humanities Research Center.

Downtown Austin Attractions & Shopping

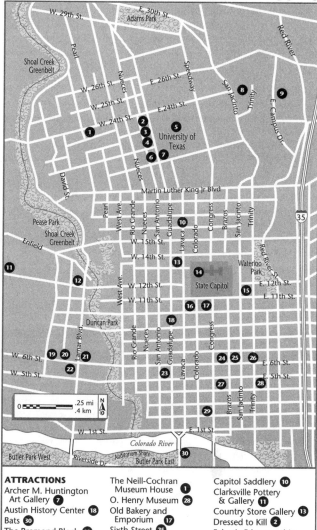

ATTRACTIONS

Archer M. Huntington Art Gallery **7**
Austin History Center **18**
Bats **30**
The Bremond Block **23**
Capitol Complex Visitors Center **15**
Driskill Hotel **24**
The Governor's Mansion **16**
Harry Ransom Humanities Research Center **7**
LBJ Library and Museum **9**
Mexic-Arte Museum **27**

The Neill-Cochran Museum House **1**
O. Henry Museum **28**
Old Bakery and Emporium **17**
Sixth Street **25**
State Capitol **14**
Texas Memorial Museum **8**
Treaty Oak **22**
The University of Texas at Austin **5**

SHOPPING

Book Woman **26**
Capitol Complex Visitors Center **15**

Capitol Saddlery **10**
Clarksville Pottery & Gallery **11**
Country Store Gallery **13**
Dressed to Kill **2**
Eclectic Ethnographic Gallery **12**
Le Cadeau **3**
Renaissance Market **4**
Sound Exchange **6**
Tesoros Trading Co. **29**
Waterloo Records and Video **21**
Whit Hanks Antiques & Decorative Arts **20**
Wiggy's **19**

The Governor's Mansion, 1010 Colorado St. ☎ 463-5518.

If the governor of Texas happens to be hosting a luncheon, members of the last tour of the mansion might notice warm smells wafting from the kitchen. Although it's one of the oldest (1856) buildings in the city, this opulent house is far from a museum piece: State law requires that the governor live here whenever he or she is in Austin.

This is not exactly a hardship, although the mansion was originally built by Abner Cook without any indoor toilets (there are now seven). The house was beautifully restored in 1979, but you can still see the scars of nails hammered into the bannister of the spiral staircase in order to break Governor Hogg's young son Tom of the habit of sliding down. The nation's first female governor, Miriam "Ma" Ferguson, entertained her friend Will Rogers in the mansion, and Governor John Connally recuperated here from gunshot wounds received when he accompanied John F. Kennedy on his fatal motorcade through Dallas. Among the many historical artifacts on display are a desk belonging to Stephen F. Austin and portraits of Davy Crockett and Sam Houston.

Come as close to opening time as you can; only a limited number of people are allowed to tour the mansion during the few hours it's open to the public. If you arrive later, you might either have a long wait or not get in at all.

Admission: Free.

Open: Tours scheduled every 20 minutes Mon–Fri 10am–11:40am (Mar–May, 9:30am–11:40am); closed weekends, some holidays, and at the discretion of the governor. **Bus:** Congress/Capitol 'Dillo, ACC/Lavaca 'Dillo.

Sixth Street, between Lavaca Ave. and I-35.

Formerly known as Pecan Street—all the east-west thoroughfares in Austin were originally named for trees—Sixth Street was once the main connecting road to the older settlements east of Austin. During the Reconstruction boom of the 1870s, the wooden wagon yards and saloons of the 1850s and 1860s began to be replaced by the more solid masonry structures you see today.

After the grand, new State Capitol was built in 1888, the center of commercial activity began shifting toward Congress Avenue; by the middle of the next century, Sixth Street had become a skid row. Restoration of the nine blocks designated a National Register District began in the late 1960s; in the 1970s, the street blossomed into a live-music venue. Now lined with more than 70 restaurants, galleries, theaters, nightspots, and shops, Austin's former main street is still rather sedate during the day, but it comes alive on weekend nights when a (mostly young) crowd throngs the sidewalks for some serious club crawling.

★ State Capitol, 11th and Congress Sts. ☎ 463-0063.

Visitors to Austin no longer have to leave disappointed that they couldn't view the city's most famous sight. Begun in 1990 and completed in time for the 1995 legislative session, a massive renovation and expansion—to the tune of $187.6 million—have restored Texas's capitol to its former glory and added a striking new underground annex.

Completed in 1888, the current capitol replaced an 1852 limestone statehouse that burned down in 1881; a land-rich but otherwise impecunious Texas government traded three-million acres of public lands to contractors to finance its construction. Gleaming pink granite was donated to the cause, but a railroad had to be built to transport the material some 75 miles from Granite Mountain, near Marble Falls, to Austin. Texas convicts labored on the project alongside 62 stonecutters brought in from Scotland.

The result was the largest state capitol in the country, second only in size to the U.S. Capitol—but measuring seven feet taller. The building covers three acres of ground; the cornerstone alone weighs 16,000 pounds and the total length of the wooden wainscoting runs approximately seven miles. A splendid rotunda and dome lie at the intersection of the main corridors; the house and senate chambers are located at opposite ends of the second level.

Almost 700,000 tons of rock were chiseled from the ground to make way for the new extension, connected to the capitol and four other state buildings by tunnels. Skylights let in natural illumination and afford spectacular views of the capitol dome. To complement the 1888 building, the annex was constructed with similar materials and incorporates many of the capitol's symbols and styles.

Admission: Free.

Open: Daily 6am–11pm; 24 hours a day during legislative sessions (held in odd years, starting in Jan, for 140 straight days; 30-day special sessions are also called sometimes). Free guided tours given every 15 minutes Mon–Fri 8:30am–4:30pm, Sat 9:30am–4:30pm, Sun 12:30–4:30pm. **Bus:** All three 'Dillo lines.

The University of Texas at Austin, Main Campus, Guadalupe and I.H.-35, Martin Luther King, Jr., Blvd., and 26th St. ☎ 471-3434.

In 1883, the 221 students and 8 teachers set to start the term at the newly established University of Texas in Austin had to meet in makeshift classrooms in the town's temporary capitol; at the time, the two-million acres of dry west Texas land that the higher educational system had been granted barely brought in 40¢ an acre for grazing. Now nearly 50,000 students occupy 120 buildings on U.T.'s main campus alone, and that arid west Texas land, which blew a gusher in 1923, has raked in more than $4 billion of oil money—two-thirds of it directed to the U.T. school system.

Two visitors centers, one at Sid Richardson Hall, next to the LBJ Library, and the other in the Arno Nowotny Building, at I-35 and Martin Luther King, Jr., Boulevard, offer maps and other campus information; they're open weekdays from 8am to 4:30pm (☎ 471-1420).

See "More Attractions," below, for details on the LBJ Library and Museum, Harry Ransom Humanities Research Center, Archer M.

Huntington Art Gallery, Texas Memorial Museum, and a tour of university sights.

2 More Attractions

Architectural Highlights

THE MOONLIGHT TOWERS

In May 1895, the first dam-generated electric current illuminated four square blocks around each of Austin's 31 new moonlight towers. Some residents of the still-rural town worried that these 165-foot-high spires would confuse the roosters, who wouldn't be able to figure out when the sun was coming up. Seventeen of these cast- and wrought-iron towers, most of them downtown, remain part of Austin's street-lighting system; you can also see one in Hyde Park, at 41st Street and Speedway.

A CEMETERY

State Cemetery, E. Seventh St. at Comal St. ☎ 478-8930.

The city's namesake, Stephen F. Austin, is the best-known resident of this east-side cemetery, established by the state in 1851. Judge Edwin Waller, who laid out the grid plan for Austin's streets and later served as the city's mayor, also rests here, as do eight former Texas governors, various fighters in Texas's battles for independence, and a woman who lived to tell the tale of the Alamo. Perhaps the most moving monument, sculpted by Elisabet Ney (see "Museums/ Galleries," below), commemorates General Albert Sidney Johnston, who died for the Confederacy at the Battle of Shiloh.

Admission: Free.

Open: Mon–Fri 8am–5pm, Sat–Sun 9am–6pm. **Bus:** 4–18 stops nearby.

HISTORIC SITES

Capitol Complex Visitors Center/Old General Land Office, 112 E. 11th St. ☎ 305-8400.

The capitol wasn't the only important member of the state complex to undergo a recent facelift: Texas also spent $4 million to gussy up its oldest surviving office building, the 1857 General Land Office. If the imposing German Romanesque structure looks a bit grand for the headquarters of an administrative agency, keep in mind that land has long been the state's most important resource. Among the employees of this important—and very political—office, in charge of maintaining records and surveying holdings, was the writer O. Henry, who worked as a draftsman from 1887 to 1891; he based two short stories on his experiences here.

The building was rededicated as a visitors center for the Capitol Complex in 1994; the Texas Department of Transportation also distributes state travel information here. A Walter Cronkite–narrated video tells the history of the complex, and changing exhibits on the first floor highlight the Capitol Preservation Project; upstairs, displays focus on the Land Office and other aspects of Texas's past.

Admission: Free.

Open: Tues–Fri 9am–4pm, Sat noon–5pm. Free tours of the building given every half hour on the hour, video ($1 adults, 50¢ children) shown every half hour on the hour. **Bus:** All three 'Dillo lines.

Driskill Hotel, 122 E. Sixth St. ☎ 474-5911.

Colonel Jesse Driskill was not a modest man; when he opened a hotel in 1886, he named it after himself, put busts of himself and his two sons over the entrances, and installed bas-relief sculptures of longhorn steers—to remind folks how he had made his fortune. Nor did he build a modest property: The ornate four-story structure, which originally boasted a skylit rotunda, has the largest arched doorway in Texas over its east entrance. So posh that the state legislature met here while the 1888 capitol was being built, the hotel has had its ups and downs over the years, but it remains *the* place for Austin politicos to host their grand events.

Bus: Convention Center/U.T. Campus 'Dillo, Congress/Capitol 'Dillo.

Frommer's Favorite Austin Experiences

Hiking & Biking   You need only stroll over to the shores of Town Lake to see why *Walking* magazine chose Austin as America's "Most Fit" city; speed walkers, joggers, and blade runners share the turf with bicyclists and hikers on one of the many trails set up by the city for its urban athletes.

Swimming at Barton Springs Pool   The bracing waters of this natural pool have been drawing Austinites to its banks for more than 100 years; if there's anything that everyone in town can agree on, it's that there's no better plunge on a hot day.

Water Sports at Lake Travis   The longest of the chain of seven Highland Lakes, Travis offers the most opportunities for folks to cavort in its clear, cool water. Whether doing your thing involves Jetskiing, snorkeling, or angling, you'll have plenty of chances to indulge here.

Bat Watching   From late March through November, thousands of bats emerge in smoky clouds from under the Congress Avenue Bridge, heading west for dinner; it's a thrilling sight, and you can thank each of the little mammals for eating as many as 600 mosquitoes per hour.

Listening to Live Music   It's not only Austin's Sixth Street that's a live-music mecca; there are plenty of terrific and inexpensive places to listen to bands all over town. If you're around at the right time, you can sit in on a taping of *Austin City Limits* and catch some first-class country-and-western acts for free.

French Legation, 802 San Marcos. ☎ **472-8180.**

The oldest residence still standing in Austin was built in 1841 for Compte Alphonse Dubois de Saligny, France's representative to the fledgling Republic of Texas. Although his home was very extravagant for the then primitive capital, the flamboyant de Saligny didn't stay around to enjoy it for very long; he left town in a huff after his servant was beaten in retaliation for making bacon out of some pigs that had dined on the diplomat's linens. In the back of the house, considered the best example of French colonial–style architecture outside Louisiana, is a re-creation of the only known authentic Creole kitchen in the United States.

Admission: $2.50 adults, 50¢ children under 10.

Open: Tues–Sun 1–5pm. **Directions:** Go east on Eighth Street, then turn left on Embassy Drive; the parking lot is on Embassy and Ninth Street.

The Neill-Cochran Museum House, 2310 San Gabriel St. ☎ **478-2335.**

Abner Cook, the architect-contractor responsible for the Governor's Mansion and many of Austin's other gracious Greek Revival mansions, built this home in 1855; it bears his trademark portico with six Doric columns and a balustrade designed with crossed sheaves of wheat. Almost all of its doors, windows, shutters, and hinges are the originals—which is rather astonishing when you consider that the house was used as the Blind Institute in 1856 and then as a hospital for Union prisoners near the end of the Civil War.

Admission: $2 adults, children under 10 free.

Open: Wed–Sun 2–5pm, guided tour only. **Bus:** ACC/Lavaca 'Dillo, U.T. shuttle.

Old Bakery and Emporium, 1006 Congress Ave. ☎ **477-5961.**

On the National Register of Historic Landmarks, the Old Bakery was built in 1876 by Charles Lundberg, a Swedish master baker, and continuously run as a confectionery until 1936; you can still see the giant oven and wooden baker's space inside. Rescued from demolition by the Austin Heritage Society, the brick-and-limestone building is one of the few unaltered structures on Congress Avenue. It now houses a gift shop, selling crafts handmade by seniors; a reasonably priced lunch room; and a hospitality desk with visitors brochures.

Admission: Free.

Open: June–Aug and Dec (before Christmas), Mon–Fri 9am–4pm, Sat 10am–3pm; rest of the year, closed Sat–Sun. **Bus:** Congress/Capitol 'Dillo.

Treaty Oak, 503 Baylor St., between Fifth and Sixth Sts.

Legend has it that Stephen F. Austin signed the first boundary treaty with the Comanches under the spreading branches of this 500-year-old live oak, which once served as the symbolic border between Anglo and Indian territory. Whatever the case, this is the sole remaining tree in what was once a grove of Council Oaks—which made the well-publicized attempt on its life in 1989 especially shocking. But almost as dramatic as the story of the tree's deliberate poisoning by an attention-seeking Austinite is the tale of its rescue by an international team of foresters. The dried wood from a major limb that they removed has been allocated to local artists, who are creating public artworks celebrating the tree.

Lakes

THE HIGHLAND LAKES

The six dams built by the Lower Colorado River Authority in the late 1930s through the early 1950s not only controlled the flooding that had plagued the areas surrounding Texas's Colorado River (not to be confused with the more famous river of the same name to the north), but also transformed the waterway into a sparkling chain of lakes, stretching some 150 miles northwest of Austin. The narrowest of them, Town Lake, is also the closest to downtown; the heart of urban recreation in Austin, it boasts a shoreline park and adjacent hike-and-bike trail. Lake Austin, the next in line, is more residential, but offers Emma Long Park as a public shore. Serious aquatic enthusiasts keep going until they reach Lake Travis, the longest lake in the chain and the one that offers the most possibilities for playing in the water. Together with the other Highland Lakes—Marble Falls, LBJ, Inks, and Buchanan—these comprise the largest concentration of freshwater lakes in Texas. See also "Recreation," below, for activity and equipment rental suggestions.

Libraries/Research Centers

Austin History Center/Austin Public Library, 810 Guadalupe St. ☎ 499-7480.

Built in 1933, the Renaissance Revival–style public library not only embodies some of the finest architecture, ironwork, and stone carving of its era, but also serves as the best resource for information about Austin from before the city's founding in 1839 to the present. The center often hosts exhibitions such as "Lost Victorian Austin," drawn from its vast archives of historical photographs and sketches.

Admission: Free.

Open: Mon–Thurs 9am–9pm, Fri–Sat 9am–6pm, Sun noon–6pm. **Bus:** ACC/Lavaca 'Dillo.

Harry Ransom Humanities Research Center, University of Texas. Harry Ransom Center, 21st and Guadalupe Sts.; Flawn Academic Center, west of the main tower. ☎ 471-8944.

The special collections of The Harry Ransom Center (HRC) contain approximately 1-million rare books, 36-million manuscripts, 5-million photographs, and more than 100,000 works of art. Most of this wealth is stashed away for scholars' use, but permanent and rotating exhibits of HRC holdings are held in two buildings: the Harry Ransom Center and the Leeds Gallery of the Flawn Academic Center. A Gutenberg Bible—one of only five complete copies in the

United States—is always on display on the first floor of the former, and you never know what else you might see: Costumes from the movie *Gone with the Wind*, the original manuscript of Arthur Miller's *Death of a Salesman*, or letters written by novelist Isaac Bashevis Singer.

Admission: Free.

Open: Harry Ransom Center, first-floor gallery, Mon–Sat 9am–5pm, Sun 1–5pm; fourth- and seventh-floor galleries, Mon–Fri 9am–4:30pm. Leeds Gallery, Mon–Fri 8:30am–4:30pm, Sat 10am–5pm. **Closed:** University holidays. **Bus:** Convention Center/ U.T. Campus 'Dillo, U.T. Shuttle.

★ **LBJ Library and Museum,** University of Texas, 2313 Red River. ☎ 482-5136.

Set on a hilltop commanding an impressive campus view, the LBJ Library contains some 40-million documents relating to the colorful 36th president, along with gifts, memorabilia, and other historical objects. Johnson himself kept an office here from 1971, when the building was dedicated, until his death in 1973. Photos trace his long political career, starting with his early successes as a state representative and continuing through to the Kennedy assassination and the Civil Rights movement; LBJ's success in enacting social programs is depicted in an Alfred Leslie painting of the Great Society. Johnson loved political cartoons, even when he was their target; examples from his large collection are among the museum's most interesting exhibits.

Admission: Free.

Open: Daily 9am–5pm. **Closed:** Christmas. **Bus:** Convention Center/U.T. Campus 'Dillo, U.T. Shuttle.

National Wildflower Research Center, 4801 La Crosse Ave. ☎ 929-3600.

Talk about fieldwork: The researchers at this complex have 42 acres of wildflowers for their personal laboratory. Founded by Lady Bird Johnson in 1982, the center is dedicated to the study and preservation of native plants—and where better to survey them than in Texas Hill Country, famous for its glorious spring blossoms? The new facility, opened in spring 1995, expands on an earlier site, with a variety of display gardens, shade pavilions, and greenhouses, along with a wildflower meadow. The admission and gift shop proceeds help fund the nonprofit organization.

Admission: $3 adults, $2 students 13 and older, seniors 60 and older, $1 children 12 and under.

Open: Mon–Fri 9am–4pm, extended to weekends late Mar through early May; call for exact dates. **Directions:** Take Loop 1 (Mo-Pac) south past Ben White Boulevard to Slaughter Lane; drive four-fifths of a mile to the Veloway leading to the center.

Museums/Galleries

Archer M. Huntington Art Gallery, University of Texas. Harry Ransom Center, 21st and Guadalupe Sts.; Art Building, 23rd St. and San Jacinto Boulevard. ☎ 471-7324.

Ranked among the top-10 university art museums in the United States, the Huntington hosts an eclectic variety of work. Among the permanent exhibits in the Harry Ransom Center are the Mari and James Michener collection of 20th-century American masters; an excellent array of Latin American art; and a rare display of 19th-century plaster casts of monumental Greek and Roman sculpture. The gallery in the Art Building is used for touring shows and student/faculty art exhibitions.

Admission: Free.

Open: Mon–Sat 9am–5pm, Sun 1–5pm. **Closed:** University holidays. **Bus:** Convention Center/U.T. Campus 'Dillo, ACC/Lavaca 'Dillo, U.T. Shuttle.

Elisabet Ney Museum, 304 E. 44th St. ☎ 458-2255.

Strong-willed and eccentric, German-born sculptor Elisabet Ney nevertheless charmed Austin society in the late 19th century; when she died, her admirers turned her Hyde Park studio into a museum. In the former loft and working area—part Greek temple, part medieval battlement—visitors can view plaster replicas of many of her pieces. Drawn toward the larger-than-life figures of her age, Ney had created busts of Schopenhauer, Garibaldi, and Bismarck by the time she was commissioned to make models of Texas heroes Stephen F. Austin and Sam Houston for an 1893 Chicago exposition. William Jennings Bryan, Enrico Caruso, Jan Paderewski, and four Texas governors were among the many visitors to her Austin studio.

Admission: Free.

Open: Wed–Sat 10am–5pm, Sun noon–5pm. **Bus:** 1, 5.

George Washington Carver Museum, 1165 Angelina St. ☎ 472-4089.

The many contributions of Austin's African American community are highlighted at this museum, the first one in Texas to be devoted to black history. Rotating exhibits of contemporary artwork share the space with photographs, videos, oral histories, and other artifacts from the community's past. Cultural events are often held here, too. The museum's collection is housed in the city's first public-library building, opened in 1926 and moved to this site in 1933; the newer George Washington Carver branch of the public library is next door.

Admission: Free.

Open: Tues–Thurs 10am–6pm, Fri–Sat noon–5pm. **Bus:** 2.

Laguna Gloria Art Museum, 3809 W. 35th St. ☎ 458-8191.

This intimate art museum sits on 28 palm- and pecan-shaded acres overlooking Lake Austin; they're believed by some to be part of a claim staked out for his retirement by Stephen F. Austin, who didn't live to enjoy the view. The lovely Mediterranean-style villa that houses the exhibits was built in 1916 by Austin newspaper publisher Hal Sevier and his wife, Clara Driscoll, best known for her successful crusade to save the Alamo from commercial development. Dedicated to 20th-century American art, the gallery hosts seven to ten shows a year; they might feature the work of Austin and central Texas artists or contemporary Mexican photographers.

Admission: $2 adults, $1 seniors and students with ID, children under 16 free. Free all day Thurs.

Open: Tues–Thurs 10am–5pm. **Bus:** 9 (Sat–Sun only). **Directions:** One mile past west end of 35th Street, at the foot of Mt. Bonnell.

MEXIC-ARTE Museum, 419 Congress Ave. ☎ 480-9373.

The first organization in Austin to promote multicultural contemporary art when it was formed in 1983, MEXIC-ARTE is now the largest art space in the city, with 24,000 square feet of exhibition room. A small permanent collection of 20th-century Mexican art—including a fascinating array of masks from the state of Guerrero—is supplemented by visiting shows, including some from Mexico, such as a major retrospective of the work of muralist Diego Rivera. The museum also programs an average of two music, theater, and performing arts events each weekend.

Admission: Suggested donation $2.

Open: Mon–Sat 10am–6pm. **Bus:** Congress/Capitol 'Dillo.

O. Henry Museum, 409 E. Fifth St. ☎ 472-1903.

When William Sidney Porter, better known as O. Henry, lived in Austin (1884–98), he published a popular satirical newspaper called the *Rolling Stone*. He also held down an odd string of jobs, including a stint as a teller at the First National Bank of Austin, where he was later accused of embezzling funds. It was while he was serving time for this crime that he wrote the 13 short stories that established his literary reputation. Recently reopened to visitors after a major restoration, the modest Victorian cottage in which O. Henry lived with his wife and daughter from 1893 to 1895 contains the family's bedroom furniture, silverware, and china, as well as the desk at which the author wrote copy for the *Rolling Stone*.

Admission: Free.

Open: Wed–Sun noon–5pm. **Closed:** Christmas, New Year's Day, Thanksgiving Day. **Bus:** Convention Center/U.T. Campus 'Dillo.

Texas Memorial Museum, University of Texas, 2400 Trinity. ☎ 471-1604.

During a whistle-stop visit to Austin in 1936, Franklin Roosevelt broke the ground for this museum, built to commemorate the centennial of Texas independence. Whatever your age, you'll probably remember going on a class trip to a place like this, with dioramas, stuffed animals, and other displays detailing the geology, anthropology, and natural history of your home state.

Three things make this museum well worth a visit: an intriguing exhibit on the history of firearms; the original zinc Goddess of Liberty that once sat on top of the capitol; and a good gift shop, with lots of ethnic crafts and educational toys.

Admission: Free, donations appreciated.

Open: Mon–Fri 9am–5pm, Sat 10am–5pm, Sun 1–5pm. **Bus:** 27.

Umlauf Sculpture Garden and Museum, 605 Robert E. Lee Rd. ☎ 445-5582.

This is a very user-friendly museum, one for people who don't enjoy being cooped up in a stuffy, hushed space. An art instructor at the University of Texas for 40 years, Charles Umlauf donated his home, studio, and more than 250 pieces of artwork to the city of Austin, which maintains the lovely native garden where much of the sculpture is displayed. Umlauf, whose pieces reside in such places as the Smithsonian Institution and New York's Metropolitan Museum, worked in many media and styles. He also used a variety of models; you'll probably recognize the portrait of Umlauf's most famous U.T. student, Farrah Fawcett.

Admission: $2 adults, $1 students, children 6 and under free.

Open: Thurs, Sat–Sun 1–4:30pm, Fri 10am–4:30pm (open until 8pm Thurs in June, July, and Aug); Tues–Wed by appointment. **Closed:** Mon. **Bus:** 63.

Neighborhoods/Historic Blocks

The Bremond Block, between Seventh and Eighth, San Antonio and Guadalupe Sts.

"The family that builds together, bonds together" might have been the slogan of Eugene Bremond, an early Austin banker who established a mini-real-estate monopoly for his own kin in the downtown area. In the mid-1860s, he started investing in land on what was once Block 80 of the original city plan; in 1874 he moved into a Greek Revival home made by master builder Abner Cook. By the time he was through, he had created a family compound, purchasing and enlarging homes for himself, two sisters, a daughter, a son, and a brother-in-law. Some were destroyed, but those that remain on what is now known as the Bremond Block are exquisite examples of elaborate late 19th-century homes. One of the homes is a bed-and-breakfast; the others are offices, not open to the public.

Hyde Park, between E. 38th and E. 45th, Duval and Guadalupe Sts.

Unlike Eugene Bremond (see above), developer Monroe Martin Shipe built homes for the middle, not upper, classes. In the 1890s, he created—and tirelessly promoted—a complex-cum-resort at the southwest edge of Austin; he even built an electric streetcar system to connect it with the rest of the city. By the middle of this century, Austin's first planned suburb had become somewhat shabby, but recent decades of gentrification have turned the tide. Now visitors can amble along pecan-shaded streets and look at beautifully restored residences, many in pleasing combinations of late Queen Anne and early Craftsman styles. Shipe's own architecturally eclectic home, at 3816 Ave. G, is a bit grander than some of the others, but not much.

Panorama

Mt. Bonnell, 3800 Mt. Bonnell Rd.

For the best views of the city and Hill Country, ascend to this mountaintop park, the highest point in Austin at 785 feet and the oldest tourist attraction in town. It has long been a favorite spot for romantic trysts; rumor had it that any couple who climbed the 106 stone steps to the top together would fall in love (an emotion often confused with exhaustion). The peak was named for George W. Bonnell, Sam Houston's Commissioner of Indian Affairs in 1836.

Admission: Free.

Open: Daily 5am–10pm. **Directions:** Take Mt. Bonnell Road one mile past the west end of W. 35th Street.

Parks & Gardens

Emma Long Park, 1600 City Park Rd. ☎ **346-1831.**

More than 1,000 acres of woodland and a mile of shore along Lake Austin make Emma Long Park—named for the first woman to sit on Austin's city council—a most appealing metropolitan space. Water activities are centered around two boat ramps and a fishing dock; there's also a protected swimming area, guarded by lifeguards on summer weekends. Camping permits are available. If you hike through the stands of oak, ash, and juniper to an elevation of 1,000 feet, you'll see the city spread out before you.

Admission: $3 per vehicle Mon–Thurs, $5 Thurs–Sun and holidays.

Open: Daily 7am–10pm. **Directions:** Exit I-35 at 290 west, then go west (street names will change to Koenig, Allendale, Northland, and F.M. 2222) to City Park Road (near Loop 360); turn south and drive 6.2 miles to park entrance.

Zilker Botanical Garden, 2220 Barton Springs Rd. ☎ **477-8672.**

There's bound to be something blooming at the Zilker Botanical Garden from March to October, but no matter what time of year you visit, you'll find this a soothing spot. The Oriental Garden created by Isamu Taniguchi is particularly peaceful; ask someone at the garden center to point out how Taniguchi landscaped the word "AUSTIN" into his design. A butterfly garden attracts gorgeous winged visitors during April and October migrations, and you can poke and prod the plants in the herb garden to get them to yield up their fragrances. One-hundred-million-year-old dinosaur tracks were discovered on the grounds in January 1991; you can view them only on tours given on Saturday mornings, May through November (call the garden or **251-1816** for times).

Admission: Free; dinosaur-track tours $2 adults, $1 students, preschoolers free.

Open: Grounds open daily 8am–7pm. Garden center open Mon–Fri 8:30am–4:30pm; Sat 1–5pm (Jan–Feb), 10am–5pm (Mar–Dec); Sun 1–5pm. **Bus:** 30.

★ **Zilker Park,** 2201 Barton Springs Rd. ☎ **476-9044.**

Comprising 347 acres, the first 40 of which were donated to the city by the wealthy German immigrant for whom the park is named, this is Austin's favorite public playground. Its centerpiece is Barton Springs (see "The Top Attractions," above), but visitors and locals also flock to the Zilker Botanical Garden, the Austin Nature Preserves, and the Umlauf Sculpture Garden and Museum, all described elsewhere in this section; see also the "Cool for Kids" and "Recreation" sections, below, for details about the Austin Nature Center, the Zilker Eagle Railroad, and Town Lake canoe rentals. In addition to its athletic fields (eight for soccer, two for softball, and one for rugby), the park also hosts a nine-hole disk (Frisbee) golf course.

Admission: Free.

Open: Daily 5am–10pm. **Bus:** 30.

Nature Preserves

City of Austin Nature Preserves, 301 Nature Center Dr.
☎ **327-5437** or **327-5478.**

Austin boasts a remarkably diverse group of natural habitats in its city-run nature preserves. At **Blunn Creek** (1100 block of St. Edward's Drive), 40 acres of upland woods and meadows are traversed by a spring-fed creek; one of the two lookout areas is made of compacted volcanic ash. The 500-acre **Forest Ridge** (8000 N. Capital of Texas Hwy.) affords wonderful views of surrounding Hill Country and Bull Creek waterfalls. Spelunkers will like **Karst** (3900 Deer Lane), which is honeycombed with limestone caves and sinkholes. Lovely **Mayfield Park** (3505 W. 35th St.) directly abuts the Barrow Brook Cove of Lake Austin; peacocks and hens roam freely around lily ponds, and trails cross over bridges in oak and juniper woods. Visitors to the rock-walled ramada at the **Zilker Preserve** (Barton Springs Road and Loop 1), with its meadows, streams, and cliff, can look out over downtown Austin. All the preserves are maintained in a primitive state with natural surface trails and no restrooms.

Admission: Free.

Open: Daily, dawn to dusk. **Directions:** To locate the city's preserves, phone one of the numbers listed above.

Westcave Preserve, Star Rte. 1, Dripping Springs. ☎ **825-3442.**

If you don't like the weather in one part of Westcave Preserve, you might like it better in another: Up to 25 degrees difference in temperature has been recorded between the highest area of this natural habitat, an arid Hill Country scrub, and the lowest, a lush riparian woodland spread across a canyon floor. Because the ecosystem here is so delicate, the 30 acres on the Pedernales River may be entered only by guided tour. No reservations are taken; the first 30 people to show up at the allotted times are allowed in.

Admission: Free.

Open: Sat–Sun, for tours at 10am, noon, 2 and 4pm (weather permitting). **Directions:** Take Hwy. 71 to Ranch Road 3238; follow the signs 15 miles to Hamilton Pool, which is across the Pedernales River Bridge from the preserve.

Wild Basin Wilderness Preserve, 805 N. Capital of Texas Hwy.
☎ **327-7622.**

Sitting on a 227-acre peninsula high above Loop 360, the Wild Basin Wilderness Preserve is a perfect place to watch the moon rise

Greater Austin Attractions and Shopping

ATTRACTIONS

Austin Children's Museum 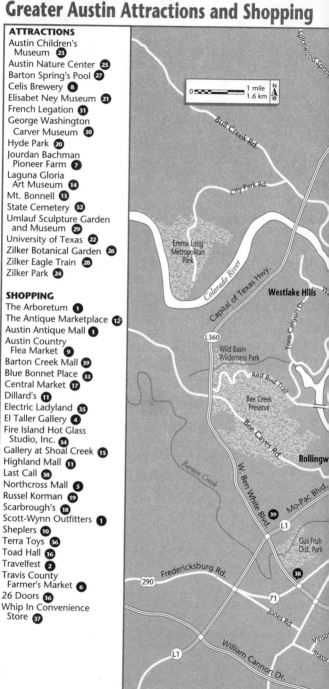23

Austin Nature Center 25

Barton Spring's Pool 27

Celis Brewery 8

Elisabet Ney Museum 21

French Legation 31

George Washington Carver Museum 30

Hyde Park 20

Jourdan Bachman Pioneer Farm 7

Laguna Gloria Art Museum 14

Mt. Bonnell 13

State Cemetery 32

Umlauf Sculpture Garden and Museum 29

University of Texas 22

Zilker Botanical Garden 26

Zilker Eagle Train 28

Zilker Park 24

SHOPPING

The Arboretum 1

The Antique Marketplace 12

Austin Antique Mall 3

Austin Country Flea Market 9

Barton Creek Mall 39

Blue Bonnet Place 33

Central Market 17

Dillard's 11

Electric Ladyland 35

El Taller Gallery 4

Fire Island Hot Glass Studio, Inc. 34

Gallery at Shoal Creek 15

Highland Mall 11

Last Call 38

Northcross Mall 5

Russel Korman 19

Scarbrough's 18

Scott-Wynn Outfitters 1

Sheplers 10

Terra Toys 36

Toad Hall 16

Travelfest 2

Travis County Farmer's Market 6

26 Doors 16

Whip In Convenience Store 37

0 — 1 mile / 1.6 km N

Spicewood Spring

Bull Creek Rd.

City Park Rd.

Emma Long Metropolitan Park

Colorado River

Capital of Texas Hwy.

Westlake Hills

Toro Canyon Dr.

L360

Wild Basin Wilderness Park

Red Bud Trail

Bee Creek Preserve

Bee Caves Rd.

Rollingw

Barton Creek

W. Ben White Blvd.

Mo-Pac Blvd.

39

L1

Gus Fruh Dist. Park

38

Fredericksburg Rd.

290

71

Jones Rd.

Vinso

L1

William Cannon Dr.

Stass

9590

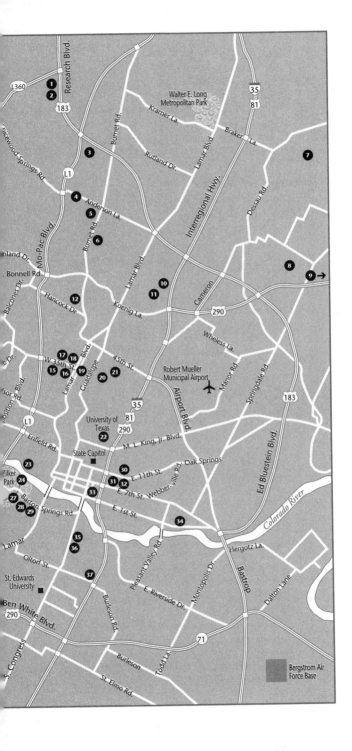

over Austin; the clarity of the night sky from here is, well, stellar. In addition to its daytime nature walks, given every weekend, Wild Basin sponsors **moonlighting** and **stargazing tours** twice a month. Call ahead for exact dates: The moonlighting tour coincides with the full moon, and stargazing is scheduled for three or four days after the new moon. This popular heavenly peak is limited to 20; make reservations as far in advance as possible.

Price: $3 adults, $1.50 ages 5–12, children free under 5.

Tours: Twice monthly, weather permitting, generally 8 or 8:30pm to 9:30 or 10pm.

Wineries & Breweries

Celis Brewery, 2431 Forbes Dr. ☎ 835-0884.

Those with a taste for highly prized Belgian beers will want to take a tour of the Celis Brewery, on the northeast side of Austin. Pierre Celis, who had made "white" beer in the village of Hoegaarden, found the spring-fed water and limestone terrain of the Austin area conducive to reproducing the beverage that had been brewed for 500 years in his native Belgian town. The brewery was built around two huge, hand-hammered copper kettles that Celis imported to give his beer the desired flavor.

Admission: Free.

Open: Tours, followed by samplings, conducted Tues–Sat at 2 and 4pm. **Directions:** Take U.S. 290 east, just past its crossing with U.S. 183; get off at Cross Park Drive, take it north to Forbes Drive.

Fall Creek Vineyards, 2.2 miles northeast of Tow.
☎ 915/379-5361.

The wines sold at this 65-acre vineyard, praised by critics around the country, amply reward the long drive up to the northwest shore of Lake Buchanan. You may have already tried a glass or two at fine restaurants in Austin; here you can sample the full range of award winners, including carnelians, Rieslings, and zinfandels. Special tours can be arranged through the Austin office (☎ **512/476-4477**).

Admission: Free.

Open: Mar–Oct Mon–Fri 11am–2pm for tasting and sales, Sat noon–5pm tours, tasting, and sales, Sun noon–4pm tasting and sales. Closed Sun from Nov–Feb. **Directions:** For the most scenic route, take Hwy. 71 (Ben White Boulevard) west to Marble Falls, and pick up Hwy. 1431 west; it'll dead-end into 261 north (called Lakeshore Drive at Lake Buchanan); when you get to 2241, take it north past Tow, where it will trail off at the vineyards.

Hill Country Cellars, U.S. Hwy. 183 north, Cedar Park.
☎ 259-2000.

Stroll under a trellised wood arbor and then enjoy the chardonnay and cabernet sauvignon grapes grown on the premises of this vineyard/winery, about 20 minutes northwest of Austin. A 200-year-old native grapevine is the centerpiece of the picnic area where various seasonal festivals are held. Winemaker Russell Smith moved back from Napa Valley to work here in his native Texas, which is newly developing a wine industry.

Admission: Free.

Open: Tasting room open daily noon–5pm; winery tours given Fri–Sun 1–4pm on the hour (or by appointment). **Directions:** Take U.S. Hwy. 183 north, four-fifths of a mile past F.M. 1431.

Slaughter Leftwich Vineyards, 4209 Eck Lane. ☎ 266-3331.

The Slaughter Leftwich vineyards produced Texas's first chardonnays in the high-plains region of Texas, but you don't have to travel out to the Lubbock area to try these award-winning bottles; just take a scenic drive to a shady lane near Austin's Lake Travis. The winery and tasting room are in a native stone structure, built to resemble those popular in the last century. If you like whites, the chardonnay is your best bet; but all the wines are reasonably priced, so it's hard to go very wrong.

Admission: Free.

Open: Daily 1–5pm for free tastings and sales; winery tour included Fri–Sun (tours are given every day except Mon from June–Sept. **Directions:** Take R.R. 620 one mile past Mansfield Dam, turn right onto Eck Lane at intersection of Hudson Bend Road and R.R. 620.

Walking Tour
University of Texas

Start   The Arno Nowotny Visitors Center.

Finish   The Littlefield Fountain.

Time   One hour, not including food breaks or visits to the museums.

Best Times   On the weekends, when the campus is less crowded (and more parking is available).

Worst Times   Morning and midday during the week when classes are in session and parking is impossible to find (beware: those tow-away zone signs mean business).

No ivy tower—although it hosts some—the University of Texas is as integral to Austin's identity as it is to its economy. To explore the vast main campus is to glimpse the city's future as well as its past: Here state-of-the-art structures—including newly installed information kiosks able to play the school's team songs for you—sit cheek by jowl with elegant examples of 19th-century architecture. The following tour points out many of the most interesting spots on campus; unless you regularly trek around the Himalayas, however, you'll probably want to drive or take a bus between some of the first seven sights (parking limitations were taken into account in this initial portion of the circuit). For a walking tour alone, begin at attraction no. 8.

Note: Stops 2, 4, 5, 6, 12, and 20 are also discussed earlier in this chapter, where their entrance hours are listed.

In 1839, the Congress of the Republic of Texas ordered a site set aside for the establishment of a "university of the first class" in Austin. Some 40 years later, when the flagship of the new University of Texas system opened, its first two buildings went up on that original 40-acre plot, dubbed College Hill. Although there were attempts to establish master-design plans for the university from the turn-of-the-century onward, they were only carried out in bits and pieces until 1930, when money from an earlier oil strike on U.T. land allowed the school to begin building in earnest. Between 1930 and 1945, consulting architect Paul Cret put his mark on 19 university buildings, most of which show the influence of his education at Paris's Ecole des Beaux-Arts. If the entire 357-acre campus will never achieve stylistic unity or anything close to it, its earliest section has a grace and cohesion that makes it a delight to stroll.

Although we start out at the oldest building owned by the university, this tour begins far from the original campus. At the frontage road of I-35 and the corner of Martin Luther King, Jr., Boulevard, you can pull into the parking lot of:

1. **The Arno Nowotny Building.** In the 1850s, many state-run asylums for the mentally ill and the physically handicapped arose on the outskirts of Austin. One of these was the State Asylum for the Blind, built by Abner Cook around 1856. The ornate Italianate-style structure soon became better known as the headquarters and barracks of General Custer, who had been sent to Austin in 1865 to reestablish order after the Civil War. Incorporated into the university and restored for its centennial celebration, the building is now one of U.T.'s two visitors bureaus.

   Take Martin Luther King, Jr., Boulevard to Red River, then drive north to the:

2. **LBJ Library and Museum,** which offers another rare on-campus parking lot; you'll want to leave your car here while you look at sights 3 through 6. The first presidential library to be built on a university campus, the huge travertine marble structure oversees a beautifully landscaped 14-acre complex. Among the museum's exhibits is a seven-eighths scale replica of the Oval Office as it looked when the Johnsons occupied the White House. In the adjoining Sid Richardson Hall are the Lyndon B. Johnson School of Public Affairs; the Barker Texas History Center, housing the world's most extensive collection of Texana; and the second of U.T.'s visitors bureaus.

   Stroll down the library steps across East Campus Drive to 23rd Street, where, next to the large Burleson bells on your right, you'll see the university's $41-million:

Walking Tour: The University of Texas

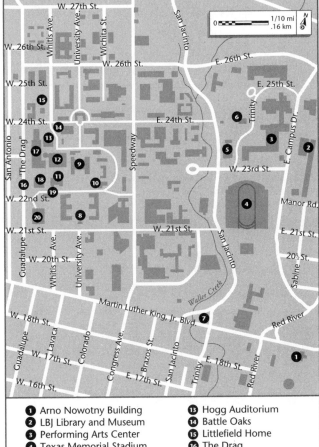

Legend:

1. Arno Nowotny Building
2. LBJ Library and Museum
3. Performing Arts Center
4. Texas Memorial Stadium
5. Art Building
6. Texas Memorial Museum
7. Santa Rita No. 1
8. Littlefield Memorial Fountain
9. Main Building and Tower
10. Garrison Hall
11. Battle Hall
12. Flawn Academic Center
13. Hogg Auditorium
14. Battle Oaks
15. Littlefield Home
16. The Drag
17. Texas Union Building
18. Goldsmith Hall
19. Sutton Hall
20. Harry Ransom Center

3. **Performing Arts Center,** which includes the 3,000-seat Bass Concert Hall, the 700-seat Bates Recital Hall, and other College of the Fine Arts auditoriums. The state-of-the-art acoustics at the Bass Concert Hall enhance the sounds of the United State's largest tracker organ: Linking contemporary computer technology with a design that goes back some 2,000 years, it has

5,315 pipes—some of them 16 feet tall—and weighs 48,000 pounds.

From the same vantage point to the left looms the huge:

4. **Texas Memorial Stadium,** where the first of the traditional U.T.–Texas A&M Thanksgiving Day games was played in 1924; the upper deck directly facing you was added in 1972. In a drive to finance the original stadium, female students sold their hair, male students their blood; U.T. alum Lutcher Stark matched every $10,000 they raised with $1,000 of his own funds. The Longhorns football team frequently draws a capacity crowd of 80,000.

Continue west on 23rd; at the corner of San Jacinto, a long staircase marks the entrance to the:

5. **Art Building,** home to the Archer M. Huntington Art Gallery. The permanent collections are in the Harry Ransom Center (see no. 20, below); this smaller space features touring exhibitions and student/faculty shows.

Walk a short distance north on San Jacinto. A stampeding group of bronze mustangs will herald your arrival at the:

6. **Texas Memorial Museum,** a monumental art moderne building designed by Paul Cret. Inside, on the first floor, the 16-foot-tall Goddess of Liberty defines the term statuesque. Liberty, who reigned atop the State Capitol dome until 1986, was designed to be viewed from more than 300 feet away; up close and personal, she's a bit crude. The museum also houses a fascinating collection of antique firearms, some carved into exotic animal shapes.

When you exit the building, take Trinity, which, curving into 25th Street, will bring you back to the parking lot of the LBJ Library and to your car. Retrace your original route along Red River until you reach Martin Luther King, Jr., Boulevard. Drive west; at the corner of San Jacinto, you'll see.

7. **Santa Rita No. 1,** an oil rig transported here from west Texas, where liquid wealth first spewed forth from it on land belonging to the university in 1923. The money was distributed between the University of Texas system, which got the heftier two-thirds, and the Texas A&M system. Though not its main source of income, this windfall has helped make the U.T. system the second richest next to Harvard.

There's no parking in the area, so it's best to pay passing obeisance to the oil god, continue on to University Avenue, and then hang a left. There are public parking places around 21st Street and University, where you'll begin your walking tour at the:

8. **Littlefield Memorial Fountain,** built in 1933. Pompeo Coppini, sculptor of the magnificent bronze centerpiece, believed that the rallying together of the nation during World War I marked the final healing of the wounds caused by the Civil War. He depicted the winged goddess Columbia riding on the bow of a battleship sailing across the ocean—represented by three rearing sea horses—to aid the Allies; the two figures on the deck represent the army and the navy.

This three-tiered fountain graces the most dramatic entrance to the university's original 40 acres. Behind you lies the State Capitol. Directly ahead of you, across an oak-shaded mall lined with heroic statues, the:

9. **Main Building and Tower** rests on the site of the university's first academic building, built in 1884. The 307-foot-high structure that now rises above the university was created by Paul Cret in 1937; it's a fine example of the beaux arts style, particularly stunning when lit to celebrate a Longhorn victory. Sadly, the Tower's many notable features—the small classical temple on top, say, or the 17-bell carillon—will always be dogged by the shadow of the carnage committed by Charles Whitman, who, in August 1966, killed 16 people before he was himself gunned down by a sharpshooter.

If you ascend the staircase on the east (right) side of the tower to the stone balustrade, you can see the dramatic sweep of the entire eastern section of campus, including the LBJ Library. The first building in your direct line of vision is:

10. **Garrison Hall,** named for one of the earliest members of the U.T. faculty, and home to the department of history. Important names from Texas's past—Austin, Travis, Houston, and Lamar—are set here in stone. The walls just under the building's eaves are decorated with cattle brands; look for the carved cow skulls and cactuses on the balcony window on the north side.

If you retrace your steps to the western (left) side of Main Building, you'll see:

11. **Battle Hall,** regarded by many as the campus's most beautiful building. Designed in 1911 by Cass Gilbert, architect of the U.S. Supreme Court building, this hall was the first to be done in the Spanish Renaissance style that came to characterize so many of the structures on this section of campus; note the terra-cotta-tiled roof and broadly arched windows. On the second floor, you can see the grand reading room of what is now the Architecture and Planning Library.

When you exit Battle Hall, go left to the northern door, which faces the much newer:

12. Flawn Academic Center. A 200,000-volume under-graduate library shares space here with exhibits from the archives of the Humanities Research Center (see no. 20, below). Among the permanent displays in the Academic Center's Leeds Gallery is a cabin furnished with the effects of Erle Stanley Gardner, Perry Mason's creator. In front of the building, Charles Umlauf's *The Torch Bearers* symbolizes the passing of knowledge from one generation to the next.

If you continue walking along the eastern side of the Academic Center, you'll pass:

13. The Hogg Auditorium, another Paul Cret building, designed in the same monumental art moderne mode as his earlier Texas Memorial Museum.

Go a few steps farther and you'll come to a group of trees that have been dubbed the:

14. Battle Oaks. The three oldest members of this small grove are said to predate the city of Austin itself. They survived the destruction of most of the grove to build a Civil War fortress, as well as a later attempt to displace them with a new Biology Building. It was this last, near-fatal skirmish that earned them their name: Legend has it that Dr. W. J. Battle, a professor of classics and an early university president, holed up in the largest oak with a rifle to protect the three ancient trees.

Just across the street at the corner of 24th and Whitis, is the impressive:

15. Littlefield Home, built in 1894 in high Victorian style. Major George W. Littlefield, a wealthy developer, cattle rancher, and banker, bequeathed more than $1 million to the university on condition that its campus not be moved to land that his rival, George W. Brackenridge, had donated. During the week, when the U.T. Development Office is open, you can enter through the east carriage driveway to see the house's gorgeous gold-and-white parlors, griffin-decorated fireplace, and other ornate details.

Walk west about a block to Guadalupe to reach:

16. The Drag—as its name suggests, the main off-campus action strip. Bookstores, fast-food restaurants, and shops line the thoroughfare, which is usually crammed with students trying to grab a bite or a book between classes. On weekends, the pedestrian mall set aside for the 23rd Street Renaissance Market overflows with crafts vendors.

Refueling Stops

A U.T. institution, **Dirty Martin's** (2808 Guadalupe St.) has been around since 1926. If you're not in the mood for Dirty's specialty, a great big greasy burger, try **Texas French Bread** (2270 Guadalupe St.), next door to the Co-op; it's just the spot for a healthy salad or sandwich and a good cup of coffee.

To get back to the university, cross Guadalupe at the traffic light in front of the huge Co-op, between 24th and 22nd Streets. You'll now be facing the west mall. On your left is the:

17. Texas Union Building, another Paul Cret creation. A beautifully tiled staircase leads up to the second level where, through the massive carved wooden doors, you'll see the Cactus Cafe, a popular coffeehouse and music venue. This bustling student center hosts everything from a bowling alley to a formal ballroom.

Immediately across the mall to the right is:

18. Goldsmith Hall, one of two adjacent buildings where architecture classes are held. Also designed by Paul Cret, this hall has beautifully worn slate floors and a palm tree–dotted central courtyard.

Walk through the courtyard and go down a few steps; to your right is the second component of the School of Architecture:

19. Sutton Hall, designed by Cass Gilbert in 1918. Like his Battle Hall, it is gracefully Mediterranean, with terra-cotta moldings, a red-tile roof, and large Palladian windows.

If you enter Sutton Hall through the double doors at the front and exit straight through the back, you'll be looking directly at the chunky, contemporary:

20. Harry Ransom Center, home to both the Humanities Research Center (HRC) and the Huntington Art Collection. The satirical portrait of a rich American literary archive in A. S. Byatt's best-selling novel *Possession* is widely acknowledged to have been based on HRC. On the first floor of this building, the center's rare Gutenberg Bible sits in front of the Huntington galleries, which host an array of 20th-century, western, classical, and Latin American art.

When you leave the building, you'll be back on 21st Street, facing the fountain where the walking tour began.

---

3   Cool for Kids

Most children will like the machine that turns pennies into capitol-dome souvenirs at the **Capitol Complex Visitors Center,** but unless your offspring are especially history minded, outdoor attractions are Austin's biggest kiddie draw. There's lots of room for children to splash around at **Barton Springs,** and even youngsters who thought bats were creepy are likely to be converted on further acquaintance with the critters. The dinosaur tracks at the **Zilker Botanical Garden** are particularly popular with kids. The following attractions are especially geared toward children.

Austin Children's Museum, 1501 W. Fifth St. ☎ 472-2499.

Offering everything from tools for tots to a soundstage for teens, this museum appeals to a wide range of ages and interests. Subtly instructive interactive exhibits include Stuffee, a huge cloth doll that can be unzipped for anatomy lessons, and plastic versions of a supermarket. Many children like to manipulate the vacation-creating computers; if you ask nicely, your offspring might show you how to use them. Along with permanent playscapes, there are also visiting exhibits, such as movable kinetic sculptures. Dance, music, or dramatic performances are held in the museum's gallery on weekends.

Admission: $2.50 adults, $2 children 2–17, children under 2 free. Free on Sun 4–5pm; inquire about the Open Door Policy (free admission to all who ask).

Open: Tues–Sat 10am–5pm, Sun noon–5pm. **Closed:** Mon, Easter Day. **Bus:** 21.

Austin Nature Center, Zilker Park, 301 Nature Center Dr. ☎ 327-8181.

A working beehive and ant farm are among the displays in the hands-on Discovery Lab at Austin's 80-acre Nature Center; the tortoises, lizards, porcupine, and vultures in the Wildlife Exhibit— among more than 50 creatures brought here because they've been orphaned or injured in the wild—also hold kids' attention. There are occasional special shows, such as lifelike robotic dinosaurs in 1994.

Admission: Donations requested; occasional special exhibits charge separately.

Open: Mon–Sat 9am–5pm, Sun noon–5pm. **Closed:** Thanksgiving Day, Christmas. **Bus:** 63.

Jourdan Bachman Pioneer Farm, 11418 Sprinkle Cut Off Rd. ☎ 837-1215.

Traveling back in time to the rural 1880s might make kids appreciate the simplicity of such modern chores as having to clear the dinner table—at least temporarily. When Harriet Bachman and Frederic Jourdan set up housekeeping in northeast Austin in 1852, cattle herders drove past their property on the Chisholm Trail. Today's visitors to what was once their farm can enter into the worlds of three typical Texas families of the late 19th century: wealthy cotton farmers, homesteaders from Appalachia, and freed slaves turned tenant farmers. Crops, clothing, food, furnishings, farm animals, and skill demonstrations all convincingly re-create an earlier era.

Admission: $2.50 adults, $1.50 children over 3.

Open: June–Aug Sun 1–5pm, Mon–Thurs 9:30am–3pm; Sept–May Sun 1–5pm, Mon–Wed 9:30am–1pm. **Directions:** Take exit 243 east off I-35 to Dessau Road, turn left and go a half mile to Sprinkle Cut Off Road and take a right.

Zilker Eagle Train, Zilker Park, 2100 Barton Springs Rd.
☎ **478-8167.**

This narrow-gauge, light-rail miniature train starts out near Barton
Springs and tootles around Zilker Park, passing Barton Creek and
Town Lake; there's a playground near the depot.

Admission: $1.25 adults, $1 children.

Open: Daily, spring and autumn 10am–dusk; summer, 10am–
7pm; winter, noon–dusk. **Bus:** 30.

4   Organized Tours

Bus Tours

Gray Line, P.O. Box 9802-557, Austin, TX 78766. ☎ **345-6789.**

In 3¹/₂ hours, Gray Line's coach tours touch on Austin's highlights,
including the State Capitol, the University of Texas, Barton Springs,
Treaty Oak, and more. The company provides complimentary pick
up and return to most motels and hotels in town.

Prices: $16 adults, $8 children 5–11.

Tours: Mon, Wed, Fri pick up 9–9:30am, return 12:30–1pm.

Customized Tours

Around Austin, 8834 Capital of Texas Hwy. North, Suite 275, Austin,
TX 78759. ☎ **345-6552.**

Mary Reynolds and her friendly, professional crew will help you do
whatever you want to do—whether it be scoping out art galleries,
taste testing the products of Hill Country wineries, or exploring the
African American history of east Austin. Although the company specializes in corporate groups, individuals are happily accommodated.
Prices depend on the length and scope of your personalized tour.

Lake Tours

Capital Cruises, Hyatt Regency Town Lake boat dock. ☎ **480-9264.**

From March through October, Capital Cruises plies Town Lake with
electric-powered boats heading out on a number of popular tours.
The bat cruises are especially big in summer, when warm nights are
perfect for the enjoyable and educational hour-long excursions; the
high point is seeing thousands of bats streaming out from under their
Congress Avenue Bridge roost. Dinner cruises, featuring fajitas from
the Hyatt Regency's La Vista restaurant, are also fun on a balmy
evening, and the afternoon sightseeing tours are a nice way to while
away an hour on the weekend.

Prices: Bat and sightseeing cruises, $8 adults, $6.50 seniors, $5
children 4–12; dinner cruises, $22 adults, $15 children.

Tours: Bat cruise, daily at sunset (call ahead for exact time),
weather permitting; sightseeing cruise, Sat–Sun at 1pm; dinner cruise,
Fri–Sun at 6pm. Reservations required for dinner cruises; for bat and
sightseeing cruises, show up at the dock a minimum of 30 minutes
in advance.

Lone Star River Boat, South shore of Town Lake, between the Congress Ave. and S. First St. Bridges. ☎ **327-1388.**

You'll set out against a backdrop of Austin's skyline and the State Capitol on this riverboat cruise and move upstream past Barton Creek and Zilker Park; 100-feet high cliffs and million-dollar estates are among the sights you'll glimpse along the way. These scenic tours, accompanied by knowledgeable narrators, last 1¹/₂ hours.

Prices: $9 adults, $6 children under 12, $7 senior citizens; half-price fares Jun–Aug Wed.

Tours: Mar–May and Sept–Oct Sat–Sun 3pm; June–Aug Tues–Sun 5:30pm, also Fri at 10:30pm. No tours Nov–Feb.

Vanishing Texas River Cruise, P.O. Box 901, Burnet, TX 78611. ☎ **512/756-6986.**

It's about 1¹/₂ hours from Austin to the Lake Buchanan dock from which these fascinating naturalist tours depart; at Burnet, drive 3 miles west on Hwy. 29 to R.R. 2341, turn right, and go 13.5 miles. A guide narrates the history of the area and points out the seasonal flora and fauna, among them bald eagles (November to March), migratory birds and wildflowers (March to May), and wild deer and turkey (June to October). There's a full-service snack bar aboard the vessel, and on Saturday nights from May through October, a sunset dinner cruise departs at 6pm ($25 including the cruise and the meal).

Prices: $15 adults, $13 seniors, students, active military, $10 children 6–12, children 5 and under free

Tours: Every day except Tues at 11am.

Train Tours

Hill Country Flyer Steam Train Excursion.

The Austin Steam Train Association restored the five historic coaches and the 1916 locomotive that you'll board for a leisurely 33-mile excursion from Cedar Park, northwest of Austin. After crossing the South San Gabriel River, the train whistles past scenic Hill Country vistas, especially pretty in spring and fall; at the end of the line— the town of Burnet, near Lake Buchanan—an old West gunfight is staged for passengers.

Prices: Coach, $24 adults, $10 children 13 and under; first class, $38 per person; Twilight Flyer coach, $20 per person, $38 per couple, first class $26 per person, $50 per couple (includes fruit-and-cheese basket and a glass of wine, beer, or soft drink).

Tours: Sat–Sun 10am (return 5:30pm); additional Twilight Flyer Tours first and third Sat of each month at 7pm, return 8:45pm; two-week advance reservations strongly suggested in high season.

Walking Tours

Some of the best guided walks I've ever taken are offered, gratis, by the **Austin Convention and Visitors Bureau (ACVB),** 201 E. Second St., 78701 (☎ **474-5171** or toll free **800/926-2282**), from March through November. Tours of the historic Bremond Block leave every Saturday and Sunday at 11pm; Congress Avenue/East

Sixth Street is explored on Thursday, Friday, and Saturday starting at 9am, Sunday at 2pm. The schedule for the new Capitol Complex tour hadn't yet been established when we went to press; phone the ACVB for current information. All tours depart *promptly* from the south entrance of the capitol; come even a few minutes late, and you'll miss out. The ACVB also publishes four excellent self-guided tour booklets, including one of Hyde Park and another of the State Cemetery; they make for interesting reading, even if you don't have time to follow the routes.

5 Sports & Recreation

Spectator Sports

There are no professional or minor-league teams in Austin, but college sports are very big, if somewhat confusing to outsiders, because all the University of Texas teams are called the Longhorns. For information about schedules, call the U.T. Athletics Ticket Office (☎ 471-3333); to order tickets, contact UTTM Charge-A-Ticket (☎ 477-6060).

BASEBALL   The **Longhorn baseball** team goes to bat from February through May at Disch-Falk Field (just east of I-35, at the corner of Martin Luther King, Jr., Boulevard and Comal). Many players from this former NCAA championship squad have gone on to the big time—for example, Roger Clemens, two-time Cy Young award winner for the Boston Red Sox.

BASKETBALL   The **Lady Longhorn basketball** and **Longhorn basketball** teams, both Southwest Conference champions, play in the Frank C. Erwin, Jr., Special Events Center (just west of I-35 on Red River between Martin Luther King, Jr., Boulevard and 15th Street) from November through March.

FOOTBALL   It's hard to tell which is more central to the success of an Austin Thanksgiving: the turkey or the U.T.–Texas A&M game. Soon to move to the Big 12 Conference, the **Longhorn football** team often fills the huge Texas Memorial Stadium (just west of I-35 between 23rd and 21st Streets, East Campus Drive and San Jacinto Boulevard) during home games, played from September through November.

Fans also turn out in droves each summer to watch the Super Bowl champion **Dallas Cowboys** in summer training camp at St. Edwards University (Congress and Woodward Avenues in south Austin). The players arrive in mid-July and stay around five to six weeks, generally practicing twice a day from Monday through Friday. Dates and local contact numbers for the team change each year; for the most up-to-date information, phone the Cowboys' office in Dallas (☎ 214/556-9960).

GOLF   Celebrities such as Joe Namath and Dennis Quaid tee off for a good cause at the **East Austin Youth Classic,** held at Barton

Creek Resort (☎ 322-4000) in April. Classic in its own way is the **Cow Patty Open,** played—where else?—in a cow pasture. The hilarious mid-October event raises money for various children's projects; contact the Austin Chamber of Commerce, P.O. Box 1967, 78767 (☎ 322-5632), for details.

HORSE RACING   Pick your ponies at **Manor Downs,** eight miles east of I-35 on U.S. 290 east (☎ 272-5581). The track is open Friday to Sunday, March through June; gates open at 11:30am, with the first post at 1:30pm. Simulcast racing for the rest of the year is in the works; call for current information.

Recreation

BALLOONING   For an uplifting experience, consider a hot-air balloon ride over Hill Country. **Airwolf Adventures** (☎ 836-2305), **Austin Aeronauts Hot Air Balloons** (☎ 440-1492), **Balloon Port of Austin** (☎ 835-6058), **Hill Country Balloons** (☎ 345-1575), **Sundance Balloon Adventures** (☎ 990-8183) are all reputable operators with FAA licensed pilots. Their scenic excursions, including champagne breakfast, generally last about an hour and cost from $150 to $175 per person.

BICYCLING   A city that has a "bicycle coordinator" on its payroll, Austin is a cyclist's dream. Call or write **Hike/Bike Trails,** 901 Riverside Dr., 78704 (☎ 440-5162), for information on the city's 32 miles of scenic paths, the most popular of which are the Barton Creek Greenbelt (7.8 miles) and the Town Lake Greenbelt (10.1 miles). The Veloway (☎ 480-3032), a 3.1-mile paved loop in Slaughter Creek Metropolitan Park, is devoted exclusively to bicyclists. You can rent bikes and get maps and other information from South Austin Bicycles, 908B W. 12th St. (☎ 322-9131), and University Cyclery, 2901 N. Lamar Blvd. (☎ 474-6696); a number of downtown hotels rent or provide free bicycles to their guests. For information on weekly road rides, phone the **Austin Cycling Association,** P.O. Box 5993, 78763 (☎ 837-3666), which also publishes a newsletter. For rougher mountain-bike routes, try the Austin Ridge Riders (☎ 454-3959).

BIRD-WATCHING   Endangered golden-cheeked warblers and black-capped vireos are among the many species you might spot around Austin. The **Travis Audubon Society** (☎ 926-8751) organizes regular birding trips and even has a rare-bird hot line (☎ 483-0952). The various parks and preserves (see "More Attractions," above) can also tell you who's flown into town.

CANOEING   You can rent canoes at **Zilker Park,** 2000 Barton Springs Rd. (☎ 478-3852), for $6 an hour; **Capital Cruises,** Hyatt Regency boat dock (☎ 480-9264), also offers hourly rentals on Town Lake. If your paddling skills are a bit rusty, the **Austin Nature Center** (☎ 327-8180) and **U.T. Recreational Sports** (☎ 471-1093) give instructional courses.

FISHING   The focus is on fly-fishing at downtown's **Austin Angler,** 312¹/₂ Congress Ave. (☎ 472-4553), an excellent place to pick up a license, tackle, and information on where to find the big ones. **Git Bit** (☎ 280-2861) provides guide service for half- or full-day bass-fishing trips on Lake Travis; prices, including equipment, start at $125 per person.

GOLF   For information about Austin's five **municipal golf courses,** call **480-3020;** all offer pro shops and equipment rental, and their greens fees are very reasonable. Among them are Hancock, which was built in 1899 and is the oldest course in Texas; and Lions, where Tom Kite and Ben Crenshaw played college golf for the University of Texas.

HIKING   Austin abounds in nature trails in its parks and preserves; see "More Attractions," above, for additional information. Contact the **Colorado River Walkers of Austin** (☎ 280-2952) or the **Sierra Club** (☎ 445-6223) if you're interested in organized hikes.

ROCK CLIMBING   Those with the urge to hang out on cliffs can call **Mountain Madness** (☎ 443-5854), which holds weekend rock-climbing courses at Enchanted Rock, a stunning granite outcropping in the Hill Country. **Texas Mountain Guides** (☎ 482-9208) let you choose between outdoor or indoor courses in the Austin area.

SAILING   Lake Travis is the perfect place to let the wind drive your sails; among the operators offering instruction and boat rentals in the Austin area are **Beach Front Boat Rentals** (☎ 258-8400), **Commander's Point Yacht Basin** (☎ 266-2333), **Dutchman's Landing** (☎ 267-4289), and **Texas Sailing Academy** (☎ 261-6193).

SCUBA DIVING   The clarity of the limestone-filtered waters of Lake Travis makes it ideal for peeking around underwater. Boat wrecks and metal sculptures have been planted on the lake bottom of the private **Windy Point Park** (☎ 266-9459), and Mother Nature has provided the park's advanced divers with an unusual underwater grove of pecan trees. Equipment rentals and lessons are available nearby from **Pisces** (☎ 258-6646) and **Scuba International** (☎ 219-9484).

SPELUNKING   The limestone country in the Austin area is rife with dark places to poke around in; in the city, two wild caves that you can crawl into with the proper training are Airman's Cave on the Barton Creek Greenbelt and Goat Cave Preserve in southwest Austin. The **University Speleological Society** (☎ 478-8051) meets twice a month on campus and takes frequent underground trips. See also Chapter 17 for other caves in nearby Hill Country.

SWIMMING   The best known of Austin's natural swimming holes is Barton Springs (see "The Top Attractions," above), but it's by no means the only one: other scenic outdoor spots to take the plunge include **Deep Eddy Pool,** 401 Deep Eddy Ave. at Lake Austin

Boulevard (☎ 472-8546), and **Hamilton Pool Preserve,** off Texas 71 on R.M. 3238 (☎ 264-2740). For lakeshore swimming, consider **Hippie Hollow** on Lake Travis, 2¹/₂ miles off R.M. 620 (☎ 473-9437), where you can let it all hang out in a series of clothing-optional coves; or **Emma Long State Park** on Lake Austin (see "More Attractions," above). You can also get into the swim at a number of free neighborhood pools; phone **476-4521** for information.

TENNIS   The very reasonably priced **Austin High School Tennis Center,** 2001 W. First St. (☎ 477-7802), **Casswell Tennis Center,** 24th Street and Lamar Boulevard (☎ 478-6268), **Pharr Tennis Center,** 4201 Brookview Dr. (☎ 477-7773), and **South Austin Tennis Center,** 1000 Cumberland Dr. (☎ 442-1466), all have enough courts to give you a good shot at getting one.

WINDSURFING   You can brush up on your windsurfing technique at **Sail & Ski Center** (☎ 258-0733) or **U.T. Recreational Sports** (☎ 471-1093); **Duck Jibe** (☎ 258-0733) offers rentals along with instruction. At Lake Travis, **Beach Front Boat Rentals** (☎ 258-8400) loans out sailboats and motorboats in addition to Windsurfers.

15

Austin Shopping

WHEN IT COMES TO ITEMS INTELLECTUAL, MUSICAL, OR INGESTIBLE, Austin is a match for cities twice its size. Shopping here has not otherwise evolved into an art, but you'll find outstanding stores in all areas.

1 The Shopping Scene

Specialty shops and art galleries are slowly filtering back to the renovated 19th-century buildings along **Sixth Street** and **Congress Avenue,** but much of Austin's shopping has moved out to the malls. Bargain hunters go farther afield to the huge collections of factory outlet stores in San Marcos and New Braunfels; see Chapter 17 for details. Little enclaves offering more intimate retail experiences can be found on **Sixth Street west of Lamar** and, nearby, north of 12th Street and West Lynn. In the vicinity of **Central Market,** between West 35th and 40th Streets and Lamar and Mo-Pac, such small shopping centers as 26 Doors and Jefferson Square are similarly charming settings for acquisition. Many stores on the Drag—the stretch of Guadalupe Street between Martin Luther King, Jr., Boulevard and 26th Street, across from the University of Texas campus—are student oriented, but a wide range of clothing, gifts, toys, and, of course, books can also be found here.

HOURS   Specialty shops in Austin tend to open around 9 or 10am, Monday through Saturday, and close at about 5:30 or 6pm; many have Sunday hours from noon until 6pm. Malls tend to keep the same Sunday schedule but, Monday through Saturday, they don't close their doors until 9pm.

2 Shopping A to Z

Antiques

In addition to the one-stop antiques markets listed below, a number of smaller shops line Burnet Road north of 45th Street.

Austin Antique Mall, 8822 McCann Dr. ☎ 459-5900.

You can spend anything from a fiver to thousands of dollars in this megacollection of past-oriented stores. More than 100 dealers in a 30,000-square-foot indoor space sell Roseville pottery, Fiesta dishes, Victorian furniture, costume jewelry, and much, much more. Think this is big? About 20 minutes north of Austin, the new Antique Mall of Texas, 1601 S. I.H.-35, Round Rock (☎ 512/218-4290), run by the same people, has double the number of stalls.

The Antique Marketplace, 5350 Burnet Rd. ☎ 452-1000.

For people who like antiques but don't enjoy speaking in hushed tones, the Antique Marketplace offers bargains and treasures in a friendly, relaxed atmosphere. You'll find a little bit of everything under the roof of this large warehouse-type building in central Austin—a lamp-restoration specialist, Czech glass, funky collectibles, and expensive furnishings.

Whit Hanks Antiques & Decorative Arts, 1009 W. Sixth St. ☎ 478-2101.

More than 50 high-quality dealers gather at tony Whit Hanks, just across the street from Treaty Oak. Even if you can't afford to buy anything, stop in to see the various craftspeople—ironsmiths, stone carvers, and cabinetmakers among them—at work. It's also fun to ogle items from fine crystal and vases to antique Chinese cabinets and neoclassical columns.

Art Galleries

Country Store Gallery, 1304 Lavaca St. ☎ 474-6222.

Occupied by the architect and the superintendent of the State Capitol during its construction in the late 19th century, this former boardinghouse now hosts the oldest art gallery in Austin and maybe all of Texas. The deer heads and branding irons on the walls complement bronzes and action paintings by well-known western artists such as Olaf Wieghorst, and provide interesting contrasts to the French impressionists and landscapes also sold here. All told, more than 2,500 pieces of all styles are available in this 7,000-square-foot space.

El Taller Gallery, 8015 Shoal Creek Blvd., Suite 109. ☎ 480-0100.

Moved recently to a new location off Mo-Pac and near Northcross Mall, this appealing showcase for southwestern art sells Santa Fe pieces at Austin prices. Amado Pena, who once owned the gallery, is represented here exclusively; you'll also find work by R. C. Gorman and other Native American artists. Handmade Pueblo pottery, Zapotec Indian weavings, and "critter" jewelry by Richard Lindsay are among the gallery's other interesting offerings.

Gallery at Shoal Creek, 1500 W. 34th St. ☎ 454-6671.

Since it opened in 1965, Shoal Creek has moved away from an exclusive emphasis on western art to encompass work from a wide range of American regions. The focus is on contemporary painting in representational or Impressionist styles—for example, Jerry Ruthven's Southwest landscapes or Nancy McGowan's naturalist watercolors. Like El Taller, this is an Austin outlet for many artists who also have galleries in Santa Fe.

Books

As might be expected, many of Austin's best bookstores are concentrated in the University of Texas area, and specifically on the Drag. **Europa,** 2406 Guadalupe St. (☎ 476-0423), has a sophisticated selection of international literature and criticism, as well as newspapers and magazines from around the world. Along with discounted reading matter, new and used, **Half-Price Books,** 3110 Guadalupe St. (☎ 451-4463, two other locations), also carries CDs, cassettes, and videos. The **University Co-Op,** 2246 Guadalupe St. (☎ 476-7211), opened in 1898, has many volumes of general interest; in addition, it has the most orange-and-white Longhorn T-shirts and mugs and other U.T. souvenirs in town.

Book People, 603 N. Lamar Blvd. ☎ **472-5050.**

In early 1995, the conjunction of Sixth Street and Lamar Boulevard acquired seriously good vibes when this expanded version of what was once primarily a New Age bookstore opened up next to a huge new Whole Foods supermarket (see "Food," below). Now stocking more than 300,000 titles ranging over a wide variety of subjects, Book People also has an extensive array of self-help videos and books on tape. Lots of intimate sitting areas and an espresso bar prevent this huge store from feeling overwhelming.

Book Woman, 324 E. Sixth St. ☎ **472-2785.**

Offering the largest selection of books by and about women in Austin, this store is also one of Texas's best feminist resource centers, the place to find out about women's organizations and events statewide. Book Woman also carries a great selection of T-shirts, cards, and posters, including a blowup of the *Texas Monthly* magazine cover of a white-leather-clad Governor Ann Richards straddling a B-I-G motorcycle.

Children's Books

Toad Hall, 1206 W. 38th St. (26 Doors). ☎ **323-2665.**

You'll find excellent reading material for toddlers to teens here, as well as a friendly staff who can offer advice about what might best suit your child's interests. One of the largest children's bookstores in the Southwest, Toad Hall also carries lots of kiddie tapes, CDs, and videos.

Crafts

Eclectic Ethnographic Gallery, 916 W. 12th St. ☎ **477-1816.**

A dazzling panoply of furniture, crafts, pottery, and paintings from around the world is beautifully presented at Eclectic, with the muted tones of antiques counterpointing the more brightly colored contemporary work. An outstanding jewelry section includes Native American pieces as well as bracelets, pins, and necklaces from Portugal, Thailand, and many other exotic places. Different countries are featured on a rotating basis.

Tesoros Trading Co., 209 Congress Ave. ☎ **479-8341.**

Colorful handwoven cloth from Guatemala; intricate weavings from Peru; glassware and tinwork from Mexico; metal-and-stone jewelry from Thailand; sequined banners from Haiti; wood carvings from Kenya . . . all these and more are available at Tesoros, which, in addition to its high-quality folk art, also offers a limited amount of furniture, dishes, and housewares from around the world. Reasonably priced items mingle with expensive treasures.

Department Store

Dillard's, Highland Mall, ☎ **452-9393;** Barton Creek Mall, ☎ **327-6100.**

This Little Rock–based chain, spread throughout the Southwest, carries a nice variety of mid- to high-range merchandise. The Barton

Creek store is slightly larger than the one in Highland Mall, but both have Texas shops with good selections of stylish western fashions.

Discount Shopping

Last Call, Brodie Oaks Shopping Center, Ben White Blvd. at S. Lamar. ☎ 447-0701.

Neiman Marcus fans will want to take advantage of Last Call, which consolidates fashions from 27 of the high-toned department stores and sells them for 50% to 75% off. Different merchandise shipments arrive every week. Not only can you find great bargains, but you needn't sacrifice the attention for which Neiman Marcus is famous by coming here; the staff is as helpful as at all the other branches, and personal shopper service is available.

Fashions

Scott-Wynne Outfitters, The Arboretum, 10000 Research Blvd., Suite 127. ☎ 346-7012.

Whether it's checked flannel hunting shirts or colorful fringed dancing skirts you're seeking, Scott-Wynne's got 'em. This large, privately owned Austin outlet features upscale outdoor lines such as Woolrich and Patagonia, as well as chic southwestern casual clothing for men and women. Attractive accessories—hats, belts, American Indian jewelry—will complement any well-dressed Texan's wardrobe.

The Whole Earth Provisions Co., 2400 San Antonio St. ☎ 478-1577.

Austin's large population of outdoor enthusiasts come here to be out-fitted in the latest earth-friendly fashions. From thermal underwear made of organically grown, unbleached cotton to state-of-the-art synthetic jackets and all the layers in between, campers, hikers, and climbers will find any item of clothing they might need, as well as the gear to go along with it. Housewares, toys, and travel books are also sold here and at a second location in south Austin, 4006 S. Lamar Blvd. (☎ 444-9974).

VINTAGE

Dressed to Kill, 2418 Guadalupe St. (The Drag). ☎ 476-3148.

An entire wall of well-preserved dresses faces one of vintage cowboy shirts, topcoats, and vests at Dressed to Kill, offering the largest and highest-quality selection of vintage clothing in town; in between are hats, scarves, shoes, and a variety of funky accessories. If you covet an item you can't afford, you might be able to work out a trade for some of your own already worn clothes.

Electric Ladyland, 1506 S. Congress Ave. ☎ 444-2002.

Feather boas, tutus, flapper dresses, angel wings, and the occasional gorilla suit overflow the narrow aisles of Austin's best known costume and vintage clothing outlet. The owner, who really *does* dress like that all the time, is a walking advertisement for her fascinating store. You can buy everyday clothes here like floral-print dresses and striped shirts—though even these require some degree of flamboy-ance—but you're likely to get sidetracked by rack after rack of outrageousness.

WOMEN

See also Le Cadeau, listed under "Gifts/Souvenirs," below.

By George, 2905 San Gabriel St. ☎ 472-5951.

Because it has suits and dressy clothes, as well as lots of pamper-yourself potpourris and bath oils, thirty- and-forty-some-things tend to frequent this By George store, while the college set stick with the more casual outlet on the Drag, 2324 Guadalupe St. (☎ 472-2731). But both shops offer hip, contemporary fashions in natural fabrics, and great purses and shoes to match. Don't feel neglected, guys: There's a By George for men two doors down from the Drag woman's store, 2346 Guadalupe St. (☎ 472-5536).

Scarbrough's, 4001 N. Lamar Blvd. (Central Park). ☎ 452-4220.

Opened in 1894 on the then prime corner of Sixth and Congress, Scarbrough's has moved around a bit since then, but it's still in the hands of the same family, now the fourth generation of Scarbroughs. If the store has achieved dowager status, its clothing is far from dowdy; women in Austin have long relied on Scarbrough's to outfit them in the latest fashions, from boot-scootin' boogie finery to glamorous gowns for the governor's ball.

Food

Central Market, 40th and Lamar. ☎ 206-1000.

All Austin was abuzz in early 1994 about the opening of the huge Central Market complex. More than just a place to buy every imag-inable food item—fresh or frozen, local or imported—this gourmet megamarket also has a restaurant section, with separate areas offer-ing cowboy, bistro, Italian, and vegetarian cuisine. A weekly news-letter announces what's fresh in the produce department; which jazz musicians are entertaining on the weekend; and which gourmet chef is holding forth at the market's Cooking School.

Travis County Farmers' Market, 6701 Burnett Rd.
☎ 454-1002.

Not only does this market offer great fresh fruit and vegetables, from all around the Austin area; it also hosts monthly festivals honoring particular crops and/or growing seasons. April, for example, honors the 1015"Y" onion, lauded as sweet, mild, and tear free, while June celebrates peaches with contests for the best peach cobbler, peach ice cream, and peach preserves.

Whole Foods, 601 N. Lamar Blvd. ☎ 476-1206.

From chemical-free cosmetics to frozen tofu burgers, Whole Foods covers the entire (organic) enchilada; it's the place to find anything edible or applicable that comes in a low-fat or otherwise pure version. Opened in March 1995, this consolidation of two already established links in the Austin health supermarket chain includes a wok deli and an on-site bakery.

Hardware, Etc.

Breed & Co. Hardware, 710 W. 29th St. ☎ 474-6679.

You don't have to be a power-drill freak to want to visit Breed & Co.: How many hardware stores, after all, have bridal registries where one can sign on for Waterford crystal? This darling of Austin do-it-your-selfers has everything from nails to tropical plants, organic fertilizer, gardening and cookbooks, pâté molds and cherry pitters. You're sure to find something here that you never knew you needed but—now that you know it exists—you have to have.

Gifts/Souvenirs

See also the Satellite Shop, listed under "Jewelry," below.

Bluebonnet Market Place, 310 Noches St. ☎ 476-3484.

Bluebonnet Market employees have arranged so many gift packets for local Austin hotels that they've become expert; all you have to do is decide how much you want to spend and what types of things you'd like to include, and they'll put together a basket for you, shrink-wrapped free of charge. More than 100 merchants gather in this converted warehouse near the Convention Center, several specializing in Texas foods, others in T-shirts, mugs, even music memorabilia. A mail center operates during the week.

Capitol Complex Visitors Center, 112 E. 11th St. ☎ 305-8400.

Over the years, visitors have admired—sometimes excessively—the intricately designed door hinges of the capitol. The gift shop at the new visitors center sells brass bookends made from the original molds used, during the capitol's renovation, to cast replacements for the hinges that had been cadged. Other terrific Texas items sold here include paperweights made from reproductions of the capitol's Texas-seal doorknobs; local food products; beautiful leather purses; and a variety of educational toys. The shop also has an excellent selection of historical books.

Le Cadeau, 2316 Guadalupe St. (The Drag). ☎ 477-7276.

"Cadeau" means gift in French, and this is the perfect place to find one, whether it be beautiful contemporary kitchenware, pottery, jewelry, clothing, bibelots, chatchkes, or knickknacks. Be forewarned: Just when you think you've got your choice narrowed down, you may suddenly realize there are two more rooms chock-full of goodies to choose from. To add to the dilemma, now there's another location, at 4001 N. Lamar Blvd. (☎ 453-6988), near 38th Street.

Glass & Pottery

Clarksville Pottery & Gallery, 1013 W. Lynn. ☎ 478-9079.

A shimmering irridescence of color greets you as you enter this pottery emporium, filled with lovely pieces created by local artisans. You'll find everything that might come in ceramic, from candleholders to bird feeders, as well as handmade kaleidoscopes and contemporary jewelry in a variety of medias. In addition to this location in the artsy Clarksville area, there's also an outlet in the Arboretum (☎ 794-8590).

Fire Island Hot Glass Studio, Inc., 3401 E. Fourth St.
   ☎ 479-0770.

This glassblowing studio, about two miles east of I-35, is a bit off-the-beaten track, but it's a treat to watch the owner/artists, Matthew LaBarbera and his wife, Teresa Ueltschey, at their delicate craft. Call ahead to find out which mornings they'll be working. You'll find their elegant perfume bottles, oil lamps, bowls, and paperweights in fine galleries around Austin, but this showroom naturally has the largest selection. If you have a certain design in mind, you can special order a set of goblets.

Jewelry

Russell Korman, 3806 N. Lamar Blvd. ☎ 451-9292.

You'd never know it from his current elegant digs, but Russell Korman got his start in Austin's jewelry trade by selling beads on the Drag. Although he's moved on to fine 14-karat gold and diamond pieces, his store still has a considerable collection of more casual sterling silver from Mexico. Prices are very competitive, even for the most formal baubles.

The Satellite Shop, 107 W. Sixth St. ☎ 477-0766.

At the historic crossroads of Congress Avenue and Sixth Street, the downtown gift shop of the Laguna Gloria Art Museum boasts a fine array of distinctive handmade jewelry. Contemporary silverwork by two Galveston sisters and fused-glass earrings and necklaces from the nearby Hill Country town of Wimberly are among the many unique items sold here. Neon, mobiles, glassware, and pottery created in Texas are also featured, as are art-related T-shirts, ties, books, cards, and posters.

Malls/Shopping Centers

The Arboretum, 10000 Research Blvd. (Hwy. 183 and Loop 360).
   ☎ 338-4437.

It's worth a trip to the far northwest part of town to a shopping center so chic that it calls itself a market, not a mall. This two-level collection of outdoor boutiques surrounding the tony Stouffer hotel doesn't include any department stores. Tasteful upscale clothing—Polo-Ralph Lauren, Jaeger—as well as specialty gift and craft shops are featured. Dining options, including a sub shop and a TGIF's, tend to be on the casual side; there's an outlet for Amy's, Austin's favorite locally made ice cream.

Barton Creek Mall, 2901 S. Capital of Texas Hwy. ☎ 327-7040.

Set on a bluff with a view of downtown, Barton Creek tends to be frequented by upscale west siders; the wide-ranging collection of more than 180 shops is anchored by Dillard's, Foley's, Sears, J. C. Penney, and Montgomery Ward. One of the newest malls in Austin, it's refined and low-key, but the fact that it includes both Frederick's of Hollywood and Victoria's Secret lingerie boutiques makes one wonder if the daytime soaps might not be onto something about the bored rich.

Highland Mall, 6001 Airport Blvd. ☎ **454-9656.**

Austin's first mall, built in the 1970s, is still one of the city's most popular places to shop; it's located at the south end of the hotel zone near the airport, just minutes north of downtown on I-35. Reasonably priced casual clothing stores like the Gap and the Limited vie with high-end shops such as Laura Ashley and Pappagallo, while Dillard's, Foley's, and J. C. Penney department stores coexist with specialty stores—Venture Map & Globe Co., say, and the Warner Bros. Studio Store. The tonier Lincoln Plaza shops are just to the south, on I-35.

Northcross Mall, 2525 Anderson Lane. ☎ **451-7466.**

A bit smaller than Highland and Barton Creek malls, Northcross is Austin's recreational shopping center, with the city's only ice-skating rink, a six-screen movie theater, and a large food court; there's even a special number that details mall events (☎ **459-FFUN**). It's also home to Oshman's Super Store, a huge sporting-goods emporium where customers can try out equipment at a batting cage, basketball court, and roller-blading surface. Bealls, the major department store, carries a variety of midrange merchandise.

26 Doors, 1206 W. 34th St. ☎ **477-1212.**

Not all the shops in 26 Doors boast the exquisite wooden antique entryways that gives this Spanish-style shopping center its name, but all are intimate and charming. Among the items sold in the specialty stores arrayed around a tiled, tree-shaded courtyard are crafts, clothing, children's books, and cheesecake.

Markets

Renaissance Market, W. 23rd and Guadalupe Sts. (The Drag).

Flash back to tie-dye days at this open-air market, selling some good-quality handmade crafts and jewelry along with cheesy, commercial items. It's theoretically open all the time, but vendors generally turn out in force on weekends only. The kids will like the jugglers, magicians, and kaleidoscopes.

FLEA MARKET

Austin Country Flea Market, 9500 Hwy. 290 east (five miles east of I.H.-35). ☎ **928-2795.**

Every Saturday and Sunday year-round, more than 500 covered spaces are filled with merchants purveying anything you might imagine—new and used clothing, fresh herbs and produce, electronics, antiques. This is the largest flea market in central Texas, covering more than 130 paved acres. There's live music every weekend—generally a spirited Latino band to step up the shopping pace.

Music

Sound Exchange, 2100A Guadalupe St. (The Drag). ☎ **476-2274.**

Come to the Sound Exchange for hard-to-find older music, imports, and releases by local bands, especially in the rock-and-roll and punk-rock genres; the walls are plastered with posters announcing upcoming Austin shows. You can get some pretty good bargains in vinyl, tape, and CDs here, and browse obscure music magazines to your heart's content.

Waterloo Records and Video, 600 N. Lamar Blvd. ☎ **474-2500.**

Carrying a huge selection of sounds of all sorts, Waterloo is always the first in town to get the new releases; if they don't have something on hand, they'll order it for you promptly. The store offers preview listening, compilation tapes of Austin groups, and tickets to all major-label shows around town; it also hosts frequent in-store promotional performances by both local and midsized national bands. For purists, there's a vinyl annex (☎ **474-2525**) with a large selection of albums.

Toys

Terra Toys, 1708 S. Congress Ave. ☎ **445-4489** or toll free **800/247-TOYS.**

Steiff teddy bears, the wooden Playmobil world, and other high-quality imported toys are among the kiddie delights at Terra, just south of the river. The store also carries a variety of miniatures, train sets, books, and dress-up clothes. For everyday children's apparel, try the owners' other place, Dragon Snaps, just down the block.

Toy Joy, 2900 Guadalupe St. ☎ **320-0090.**

The name says it all; the only question is whether kids or grown-ups will have more Toy Joy here. Ambi and San Rio are among the appealing children's lines sold in the large back room; up front things like lava lamps and cartoon character watches keep both Generation X and Baby Boomers endlessly fascinated. This store has some great Japanese toys, but for the full range—including a four-foot-high radio-controlled Godzilla and Astro Boy videos—check out the new branch, opened down the road on the Drag, 2100B Guadalupe St. (☎ **472-2262**). Both stores stay open until midnight on Friday and Saturday.

Travel

Travelfest, 9503 Research Blvd. ☎ **418-1515.**

A concept whose time has clearly come, the country's first all-inclusive travel shop offers guidebooks, luggage, cameras, binoculars, over-the-counter medicines, travel-sized containers, and a full-service travel agency under one roof. Those planning a trip of any sort can come in and browse various useful directories or attend the (mostly free) travel-related seminars held three or four nights a week.

Western Stores

Capitol Saddlery, 1614 Lavaca St. (between 16th and 17th Sts.).
☎ **478-9309.**

Even if *Mr. Ed* reruns on Nickelodeon are the closest you usually
come to a horse, you'll be tempted to bring home a saddle, so
beautiful is the leatherwork at this three-level western store near the
capitol. The custom-made boots, immortalized in a song by Jerry Jeff
Walker, are more practical but still a bit dear, with prices starting at
around $500. There are always the hand-tooled ranger belts, purses,
or even used leather chaps; it's hard to walk out of here without
buying *something*.

Sheplers, 6001 Middle Fiskville Rd. ☎ **454-3000.**

Adjacent to Highland Mall and especially convenient to those staying in the hotel zone north of the airport, Austin's huge branch of
this growing chain of western-wear department stores has everything
the well-dressed urban cowboy or cowgirl could require. If you get a
sudden urge for a concho belt or bola tie when you get back home,
call toll free **800/835-4004** for a mail-order catalog.

Wine & Beer

Whip in Convenience Store, 1950 S. I-35. ☎ **442-5337.**

Be it lager or stout, produced in Hill Country or New Delhi—if it's
legally imported into Texas, you can get it here. At a conservative
estimate, the cooler is filled with 220 different types of beer at any
given time, with even more come Oktoberfest or other special
beer-producing seasons. You can pick up munchies to go with your
brews at this large convenience store; if you're lucky, you might also
be able to find some great beer steins or mugs.

Wiggy's, 1130 W. Sixth St. ☎ **474-WINE.**

If liquor and tobacco are among your vices, Wiggy's can help you
indulge in high style. In addition to its extensive selection of wines
and single-malt scotches, this friendly west-end store also carries an
array of imported smokes, including humidified cigars. Prices are
reasonable and the staff is very knowledgeable.

16

Austin Nights

Gɪᴠᴇɴ ᴛʜᴇ ʟᴏɴɢ ʀᴇᴀᴄʜ ᴏꜰ ɪᴛꜱ ʙᴏᴅy ᴏꜰ ᴘᴇʀꜰᴏʀᴍɪɴɢ ᴀʀᴛꜱ, ɪᴛ ᴡᴏᴜʟᴅ ʙᴇ hard to imagine an itch for entertainment, high or low, that Austin couldn't scratch. Live-music freaks enjoy a scene rivaling those of Nashville, New Orleans, or Seattle, while culture vultures have local access to everything from classic lyric opera to high-tech modern dance.

The best single source for what's on around town is the free *Austin Chronicle,* distributed in hundreds of outlets every Thursday; listings in the various weekend entertainment sections of the *Austin American-Statesman* are more diffuse. The **Austin Circle of Theaters Hotline** (☎ 320-7168) can tell you what's on the boards each week. For up-to-date club action, call the **Entertainment Hotline** (☎ 832-4094). If you want to know who's kicking around, phone **Danceline** (☎ 474-1766).

The **Ticketmaster** number for the University of Texas, the locus for most of the city's performing-arts events, is **477-6060;** Paramount Theatre events can also be booked at this number. The Box Office (☎ **499-TIXS**) handles phone charges for many of the smaller theaters in Austin and can give you supplementary information— what to wear, for example, or what restaurants are nearby—about all of them.

You can call **AusTix** (☎ **397-1450** or **320-7168**), the city's half-price theater outlet, for a recorded listing of what's currently being discounted, and then buy tickets at the Dougherty Arts Center, 1110 Barton Springs Rd. (open Wednesday to Friday 11:30am to 1:30pm and 4:30 to 6:30pm), or the Austin Visitors Center, 201 E. Second St. (open Thursday, Friday, and Saturday 11:30am to 1:30pm).

Free Entertainment

Starting in late April or early May, the city sponsors 10 weeks of no-cost Wednesday night concerts at Auditorium Shores, and Sunday afternoon concerts at the Zilker Hillside Theater. Barring classical, they run the gamut of musical styles, from rock and reggae to country and western and Latin. Call **440-1414** for current schedules of these two series and of the free **Zilker Park Jazz Festival** in September. Every other Wednesday night from June through August, the upscale Arboretum shopping center (10000 Research Blvd.) hosts a **Blues on the Green** concert series in their open-air courtyard; phone **338-4437** for details. Some 70,000 people turn out to cheer the "1812 Overture" and the fireworks at the Austin Symphony's **Fourth of July Concert** at Auditorium Shores (☎ **476-6064**).

The long-running (since 1975) *Austin City Limits,* which has showcased such major country-and-western talent as Lyle Lovett, Garth Brooks, Reba McEntire, and Mary Chapin Carpenter, is taped live from August through December at the KLRU-TV studio. Free tickets are distributed on a first-come, first-served basis, one to three days before each taping. Phone the show's hot line at **512/471-4811,** ext. 310, for details.

From mid-July through late August, the Zilker Hillside Theater hosts major **musical productions** (☎ **397-1463**). The summer **Austin Shakespeare Festival** is often held at the theater, too; call **454-BARD** for up-to-date information about locations and dates.

The first weekend in June, the **Austin Contemporary Ballet** plié for the nonpaying public. Performances usually take place at the Zilker Hillside Theater; call **892-1298** for details.

1 The Performing Arts

In addition to having its own symphony, theater, ballet, lyric opera, and modern-dance companies, Austin draws major international talent to town. Much of the action, local and imported, goes on at the University of Texas's Performing Arts Center, but some terrific outdoor venues take advantage of the city's abundant greenery and mild weather.

Major Performing Arts Companies

OPERA & CLASSICAL MUSIC

Austin Chamber Music Center, 4930 Burnet Rd. ☎ **454-7562.**

This teaching-and-performing group often plays at the Central Presbyterian Church downtown. They also host visiting national and international artists—for example, the resident chamber music orchestra from Juilliard.

Austin Choral Union, 809 Rio Grande St. ☎ **472-9600.**

According to the *Chronicle*'s 1994 reader's poll, the best local vocals are performed by this official choral group of the Austin Symphony. The highly acclaimed 160-member oratorio ensemble puts on approximately eight performances per year (three with the symphony), ranging from early baroque to contemporary; you might be able to catch them during one of their seasonal church appearances.

Major Concert & Performance Halls

Austin Convention Center. ☎ **476-5461.**

Capitol City Playhouse. ☎ **472-1855.**

Dougherty Arts Center Theater. ☎ **397-1468.**

Hyde Park Theater. ☎ **499-8497.**

Live Oaks Theater. ☎ **472-5143.**

Palmer Auditorium/City Coliseum. ☎ **472-5111.**

Paramount Theatre. ☎ **472-5411.**

Performing Arts Center/U.T. ☎ **471-1444.**

Zachary Scott Theatre. ☎ **476-0541.**

Symphony Square. ☎ **476-6064.**

Zilker Hillside Theater. ☎ **397-1463.**

Austin Lyric Opera, 1111 W. Sixth St. ☎ **472-5927** or **472-5992** (box office).

Austin's first professional opera company, started in 1985, presents three productions a year at the Bass Concert Hall. Major international artists as well as performers of national stature hit the high notes in such operas as Gounod's *Faust,* Verdi's *Rigoletto,* and Puccini's *Madama Butterfly,* which is on the program for the 1994–95 season.

Tickets: $12–$72.

Austin Symphony, 1101 Red River St. ☎ **476-6064** or **476-4626** (box office).

A resident in Austin since 1911, the symphony performs most of its classical works—including a popular children's series—at Bass Concert Hall; guest artists in the 1994–95 season include Van Cliburn and Joshua Bell. The informal Pops shows play to a picnic table-seated crowd at the Palmer Auditorium. There's also a Summer Festival at Symphony Square. Maestro Sung Kwak is the resident conductor.

Tickets: Classical, $8–$22; Pops, $10–$22; children's concerts, $4–$5 (children), $5–6 (adults); Summer Festival, $6–10.

Theater

Capitol City Playhouse, 214 W. Fourth St. ☎ **472-1855** or **472-2966** (box office).

Though off-Broadway fare such as *Streamers* and *Always Patsy Cline* is the focus of Capitol City, the Jose Greco Dance Company often turns up at this 1890s theater, in downtown's west-side arts district. The resident company also produces original work, including that of the winners of the Texas Young Playwrights competition, which it hosts every year. Wednesday and Thursday performances follow a complimentary buffet.

Tickets: $10–$21.

Hyde Park Theatre, 511 W. 43rd St. ☎ **452-6688** or **499-8497** (box office).

This intimate neighborhood theater in Austin's historic Hyde Park district presents innovative, contemporary work at night and children's plays during the day. Most are produced by the theater's semiprofessional resident company, but even if the space is leased out, you can expect the pieces performed here to be intellectually engaging. The early fall Fronterafest showcases local dance, music, and performance art as well as theater.

Tickets: $10 on average.

Live Oaks Theater, 200 Colorado St. ☎ **472-1855** or **472-5143** (box office).

Austin's most professional theater puts on a wide variety of work, from acclaimed romantic comedies like *She Loves Me* and serious political dramas such as *Death and the Maiden* to lesser known pieces by Texas-based playwrights. Readings from nationwide participants in the Harvest Festival of New Plays are held in the fall; the play that wins the contest is produced during the season.

Tickets: $16–$18.

Mary Moody Northen Theatre of St. Edward's University,

3001 S. Congress Ave. ☎ **448-8483** or **448-8484** (box office).

U.T.'s College of Fine Arts is not the only act in town: St. Edward's University also has a thriving theater department, which gets support for its performances from a variety of professional directors and guest actors. The 1994–95 season ranged from the rock classic *Hair* to the classic *Pygmalion* by George Bernard Shaw. Three shows are presented in a six-week summer-stock series.

Tickets: $10 adults, seniors $8, students $5.

Vortex Repertory Company, Planet Theater, 2307 Manor Rd.

☎ **472-2644** or **478-LAVA** (box office)

A converted warehouse with an outdoor courtyard and café, the new Planet Theater (just east of the University of Texas and I-35) complements Vortex's avant-garde program. The company premieres such cutting-edge work as *Unidentified Human Remains* and *Beirut,* and presents national touring artists like the Flirtations, a gay a cappella group, and performance artist Holly Hughes.

Tickets: Prices average around $10, with discounts available for students and seniors.

Zachary Scott Theatre Center, 1510 Toomey Rd. (John E.

Whisenhunt Arena Stage) or 1421 W. Riverside Dr. (Kleburg Stage), ☎ **476-0594** or **476-0541** (box office).

Austin's oldest theater, incorporated in 1933, features Broadway shows such as *Dream Girls* and *The Sisters Rosenzweig,* as well as musical revues, serious drama, and, occasionally, children's plays. Works are performed at two adjacent theaters—one a three-sided thrust stage, the other in the round—at the edge of Zilker Park; it's a sneaker's throw from the parking lot to the hike-and-bike trail.

Tickets: $12–$18.

Dance ―――――――――――――――――――――――――――――――――――

Ballet Austin, 3004 Guadalupe St. ☎ **476-9051** or **476-2163** (box

office).

This company's 20 professional dancers leap and bound in such classics as *The Nutcracker* and *Coppelia,* as well as in such contemporary original pieces as *Myths and Mythology,* with electroacoustic accompaniment. Among the many places Ballet Austin has toured is Cyprus, where artistic director Lambros Lamrou was born. When in town, they perform at Bass Concert Hall or, for children's shows, the Paramount Theatre.

Tickets: $6–$39.

Sharir Dance Company, 1501 W. Fifth St. ☎ **458-8158.**

An aptly high-tech ensemble for on-line Austin, Sharir stretched the boundaries of dance toward virtual reality in 1994 when the company included video projections and computer-generated images in its choreography. New forms have always been key to this exciting postmodern troupe, in residence at the University of Texas's College of Fine Arts. Most of the Austin performances are held at the college's Performing Arts Center, but outdoor environmental pieces are currently in the planning stages.

Tickets: $12 (students and senior discounts available).

Major Concert Halls & All-Purpose Auditoriums

The Paramount Theatre, 713 Congress Ave. ☎ **472-5411** or ☎ **472-5470** (box office).

The Marx Brothers, Sarah Bernhardt, Helen Hayes, and Katharine Hepburn all entertained at this former vaudeville house, which opened as the Majestic Theater in 1915 and functioned as a movie palace for 50 years. Restored to its original opulence, the Paramount now hosts Broadway shows; visiting celebrity performers; local theatrical productions, including an impressive Kids Classic series; and, in the summer, old-time films.

Tickets: Broadway shows, $20–$40; concerts, around $20; dance shows, $15–$20; Kids Classic shows, $10; film series, $3.50–$5.

The Performing Arts Center, University of Texas Campus. ☎ **471-1444.**

Along with local talent, a dazzling array of international and national stars shine at the Performing Arts Center, the hub of the University of Texas's College of Fine Arts and of the city's cultural scene. The 1994–95 roster alone features Isaac Stern, Victor Borge, Mel Tormé, Laurie Anderson, Los Lobos, the Joffrey Ballet, and the Alvin Ailey American Dance Theatre. The state-of-the-art **Bass Concert Hall** (23rd Street and East Campus Drive), which seats 3,000, is the complex's flagship theater and host to its central box office. Other main venues include the **Bates Recital Hall** (Music Building, 2500 block of East Campus Drive), known for its excellent acoustics; the 400-seat **McCullough Theatre** (2400 Block of East Campus Drive), where dance performances are frequently held; and the **B. Iden Payne Theatre** (23rd and San Jacinto), a slightly larger venue, seating 600 to 700 for its theatrical productions.

Tickets: $6–$50 (most around $10–$25).

Symphony Square, 11th and Red River Sts. ☎ **476-6064.**

Home to the Austin Symphony Orchestra's offices, this entertainment complex comprises an outdoor amphitheater and four historic structures dating from 1871 to 1877; the triangular Hamilton building, the only one original to the site, belonged to the city's first African American legislator. A narrow Waller Creek runs between the seats and the stage of the amphitheater, where the symphony's Summer Music Festival is held. Also in the summer, every Wednesday from 9:30 until about 11:30am, kids can try out various orchestral instruments in the symphony's version of a petting zoo.

Zilker Hillside Theater, Zilker Park, across from Barton Springs Pool. ☎ **397-1463.**

More than 5,000 people can perch on this natural grassy knoll to watch free, city-sponsored performances, including dance, drama, symphony, and jazz. The summer musical series, featuring *Joseph and the Amazing Technicolor Dream Coat* in 1995, started in the late 1950s and is the longest running one in the United States. Seating is first-come, first-served; bring your own blanket or lawn chairs.

2   The Club & Music Scene

The 1972 appearance at the Armadillo World Headquarters of country-and-western "outlaw" Willie Nelson, uniting hippies and rednecks in a common musical cause, is often credited with the birth of the live-music scene on Austin's Sixth Street. Although the Armadillo is defunct and Sixth Street is past its creative prime—with some notable exceptions, it caters pretty much to a rowdy college crowd—live music in Austin is very much alive, just more geographically diffuse. Some clubs, like Antone's, have always been off-the-beaten path; others, like the Backyard, are newly expanding the boundaries of Austin's musical terrain. Poke around; you can never tell which dive might turn up the likes of Janis Joplin, Stevie Ray Vaughan, or Jimmie Dale Gilmore, all of whom played local gigs. Categories of clubs in a city known for crossover are often very rough approximations; those that completely defy typecasting are dubbed "eclectic." Cover charges range from $2 to $6, with free or cheap drinks usually included when prices are at the high end.

Comedy Clubs

Esther's Follies, 525 E. Sixth St. ☎ **320-0553.**

You might miss a couple of the punchlines if you're not in on the latest twists and turns of local politics, but the no-holds-barred Esther's Follies doesn't spare Washington, either. It's very satirical, very irreverent, very Austin.

Performances: Thurs 8pm, Fri–Sat 8 and 10pm.
Prices: $10 Thurs, $12 Fri, $14 Sat; $4 off for students.

The Velveeta Room, 525 E. Sixth St. ☎ **469-9116.**

For one-stop comedy consumption, go straight from Esther's to the Velveeta Room next door. This deliberately cheesy club serves more standard stand-up, local as well as national. Thursday is open mike night, while jocks are the target of Saturday's Comedy Sportz.

Performances: Thurs 9:30pm, Fri–Sat 8, 9:30, and 11:30pm.
Prices: $2 Thurs, $4 Fri, $6 Sat.

Folk & Country

Broken Spoke, 3201 S. Lamar Blvd. ☎ **442-6189.**

This is the genuine item, a western honky-tonk with a wood plank floor and a cowboy-hatted, two-steppin' crowd. Still, it's in Austin, so don't be surprised if the band wears Hawaiian shirts, or if tongues are firmly in cheek for some of the songs. Photos of Hank Williams, Tex Ritter, and other country greats line the walls of the club's "museum." You can eat in a large, open room out front, or bring your long necks back to a table overlooking the dance floor.

Cactus Cafe, Texas Union, University of Texas Campus. ☎ 475-6515.

A small, dark cavern with great acoustics and a fully stocked bar, U.T.'s Cactus Cafe is singer/songwriter heaven, a place where dramatic stage antics take a backseat to engaged showmanship. The attentive listening vibes attract talented solo artists like Steve Forbert and Vic Chestnutt, along with well-known acoustic combos.

★ **Continental Club,** 1315 S. Congress Ave. ☎ 441-2444.

Although it also showcases rock, rockabilly, and new-wave sounds, the Continental Club holds on to its roots in traditional country, celebrating events such as Hank Williams's birthday. A small, smoky club with high stools and a pool table in the back room, this is a not-to-be-missed Austin classic. Tuesday night's happy hour brings on the blues.

Jazz & Blues

★ **Antone's,** 2915 Guadalupe St. ☎ 474-5314.

Clifford Antone's place is as open-minded as any in Austin; Willie Nelson celebrated his 60th birthday here and country-and-western crossover bands like the Austin Lounge Lizards turn up all the time. But in this dark, cavernous room, where Stevie Ray Vaughan was once a regular, the strains of a blues guitar are still the most likely to be heard. When major blues artists venture down this way—for example, Buddy Guy, Etta James, or Edgar Winter—you can be sure they'll either be playing Antone's or stopping by for a surprise set.

Elephant Room, 315 Congress Ave. ☎ 473-2279.

Film stars on location in Austin mingle with T-shirted students and well-dressed older aficionados at this intimate downtown venue, as dark and as smoky as a jazz bar should be. The focus is on contemporary and traditional jazz, though the bill branches out to rock on occasion.

Pearl's Oyster Bar, 9003 Research Blvd. ☎ 339-7444.

Some jazz acts join Texas rhythm-and-blues bands seven nights a week in a funky New Orleans atmosphere. Settle in here for some good seafood and beer along with the blues.

Top of the Marc, 618 W. Sixth St. ☎ 472-9849.

A standout in a town surprisingly weak on jazz, Top of the Marc draws a sophisticated crowd to hear artists like the Duke Ellington Orchestra as well as favorite local bands. You can enjoy hot pastrami (see "Katz's" in Chapter 13) and cool sounds in a chic black-and-white room or an outdoor roof deck.

Rock

Electric Lounge, 302 Bowie St. ☎ 476-FUSE.

The barometer of Austin's rock/pop scene, the Electric Lounge is the town's main showcase for local up-and-coming bands. If you squint at the dimly lit corner stage and concrete-block walls, you'll have no trouble imagining you're in someone's garage.

Emo's, 603 Red River St. ☎ 477-EMOS.

Austin's last word in punk rock and all its mutations, Emo's draws acts of all sizes and flavors. Free admission makes this *the* place for Austin's college crowd to see and be seen. There are pool tables and pinball machines out front, picnic tables on the outside patio.

Liberty Lunch, 405 W. Second St. ☎ 477-0461.

This huge converted warehouse, with a concrete floor sloping down to a large stage, has a long-standing reputation for presenting the widest range of midscale rock and roll of any club in Austin. Expect to see acts ranging from Los Lobos to the Cowboy Junkies to Violent Femmes; hardcore metal and reggae bands turn up, too. Be sure to check out the great tropical mural.

Maggie Mae's, 512 Trinity St. ☎ 478-8541.

Good rock bands and a great selection of beer set Maggie Mae's apart from the collegiate-crowded clubs lining Sixth Street. The dining deck upstairs isn't exactly quiet, but you can usually make out what your dinner companion is saying.

Eclectic

★ The Backyard, 13101 Hwy. 71 west, Bees Cave. ☎ 236-4146.

A terrific sound system and a casual country atmosphere have helped make this one of the hottest new venues in town. Since it opened in 1993, the Allman Brothers, Chet Atkins, Joan Baez, Jimmy Cliff, Leonard Cohen, Chick Corea, Willie Nelson, and Warren Zevon have all played the terraced outdoor amphitheater, which is shaded by ancient live oaks. Come early for dinner; a committedly Texas menu (barbecue, Tex-Mex, steaks, and burgers) is reasonably priced and good.

Prices: $6–8 local acts, $12–$24 national acts.

Hole in the Wall, 2538 Guadalupe St. ☎ 474-5314.

This intimate club, on the Drag just off the U.T. campus, has a long-standing tradition of trying anything once. It's a great coup for local performers to be booked here, and the audience often gets to say, "We saw them when" about popular Texas bands that later hit it big.

★ La Zona Rosa, 612 W. Fourth St. ☎ 482-0662.

Another Austin classic, LZR mixes a Tex-Mex menu with high-quality music ranging from Latino and alternative country to punk rock. A renovated garage brightly painted with monsters and filled with kitschy memorabilia is an appropriately outrageous setting for the club's cutting-edge sounds.

Dance Clubs & Discos

Dancing fools head for the heart of the downtown, where they can hop from one club to another within a five-block radius. The **404 Club,** 404 Colorado St. (☎ **499-0088**), is the foremost gay/lesbian/straight/meat market/dance bar in the city; all orientations also mix it up at **Ohms,** 611 E. Seventh St. (☎ **472-7136**), another great dance club. **Nexus,** 305 W. Fifth St. (☎ **472-5288**), which has a country-and-western flavor, and **Hollywood,** 113 San Jacinto Blvd. (☎ **480-9627**), both attract a largely lesbian crowd. An alternative, college-age group turns out at **Infinity,** 600 E. Sixth St. (☎ **499-8700**). **Proteus,** 501 E. Sixth St. (☎ **472-8922**), often holds raves; **Paradox,** 311 E. Fifth St. (☎ **469-7615**), **Medusa's,** 612 E. Sixth St. (☎ **499-8700**), **Mirage,** 222 E. Sixth St. (☎ **474-7531**), and **5th St. Station,** 505 E. Fifth St. (☎ **478-6065**), are also very popular.

3 The Bar Scene

Brew Pubs

The Armadillo Brewing Co., 419 E. Sixth St. ☎ **322-0039.**

Shiny copper vats make a nice contrast to the limestone walls of this historic downtown building, only recently turned brew pub. A reasonably priced menu—filled with thirst-inspiring items, naturally—complements such beers as the rich, amber Road Kill Red and the refreshing, light Axes Pale Ale (much more appetizing than their names).

The Waterloo Brewing Company, 401 Guadalupe St. ☎ **477-1836.**

The first brew pub in Texas—do-it-yourself suds weren't legal in the state until late 1993—Waterloo has a decent dining room on the first floor, a game room upstairs, and four good microbrews on tap. The full-bodied O. Henry's Porter is practically a meal in itself.

Specialty Bars

GAY BARS

Chances, 900 Red River St. ☎ **472-8273.**

A friendly group of older and college-age women mingle in this low-key bar, with a single pool table and a huge volleyball court outside. Lots of up-and-coming bands play here, either on the tiny indoor stage or the larger amphitheater-like platform on the patio.

Oilcan Harry's, 211 W. Fourth St. ☎ **320-8823.**

This is the place to come to find a buttoned-down, Brooks Brothers kind of guy; its name notwithstanding, this slick downtown men's bar attracts a clean-cut, upscale crowd. There's dancing here, but not with the same frenzy as at many of the other clubs.

HISTORIC BAR

Scholz Garten, 1607 San Jacinto Blvd. ☎ 477-4171.

Since 1866, when councilman August Scholz first opened his tavern near the State Capitol, every Texas governor has visited it at least once (and many quite a few more times). Although it's no longer in the hands of the German singing society that ran it for decades, this huge beer hall and garden still gets a lot of rousing songs when the University of Texas teams win their games. It's a great place to drink in some Austin history.

LOCAL BAR

Cedar Door, 910 W. First St. ☎ 473-3712.

"Cheers" with a redwood deck looking out on Town Lake, the Cedar Door is Austin's favorite local, drawing a group of potluck regulars ranging from hippies to journalists and politicos. The beer's cold, the drinks are strong, and to lots of folks it feels like home.

PIANO BAR

Driskill Hotel, 604 Brazos St. ☎ 474-5911.

Sink into one of the plush chairs arrayed around a grand piano and enjoy everything from blues to show tunes in the opulent upper-lobby bar of Austin's only historic hotel. A pianist accompanies the happy-hour hors d'oeuvres munching (nightly from 5 to 7pm), but the ivory thumping doesn't get going in earnest until 9pm on Thursday, Friday, and Saturday, when people start singing along.

4 More Entertainment

Movies

It's almost harder to find mainstream movies in Austin than it is to locate foreign films in most other cities; nearly every cinema in town devotes at least one screen to something off Hollywood's beaten track. In the university area, the largest concentration of art films can be found at the **Dobie Theatre,** 2021 Guadalupe St., on the Drag (☎ 472-FILM), and at the two venues of the **Texas Union Film Series,** U.T. Campus, Texas Union Building and Hogg Auditorium (☎ 471-1945). The **Village Cinema Art,** 2700 W. Anderson Lane (☎ 451-8352), across from Northpark Mall, also exclusively showcases low-budget and imported fare.

Virtual Reality

For high-tech interactive adventures, head for the **Virtual Reality Gaming Center,** 2118 Guadalupe St. (☎ 478-5544), where you can either conquer monsters in your own three-dimensional world, or join others in vivid imaginary melees. Although it's on the U.T. Drag, the center draws families as well as students. Rates are $3 for 15 minutes, with discounts for an hour's play and for groups of four or more. The center is open 11am until midnight, Tuesday through Sunday.

17

Easy Excursions from San Antonio & Austin

A RISING AND FALLING DREAMSCAPE OF LAKES AND RIVERS, SPRINGS AND caverns, **Hill Country** is one of Texas's prettiest regions, especially in early spring when wildflowers daub it with every pigment in nature's palette. Dotted with quaint Teutonic towns—more than 30,000 Germans emigrated to Texas during the great land-grant years of the Republic—and birthplace of one of the U.S.'s more colorful recent presidents, the region also presents a riveting tableau of the state's history.

San Antonio lies at the southern edge of Hill Country, while Austin is the northeastern gateway to the region. The following tour traces a roughly circular route from San Antonio, but it's only 80 miles between the two cities; distances in this area are sufficiently short that you can design excursions based on your point of origin and your particular interests. If you have lots of leisure time, contact the **Hill Country Tourism Association,** 1700 Sidney Baker, Suite 200, Kerrville, 78028 (☎ **210/895-5505**), for information about additional things to see and do in the area; they can also send you a schedule of the many food-and-music fests celebrated here throughout the year.

1 Boerne

From San Antonio, it's a straight shot north for 30 miles on I-10 to Boerne (rhymes with "journey"). A popular health resort in the 1880s, the little (2.2-mile) town was first settled 30 years earlier by freedom-seeking German intellectuals; it was named after German firebrand journalist, Ludwig Börne. A gazebo with a Victorian cupola in the center of the main plaza often hosts concerts by the 133-year-old Boerne Village Band, the oldest continuously operating German band in the world outside Germany. A number of the town's 19th-century limestone buildings house small historical museums, boutiques, and restaurants, but Boerne's biggest draw for many is its antiques shops—more than 20 line the "Hauptstrasse," or main street. For a self-guided tour, stop in at the **Boerne Chamber of Commerce,** 1 Main Plaza, 78006 (☎ **210/249-8000**).

In Boerne City Park, you can explore four distinct ecosystems via short treks on the **Cibolo Wilderness Trail.** Nearby attractions include the **Cascade Caverns,** south of Boerne, exit 543 on 1-10 (☎ **210/755-8080**), an active cave that boasts huge chambers, a 90-foot underground waterfall, and comfortable walking trails. It's also easy to tour the stalactite- and stalagmite-filled **Cave Without a Name,** Kreuzberg Road, 12 miles northeast of Boerne (☎ **210/537-4212**); a naming contest held when the cavern was discovered in 1939 was won by a little boy who wrote that it was too pretty to name (the $500 he earned put him through college). Rafters and canoers enjoy **Guadalupe River State Park,** about 13 miles east of Boerne, off Hwy. 46 on P.R. 31 (☎ **210/438-2656**), comprising more than 1,900 acres surrounding a lovely, cypress-edged river. Keep an eye out: You might spot white-tailed deer, coyotes, armadillos, or even a rare golden-cheeked warbler here.

If you'd like to stay overnight, try the two-story **Ye Kendall Inn,** 128 W. Blanco, Boerne, 78006 (☎ **210/249-2138**), opened as a lodging for stagecoach passengers in 1859 and restored as a bed-and-breakfast in 1990. The eight rooms ($80) and three suites ($125) are all nicely furnished with Victorian antiques. **Scuzzi** (☎ **210/249-8886**), also in the inn, serves good northern Italian cuisine in an elegant atmosphere.

2 Castroville

For a look at a unique old-world culture, take U.S. 90 west some 20 miles from San Antonio to Castroville, founded on a scenic bend of the Medina River in 1844. Two years earlier, Henri Castro, a Portuguese-born Jewish Frenchman, had received a 1.25-million-acre grant from the Republic of Texas in exchange for a commitment to colonize the land. Second only to Stephen F. Austin in the number of settlers he brought over, Castro recruited most of his 2,134 émigrés from the Rhine Valley, and especially from the French province of Alsace. You can still hear Alsatian, an unwritten dialect of German, spoken by some of the older members of town, but, sadly, the language is likely to die out of the area when they do.

Almost 100 of the original settlers' unevenly slope-roofed houses remain in Castroville, some still occupied by the builders' ancestors; the oldest standing structure, the **First St. Louis Baptist Church,** went up in 1846 on the corner of Angelo and Moy. Many of the European-style headstones in the **cemetery** at the western edge of town, where Henri Castro's wife, Amelia, is buried, date back to the 1840s. A gristmill and wood-and-stone dam are among the interesting artifacts at the **Landmark Inn State Historical Park,** 402 Florence St. (☎ **210/931-2133**); Robert E. Lee is said to have stayed at what was then the Vance Hotel. The **Castroville Chamber of Commerce,** 802 London St., 78009 (☎ **210/538-3142**), can provide details about the town's other historical buildings, as well as about its many boutiques and antiques shops.

Get a delicious taste of the past at **Haby's Alsation Bakery,** 207 U.S. 90 east (☎ **210/538-2118**), owned by the Tschirhart family since 1948 and featuring apple fritters, strudel, stollen, breads, and coffee cakes. Among the specialties of the **Alsatian Restaurant,** 403 Angelo St. (☎ **210/931-3260**), set in a charming 19th-century cottage, is the delicious Strasbourg chicken, served with sauerkraut and red cabbage. The **Landmark Inn** (see above), now a bed-and-breakfast, offers eight rooms beautifully appointed with pieces from the 1940s. Prices for a double with a private bath are $55, with a shared bath, $50; none of the rooms have phones or TVs.

3 Bandera

North of Castroville and west of Boerne, Bandera is a slice of life out of the old West; everything and everybody here seems to have come straight off a John Ford film set. Established as a lumber camp in

Excursions from San Antonio and Austin

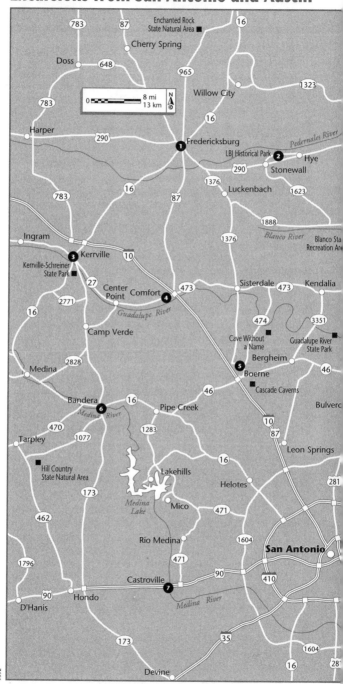

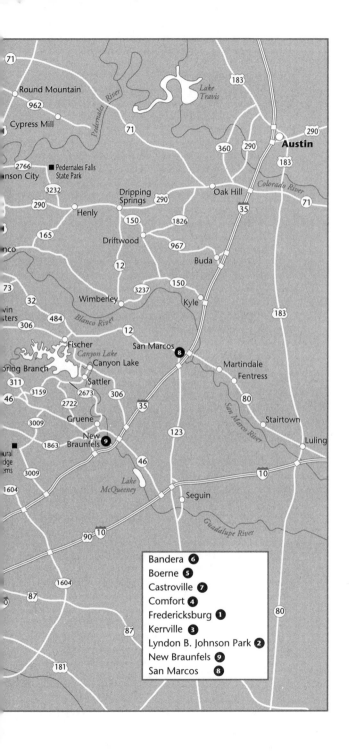

Bandera **6**
Boerne **5**
Castroville **7**
Comfort **4**
Fredericksburg **1**
Kerrville **3**
Lyndon B. Johnson Park **2**
New Braunfels **9**
San Marcos **8**

1853, this popular guest-ranch center still has the feel of the frontier: Not only are many of its historic buildings intact—including **St. Stanislaus** (1855), the second-oldest Polish church in the country—but people are as genuinely friendly as any you might imagine from America's small-town past.

Take your time strolling along Main Street; be sure to stop in at the **Bandera Forge** (☎ 210/796-7184), a working blacksmith shop where you can design your own branding iron, and at **Sim's Spur Company** (☎ 210/796-3716), where intricate spurs and bits are made by hand. If all this puts you in the mood to mount your own nag, the **Bandera County Convention & Visitors Bureau,** P.O. Box 171, 78003 (☎ 210/796-3045 or toll free 800/364-3833), can help you find a horseback tour. It's also the place to check whether any rodeos or roping exhibitions are in the area; you're especially likely to catch them in summer.

When you're ready to put on the feed bag, try Main Street's **O.S.T.** (☎ 210/796-3636), named for the Old Spanish Trail which used to run through Bandera; serving up down-home Texas and Tex-Mex victuals since 1921, this café has a room dedicated to the Duke and other cowboy film stars. At night, don't miss **Arkey Blue's Silver Dollar Saloon** (☎ 210/796-8826), a genuine spit-and-sawdust cowboy honky-tonk; Hank Williams, Sr., carved his name on one of the tables. When there's no band on, plug a quarter in the old jukebox and play a country ballad by owner Arkey.

For the full flavor of this region, plan to stay at one of Bandera's many guest ranches. At the **Dixie Dude Ranch,** P.O. Box 548, Bandera, 78003 (☎ 210/796-7771 or toll free 800/375-Y'ALL), you're likely to see white-tailed deer or wild turkeys as you trot on horseback through a 725-acre spread. Tubing on the Medina River is among the many things you might do during the day at the **Mayan Ranch,** P.O. Box 577, Bandera, 78003 (☎ 210/796-3312 or 460-3036). Both places provide lots of additional western fun for their guests—maybe two-step lessons, cookouts, hayrides, singing cowboys, or trick-roping exhibitions. Rates (at the Dixie Dude Ranch, from $80 to $85 per person per night, at the Mayan Ranch, $95 to $115 per person per night) include three home-cooked meals, two trail rides, and most of the other activities.

About 20 miles southeast of town (take Hwy. 16 to R.R. 1283), **Medina Lake** is the place to hook crappie, white or black bass, and, especially, huge yellow catfish; the public boat ramp is on the north side of the lake, at the end of P.R. 37. The Convention & Visitors Bureau can provide names of various outfitters to those who want to kayak, canoe, or tube down the Medina River. You can canter through The **Hill Country State Natural Area,** 10 miles southwest of Bandera (☎ 210/796-4413), the largest state park in Texas allowing horseback riding, but if you're happier betting on than getting on a horse, head for **Bandera Downs** (☎ 210/796-7781 or toll free 800/572-2332), on Hwy. 16 approximately a mile south of town.

EN ROUTE TO KERRVILLE   Both of the roads from Bandera to Kerrville are scenic and each has its distinct allure. If you take the longer Hwy. 16 route—37 miles compared to 26—you'll pass through **Medina**. You won't doubt the little town's claim of being the Apple Capital of Texas when you come to Love Creek Orchards Cider Mill and Country Store on the main street; along with apple pies and other fresh-baked goods, you can buy apple cider, apple syrup, apple butter, apple ice cream . . . you can even have an apple sapling shipped back home to you.

Military buffs might want to take the more direct Hwy. 173, which passes through **Camp Verde** (1856–69), the former headquarters of the short-lived U.S. Army camel cavalry. Widespread ignorance of their habits and the onset of the Civil War led to the abandonment of the attempt to introduce "ships of the desert" into dry Southwest terrain, but the commander of the post had great respect for his humpbacked recruits. There's little left of the fortress itself, but the old General Store & Post Office is intact. You can pick up postcards here as well as fixings for a picnic at the pleasant roadside park nearby.

4   Kerrville

With a population of about 20,000, Kerrville is larger than the other Hill Country towns so far explored. Now a popular retirement and tourist area, it was founded in the 1840s by Joshua Brown, a shingle-maker attracted to the area's many cypresses. A rough-and-tumble camp surrounded by more civilized German towns, Kerrville soon became a ranching center for longhorn cattle and, more unusually, for Angora goats, eventually turning out the most mohair in the United States. Lauded in the 1920s for its healthful climate, Kerrville began to draw youth camps, sanitoriums, and artists.

Prime among the town's cultural attractions is the **Cowboy Artists of America Museum,** 1550 Bandera Hwy. (☎ 210/896-2553), with various visions of the West displayed in a striking southwestern-style building. For a glimpse of affluent Hill Country life in the early days, visit the **Hill Country Museum,** 226 Earl Garrett St. (☎ 210/896-8633), a mansion built of native stone for pioneer rancher Capt. Charles Schreiner. **Old Republic Square** (off Lemos, between Main and Water Streets) hosts a collection of quaint gift shops and boutiques. Combine lunch with antiquing at the nearby **Water Street Antique Co.,** 820 Water St. (☎ 210/257-5044), a restored turn-of-the-century building with a charming tearoom. Just down the block, **Artisan Accents,** 826 Water St. (☎ 210/896-4220), sells beautiful contemporary crafts. For fine gold and silver jewelry, visit **James Avery Craftsman,** 3¹/₂ miles north of Kerrville on Harper Road (☎ 210/895-1122).

Outdoor enthusiasts will enjoy **Kerrville-Schreiner State Park,** 2385 Bandera Hwy. (☎ 210/257-5392), a 500-acre green space boasting seven miles of hiking trails, as well as swimming and boating on the Guadalupe River. Sika deer, Corsican sheep, and the rare scimitar-horned oryx are among the species you can capture for your photo album on the **Kerrville Camera Safari,** 2301 Sidney Baker north (☎ **210/792-3600**), a drive-through wildlife ranch. The **Kerrville Convention & Visitors Bureau,** (1700 Sidney Baker, Suite 2, 78028 (☎ **210/896-1155** or toll free **800/221-7958**), can give you a map and clue you into more of the town's attractions; ask about the huge Kerrville Folk Festival, which draws fans from around the country.

You'll have to make a reservation to visit the **Y.O. Ranch,** 32 miles from Kerrville, off Hwy. 41, Mt. Home, 78058 (☎ **210/640-3222**). Originally comprising 550,000 acres purchased by Charles Shreiner in 1880, the Y.O. is now a 40,000-acre working ranch known for its exotic wildlife as well as for its Texas longhorn cattle. You can go out for a horseback ride and lunch during the day or stay overnight, if you don't mind sleeping under a furry hunting trophy.

The **Holiday Inn Y.O. Ranch Hotel and Conference Center,** 2033 Sidney Baker, Kerrville, 78028 (☎ **210/257-4440** or toll free **800-HOLIDAY**)—not near the ranch but in Kerrville itself—offers large and attractive western-style quarters; its Sam Houston dining room features wild game and big steaks, and the saloon serves up live music with its whisky. Doubles range from $68 to $88, depending on the season.

5 Comfort

The most direct route from Kerrville to Fredericksberg is via Hwy. 16 north, but if you have time, detour 18 miles southeast along Hwy. 27 to seek Comfort. The freethinking German immigrants who founded the town in 1852 were originally going to name it *gemütlichkeit*—a more difficult-to-pronounce native version of its current name—when they arrived at this welcoming spot after an arduous journey from New Braunfels. The rough-hewn limestone buildings in the center of Comfort may comprise the most complete 19th-century business district in Texas; some of the offices were designed by architect Alfred Giles, who also left his distinctive mark on San Antonio's streets. The earliest church in town was built some 40 years after the first settlers arrived; during the initial period, the founders' antireligious beliefs, for which they had been persecuted in the old country, prevailed.

Among the town's many antiques shops, one of the most interesting is **Comfort Common,** 818 High St., Comfort, 78013 (☎ **210/995-3030**), on the ground floor of the 19th-century Faust-Ingenhuett Hotel; the latter is now a popular bed-and-breakfast (rates run from $55 to $90). Don't miss the **Ingenhuett Store,** 830 High St. (☎ **210/995-2149**), operated by the same German American family since 1880, or the *Treue der Union* **(True to the Union) Monument** (High Street, between Third and Fourth Streets), erected in 1866 to commemorate 36 antislavery settlers who were killed by Confederate soldiers when they tried to defect to Mexico. Outside of national cemeteries, this striking obelisk is the only monument to the Union in former Confederate territory. The **Comfort Chamber of Commerce,** P.O. Box 777, Comfort, 78013 (☎ **210/995-3131**), on Seventh and High Streets, is open limited hours.

If you missed the **bats** in Austin, you've got a chance to see even more in an abandoned railroad tunnel supervised by the Texas Parks and Wildlife Department. From Comfort, take Hwy. 473 north four or five miles. When the road winds to the right toward Sisterdale, keep going straight; in another eight or nine miles, you'll spot a parking lot and a mound of large rocks on top of a hill. During migration season (May to November), you can watch as many as $2^1/_2$ million Mexican free-tailed bats set off on a food foray at around dusk. State-sponsored naturalist tours are given every Thursday and Saturday evening from June through October; call **210/868-7304** for details.

6 Fredericksburg

A popular weekend retreat for San Antonians and Austinites, Fredericksburg is devoted to its European past. Baron Ottfried Hans von Meusebach was one of 10 nobles who formed a society designed to help Germans resettle in Texas, where they would be safe from political persecution and economic hardship. In 1846, he took 120 émigrés in ox-drawn carts from New Braunfels to this site, which he named for Prince Frederick of Prussia; the town's mile-long main street is still wide enough for a team of oxen to turn around in. The permanent peace treaty Meusebach negotiated with the Comanches in 1847, and the gold rush of 1849—Fredericksburg was the last place the California-bound prospectors could get supplies—both helped the town thrive.

The **Convention & Visitors Bureau,** 106 N. Adams, 78624 (☎ **210/997-6523**), can direct you to the many points of interest in the town's historic district. These include a number of little **Sunday Houses,** built by German settlers in distant rural areas because they needed a place to stay overnight when they came to town to trade or attend church. You'll also notice many homes built in the Hill Country version of the German *fachwerk* design, made out of limestone with diagonal wood supports. The unusual octagonal **Vareins Kirche** (Society Church) in Market Square once functioned as a town hall, school, and storehouse; a 1935 replica of the original 1847 building now holds the archives of the Gillespie County Historical Society. The Historical Society also maintains the **Pioneer Museum Complex,** 309 W. Main St. (☎ **210/997-2835**), anchored by the 1849 Kammlah House, which was a family residence and general store until the 1920s; among the other historical structures here are a one-room schoolhouse and a blacksmith's forge. The 1852 Steamboat Hotel, originally owned by the grandfather of World War II naval hero Chester A. Nimitz, is now home to the exhibits of the **Admiral Nimitz Museum State Historical Park,** 340 E.

Main St. (☎ 210/997-4379); also in the park are the Japanese Garden of Peace and the History Walk of the Pacific War—three acres of large World War II relics. More than 100 **specialty shops,** many of them in mid-19th century houses, feature work by Hill Country artisans; you can take a tour of a dulcimer factory (715 S. Washington), see a glassblowing studio (109 E. Main St.), or watch candles being made (155 & 121 E. Main St.).

When you're ready for some fortification, the **Altdorf Biergarten,** 301 W. Main St. (☎ 210/997-7865), and **Friedhelm's Bavarian Inn,** 905 W. Main St. (☎ 210/997-6300), both feature hearty German schnitzels, dumplings, and Sauerbraten, and large selections of beer. For a lighter menu, stop in at the **Peach Tree Tea Room,** 210 S. Adams St. (☎ 210/997-9527), which has a gift gallery, too. About 11 miles north of Fredericksburg on I-87, the **Hill Top Cafe** (☎ 210/997-8922) serves good Cajun and Greek food; you might find the owner, a former member of the band Asleep at the Wheel, very much awake at the piano.

Fredericksburg is the perfect place to try an overnight stay in a *gastehaus* (guest cottage); many historic homes have been converted into romantic havens replete with robes, fireplaces, and even spas. For a booklet detailing some of the most interesting ones, contact **Gastehaus Schmidt,** 231 W. Main St., Fredericksburg, 78624 (☎ 210/997-5612). Both **Bed & Breakfast of Fredericksburg,** 619 W. Main St., Fredericksburg, 78624 (☎ 210/997-4712), and **Be My Guest,** 402 W. Main St., Fredericksburg, 78624 (☎ 210/997-7227), include more traditional bed-and-breakfasts among their listings.

One of the many attractions in the Fredericksburg vicinity is **Lady Bird Johnson Municipal Park,** two miles southeast on Hwy. 16 (☎ 210/997-4202), with an 18-hole golf course, a tennis court, and a 17-acre lake for fishing. Lots of well-known performers turn up in the dance hall of **Luckenbach** (11 miles southeast on R.R. 1376), immortalized in a song by Waylon Jennings and Willie Nelson; there's not much else in the tiny town—listed under "L" in the Fredericksburg section of the county telephone directory— except a bar and a general store. Three wineries near Fredericksburg all offer tastings and tours: **Oberhellmann Vineyards,** 14 miles north on Hwy. 16 (☎ 210/685-3297), **Pedernales Vineyards,** 41$\frac{1}{2}$ miles south on Hwy. 16 South (☎ 210/997-8326), and **Grape Creek Vineyard,** 9 miles east on Hwy. 290 (☎ 210/644-2710). For a scenic loop drive, head northwest to Willow City; the 13-mile route, which leads back to Hwy. 16, is especially spectacular in wildflower season. Take F.M. 965 some 18 miles north to reach **Enchanted Rock State Park** (☎ 915/247-3903), a 640-acre, pink granite dome which draws thousands of hikers each year. The creaking noises that emanate from it at night—likely caused by the cooling of the rock's outer surface—led the area's Indian tribes to believe the rock was inhabited by evil spirits.

7 Lyndon B. Johnson Parks

Welcome to Johnson territory, where the forebears of the 36th president settled almost 150 years ago. Even before he attained the country's highest office, Lyndon Johnson was a local hero whose successful fight for funding of a series of dams provided the region with inexpensive water and power. If you can, make a day out of a visit to LBJ's boyhood home and the sprawling ranch that became known as the Texas White House; even those who don't usually feel drawn to the past are likely to find themselves fascinated by Johnson's frontier lineage. Consider bringing along a picnic to enjoy at the state park; there are also quite a few restaurants in Johnson City.

From Fredericksburg, take U.S. 290 east for 16 miles to the entrance of the **Lyndon B. Johnson State and National Historical Parks at LBJ Ranch,** (Box 238, Stonewall, 78744 (☎ **512/868-7128** or **512/644-2420**), co-run by the Texas Parks and Wildlife Department and the National Park Service. Tour buses depart regularly from the Visitors Center to the still-operating Johnson Ranch; you probably won't spot Lady Bird Johnson, who spends about a third of her time here, but don't be surprised to see longhorn cattle being grazed.

Crossing over the swift-flowing Pedernales River to fields filled with phlox, Indian blanket, and other wildflowers, one can easily see why Johnson loved this land and why, discouraged from running for a second presidential term, he came back here to lick his wounds and, all too soon, to die. A reconstructed version of the former president's modest birthplace lies close to his final resting place, shared with five generations of Johnsons. On the side of the river from which you started out, period-costumed guides at the Sauer-Beckmann Living History Farm give visitors a look at typical Texas-German farm life at the turn of the century; the midwife who attended LBJ's birth grew up here. Nearby, you can take advantage of a swimming pool (open only in summer) and lots of picnic spots.

Admission: $2 per person for bus tours; all other areas are free.

Open: All State Park buildings, including the Visitors Center, are open daily 8am–5pm except Christmas; the Sauer-Beckmann Living History Farm is open daily 8am–4pm except Christmas; the Nature Trail, grounds, and picnic areas are open until 10pm daily. National Park Service tours of the LBJ Ranch, lasting from 1 to 1½ hours, depart from the State Park Visitors Center daily 10am to 4pm except Christmas (tours may be shortened or cancelled due to excessive heat and humidity).

It's 14 miles farther east along U.S. 290 to **Johnson City,** named for founder James Polk Johnson, who was LBJ's cousin. The Boyhood Home—the house on Ninth Street where Lyndon was raised after the age of five—is the centerpiece of this unit of the **Lyndon B. Johnson National Historical Park,** P.O. Box 329, Johnson City, 78636 (☎ **210/868-7128**). The modest white clapboard structure that the family occupied from 1913 on was a hub of intellectual and political activity: LBJ's father, Sam Ealy Johnson, Jr., was a state legislator and his mother, Rebekah, was one of the few college-educated women in the country at the time. From here you can walk over to the Johnson Settlement, where LBJ's grandfather, Sam Ealy Johnson, Sr., and his great uncle, Jessie, engaged in successful cattle speculation in the 1860s. The rustic dogtrot cabin out of which they ran their business is still intact. Before exploring the two sites, pick up a map and background information at the new Visitors Center (take F Street to 10th Street; you'll see the signs).

Admission: Free.

Open: The Boyhood Home, Visitors Center, and Johnson Settlement are all open 9am–5pm daily except Christmas and New Year's Day.

If you're heading on to Austin, take a short detour from U.S. 290 to **Pedernales Falls State Park,** nine miles east of Johnson City on F.R. 2766 (☎ 210/868-7304). When the flow of the Pedernales River is normal to high, the stepped waterfalls that give the 4,860-acre park its name are dramatic.

8 San Marcos

It's a quick 26 miles south via I-35 from Austin to San Marcos. The temporary site of two Spanish missions in the late 1700s, the town was settled by Anglos in the middle of the 19th century and is now home to Southwest State University, the alma mater of Lyndon Johnson and of singer George Strait. But it is San Marcos's geology, rather than its history, that interests most visitors.

In the center of town, clear, cool springs, which keep a constant temperature of 72 degrees, well up from the Balcones Fault to form Spring Lake. On its shores sits **Aquarena Springs Resort,** 1 Aquarena Springs Dr. (☎ 512/396-8900 or toll free 800/999-9767), renowned for glass-bottomed boats from which you can view some of the rare flora and fauna that the springs support, as well as for Ralph the Swimming Pig, who performs at a submarine theater. The **San Marcos River,** which begins at Spring Lake, attracts many canoers and rafters; between May and September, the local Lions Club (☎ 512/392-8255) rents inner tubes and operates a river shuttle at City Park. When the Balcones Fault was active some 30 million years ago, an earthquake created the cave at the center of **Wonder World,** Prospect Street, off Bishop (☎ 512/392-3760 or toll free 800/782-7653, ext. 2283); in addition, you can see water flowing upward at an Anti-Gravity House.

Serious shoppers arrive in droves at the two factory outlet malls, located a few miles south of downtown. Take exit 200 from I-35 for both the **Tanger Factory Outlet Center** (☎ 512/396-7444 or toll free 800-4TANGER) and the larger **San Marcos Factory Shops** (☎ 512/396-2200), across the street. Among the more than 100 stores, you'll find everything from Donna Karan and Brooks Brothers to American Tourister and Black & Decker.

For antiques and crafts, head out to **Wimberly,** 15 miles north-west of San Marcos. Lots of arty boutiques surround the quaint town square, where the Chamber of Commerce (☎ **512/847-2201**) can help orient you. If it's a Stetson or fedora you're after, get off I-35 at Buda (exit 220, about halfway between Austin and San Marcos); on the access road on the east side of the highway, you'll see **Texas Hatters** (☎ **512/295-HATS** or **441-HATS**), in business for more than 50 years. You can spend hours just poring over photos of an unlikely mix of famous customers: Tip O'Neill, George Bush, and the king of Sweden; Al Hirt and Willie Nelson; Peter Fonda and Arnold Schwarzenegger—to name just a few.

The **San Marcos Convention & Visitors Bureau,** 202 N. C. M. Allen Pkwy., 78666 (☎ **512/353-3435** or toll free **800/782-7653,** ext. 177), can provide you with a complete list of places to eat and stay in town. **Pepper's at the Falls,** 100 Sessoms Dr. (☎ **512/396-5255**), serving burgers, grilled chicken, fajitas, and the like, offers great views of the San Marcos River. You're preordained at **Kismet,** 220 N. Edward Geary (☎ **512/757-6760**), to enjoy tasty, healthful food; good live bands on Friday and Saturday nights; and the *New York Times* on Sunday morning.

Guests can book ladies-only and murder-mystery weekends at the **Crystal River Inn,** 326 W. Hopkins, San Marcos, 78666 (☎ **512/396-3739**); rooms in this friendly Victorian bed-and-breakfast run from $45 to $85, suites from $70 to $100. In addition, there are lots of places to spend the night in Wimberly. The **Blair House,** No. 1 Spoke Hill Rd., Wimberly, 78676 (☎ **512/847-8828**), a luxurious country inn on 85 acres, is particularly recommended. Four of the six rooms in the Texas limestone ranch complex have Jacuzzis; rates ($100 to $125) include a full gourmet breakfast. For details and reservations on other lodgings in Wimberly, contact **Country Inn-keepers** (☎ toll free **800/230-0805**), **Hill Country Accommodations** (☎ toll free **800/926-5028**), **See You in the Morning** (☎ toll free **800/773-3968**), or **Wimberly Lodging** (☎ toll free **800/460-3909**).

San Marcos is a convenient jumping-off point for one of Texas's most breathtaking drives; take R.M. 12 west to R.R. 32 to reach the **Devil's Backbone,** a 30-mile, switchback-filled route affording spectacular Hill Country views.

9 New Braunfels

Continue south another 16 miles along I-35 to reach New Braunfels, at the junction of the Comal and Guadalupe Rivers. German settlers were brought here in 1845 by Prince Carl of Solms-Braunfels, the commissioner general of the Society for the Protection of German Immigrants in Texas; members of the same group continued on to found Fredericksburg. Although Prince Carl returned to Germany within a year to marry his fiancée, who refused to join him in the wilderness, his colony prospered; by the 1850s, New Braunfels was the fourth-largest city in Texas after Houston, San Antonio, and Galveston.

At the **New Braunfels Chamber of Commerce,** 390 S. Seguin, 78130 (☎ **512/625-2385** or toll free **800/572-2626**), you can pick up a pamphlet mapping out an antique-lovers' crawl. Those who want to remain in the modern world of retail can explore more than 40 shops in **Mill Store Plaza,** 651 Hwy. 81 East (☎ **210/620-6806**), another popular factory outlet mall.

Of note on the 69-point historic walking tour of midtown, also available at the Chamber of Commerce, are the ornate Romanesque Gothic Comal County Courthouse (1898) on Main Plaza and the nearby Jacob Schmidt Building (193 W. San Antonio), built on the site where William Gebhardt, of canned chili fame, perfected his formula for chili powder in 1896. The **Hummel Museum,** 199 Main Plaza (☎ **210/625-5636** or toll free **800/456-4866**), displays the world's largest collection of drawings by Sister M. I. Hummel; the popular German figurines they inspired can be purchased in the museum's gift shop. Prince Carl never did build a planned castle for his sweetheart, Sophia, on the elevated spot where the **Sophienburg Museum,** 401 W. Coll (☎ **210/629-1900**), now stands, but it's nevertheless an excellent place to learn about the history of New Braunfels and other Hill Country settlements. The **Museum of Texas Handmade Furniture,** 1370 Church Hill Dr. (☎ **210/629-6504**), also sheds light on local domestic life of the last century. You can tour some of the historic homes on **Conservation Plaza;** ask for directions at the Chamber of Commerce, or phone **210/629-2943.**

Four miles northwest of downtown New Braunfels, the once sleepy village of **Gruene** (pronounced "Green") is now crowded with day-trippers browsing the specialty shops in its restored buildings; try H. P. Gruene Antique Mall for reasonably priced and fun nostalgia. Lyle Lovett and Garth Brooks are among the big names who've played at Gruene Hall (☎ **210/606-1281**), the oldest country-and-western dance hall in Texas.

Gruene also figures among the area's impressive array of places to get wet, most of them open only in summer. Outfitters who can help you ride the Guadalupe River rapids on raft, tube, canoe, or inflatable kayak include **Rockin "R" River Rides** (☎ **210/625-2800** or toll free **800/55-FLOAT**) and **Gruene River Company** (☎ **210/625-2800**), both on Gruene Road just south of the Gruene Bridge. The going's a bit smoother at downtown New Braunfels' **Landa Park** (☎ **210/608-2165**), where you can either swim in the largest spring-fed pool in Texas or calmly float in an inner tube down the state's smallest ($2^1/_2$ miles) river; you can also rent paddleboats or glass-bottom boats here. **Schlitterbahn,** 400 N. Liberty (☎ **210/625-2351**), Texas's biggest water park, features gigantic slides, rides, and pools, as well as the world's first uphill water coaster. Even if you don't want to immerse yourself, you might take the lovely 22-mile drive along the Guadalupe River from downtown's Cypress Bend Park to Canyon Lake, which is perfect for scuba diving because of its clarity.

Natural Bridge Caverna, 26495 Natural Bridge Caverns Rd. (☎ 210/657-6101), 12 miles west of New Braunfels, is named for the 60-foot limestone arch spanning its entryway. More than a mile of huge rooms and passages are filled with stunning, multi-hued formations.

Many of the best spots to eat and sleep in New Braunfels have interesting histories. The oldest restaurant in town, **Krause's Cafe,** 148 S. Castell (☎ 210/625-7581), serves substantial German dishes and blue-plate specials in a diner-type setting. In Gruene, the **Grist Mill Restaurant,** 1287 Gruene Rd. (☎210/625-0684), a converted 100-year-old cotton gin, has a Texas casual menu including catfish, burgers, and chicken-fried steak. For upscale American and continental fare in a *gemütlich* atmosphere, try **Wolfgang's Keller,** 295 E. San Antonio St. (☎ 210/625-9169), in the cellar of the Prince Solmes Inn.

The **Prince Solmes Inn,** 295 E. San Antonio St., New Braunfels, 78130 (☎ 210/625-9169), has been in continuous operation since it opened its doors to travelers in 1898. A prime downtown location, tree-shaded courtyard, and accommodations beautifully decorated in florid high Victorian style have put rooms ($50 to 95) and suites ($95 to $125) at this bed-and-breakfast in great demand. For a river view, consider the **Gruene Mansion Inn,** 1275 Gruene Rd., New Braunfels, 78130 (☎ 210/629-2641), another bed-and-breakfast. Here you have a choice of staying in an 1875 plantation house or in one of the surrounding former barns that have been converted to rustic, elegant cottages; accommodations for two go from $85 to $125 per night. If you're planning to come to town during *wurstfest* (late October through early November), be sure to book far in advance.

18

For Foreign Visitors

ALTHOUGH AMERICAN FADS AND FASHIONS HAVE SPREAD ACROSS Europe and other parts of the world so that America may seem like familiar territory before your arrival, there are still many peculiarities and uniquely American situations that any foreign visitor will encounter.

A   Preparing for Your Trip

Entry Requirements

DOCUMENT REGULATIONS   Canadian citizens may enter the United States without visas; they need only proof of residence.

Citizens of the United Kingdom, New Zealand, Japan, and most western European countries traveling on valid passports may not need a visa for fewer than 90 days of holiday or business travel to the United States, providing that they hold a round-trip or return ticket and enter the United States on an airline or cruise line participating in the visa-waiver program.

(Note that citizens of these visa-exempt countries who first enter the United States may then visit Mexico, Canada, Bermuda, and/or the Caribbean islands and then reenter the United States, by any mode of transportation, without needing a visa. Further information is available from any U.S. embassy or consulate.)

Citizens of countries other than those stipulated above, including citizens of Australia, must have two documents:

- a valid **passport,** with an expiration date at least six months later than the scheduled end of the visit to the United States; and
- a **tourist visa,** available without charge from the nearest U.S. consulate. To obtain a visa, the traveler must submit a completed application form (either in person or by mail) with a $1^1/_2$-inch square photo and demonstrate binding ties to a residence abroad.

Usually you can obtain a visa at once or within 24 hours, but it may take longer during the summer rush from June to August. If you cannot go in person, contact the nearest U.S. embassy or consulate for directions on applying by mail. Your travel agent or airline office may also be able to provide you with visa applications and instructions. The U.S. consulate or embassy that issues your visa will determine whether you will be issued a multiple- or single-entry visa and if there will be any restrictions regarding the length of your stay.

MEDICAL REQUIREMENTS   No inoculations are needed to enter the United States unless you are coming from, or have stopped over in, areas known to be suffering from epidemics, particularly cholera or yellow fever.

If you have a disease requiring treatment with medications containing narcotics or drugs requiring a syringe, carry a valid signed prescription from your physician to allay any suspicions that you are smuggling drugs.

CUSTOMS REQUIREMENTS   Every adult visitor may bring in free of duty: one liter of wine or hard liquor; 200 cigarettes or 100 cigars (but no cigars from Cuba) or three pounds of smoking tobacco; $100 worth of gifts. These exemptions are offered to travelers who spend at least 72 hours in the United States and who have not claimed them within the preceding six months. It is altogether forbidden to bring into the country foodstuffs (particularly cheese, fruit, cooked meats, and canned goods) and plants (vegetables, seeds, tropical plants, and so on). Foreign tourists may bring in or take out up to $10,000 in U.S. or foreign currency with no formalities; larger sums must be declared to Customs on entering or leaving.

Insurance

There is no national health system in the United States. Because the cost of medical care is extremely high, we strongly advise every traveler to secure health coverage before setting out.

You may want to take out a comprehensive travel policy that covers (for a relatively low premium) sickness or injury costs (medical, surgical, and hospital); loss or theft of your baggage; trip-cancellation costs; guarantee of bail in case you are arrested; costs of accident, repatriation, or death. Such packages (for example, "Europe Assistance" in Europe) are sold by automobile clubs at attractive rates, as well as by insurance companies and travel agencies.

Money

CURRENCY & EXCHANGE   The U.S. monetary system has a decimal base: one American **dollar ($1)** = 100 **cents (100¢).**

Dollar bills commonly come in $1 ("a buck"), $5, $10, $20, $50, and $100 denominations (the last two are not welcome when paying for small purchases and are not accepted in taxis or at subway ticket booths). There are also $2 bills (seldom encountered).

There are six denominations of coins: 1¢ (one cent or "penny"), 5¢ (five cents or "a nickel"), 10¢ (ten cents or "a dime"), 25¢ (twenty-five cents or "a quarter"), 50¢ (fifty cents or "a half dollar"), and the rare $1 piece.

TRAVELER'S CHECKS   Traveler's checks denominated in U.S. dollars are readily accepted at most hotels, motels, restaurants, and large stores. But the best place to change traveler's checks is at a bank. Do not bring traveler's checks denominated in other currencies.

CREDIT CARDS   The method of payment most widely used is the credit card: VISA (BarclayCard in Britain), Mastercard (EuroCard in Europe, Access in Britain, Chargex in Canada), American Express, Diners Club, Discover, and Carte Blanche. You can save yourself trouble by using "plastic money" rather than cash or traveler's checks in most hotels, motels, restaurants, and retail stores (a growing number of food and liquor stores now accept credit cards). You must have a credit card to rent a car. It can also be used as proof of identity (often carrying more weight than a passport), or as a "cash card," enabling you to draw money from banks that accept them.

Note: The "foreign-exchange bureaus" so common in Europe are rare even at airports in the United States, and nonexistent outside major cities. Try to avoid having to change foreign money, or traveler's checks denominated other than in U.S. dollars, at a small-town bank, or even a branch in a big city; in fact, leave any currency other than U.S. dollars at home—it may prove more nuisance to you than it's worth.

Safety

GENERAL   While tourist areas are generally safe, crime is on the increase everywhere, and U.S. urban areas tend to be less safe than those in Europe or Japan. Visitors should always stay alert. This is particularly true of large U.S. cities. It is wise to ask the city's or area's tourist office if you're in doubt about which neighborhoods are safe. Avoid deserted areas, especially at night. Don't go into any city park at night unless there is an event that attracts crowds—for example, New York City's concerts in the parks. Generally speaking, you can feel safe in areas where there are many people, and many open establishments.

Avoid carrying valuables with you on the street, and don't display expensive cameras or electronic equipment. Hold on to your pocketbook, and place your billfold in an inside pocket. In theaters, restaurants, and other public places, keep your possessions in sight.

Remember also that hotels are open to the public, and in a large hotel, security may not be able to screen everyone entering. Always lock your room door—don't assume that once inside your hotel you are automatically safe and no longer need be aware of your surroundings.

DRIVING   Safety while driving is particularly important. Question your rental agency about personal safety, or ask for a brochure of traveler safety tips when you pick up your car. Obtain written directions, or a map with the route marked in red, from the agency showing how to get to your destination. And, if possible, arrive and depart during daylight hours.

Recently more and more crime has involved cars and drivers. If you drive off a highway into a doubtful neighborhood, leave the area as quickly as possible. If you have an accident, even on the highway, stay in your car with the doors locked until you assess the situation or until the police arrive. If you are bumped from behind on the street or are involved in a minor accident with no injuries and the situation appears to be suspicious, motion to the other driver to follow you. *Never* get out of your car in such situations. You can also keep a premade sign in your car which reads: PLEASE FOLLOW THIS VEHICLE TO REPORT ACCIDENT. Show the sign to the other driver and go directly to the nearest police precinct, well-lighted service station, or all-night store.

If you see someone on the road who indicates a need for help, do *not* stop. Take note of the location, drive on to a well-lighted area, and telephone the police by dialing **911.**

Park in well-lighted, well-traveled areas if possible. Always keep your car doors locked, whether attended or unattended. Look around you before you get out of your car, and never leave any packages or valuables in sight. If someone attempts to rob you or steal your car, do *not* try to resist the thief/carjacker—report the incident to the police department immediately.

You may wish to contact the San Antonio Convention & Visitors Bureau, P.O. Box 2277, San Antonio, TX 78298 (☎ toll free **800/447-3372**), or the Austin Convention and Visitors Bureau, 201 E. Second St., Austin TX 78701 (☎ toll free **800/926-2282**), before you go for advice on safety precautions.

B   Getting to & Around the U.S.

Travelers from overseas can take advantage of the APEX (Advance Purchase Excursion) fares offered by all the major U.S. and European carriers. Aside from these, attractive values are offered by Icelandair on flights from Luxembourg to New York and by Virgin Atlantic Airways from London to New York/Newark.

Houston is the hub for international flights into Texas. **Air Canada** (☎ toll free **800/776-3000**) offers direct flights from Toronto to Houston; **Continental** (☎ toll free **800/231-0856**) and **British Airways** (☎ toll free **800/247-9297**) both have daily non-stop service from London.

Some large American airlines (for example, TWA, American Airlines, Northwest, United, and Delta) offer travelers on their transatlantic or transpacific flights special discount tickets under the name **Visit USA,** allowing travel between any U.S. destinations at minimum rates. They are not on sale in the United States, and must, therefore, be purchased before you leave your foreign point of departure. This system is the best, easiest, and fastest way to see the United States at low cost. You should obtain information well in advance from your travel agent or the office of the airline concerned, since the conditions attached to these discount tickets can be changed without advance notice.

The visitor arriving by air, no matter what the port of entry, should cultivate patience and resignation before setting foot on U.S. soil. Getting through Immigration control may take as long as two hours on some days, especially summer weekends. Add the time it takes to clear Customs and you'll see that you should make very generous allowance for delay in planning connections between international and domestic flights—an average of two to three hours at least.

In contrast, travelers arriving by car or by rail from Canada will find border-crossing formalities streamlined to the vanishing point. And air travelers from Canada, Bermuda, and some places in the Caribbean can sometimes go through Customs and Immigration at the point of departure, which is much quicker and less painful.

For further information about travel to San Antonio and Austin, see the "Getting There" sections of Chapters 2 and 10, respectively. International visitors can also buy a **USA Railpass,** good for 15 or 30 days of unlimited travel on Amtrak. The pass is available through many foreign travel agents. Prices in 1994 for a 15-day pass are $208 off-peak, $308 peak; a 30-day pass costs $309 off-peak, $389 peak. (With a foreign passport, you can also buy passes at some Amtrak offices in the United States, including locations in San Francisco, Los Angeles, Chicago, New York, Miami, Boston, and Washington, D.C.) Reservations are generally required and should be made for each part of your trip as early as possible.

Visitors should also be aware of the limitations of long-distance rail travel in the United States. With a few notable exceptions (for instance, the Northeast Corridor line between Boston and Washington, D.C.), service is rarely up to European standards: Delays are common, routes are limited and often infrequently served, and fares are rarely significantly lower than discount airfares. Thus, cross-country train travel should be approached with caution.

The cheapest way to travel the United States is by bus. Greyhound, the nation's nationwide bus line, offers an **Ameripass** for unlimited travel for 7 days (for $250), 15 days (for $350), and 30 days (for $450). Bus travel in the United States can be both slow and uncomfortable, so this option is not for everyone.

Fast Facts: For the Foreign Traveler

Automobile Organizations   Auto clubs will supply maps, suggested routes, guidebooks, accident and bail-bond insurance, and emergency road service. The major auto club in the United States, with 955 offices nationwide, is the American Automobile Association (AAA). Members of some foreign auto clubs have reciprocal arrangements with the AAA and enjoy its services at no charge. If you belong to an auto club, inquire about AAA reciprocity before you leave. The AAA can provide you with an International Driving Permit validating your foreign license. You may be able to join the AAA even if you are not a member of a reciprocal club. To inquire, call toll free **800/336-4357.** In addition, some automobile-rental agencies now provide these services, so you should inquire about their availability when you rent your car.

Automobile Rentals   To rent a car you need a major credit card. A valid driver's license is required, and you usually need to be at least 25. Some companies do rent to younger people but add a daily surcharge. Be sure to return your car with the same amount of gas you started out with; rental companies charge excessive prices for gasoline. All the major car-rental companies are represented in Texas; for details about San Antonio and Austin, see the "Getting Around" sections of Chapters 3 and 11, respectively.

Business Hours   **Banks** are open weekdays from 9am to 3 or 4pm, although there's 24-hour access to the automatic tellers (ATMs) at most banks and other outlets. Generally, **offices** are open weekdays from 9am to 5pm. **Stores** are open six days a week, with many open on Sunday, too; department stores usually stay open until 9pm at least one day a week.

Climate   See "When to Go" in Chapter 2.

Currency   See "Money" in "Preparing for Your Trip," above.

Currency Exchange   You will find currency-exchange services in major airports with international service. Elsewhere, they may be quite difficult to come by. In New York, a very reliable choice is Thomas Cook Currency Services, Inc., which has been in business since 1841 and offers a wide range of services. They also sell commission-free foreign and U.S. traveler's checks, drafts, and wire transfers; they do check collections as well (including Eurochecks). Their rates are competitive and service excellent. They maintain several offices in New York City (telephone number for the Fifth Avenue office is **212/757-6915**), at the JFK Airport International Arrivals Terminal (☎ **718/656-8444**), and at La Guardia Airport in the Delta terminal (☎ **718/533-0784**).

Currency Exchange   You'll find currency-exchange facilities at the San Antonio International Airport. In Austin, a number of Bank One branches around town provide this service; there's also an American Express Travel Service Office at 2943 W. Anderson Lane (☎ **512/452-8166**).

Drinking Laws   See "Liquor Laws" in "Fast Facts: San Antonio," Chapter 3, and "Fast Facts: Austin," Chapter 11.

Electricity   The United States uses 110 to 120 volts, 60 cycles, compared to 220 to 240 volts, 50 cycles, as in most of Europe. In addition to a 100-volt converter, small appliances of non-American manufacture, such as hair dryers or shavers, will require a plug adapter, with two flat, parallel pins.

Embassies & Consulates   All embassies are located in the national capital, Washington, D.C.; some consulates are located in major cities, and most nations have a mission to the United Nations in New York City. Foreign visitors can obtain telephone numbers for their embassies and consulates by calling "Information" in Washington, D.C. (☎ **202/555-1212**).

There's a Canadian consulate in Dallas, 750 N. St. Paul St., Suite 1700, 75201 (☎ **214/922-9806**). Houston is home to consulates for the United Kingdom, 1000 Louisiana St., 77002 (☎ **713/659-6270**), and for Australia, 1990 Post Oak Blvd., Suite 800, 77056 (☎ **713/629-9131**).

Emergencies   Call **911** to report a fire, call the police, or get an ambulance.

If you encounter traveler's problems, check the local directory to find an office of the Traveler's Aid Society, a nationwide, nonprofit, social-service organization geared to helping travelers in difficult straits. Their services might include reuniting families separated while traveling, providing food and/or shelter to people stranded without cash, or even emotional counseling. If you're in trouble, seek them out.

Gasoline [Petrol]   One U.S. gallon equals 3.75 liters, while 1.2 U.S. gallons equals one imperial gallon. You'll notice there are several grades (and price levels) of gasoline available at most gas stations. And you'll also notice that their names change from company to company. The unleaded ones with the highest octane are the most expensive (most rental cars take the least expensive "regular" unleaded) and leaded gas is the least expensive, but only older cars can take this any more, so check if you're not sure.

Holidays   On the following legal national holidays, banks, government offices, post offices, and many stores, restaurants, and museums are closed:

January 1 (New Year's Day)
Third Monday in January (Martin Luther King, Jr., Day)
Third Monday in February (Presidents Day, Washington's Birthday)
Last Monday in May (Memorial Day)
July 4 (Independence Day)
First Monday in September (Labor Day)
Second Monday in October (Columbus Day)
November 11 (Veteran's Day/Armistice Day)
Last Thursday in November (Thanksgiving Day)
December 25 (Christmas)

Finally, the Tuesday following the first Monday in November is Election Day, and is a legal holiday in presidential-election years.

Languages   Major hotels may have multilingual employees. Unless your language is very obscure, they can usually supply a translator on request. Many people in San Antonio are fluent in Spanish.

Legal Aid   The foreign tourist, unless positively identified as a member of the Mafia or of a drug ring, will probably never become involved with the American legal system. If you are pulled up for a minor infraction (for example, of the highway code, such as speeding), never attempt to pay the fine directly to a police officer; you may wind up arrested on the much more serious charge of attempted bribery. Pay fines by mail, or directly into the hands of the clerk of the court. If accused of a more serious offense, it's wise to say and do nothing before consulting a lawyer. Under U.S. law, an arrested person is allowed one telephone call to a party of his or her choice. Call your embassy or consulate.

Mail If you want your mail to follow you on your vacation and you aren't sure of your address, your mail can be sent to you, in your name, c/o General Delivery at the main post office of the city or region where you expect to be. The addressee must pick it up in person and produce proof of identity (driver's license, credit card, passport, etc.).

Generally to be found at intersections, mailboxes are blue with a red-and-white stripe and carry the inscription U.S. MAIL. If your mail is addressed to a U.S. destination, don't forget to add the five-figure postal code, or ZIP (Zone Improvement Plan) Code, after the two-letter abbreviation of the state to which the mail is addressed (CA for California, FL for Florida, NY for New York, and so on).

Newspapers/Magazines National newspapers include the *New York Times, USA Today,* and the *Wall Street Journal.* National news weeklies include *Newsweek, Time,* and *U.S. News & World Report.* There's only one major daily newspaper in San Antonio and Austin: the *San Antonio-Express* and the *Austin-American Statesman,* respectively.

Radio & Television Audiovisual media, with four coast-to-coast networks—ABC, CBS, NBC, and Fox—joined in recent years by the Public Broadcasting System (PBS) and the cable network CNN, play a major part in American life. In big cities, televiewers have a choice of about a dozen channels (including the UHF channels), most of them transmitting 24 hours a day, without counting the pay-TV channels showing recent movies or sports events. All options are usually indicated on your hotel TV set. You'll also find a wide choice of local radio stations, each broadcasting particular kinds of talk shows and/or music—classical, country, jazz, pop, gospel—punctuated by news broadcasts and frequent commercials.

Safety See "Safety" in "Preparing for Your Trip," above.

Taxes In the United States there is no VAT (Value-Added Tax) or other indirect tax at a national level. Every state, and each city in it, has the right to levy its own local tax on all purchases, including hotel and restaurant checks, airline tickets, and so on. In San Antonio, the sales tax is $7^3/4$%; in Austin, it's 8%.

Telephone, Telegraph, Telex The telephone system in the United States is run by private corporations, so rates, especially for long-distance service, can vary widely—even on calls made from public telephones. Local calls in the United States usually cost 25¢. Generally, hotel surcharges on long-distance and local calls are astronomical. You are usually better off using a public pay telephone, which you will find clearly marked in most public buildings and private establishments as well as on the street. Outside metropolican areas, public telephones are more difficult to find. Stores and gas stations are your best bet.

Most long-distance and international calls can be dialed directly from any phone. For calls to Canada and other parts of the United States, dial 1 followed by the area code and the seven-digit number. For international calls, dial 011 followed by the country code, city code, and the telephone number of the person you wish to call.

For reversed-charge or collect calls, and for person-to-person calls, dial 0 (zero, *not* the letter "O") followed by the area code and number you want; an operator will then come on the line, and you should specify that you are calling collect, or person-to-person, or both. If your operator-assisted call is international, ask for the overseas operator.

For local directory assistance ("information"), dial 411; for long-distance information, dial 1, then the appropriate area code and **555-1212.**

Like the telephone system, telegraph and telex services are provided by private corporations like ITT, MCI, and above all, Western Union, the most important. You can bring your telegram in to the nearest Western Union office (there are hundreds across the country), or dictate it over the phone (a toll-free call, **800/325-6000**). You can also telegraph money, or have it telegraphed to you, very quickly over the Western Union system.

Telephone Directory   There are two kinds of telephone directories available to you. The general directory is the so-called White Pages, in which private and business subscribers are listed in alphabetical order. The inside front cover lists the emergency number for police, fire, and ambulance, and other vital numbers (like the Coast Guard, poison-control center, crime-victims hotline, and so on). The first few pages are devoted to community-service numbers, including a guide to long-distance and international calling, complete with country codes and area codes.

The second directory, printed on yellow paper (hence its name, *Yellow Pages*), lists all local services, businesses, and industries by type of activity, with an index at the back. The listings cover not only such obvious items as automobile repairs by make of car, or drugstores (pharmacies), often by geographical location, but also restaurants by type of cuisine and geographical location, bookstores by special subject and/or language, places of worship by religious denomination, and other information that the tourist might otherwise not readily find. The *Yellow Pages* also include city plans or detailed area maps, often showing postal ZIP Codes and public transportation routes.

Time   The United States is divided into four time zones (six, if Alaska and Hawaii are included). From east to west, these are: eastern standard time (EST), central daylight time (CDT), mountain standard time (MST), Pacific standard time (PST), Alaska standard time (AST), and Hawaii standard time (HST). Always keep changing time zones in mind if you are traveling (or even telephoning) long distances in the United States. For example, noon in New York City

(EST) is 11am in Chicago (CDT), 10am in Denver (MST), 9am in Los Angeles (PST), 8am in Anchorage (AST), and 7am in Honolulu (HST).

Most of Texas, including San Antonio and Austin, is on Central Time; the far western part of the state, around El Paso, observes Mountain Time (clocks are set one hour earlier). Daylight saving time is in effect from the last Sunday in April through the last Saturday in October (actually, the change is made at 2am on Sunday) except in parts of Arizona, Hawaii, part of Indiana, and Puerto Rico. Daylight saving time moves the clock one hour ahead of standard time.

Tipping This is part of the American way of life, on the principle that you must expect to pay for any service you get. Here are some rules of thumb:

Bartenders: 10% to 15%.

Bellhops: at least 50¢ per piece; $2 to $3 for a lot of baggage.

Cab drivers: 15% of the fare.

Cafeterias, fast-food restaurants: no tip.

Chambermaids: $1 a day.

Checkroom attendants (restaurants, theaters): $1 per garment.

Cinemas, movies, theaters: no tip.

Doormen (hotels or restaurants): not obligatory.

Gas-station attendants: no tip.

Hairdressers: 15% to 20%.

Redcaps (airport and railroad station): at least 50¢ per piece, $2 to $3 for a lot of baggage.

Restaurants, nightclubs: 15% to 20% of the check.

Sleeping-car porters: $2 to $3 per night to your attendant.

Valet parking attendants: $1.

Toilets Foreign visitors often complain that public toilets are hard to find in most U.S. cities. True, there are none on the streets, but the visitor can usually find one in a bar, restaurant, hotel, museum, department store, or service station—and it will probably be clean (although the last-mentioned sometimes leaves much to be desired). Note, however, a growing practice in some restaurants and bars of displaying a notice that "toilets are for the use of patrons only." You can ignore this sign, or better yet, avoid arguments by paying for a cup of coffee or soft drink, which will qualify you as a patron. The cleanliness of toilets at railroad stations and bus depots may be more open to question, and some public places are equipped with pay toilets, which require you to insert one or more coins into a slot on the door before it will open.

The American System of Measurements ——————

Length

1 inch (in.)	=	2.54cm					
1 foot (ft.)	=	12 in.	=	30.48cm	=	.305m	
1 yard (yd.)	=	3 ft.			=	.915m	
1 mile (m)	=	5,280 ft.					= 1.609km

To convert miles to kilometers, multiply the number of miles by 1.61. Also use to convert speeds from miles per hour (m.p.h.) to kilometers per hour (kmph).

To convert kilometers to miles, multiply the number of kilometers by .62. Also use to convert kmph to m.p.h.

Capacity

1 fluid ounce (fl. oz.)			=	.03 liters	
1 pint (pt.)	=	16 fl. oz.	=	.47 liters	
1 quart (qt.)	=	2 pints	=	.94 liters	
1 gallon (gal.)	=	4 quarts	=	3.79 liters	=	.83 Imperial gal

To convert U.S. gallons to liters, multiply the number of gallons by 3.79.

To convert liters to U.S. gallons, multiply the number of liters by .26.

To convert U.S. gallons to Imperial gallons, multiply the number of U.S. gallons by .83.

To convert Imperial gallons to U.S. gallons, multiply the number of Imperial gallons by 1.2.

Weight

1 ounce (oz.)			=	28.35g			
1 pound (lb.)	=	16 oz.	=	453.6g	=	.45 kg	
1 ton			=	2,000 lb.	=	907kg	= .91 metric tons

To convert pounds to kilograms, multiply the number of pounds by .45.
To convert kilograms to pounds, multiply the number by kilograms by 2.2.

Area

1 acre			=	.41ha		
1 square mile	=	640 acres	=	2.59ha	=	2.6km

To convert acres to heactares, multiply the number of acres by .41.
To convert hectares to acres, multiply the number of hectares by 2.47.
To convert square miles to square kiometers, multiply the number of square miles by 2.6.
To convert square kilometers to square miles, multiply the number of square kilometers by .39.

Temperature

To convert degrees Farenheit to degrees Celsius, subtract 32 from °F, multiply by 5, then divide by 9 (example: 85°F − 32 x 5/9 = 29.4°C).

To convert degrees Celsius to degrees Fahrenheit, multiply °C by 9, divide by 5, and add 32 (example: 20°C x 9/5 + 32 = 68°F).

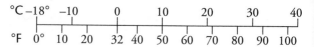

Index

AUSTIN

NOTES

NOTES

NOTES

NOTES

NOTES

NOTES

Now Save Money On All Your Travels By Joining FROMMER'S™ TRAVEL BOOK CLUB The World's Best Travel Guides At Membership Prices!

Frommer's Travel Book Club is your ticket to successful travel! Open up a world of travel information and simplify your travel planning when you join ranks with thousands of value-conscious travelers who are members of the Frommer's *Travel Book Club.* Join today and you'll be entitled to all the privileges that come from belonging to the club that offers you travel guides for less to more than 100 destinations worldwide. **Annual membership is only $25.00 (U.S.) or $35.00 (Canada/Foreign).**

The Advantages of Membership:

1. Your choice of **three free** books (any **two** Frommer's Comprehensive Guides, Frommer's $-A-Day Guides, Frommer's Walking Tours or Frommer's Family Guides—plus **one** Frommer's City Guide, Frommer's City $-A-Day Guide or Frommer's Touring Guide).

2. Your own subscription to the **TRIPS & TRAVEL** quarterly newsletter.

3. You're entitled to a **30% discount** on your order of any additional books offered by the club.

4. You're offered (at a small additional fee) our **Domestic Trip-Routing Kits.**

Our **Trips & Travel** quarterly newsletter offers practical information on the best buys in travel, the "hottest" vacation spots, the latest travel trends, world-class events and much, much more.

Our **Domestic Trip-Routing Kits** are available for any North American destination. We'll send you a detailed map highlighting the best route to take to your destination—you can request direct or scenic routes.

Here's all you have to do to join:

Send in your membership fee of $25.00 ($35.00 Canada/Foreign) with your name and address on the form below along with your selections as part of your membership package to the address listed below. Remember to check off your three free books.

If you would like to order additional books, please select the books you would like and send a check for the total amount (please add sales tax in the states noted below), plus $2.00 per book for shipping and handling ($3.00 Canada/Foreign) to the address listed below.

FROMMER'S TRAVEL BOOK CLUB
P.O. Box 473
Mt. Morris, IL 61054-0473
(815) 734-1104

[ ] **YES!** I want to take advantage of this opportunity to join Frommer's Travel Book Club.

[ ] My check is enclosed. Dollar amount enclosed_____*
(all payments in U.S. funds only)

Name _____

Address _____

City _____ State _____ Zip _____

Phone ( ) _____(In case we have a question regarding your order).

All orders must be prepaid.

To ensure that all orders are processed efficiently, please apply sales tax in the following areas: CA, CT, FL, IL, IN, NJ, NY, PA, TN, WA and CANADA.

*With membership, shipping & handling will be paid by Frommer's Travel Book Club for the three FREE books you select as part of your membership. Please add $2.00 per book for shipping & handling for any additional books purchased ($3.00 Canada/Foreign).

Allow 4-6 weeks for delivery for all items. Prices of books, membership fee, and publication dates are subject to change without notice. All orders are subject to acceptance and availability.

Please send me the books checked below:

FROMMER'S COMPREHENSIVE GUIDES

*(Guides listing facilities from budget to deluxe,
with emphasis on the medium-priced)*

	Retail Price	Code		Retail Price	Code
☐ Acapulco/Ixtapa/Taxco, 2nd Edition	$13.95	C157	☐ Jamaica/Barbados, 2nd Edition	$15.00	C149
☐ Alaska '94-'95	$17.00	C131	☐ Japan '94-'95	$19.00	C144
☐ Arizona '95 (Avail. 3/95)	$14.95	C166	☐ Maui, 1st Edition	$14.00	C153
☐ Australia '94-'95	$18.00	C147	☐ Nepal, 2nd Edition	$18.00	C126
☐ Austria, 6th Edition	$16.95	C162	☐ New England '95	$16.95	C165
☐ Bahamas '94-'95	$17.00	C121	☐ New Mexico, 3rd Edition (Avail. 3/95)	$14.95	C167
☐ Belgium/Holland/ Luxembourg '93-'94	$18.00	C106	☐ New York State '94-'95	$19.00	C133
☐ Bermuda '94-'95	$15.00	C122	☐ Northwest, 5th Edition	$17.00	C140
☐ Brazil, 3rd Edition	$20.00	C111	☐ Portugal '94-'95	$17.00	C141
☐ California '95	$16.95	C164	☐ Puerto Rico '95-'96	$14.00	C151
☐ Canada '94-'95	$19.00	C145	☐ Puerto Vallarta/ Manzanillo/Guadalajara '94-'95	$14.00	C135
☐ Caribbean '95	$18.00	C148			
☐ Carolinas/Georgia, 2nd Edition	$17.00	C128	☐ Scandinavia, 16th Edition (Avail. 3/95)	$19.95	C169
☐ Colorado, 2nd Edition	$16.00	C143	☐ Scotland '94-'95	$17.00	C146
☐ Costa Rica '95	$13.95	C161	☐ South Pacific '94-'95	$20.00	C138
☐ Cruises '95-'96	$19.00	C150	☐ Spain, 16th Edition	$16.95	C163
☐ Delaware/Maryland '94-'95	$15.00	C136	☐ Switzerland/ Liechtenstein '94-'95	$19.00	C139
☐ England '95	$17.95	C159	☐ Thailand, 2nd Edition	$17.95	C154
☐ Florida '95	$18.00	C152	☐ U.S.A., 4th Edition	$18.95	C156
☐ France '94-'95	$20.00	C132	☐ Virgin Islands '94-'95	$13.00	C127
☐ Germany '95	$18.95	C158	☐ Virginia '94-'95	$14.00	C142
☐ Ireland, 1st Edition (Avail. 3/95)	$16.95	C168	☐ Yucatan, 2nd Edition	$13.95	C155
☐ Italy '95	$18.95	C160			

FROMMER'S $-A-DAY GUIDES

(Guides to low-cost tourist accommodations and facilities)

	Retail Price	Code		Retail Price	Code
☐ Australia on $45 '95-'96	$18.00	D122	☐ Israel on $45, 15th Edition	$16.95	D130
☐ Costa Rica/Guatemala/ Belize on $35, 3rd Edition	$15.95	D126	☐ Mexico on $45 '95	$16.95	D125
			☐ New York on $70 '94-'95	$16.00	D121
☐ Eastern Europe on $30, 5th Edition	$16.95	D129	☐ New Zealand on $45 '93-'94	$18.00	D103
☐ England on $60 '95	$17.95	D128			
☐ Europe on $50 '95	$17.95	D127	☐ South America on $40, 16th Edition	$18.95	D123
☐ Greece on $45 '93-'94	$19.00	D100			
☐ Hawaii on $75 '95	$16.95	D124	☐ Washington, D.C. on $50 '94-'95	$17.00	D120
☐ Ireland on $45 '94-'95	$17.00	D118			

FROMMER'S CITY $-A-DAY GUIDES

	Retail Price	Code		Retail Price	Code
☐ Berlin on $40 '94-'95	$12.00	D111	☐ Madrid on $50 '94-'95	$13.00	D119
☐ London on $45 '94-'95	$12.00	D114	☐ Paris on $50 '94-'95	$12.00	D117

FROMMER'S FAMILY GUIDES
(Guides listing information on kid-friendly hotels, restaurants, activities and attractions)

	Retail Price	Code		Retail Price	Code
☐ California with Kids	$18.00	F100	☐ San Francisco with Kids	$17.00	F104
☐ Los Angeles with Kids	$17.00	F103	☐ Washington, D.C.		
☐ New York City with Kids	$18.00	F101	with Kids	$17.00	F102

FROMMER'S CITY GUIDES
(Pocket-size guides to sightseeing and tourist accommodations and facilities in all price ranges)

	Retail Price	Code		Retail Price	Code
☐ Amsterdam '93-'94	$13.00	S110	☐ Montreal/Quebec City '95	$11.95	S166
☐ Athens, 10th Edition (Avail. 3/95)	$12.95	S174	☐ Nashville/Memphis, 1st Edition	$13.00	S141
☐ Atlanta '95	$12.95	S161	☐ New Orleans '95	$12.95	S148
☐ Atlantic City/Cape May, 5th Edition	$13.00	S130	☐ New York '95	$12.95	S152
☐ Bangkok, 2nd Edition	$12.95	S147	☐ Orlando '95	$13.00	S145
☐ Barcelona '93-'94	$13.00	S115	☐ Paris '95	$12.95	S150
☐ Berlin, 3rd Edition	$12.95	S162	☐ Philadelphia, 8th Edition	$12.95	S167
☐ Boston '95	$12.95	S160	☐ Prague '94-'95	$13.00	S143
☐ Budapest, 1st Edition	$13.00	S139	☐ Rome, 10th Edition	$12.95	S168
☐ Chicago '95	$12.95	S169	☐ St. Louis/Kansas City, 2nd Edition	$13.00	S127
☐ Denver/Boulder/Colorado Springs, 3rd Edition	$12.95	S154	☐ San Diego '95	$12.95	S158
☐ Dublin, 2nd Edition	$12.95	S157	☐ San Francisco '95	$12.95	S155
☐ Hong Kong '94-'95	$13.00	S140	☐ Santa Fe/Taos/ Albuquerque '95 (Avail. 2/95)	$12.95	S172
☐ Honolulu/Oahu '95	$12.95	S151	☐ Seattle/Portland '94-'95	$13.00	S137
☐ Las Vegas '95	$12.95	S163	☐ Sydney, 4th Edition	$12.95	S171
☐ London '95	$12.95	S156	☐ Tampa/St. Petersburg, 3rd Edition	$13.00	S146
☐ Los Angeles '95	$12.95	S164	☐ Tokyo '94-'95	$13.00	S144
☐ Madrid/Costa del Sol, 2nd Edition	$12.95	S165	☐ Toronto '95 (Avail. 3/95)	$12.95	S173
☐ Mexico City, 1st Edition	$12.95	S170	☐ Vancouver/Victoria '94-'95	$13.00	S142
☐ Miami '95-'96	$12.95	S149	☐ Washington, D.C. '95	$12.95	S153
☐ Minneapolis/St. Paul, 4th Edition	$12.95	S159			

FROMMER'S WALKING TOURS

*(Companion guides that point out the places
and pleasures that make a city unique)*

	Retail Price	Code		Retail Price	Code
□ Berlin	$12.00	W100	□ New York	$12.00	W102
□ Chicago	$12.00	W107	□ Paris	$12.00	W103
□ England's Favorite Cities	$12.00	W108	□ San Francisco	$12.00	W104
□ London	$12.00	W101	□ Washington, D.C.	$12.00	W105
□ Montreal/Quebec City	$12.00	W106			

SPECIAL EDITIONS

	Retail Price	Code		Retail Price	Code
□ Bed & Breakfast Southwest	$16.00	P100	□ National Park Guide, 29th Edition	$17.00	P106
□ Bed & Breakfast Great American Cities	$16.00	P104	□ Where to Stay U.S.A., 11th Edition	$15.00	P102
□ Caribbean Hideaways	$16.00	P103			

FROMMER'S TOURING GUIDES

*(Color-illustrated guides that include walking tours,
cultural and historic sites, and practical information)*

	Retail Price	Code		Retail Price	Code
□ Amsterdam	$11.00	T001	□ New York	$11.00	T008
□ Barcelona	$14.00	T015	□ Rome	$11.00	T010
□ Brazil	$11.00	T003	□ Tokyo	$15.00	T016
□ Hong Kong/Singapore/ Macau	$11.00	T006	□ Turkey	$11.00	T013
□ London	$13.00	T007	□ Venice	$ 9.00	T014

---

*Please note: If the availability of a book is several months away, we may
have back issues of guides to that particular destination.
Call customer service at (815) 734-1104.*